The Myth of the M...
Homosexual

LIBRARY

The Myth of the Modern Homosexual

Queer History and the Search for Cultural Unity

Rictor Norton

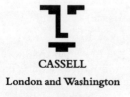

CASSELL
London and Washington

For a catalogue of related titles in our
Sexual Politics list
please write to us at an address below

Cassell
Wellington House
125 Strand
London WC2R 0BB

PO Box 605
Herndon
Virginia 20172

First published 1997

British Library Cataloguing in Publication Data
A catalogue record for this book is available from the British Library.

Library of Congress Cataloging-in-Publication Data
Norton, Rictor, 1945–
    The myth of the modern homosexual: queer history and the search
for cultural unity/Rictor Norton.
       p.   cm.
    Includes bibliographical references and index.
    ISBN 0-304-33891-5—ISBN 0-304-33892-3 (pbk.)
    1. Homosexuality, Male—History.   2. Gays—History.
  3. Homosexuality—History.   I. Title.
    HO76.25.N67 1997
    306.76'62'09–dc21   97–7785
       306. 766 NOR   CIP
ISBN 0 304 33891 5 (hardback)

     0 304 33892 3 (paperback)

Designed and typeset by Ben Cracknell Studios
Printed and bound in Great Britain by Biddles Ltd,
Guildford and King's Lynn

Contents

Preface

When I read *A Queer Reader* (Higgins, 1993) I was amused to find myself quoted for having once said:

> to be honest, gay persons are not just plain folk, we are quite extraordinary. ... We are not – heaven forbid – 'the same as' heterosexuals, but are uniquely different with our own positive and lasting contributions to humanity. Some of us are pederasts. Some of us are sado-masochists. Some of us are hustlers. Some of us are frenzied fairies in drag. In other words: we have amongst our ranks – in our culture – a wealth and variety of collectively liberating experience undreamt of by merely mortal heterosexuals. We are Hamlet and his father in heaven and hell, while they are Horatio with his plodding commonsense.

The excerpt was headed 'Superior Persons', though my own more abstruse title was 'The Phoenix of Sodom'. The words came from an article I wrote for *Gay News* in 1974, shortly after joining the full-time staff of the fortnightly newspaper, as an explanation of why I researched gay history and early gay literature. I reread the article as I worked on this present book to see if I still felt the same twenty years later. Some of the 'revolutionary' rhetoric is rather embarrassing today, but my ideal of the queer historian remains the same: to liberate gay pride by liberating queer history and queer culture from that secret closet to which heterosexual history had consigned them; to celebrate the uniqueness and diversity of gay peoples rather than presenting them as just plain folk; to challenge the notion that the features of queer culture throughout history are little more than symptoms of pathological oppression, internalized guilt, repression or sublimation. I saw then, and I see today, 'the dilemma of integrating our liberation with our own culture. The less radical part of the gay liberation movement, as it exhibits itself in the public forum, is not so much political as politic ... nearly all of the programmes for "our" gay liberation (manifestos, gay organizations, gay conferences, etc.) seem to imply that we will be liberated only by freeing ourselves *from* our own gay culture rather than by freeing ourselves *for* our own gay culture.'

Queer historians do have a role to play in ensuring that the revelation of a person's queer sexuality comes to be seen as neither abnormal nor infamous, but I think it is mistaken to argue that we are 'virtually normal' and have no history except as victims or activists.

Rictor Norton
January 1997

Acknowledgements

A work of this nature could not have been written without the aid of the comprehensive articles in the *Encyclopedia of Homosexuality* (Dynes, 1990), to which I am deeply indebted.

For help in collecting the illustrations I would like to thank the staff of the British Library and the Museo del Prado; Pat Sewell, Principal District Archivist, Calderdale District Archives; Andy Chopping, Museum of London Archaeology Service; and Greg Reeder for sending me photographs of the tomb of Niankhkhnum and Khnumhotep. I am especially grateful to Keith Cavers for several helpful discussions concerning the nature of visual evidence, and for allowing me to publish a number of illustrations from his extensive collection of material on the history of drag queens and persons of the third sex.

Part I

Social Constructionism and Other Myths

The Search for Cultural Unity

Many of the early gay liberationists – like most activists in nationalist and ethnic movements – believed, I think correctly, that knowledge of history plays an important role in the development of solidarity: a consciousness of cultural community provides the necessary strength for collective action to overcome oppression. Jonathan Katz's *Coming Out: A Documentary Play about Gay Life and Liberation in the United States of America* (1975) uses some two dozen significant moments in American gay history to promote enthusiasm for the struggle, including the 'Boys of Boise' witch-hunt, the Stonewall riots, notable raids and trials in Chicago and New York, and vignettes of Horatio Alger, Willa Cather, Allen Ginsberg, Gertrude Stein and Walt Whitman. Gay heritage also formed the basis of one of the earliest pieces of agitprop performed by the Gay Sweatshop theatre company in London in 1976. *As Time Goes By*, by Noel Greig and Drew Griffiths, contains European queer-cultural set pieces, including the male brothel of the Cleveland Street Scandal in the 1890s, Edward Carpenter and George Merrill at home in Millthorpe, and a scene in which two drag entertainers sing to Magnus Hirschfeld 'Dear Darling Doctor Magnus'.

The simple fact of queer survival is itself inspiring and empowering:

> the history of gay people shows that despite repression, secrecy and shame, we as a people have nonetheless survived, have insisted on our specialness, have developed coping strategies for survival; and therefore this history can provide real inspiration to everyone else to be just as different as they really are – to summon up the courage to insist on their specialness being respected. (Duberman, 1991)

Several queer historians opted for this discipline specifically because it falls within the liberation agenda, as did D'Emilio (1992): 'My allegiance to the academic world was, at best, tenuous; only the conviction that the movement would be strengthened by the retrieval of its hidden early history kept me at it.'

Queer history was also important to the earlier 'homophile' movement. ONE Institute opened in Los Angeles in 1956 and began offering its course on Homosexuality in History in 1957; this was followed by The History of the Homophile Movements of Europe, in 1958–9, which included visiting lectures by men who personally knew Magnus Hirschfeld; and in 1959–60 The Homosexual in American Society or Sociology of Homosexuality was a course designed specifically to examine two new ideas: that a 'homosexual minority' and a 'homosexual culture' existed (Legg, 1994). In the same year, Jim Kepner began his very thorough seminars on Homosexuality in Modern German History: From Frederick the Great through Hitler; Don Slater began teaching The Gay Novel in 1960, the year in which the Institute issued 'A Declaration of Homosexual Rights'. Christopher Isherwood was a director of ONE's affiliate Institute for the Study of Human Resources from 1976 to 1984, and he researched much of *Christopher and His Kind* (1977) in ONE Institute's Blanche M. Baker Memorial Library and Archives. A fellow director was Laud Humphreys, author of *Tearoom Trade* and *Out of the Closets, the Sociology of Homosexual Liberation* (1972). Vern L. Bullough, Professor of History at California State University, Northridge, was closely involved with the Institute from the late 1960s, notably contributing some two thousand entries from his research towards the compilation of *A Bibliography of Homosexuality*, published in 1976. From 1981 the ONE Institute Graduate School was licensed by the state education authority to offer courses leading to accredited Master of Arts and Doctor of Philosophy degrees in Homophile Studies. One of the first dissertations was Michael H. Lombardi's *The Writings of Karl Heinrich Ulrichs* (1984) (his translation of Ulrichs's complete writings was published in 1988).

ONE Inc. is resentful that its activities and publications are so lightly dismissed by social constructionist historians such as John D'Emilio (1992), who claims that when he started graduate school in 1971 '"gay history" was a term not yet invented'. In fact 'homophile history' had existed as a term in the 1950s, and as a concept since the 1870s. There is a New York versus California element in gay politics, New York being the base for 'progressive' politically based social constructionism, and California representing the more personal, developmental, cultural, 'lifestyle' and New Age essentialism, much satirized by the New York set with its greater access to publishing power bases and the media. In rewriting the history of the homophile emancipation movement, the New York branch of gay liberation has attempted to reserve most of the credit for itself. In response, Dorr Legg's (1994) book attempts to set the record straight, and certainly establishes the fact that an enormous cultural educational programme existed some fifteen years before the supposed 'birth' of gay liberation in 1969 in New York's Stonewall riots.

In 1957 Henry (Harry) Hay began working on an article which nearly matches the title of this present book: 'The Homophile in Search of an Historical Context and Cultural Contiguity'. Though a paid-up member of the Communist Party, Hay took the essentialist approach, emphasizing the importance of anthropological evidence of cross-cultural unity in variety, for example of initiation rituals and transgender persons: 'all their *thousand modifications* are facts in a single series, and only ring the changes upon some one impulse or necessity that is implicit in the generic situation'. Harry Hay had begun promoting his concept of 'the Homosexual Minority' in 1948, and under his guidance in 1950 the Mattachine Society Mission and Purposes stated that it was 'possible and desirable that a highly ethical homosexual culture emerge, as a consequence of its work, paralleling the emerging culture of our fellow minorities – the Negro, Mexican and Jewish Peoples'. Charles Rowland, another founder of the Society, in his article 'The Homosexual Culture' (*ONE Magazine*, May 1953) 'strongly defended the proposition that homosexuals constitute a minority with a distinctive culture'. During the Mattachine Constitutional Convention on 11 April 1953, and its continuation a month later, 'the words *minority* and *culture* triggered major disputes on several occasions during the proceedings' (Legg, 1994).

But no one seemed to dispute the fundamental fallacy of the view that a minority culture has to make a contribution to its 'parent culture', that it be of value to society at large, as stated in an article on 'Homosexual Culture' by Julian Underwood in 1960: 'Homosexuals can claim to be a distinct cultural minority only as it can be proven that they make a group contribution to the dominant culture which is the specific outcome of the homosexual temperament.' Most of the discussion since the early 1960s has rested upon this fundamental misuse of the term 'minority', which partly arises from the moral force attached to the 'majority' in American democratic philosophy. The truth is that any contribution from one culture to another is wholly irrelevant to whether or not that culture is distinctive. Romany gypsies may or may not make a contribution to the societies in which they reside, but they are nevertheless a distinctive ethnic culture within society. The three 'fellow minorities' originally mentioned by Hay – Mexicans, blacks and Jews – are not offsprings of a 'parent' white American culture. They may be dominated and oppressed by white Anglo-Saxon Protestant American society, but they nevertheless have their own culture and their own history.

And queers, like Mexicans, blacks and Jews, draw strength from an awareness of their own culture and history. 'What gives any group of people distinction and dignity is its culture. This includes a remembrance of the past and a setting of itself in a world context whereby the group can see *who it is* relative to everyone else' (Grahn, 1984). The search for cultural unity in the queer past is relevant even in the age of AIDS when attention is urgently focused upon the immediate present and near future. In Paul Monette's *Borrowed Time* (1988) a man and his lover who is dying from AIDS visit Greece: 'Impossible to measure the symbolic weight of the place for a gay man. ... Ancient places "confirm" a person, uniting a man to the past and thus the future.'

Social constructionism

During the past half-generation the history of homosexuality has been dominated by social constructionist dogma. I should perhaps make it clear that I shall not be analysing social constructionist theory about the alleged 'constructs' of sex, gender, race and class, or in other fields such as literature, art and the cinema, except as they impinge directly upon the concept with which I am concerned: homosexuality in history. The social constructionists in this field include Mary McIntosh, Jeffrey Weeks, Kenneth Plummer, Robert Padgug, David M. Halperin, John D'Emilio, Michel Foucault, Sheila Jeffreys, Jonathan Ned Katz (in his later work) and, to a lesser extent, less dogmatic theorists such as David F. Greenberg and George Chauncey. The school is sometimes called 'cultural constructivism', which hides its political agenda; their 'history' invariably focuses upon the nineteenth century, the era of bourgeois capitalism capable of being subjected to Marxist/Maoist economic analysis. Jeffrey Weeks was a founding member of the *Gay Left* collective, refugees from the collapsed Gay Marxist Group, whose magazine was published twice a year during the mid to late 1970s with the aim of disseminating socialist theory *vis-à-vis* gay oppression; he later became editor of the radical *History Workshop Journal*. Members of the Lesbian History Group founded in 1984, notably Sheila Jeffreys, were involved with the London Feminist History Group, and had much the same political aims. In 1974 Jonathan Katz invited John D'Emilio to join the gay men's study group 'convened to explore the utility of Marxist theory for understanding gay oppression. We met weekly for a period of almost two years ... I came away from those readings and discussions with tools for intellectual analysis that still inform the gay history I write' (D'Emilio, 1992). When these theorists talk about 'social constructs' they are referring specifically to ideologies constructed by bourgeois society in order to control the working classes. Towards the late 1980s much of this political agenda was hidden behind some very sophisticated theorizing, but these are the bare bones that are fairly easy to read between the lines.

The social constructionists maintain that significant shifts took place in the nineteenth century (this is when their political theory requires them to have taken place as part of the dialectics of revolution). By defining 'the homosexual' as 'the modern homosexual', the social constructionists are able to redefine the modern homosexual, who merely has 'class *awareness*', as the politicized homosexual, whose 'class *consciousness*' enables him or her to radically question such concepts as gender. The aim is to fight the class war so that 'homosexuals' (and 'men' and 'women') disappear as a class. I have much sympathy with the feminist position that heteropatriarchy is a social construct through which women are subjugated; but I have even greater sympathy with the lesbian-feminist position that lesbianism is 'natural' while 'compulsory heterosexuality' is the 'political institution', and that it is only the latter, and not the former, that requires deconstruction (Rich, 1993). The class war is an essential feature of social constructionist theory – if historical evidence can be produced which establishes the existence of the homosexual role and identity before capitalism, then the materialist theory starts to collapse. The dating of the emergence of the queer subculture, though crucial to the theory, is its weakest part.

> A curious outcome of ... centuries of oppression is that when the first writings on homosexuality reached the general public at the end of the nineteenth century, some individuals revealed to psychiatrists that, although they had responded solely to members of their own sex since adolescence, until then they imagined themselves unique in the whole world. They had 'constructed' their own sexual consciousness without any social input – a feat that should be impossible according to social constructionist postulates.
> (W. R. Dynes, 'Social Construction Approach', *EH*)

It is very easy for historians to establish that most of the sexual categories which are supposed to have arisen under modern capitalism in fact existed much earlier. It is nevertheless important to pursue this relatively easy branch of demolition, because the nineteenth century date is one of the major props of social constructionism, without which its economic/control analysis of homosexuality becomes meaningless. Any work which demonstrates the existence of significant 'constructs' before 1800 will tend to undermine Foucault's theories about the 'ruptures' between the 'epistemes' of the Classical Period and those of the Modern Period.

Political correctness has unfortunately relegated 'gay history' to the recent and contemporary account of the gay emancipation movement. But to place this movement in its proper historical perspective we must revert to some of the principles of 'queer history'. Jeffrey Weeks (1991) and other social constructionists have stressed 'the vital importance of distinguishing between behaviour, role, and identity in any sociological or historical approach to the subject of homosexuality'. On the contrary, I believe it is vital to recognize the integrity, unity and ambiguity of the experience that is falsified by over-intellectual analysis.

One of the reasons why many contemporary lesbian and gay theorists fail to appreciate that homosexuals existed before 1869 is the politically correct view that terms such as 'queer', 'faggot' and 'queen' are not nice, and especially since the late 1960s people have endeavoured to use the phrase 'gay and lesbian' wherever possible. There are certain men who lived before 1869 whom I would feel uneasy to call 'gay' or 'homophile', but I would not hesitate to call them queer or even silly old queens. Many of the mollies of the early eighteenth century were undoubtedly queens, whose interests and behaviour are virtually indistinguishable from queens I have known in the early 1960s (and later). I use the word 'queer' in such a way as to subsume the meanings of words such as homosexual, homophile, homoerotic and homosocial – all of which I think involve false distinctions rather than continuity (homosociality is little more than homosexuality with a fig leaf) – within the meanings of queer, faggot, dyke and gay, which more accurately reflect the working-class reality which formed gay (sub)cultures, whose authenticity middle-class lesbians and gays began denying in the 1950s and 1970s. My emphasis will be upon ethnic autonomy rather than assimilation (reflecting the separatist stance of contemporary 'queers'). 'Gay and lesbian' is perfectly acceptable for life since the 1960s, but most of my focus is upon the earlier past. 'Queer' was the word of preference for homosexuals as well as homophobes for the first half of the twentieth century, and of course is being reclaimed today in defiant rather than defensive postures. In English during the eighteenth and most of the nineteenth century the words of preference were 'molly' and 'sapphist', for which good modern equivalents are 'queer' and 'dyke'. During the seventeenth century and earlier the commonest terms were 'sodomite' and 'tribade', for which, again, precise modern equivalents are 'queer' and 'dyke'. In ancient and indigenous and premodern cultures the nearest modern equivalents are 'queer' and 'tomboy'. And the nearest modern equivalent for the nineteenth-century term 'homosexual' is: queer.

I add my voice to the widespread dissatisfaction with social constructionist thought, whose initial premises have been constantly reinforced by restatement and incestuous quotation among constructionist colleagues rather than supported by scholarly research. The approach quickly became authoritarian and totalitarian, insisting that only one method be used and that certain questions could not be asked:

> There remains today a fundamental divide between historians who believe that one should first decide what questions require answers, then wring answers out of whatever material is available, however unsatisfactory, and historians who prefer to be guided by the available material and to ask only those questions to which the material provides well-substantiated answers. (Marwick, 1989)

Social constructionists have even redefined the word 'experience' as a product of discourse, so 'evidence' itself is a social construct (Scott, 1993). The notion that there can be a social constructionist history is a contradiction in terms.

It was quickly recognized that social constructionism seemed to be founded upon historical ignorance, and it is no longer possible to dismiss this ignorance as a product of youthful overenthusiasm for a new idea. The recent argument that the debate between essentialists and social constructionists is 'arid and false' is an effort by social constructionists to consolidate their position in the face of the increasing recognition that by the end of the 1980s more and more historical evidence was coming to light and undermining their theories, which after twenty years of increasing abstruseness were still no more than unsupported working hypotheses. Marwick's (1989) judgement on Foucault's major works is that they are

> philosophical, intuitive, and imaginative, and lacking in effective historical underpinning ... there has been the production of ever more complex, more abstract, and more uncompromising theory in which anything so mundane as what actually happens in real human societies seems to become less and less relevant. ... With someone like Foucault it is probably truer to say that he sought refuge in imaginative leaps of greater and greater incredibility, rather than in any coherent theory.

Camille Paglia (1994) more forcefully judges Foucault to have been a glib game-player who took very little research a very long way. ... Leftists have damaged their own cause ... by their indifference to fact, their carelessness and sloth, their unforgivable lack of professionalism as scholars. ... My first proposal for the gay world: Get rid of dead abstract 'theory' and rabid social constructionism, the limp legacy of academic know-nothings.

The absence of historical underpinning to social constructionist theory can be readily demonstrated. 'The most vulnerable claim [of the constructionists] is that the notion of the homosexual as a distinct "species" originated only about a hundred years ago, an invention of the medical profession or the product of capitalist urbanization' (Greenberg, 1988); the materials gathered by Greenberg's exhaustive review of research

> make abundantly clear that the world was neither conceptually nor behaviorally polymorphously perverse prior to the Industrial Revolution. ... Foucault, who held a chair in the history of ideas, assumed too readily that intellectuals are the sole repository of conceptual invention and simply imposed a new hegemonic discourse on passive recipients.

On the whole, a strictly social constructionist strategy has ended up throwing the baby out with the bath water. As Anthony Julius notes in his review of *The Jew in the Text: Modernity and the Construction of Identity* (1995) (essays collected by Linda Mochlin and Tamar Garb), if we take the view that what we hold to be our most private self is itself a construct, then

> two unappealing consequences follow. First, if all Jews are 'constructed', then the difference between 'fictional' and 'real' Jews, or between fictional Jews that are merely 'stereotypical' and those that are fully realised, is not very important. Second, giving an account of individual suffering, of the violations of self, ceases to be interesting. ... If, as one contributor says, '"Real Jews" and "fictitious Jews" occupy the same representational theatre', then you disable yourself from protesting: 'I have been misrepresented!' ... One cannot write about persecution in a language in which that experience is invisible.

Spencer (1995) rightly rejects Foucault's position that 'The sensuality of those who did not like the opposite sex was hardly noticed in the past.' Rather than the end of the nineteenth century, Spencer, with a much better survey of the available historical evidence, places a noticeable shift at the beginning of the medieval period:

> the concept of bisexuality was discarded from the consciousness of society, [and] a polarity began to establish itself between the Other (what is repressed) and the Self (which is publicly acknowledged); between that which will later be called homosexual, which must be hidden, and the status quo, the heterosexual, which needs to be publicly enhanced. Human sexual nature, in the way it was considered socially, was divided into two parts, homosexual and heterosexual, as if they were mutually exclusive.

This itself is not a very satisfactory 'grand theory', for there are many examples prior to the thirteenth century that show an awareness of a predominantly homosexual orientation, and, equally, many contemporary queers who do not regard themselves as being exclusively homosexual.

My aim in the present book will be to examine the nature of queer history, with a focus upon historiographical issues that have not been adequately addressed by historians in the 1980s and 1990s, who have largely failed to recognize the difference between attitudes towards homosexuals and the experiences of queers, and who have built up theories that have no empirical foundations in history. The myth that the homosexual was born circa 1869 is easily demolished, but beyond that I aim to show that the social constructionist emperor has no clothes. I will argue that a typology of queer personalities and relationships and the characteristic features of a queer culture arise from a core of queer desire and are not wholly configured by the regulation of that desire. Queer history properly considered is the attempt to recover the authentic voice of queer experience rather than simply to document suppression or oppression.

Essentialism

My position is sited within the essentialist camp, and I hope to expose some of the fallacies of social constructionist theory, which I see as the main impediment to the understanding of queer history. The history of ideas (and ideologies) is enormously interesting and valuable, but it is tragic that homosexuals have been subsumed *totally* under the idea of the homosexual. The result is little better than intellectual ethnic cleansing. In the social constructionist view, knowledge is constructed, deconstructed and reconstructed through ideological discourse. In my essentialist view, knowledge is discovered, repressed, suppressed and recovered through history and experience. Social constructionism emphasizes revolutionary development (the dialectic); I see evolutionary development, cultural growth and permutation, and sometimes mere change in fashion. Rather than the word 'construct', which implies building from scratch according to an arbitrarily chosen blueprint, I prefer 'consolidate' or 'forge', implying that the basic material already exists but can be subjected to shaping and polishing.

'Cultural constructs' are sometimes set up in opposition to 'universal truths' in an effort to force essentialists into an impossibly idealistic corner, but 'culture' is a concept that can be claimed by essentialists as well as by social constructionists. The essentialist position is that queer culture is organic rather than artificial. Social constructionists see culture as a construct whose arbitrary foundation is determined by the builder; I see culture as the cultivation of a root, and I shall be developing the ethnic view that queer culture grows naturally from personal queer identity and experience and is self-cultivated by queers rather than by the ideology and labels of straight society. I have no objection if critics wish to call me an 'essentialist' pure and simple, because I believe that homosexuals are born and not made. However, I also believe that queers fashion their own culture (using their own resources rather than being imposed upon by society), and that will be a significant focus of my own version of essentialism, which might be called 'queer cultural essentialism'. I take the view that there is a core of queer desire that is transcultural, transnational and transhistorical, a queer essence that is innate, congenital, constitutional, stable or fixed in its basic pattern. However, I distinguish between queer persons, queer sexual acts and behaviour, and queer social interactions, and try not to confuse the constancy of the desire with the variability of its expression. Personal queer identity arises from within, and is then consolidated along lines suggested by the collective identity of the queer (sub)culture.

In the theoretical literature it is generally assumed that essentialism is the same as uniformism/conformism (often made explicit in lesbian-feminist theory). But the view that homosexuality is a monolith is not at all an essential feature of essentialism. The essentialist does not say there is only *one* gay root; in fact a *diversity of roots* has been a key feature of essentialism since the early 1970s (witness the title of the two-volume collection of essays from *Gay Sunshine: Gay Roots*). It is really social constructionist theorists who have forced essentialism into this straitjacket, just as they have forced gay experience into the political straitjacket.

I have no problem in reconciling the view that queer desire is innate but that it also expresses itself in sexual or social actions and (sub)cultures that may reflect to a greater or lesser degree the time and place in which they occur. Self-presentation can be carefully constructed while being founded upon an innate self-conception. There should be no difficulty in recognizing, for example, that modern British gay consciousness was well in place before American styles of presenting gayness were deliberately imported into Britain: 'Michael Glover, who started the London Apprentice [pub], had seen leather bars and cruise bars in the States and it was his intention to bring that style of bar to London' (Healy, 1996). The specific sexual custom of fistfucking appeared first in America and was exported to Europe and Japan, probably in the year 1971, but it is not likely that an entirely new *mentalité* arose in that year, or even that decade.

Beneath a (fairly limited) variety of customs that differ from culture to culture lies the phenomenon of queer desire. That desire need not necessarily be expressed through sexual acts: queer culture and queer 'sexuality' go beyond genital sexuality. Henry James, as he walked along the river in Oxford in 1869, seeing the punts full of 'the mighty lads of England, clad in white flannel and blue, immense, fair-haired, magnificent in their youths', felt that his heart 'would crack with the fullness of satisfied desire' (cited by Kaplan, 1992). This kind of diffuse homoerotic passion for golden lads or lasses is a central feature of gay and lesbian culture, whether or not it reflects the sexual longing and nostalgia that can arise from 'sublimation', and even though its avenues of expression are often restricted and controlled by society in ways specific to each society. Homosexuality is a broad stream which continues to run despite being dammed up and channelled off by social control. The evidence of history points to repression rather than construction as the shaping force of queer identity and culture. The opportunities for expressing queer desire have been increasingly restricted in modern times, but the desire remains the same. The inner drive has simply been repressed or liberated to varying degrees from one era and culture to another. Trevisan's (1986) history of homosexuality in Brazil more or less confirms the perception of the early travellers to southern countries that there exists a 'Carnival instinct', an 'indisputable taste for lechery', a homoeroticism that gives the *bunda*, the backside, a privileged place:

> Any attempt at the historical systemisation of homosexuality as
> experienced by Brazilians will be less the history of permissiveness
> arising from the mechanisms of social control (from the Inquisition

and police censorship to psychiatry and academic science) and more the insurrection of vestiges of an uncontrolled desire which flourishes underground, in the backyards of the provinces and the public conveniences of large cities.

The queer historian can adopt an essentialist position without having to clearly specify which popular scientific theory is regarded as most correct. Although the essentialist position assumes a physiological grounding, it is not incumbent upon a historian to offer biological theories concerning brain structure, chromosomes, hormones and genes. The business of the historian, as opposed to, say, the geneticist, is to examine historical evidence for or against the issue of constitutionality itself. The historian of homosexuals in Renaissance Venice need acquire no more expertise in the field of genetics than a historian of immigration patterns of the gypsies (travellers) in the Balkans.

Earlier biological studies which tried to show a link between sexual orientation and the physical development of the genitalia proved inconclusive and have been abandoned. Current studies purporting to show a link between sexual orientation and hormonal influence upon the brain and genetic make-up may similarly prove inconclusive. The studies of Simon LeVay (for example *The Sexual Brain*, 1993), and others whose work has led to tabloid headlines about 'the gay gene', have provoked serious criticism of methodological failings in defining the deviant group, of the inadequate control of many variables and the inability to quantify very tiny differences in measurements of brain tissue (Vines, 1992). The brain continues to develop for several years after birth, but the degree to which this allows for 'social' influences is debatable. The psychoanalytical theory that homosexuality is 'acquired' by experience during, say, the first three years of childhood may never be proved or disproved by historical research; recollections by modern persons about their first three years are untrustworthy, and testimony about the very early childhood of homosexuals in ancient and premodern periods is scarce. But in any case the idea that queerness is 'nature nurtured' is still an essentialist position rather than a compromise between the born versus bred argument; the social constructionist position completely turns its back upon nature. Rather like exclusive heterosexuality, social constructionism lies solely at point 0 on the Kinsey scale: points 1 to 6 are all essentialist to a greater or lesser extent.

Historical research tends to support the essentialist position that queer desire is congenital and then constituted into a meaningful queer identity during childhood. The message of abundant personal testimony on the subject, in a wide range of sources, from fifteenth-century Italy to late twentieth-century Thailand, from biographies and autobiographies to novels, is that *queerness dawns* around the age of 7, or, if it comes later, that it is something that has lain dormant in the personality, but was always there. Chosen as the spokesperson for the 1988 World Expo in Australia because she was the only one living who had attended the 1888 Expo, E. M. 'Monte' Punshon, who died in 1989 at the age of 106, revealed to the media that 'she had known she was a lesbian for nearly a century – since the age of six' (Richards, 1990).

Gender nonconformity

Queerness at an early age is usually recollected as a positive rather than a negative feeling, a suggestion that it is *not* something constructed by stigma, because the awareness precedes the age at which internalized stigmatization could be activated. However, 'gender constructs' could possibly occur at a very early age, and gender roles are often used to support social constructionist arguments. The view that children are wholly conditioned by their parents ignores the fact that 'children are born with differing temperaments which to some degree determine how they will be treated by parents and others' (Legg, 1994). The 1981 Kinsey Institute studies of possible correlates between homosexuality and other factors such as class, siblings, etc., 'came up with almost nothing. They very nearly found that the only powerful predictor of adult homosexuality is childhood gender nonconformity, a finding that has been replicated often, both retrospectively and prospectively' (J. D. Weinrich, 'Sociobiology', *EH*). However, to posit gender nonconformity as somehow 'causing' homosexuality begs the question 'what causes the gender nonconformity? Researchers have suggested that at some level, the child and family know from an early point that the child is sexually "different"' (R. C. Savin-Williams, 'Youth', *EH*).

John Tanner (1780–1847), who lived with the North American Indians for the last thirty years of his life, and who was constantly approached by a 50-year-old man who had already lived with many husbands and now wanted to live with him, said that among the Objibbeway the *berdache* 'are commonly called A-go-kwa, a word which is expressive of their *condition*' (cited by Legg, 1994). A common theme is that the two-spirit individual is destined to be the way he or she is. Usually this calling is discovered in early childhood; at one extreme, the infant who picks up a female article of clothing or occupation rather than the male objects which have been placed in a circle near it will be 'dedicated' to the two-spirit life, and this has been used to argue for social conditioning. But the ritual could well be a case of retrospective rationalization, as parents explain and justify their children's personality, in the same way that the dreams 'authorizing' these transformations are often 'recalled' after the event. An observer of *berdache* among the Crow of the Plains in 1903 explained, 'I was told that when very young, those persons manifested a decided preference for things pertaining to female duties'; while another observer of the Miami said, 'There were men who are bred for this purpose from their childhood' from the first moment they are seen picking up a spindle etc., but most of the evidence suggests that they were 'self-recruited' (Whitehead, 1993).

There were also female *berdache*, for example the *hwame* among the Mohave, though their role seems to have been less clearly institutionalized. Female transvestites, for example in the Cocopa, where young girls manifest 'male proclivities indicated by a desire to play with boys, make bows and arrows, hunt birds and rabbits', and among the Yuman the *kwe'rhame* are rare, but they too 'realize their character through a dream at puberty', characteristically dreaming of men's weapons: 'As a small child the kwe'rhame plays with boys' toys' (cited by Whitehead, 1993). In other words, like a good many modern lesbians, they were born tomboys.

Most *berdache* are described by themselves and their societies as comprising a 'third sex/gender', yet modern anthropologists concentrate on culture and custom and generally do not spend much time commenting upon their physiological – that is, essentialist – characteristics: 'Spontaneous use of female speech patterns, a piping voice, or feminine ways of laughing and walking are sometimes mentioned as identifying the budding berdache' (Whitehead, 1993). There is abundant evidence that the *berdache* – exactly like most lesbians and gay men – have an innate nature that resists being heterosexually constructed. The Mohave, like many other tribes, explained it thus in 1937:

> When there is a desire in a child's heart to become a transvestite, that child will act different. It will let people become aware of that desire. They may insist on giving the child the toys and garments of its true sex, but the child will throw them away and do this every time there is a big [social] gathering. (Cited by Whitehead, 1993)

The *berdache* were noted for being exclusively homosexual from the moment they took on the characteristic identity/role until their death (Greenberg, 1988) (though they paired off with non-*berdache* men). The common view that they wore the clothes of the other sex is an oversimplified stereotype; it is more accurate to say that they wore *some* clothes of the other sex, which reflects their third-sex (or 'two-spirit') status; indeed more recent anthropologists describe such behaviour as 'mixed-gender' rather than 'cross-gender' or 'cross-dressing' (a term coined by Edward Carpenter in 1911), to get away from the simplistic idea of 'reversal' or 'inversion'. Greenberg points out that the dichotomous view of gender used by anthropologists is inadequate, but he then uses the prejudicial phrase 'partial or incomplete transformation' to accord with his view that the 'core' of the phenomenon is based upon gender rather than orientation. Whitehead (1993) similarly argues that 'for Native Americans, occupational pursuits and dress/demeanor were the important determinants of an individual's social classification, and sexual object choice was its trailing rather than its leading edge'.

This kind of foreground versus background debate, however, obscures the central point, that the *berdache* has a unified sexual/cultural identity in which sexuality is as fundamental as gender. Homosexuality is so closely tied up with the *berdache* identity that to assert that gender is '*the* important determinant' is prescriptive rather than descriptive. Homosexuality is the constant in the *berdache*; their gender behaviour is variable (for example, ranging from mostly male to mostly female clothing or occupations). Gender dress/demeanour is most sharply marked when a *berdache* marries a man: what is never adequately considered is the possibility that the other-gender option was adopted *after* the homosexual relationship was chosen, to allow for the efficient division of labour in 'husband–wife' couples. The active/passive roles of the *berdache* and his husband are not necessarily fixed in private, only in public: a Hupa *berdache* says of his partner, 'As far as it was publicly known, he [the husband] was the man. But in bed there was an exchange of roles. They have to keep an image as masculine, so they always ask me not to tell anybody' (cited by Williams, 1986).

Part of the social constructionist analysis of the 'gender role' of the *berdache* depends upon the allegation that the husband (and the wife, in the case of the female *berdache*) is simply a man (or woman) rather than publicly categorized into a role. However, this is not strictly true: husbands of *berdaches* and wives of *hwame* were frequently the butt of social ridicule, a 'kidding' or 'teasing' severe enough to break up such marriages: in other words, a homosexual/heterosexual dichotomy clearly functioned here (Williams, 1986). McIntosh (1968) paradoxically acknowledges this yet ignores it in her discussion of the homosexual role. The view that husbands of *berdaches* do not form a peculiar category is contradicted by George Catlin's famous paintings and descriptions in the 1830s of the 'Dance of the Berdache'. These in fact feature what he called the 'society ... of odd fellows', which consists of those who have had sex with the *berdache* dancing around him and making a public proclamation of that fact; only the partners of the *berdache* are allowed to join the dance and to partake of the feast afterwards (Legg, 1994). No native American term is given for these 'odd fellows', but the distinctive category was nevertheless institutionalized by this ritual.

The shamans of Siberia and Central Asia have many features in common with the *berdache*, though the phenomenon is more closely associated with ritual ecstasy or trance states. Transvestism is important to the role, and there is an institutionalized role for female shamans. The male shamans regard themselves as the 'wife' of a supernatural 'husband', and they marry men less frequently than do the *berdache*. It is important to recognize the distinctive religious function of the shamans, but it is also a fact that homosexuals have a professional monopoly on this role. It is by no means a modern gay anachronism to suggest, as did Edward Carpenter, that shamanism springs from homosexual orientation, or that 'In the whole process the homosexual–transvestite orientation is primary, the shamanic calling secondary' (W. Johansson, 'Shamanism', *EH*).

The *hijras* of modern India – mostly transvestite or transsexual male prostitutes who perform music and dance at important social festivals – have been reduced to specifically gender phenomena by modern theorists despite the overriding importance of homosexuality in their lives. The *hijras* are of course 'constructed', in the sense that they castrate themselves, but they maintain that their *hijra* identity predates that castration and is specifically a homosexual identity. Today, *hijras* are conscious that they are part of the historical tradition of court eunuchs, when they wore male rather than female clothing (Dalrymple, 1993). Shakuntala, a *hijra* interviewed in 1981, emphasized:

> In many places men who are perfect men have joined this community only for the sake of earning a living. This is not good. Only men who have not spoiled any lady or got any children should come into the hijra company. You should not have had any affairs with ladies, not have loved ladies, or done any sexual thing with

them or have married a lady. We true hijras are like this from childhood. From a small age we like to dance and dress as women. Even when we go away from this world, in our death, we must wear the sari. That is our desire. (Nanda, 1993)

The gender of *hijras* is a specifically queer gender – 'neither man nor woman'. They deliberately exaggerate or burlesque female dress and mannerisms; their sexually suggestive behaviour and coarse speech and gestures (notably their habit of lifting their skirt to display their mutilated genitals) would be outrageous for women; they smoke the hookah which is reserved for men (Nanda, 1993). A modern outrageous queen would recognize a sister in the *hijra* and his kin. Margaret Mead tells a story that demonstrates instant recognition between an Omaha Indian *berdache* and a modern Japanese homosexual who visited her in the field in 1961: the Japanese man 'was not a transvestite but ... had a complete repertoire of homosexual postures. Within an hour of his arrival, the single berdache in the tribe turned up and tried to make contact with him' (cited by Weinrich, 1987).

Most queers are as recognizable for their characteristic speech, mannerisms and bearing as are Jamaicans, Italians, Pakistanis or any other ethnic group. The long-running British television series *Out on Tuesday* (later called *Out*) demonstrated this to an embarrassing degree for politically correct viewers: letters to the gay press complained about the choice of 'obvious gay types' for respondents/interviewees, unable to accept that we are *all* obvious gay types. I am sure that an aural analysis of the programme would result in a scientific chart of 'the gay voice'.

'Do queers walk funny?' is a question still half-seriously debated in Internet queer newsgroups, the general consensus being that the walk imitates female prostitutes. But men who lived in the 1930s and 1940s when swishing was especially noticeable felt that the real construct was the exaggeratedly masculine walk of heterosexual men. 'Men, with their B.M. [Bloody Manly] walk, were so terribly difficult to emulate. The biggest give away was the gay walk. The trouble was, if you were sent up, the camper you walked' (Skinner, 1978). Quentin Crisp remarked upon the Dilly boys in the 1920s:

A passer-by would have to be very innocent indeed not to catch the meaning of the mannequin walk and the stance in which the hip was only prevented from total dislocation by the hand placed upon it. ... The strange thing about 'camp' is that it has become fossilized. The mannerisms have never changed. If I were now to see a woman sitting with her knees clamped together, one hand on her hip and the other lightly touching her back hair, I should think, 'Either she scored her last social triumph in 1926 or it is a man in drag.' (Cited by Miller, 1995)

However, 'camp stylization' can be traced much further back than the 1920s. Grahn (1984) points out that not all 'femme' faggotry imitates female mannerisms:

> Some of it is an independent Gay cultural tradition ... handed along from faggot to faggot. ... It is commonly supposed that faggots lisp in imitation of women. Modern women, however, do not lisp. ... But the sweet sibilant faggot speech is peculiar to Gay men, and completely distinctive. For the most part faggots learn their particular manner of speaking from each other.

Lisping is cited as an affectation in works by Shakespeare and Chaucer; it is not impossible, as Grahn suggests, that it was once a special courting speech or a ceremonial language of court. The alleged stereotype of the mincing queen has not changed significantly since Adamantios portrayed him in the second century:

> You can recognize him by his provocatively melting glance and by the rapid movement of his intensely staring eyes. ... His head is tilted to the side, his loins do not hold still, and his slack limbs never stay in one position. He minces along with little jumping steps; his knees knock together. He carries his hands with palms turned upward. He has a shifting gaze, and his voice is thin, weepy, shrill, and drawling. (Cited by Aldrich, 1993)

Identity

Social constructionists themselves acknowledge that despite an intellectual commitment to their theories, they often operate 'as if' their sexual identity were innate:

> Myself, in the main I agree with Fuss [Diana Fuss, *Essentially Speaking: Feminism, Nature and Difference*, 1989] that 'lesbian' is a historical construction of comparatively recent date, and that there is no eternal lesbian essence outside the frame of cultural change and historical determination. However, this strictly intellectual definition wouldn't stop me *feeling*, and sometimes

behaving, as though the total opposite were true. ... We need our dream of a lesbian nation, even as we recognise its fictionality.
(S. Munt, *New Lesbian Criticism*, 1992, quoted by Bradby, 1993)

This is a very revealing admission from a leading lesbian feminist, which raises a host of problems: how can one found an identity upon a known falsehood? My own feeling is that Munt has been led against her will into adopting the fashionable theory of social constructionism. In a similar way, nearly all gay and lesbian critics of literature and the cinema feel compelled to use the fashionable post-structuralist theory of the death of the author, while at the same time they find it impossible not to hypothesize the existence of the author when discussing any lesbian or gay texts.

The real problem is that social constructionists will happily jettison both history and personal experience if they contradict political theory. John D'Emilio (1992) saw his first queers during his initial visits to Broadway as a 15-year-old high-school student:

> three young men, thin as toothpicks, with long teased hair, mascara, rouge, and powder on their faces, their fingers fluttering in front of them. ... As with so many of my other early instances of 'discovery,' I wonder now just how I *knew* they and I had something in common. No one had ever spoken to me about drag queens, or effeminacy, or homosexuality, or the connections among them. Yet I knew. ... I, and so many of the gay men I met in the succeeding years, would wax lyrical about our sixth gay sense, about the sharply honed ability we all possessed to recognize 'members of the tribe.' Now I think that's all hogwash. It ignores the hundreds of legs that didn't press back [in subway cars] and eyes that didn't return the gaze.

In my view this illustrates a politically correct renunciation of a perception that *did* exist and which can be documented in the lives of a vast number of queer men and women throughout history. The queer gaze is immediately recognizable, whether one participates in it or just observes; as a man who cruised Leicester Square during the Second World War explained, 'The eyes, the eyes, they're a dead giveaway. ... If someone looks at you with a lingering look, and looks away, and then looks at you again' (Chauncey, 1994). Like countless others, I can recognize a gay man at fifty feet, by sight or by sound. I can tell if a man is gay by the way he walks, by the inflections in his voice, by the way he steps out of a car. It is not simply a matter of being effeminate or even camp; as Donald

Webster Cory said in the 1950s, there are signs 'neither masculine nor feminine, but specifically and peculiarly homosexual'. When these features are exaggerated they become the mincing gait, the high-pitched, haughty or ironic voice and lisp, the self-conscious display of the body and the flutter of the fingers. 'The special language of a queen, or even an ordinary garden-variety faggot, is so distinct I find I can distinguish it even in a crowd of men in a restaurant or on the street, far from any Gay scene' (Grahn, 1984). To assert that various queer gestures and signs are 'culturally specific' is to ignore the evidence that a quite limited number of gestures and signs marks out the effeminate/camp man and the butch woman across a very wide range of cultures and across several thousand years. A 'third sex' category is almost universally discernible even while the 'manly' and 'feminine' elements that go into that category differ.

If anything tends to disprove the idea that personality and behaviour are purely the results of choice and will (including the imposition of the will of others), it is homosexuality. The idea that one can choose to be queer arose as part of the political agenda for social change in the 1970s and 1980s, and personal testimony of this phenomenon is limited mainly to lesbian feminists (for example, Dell Richards). The 'freedom of choice' within the gay emancipation movement was not initially cast as a political choice; it originally meant freedom *to be* homosexual without harassment, freedom to express oneself publicly and to follow one's path; homosexuality itself was a given, which one could choose to fight against, to hide or to accept and even celebrate: the emphasis was upon choosing one's authentic self. Homosexuality is not a political choice; it is dictated by the imperatives of desire.

The historical record demonstrates that, on the contrary, many homosexuals chose heterosexuality and failed to maintain it because choice is less powerful than destiny. The idea that sexual identity is 'malleable' to the degree that social constructionists believe seems to me absurd. Abundant evidence demonstrates that sexual orientation cannot be changed even for men who are strongly motivated to change and who have voluntarily undergone extensive psychiatric therapies, involving the use of drugs and hormone injections, behaviour modification techniques, electric shock therapy, etc., in an effort to turn straight. The main result has been to make many therapists rich while shattering the lives of countless homosexuals. The widespread failure of such therapies has led to their virtual abandonment except by psychiatric institutions supported by the radical religious right in America. Most therapists now advise their clients to accept themselves and concentrate on *managing* their identities in a positive fashion; it is recognized, in effect, that their queerness is part of their essential nature and cannot be changed. The development of penile plethysmography (measurement of penile volume change during sexual arousal) by Czech researcher Kurt Freund in the 1970s demonstrated that men who said they had been 'cured' of homosexual desires by aversion therapy in fact still possessed a *scientifically measurable* desire for homosexual relations. This prompted Freund to give up aversion therapy, while other researchers confirmed his findings that it was nearly impossible to change sexual orientation. Plethysmographic research has also demonstrated the validity of anecdotal evidence that very few men are equally aroused by men and women: that is, a 'bisexual orientation' is rare. This scientific technique confirms the essentialist position:

> it has established the validity of talking about one's sexual orientation, since it can establish that it exists independently of what one consciously reports ... it has challenged the notion that one's sexual proclivities are mere preferences on the level of what route one prefers to drive to work. (James D. Weinrich, 'Plethysmography', *EH*)

Ray Evans in a 1961 article in *ONE Institute Quarterly of Homophile Studies* took the view that biological factors are important and perhaps crucial to the homophile personality and behaviour, and his basic conclusions have not been undermined by an additional thirty-five years of research:

> the very fact that throughout the mammalian scale, a great many more males than females engage in homosexual behavior is in itself suggestive of a constitutional factor.

> Despite innumerable case histories and expansive psychoanalytic 'explanations', there is no incontrovertible evidence as to how homosexuality is acquired through life experiences. There is no known set of conditions which invariably leads to its development.

> When virtually all pressures and attitudes of parents and society tend to teach and enforce heterosexual behavior, it is perplexing how anyone learns to be homosexual. (Legg, 1994)

'Homosexualities'

The cultural relativism observed by the social constructionists has been very much exaggerated. The essentialist does not reject the notion that there are 'homosexualities' rather than a single monolithic homosexuality. It is obvious that the ways of being homosexual sometimes vary in different historical periods and in different cultures. But they are not infinitely different; in fact the differences are not very wide (perhaps there are not even so many as a dozen different homosexualities). Dynes and Donaldson (1992) distinguish only seven models of male homosexual relationships (with somewhat fewer lesbian counterparts): age-differentiated (institutionalized *paiderastia* as in ancient Greece); ephebophilia (adult passive males with 17- to 21-year-old active masculine males); gender-differentiated (for example, the *berdache*); androphilia (reciprocal same-status adults as in contemporary North America); adolescent experimentation; situational (heterosexuals deprived of women); and 'dominance-enforcement' (power roles as alleged for ancient Rome). Eight hundred years ago Richard of Devizes in his *Chronicle of the Times of King Richard the First* (1192) described at least four classes of males (who probably comprised a queer subculture) who still figure prominently in today's queer typology: *glabriones* ('smooth-cheeked, pretty, effeminate boys'), *pusiones* ('little hustlers, kept boys'), *molles* ('effeminates') and *mascularii* ('man-lovers') (W. Houser, 'London', *EH*). Vicinus (1993) agrees with Steven Epstein that there are only a limited number of 'sexual scripts' by which we are all 'typecast', and she suggests there are only four lesbian types – 'transvestite, romantic friend, occasional lover, and androgynous woman' – and only a few types of lesbian relationship, for example, romantic friendship and butch/femme. She cannot reconcile the claim that modern sexual identity is socially constructed and historically specific with her historical perception that 'same-sex erotic attraction appears to be transhistorical and transcultural and to appear repeatedly in a limited range of behaviors'.

The assertion that there are an infinite number of homosexualities is a political statement rather than an observable fact. Not only have a very limited number of homosexual paradigms been observed throughout history and throughout different cultures, but they are very often found concurrently in a single culture. These models display more similarities to one another than do individual cultures, and it is remarkable that queer (sub)cultures have more in common with each other than with the larger cultures of which they are a part. Empirical research has not borne out the universal–polymorphous hypothesis, nor has it discovered a very wide range of configurations of erotic pleasure. 'The conclusion is inescapable: since cultures are legion but sexual arrangements are few, there can be no one-to-one correlation of culture and sexual-orientation typing' (S. Donaldson and W. R. Dynes, 'Typology', *EH*).

Discourse and shifts

Most social constructionists, taking their cue from Weeks and Foucault, concentrate on the 'discourse' of homosexuality, namely the discussion and investigation of homosexuality by professional sexologists and physicians, and ignore the evidence that falls outside that discourse. But if anything suggests that experiential reality exists outside of discourse, it is the feeling of thousands of homosexuals of a desire *for which they have no name*. Even when we examine the professional discourse, repeatedly we find instances of a dawning awareness among heterosexuals (especially the middle classes) of the existence of a world of homosexuals (especially among the working classes) which homosexuals have known about for decades and even centuries. As W. Dorr Legg expressed it in 1962, after reviewing the notable gap in the sociological literature: 'Are social scientists actually unaware of phenomena that are common knowledge to every street urchin? Do these scholars suffer from some sort of in-group myopia?' (Legg, 1994). The answer lay in their class: the middle classes are puritans, and have little connection with the lower classes. Symonds, for example, in the 1870s, was actively engaged in the discourse before he discovered the reality with a Guardsman; the truth dawned for him not as a result of discourse, but after seeing 'a rude *graffito* scrawled with slate-pencil upon slate. It was of so concentrated, so stimulative, so penetrative a character – so thoroughly the voice of vice and passion in the proletariat – that it pierced the very marrow of my soul. "Prick to prick, so sweet".' There are also many cases in which the authorities, those who supposedly define and create the homosexual construct, began an investigation which suddenly revealed to their astonishment a large underworld, which becomes so threatening that it put a halt to the inquiry. The investigation of the gay subculture at the Newport Naval Training Station led to the arrest of twenty sailors and sixteen civilians in 1919, at which point the chairman of the court ordered the chief investigator to curtail the investigation, warning, 'If your men [the decoys] do not knock off, they will hang the whole state of Rhode Island' (Chauncey, 1985). So even within the discourse what we are often

25

dealing with is social *discovery* rather than social *construction*. A key feature of the homosexual 'discourse' during the 1950s and early 1960s consisted of ordinary homosexuals successfully persuading the sociologists to recognize them and to begin basing their theories on the majority of homosexuals who had never consulted psychiatrists or been arrested. It was this line of sociological enquiry, by the likes of Evelyn Hooker, whose pool was drawn from acquaintances of her ordinary gay friends, which successfully began to deconstruct the models constructed by psychiatry and the law.

Social constructionist discourse is fond of hyperbole such as 'crucial change', 'massive shift', 'distinctively new', 'profoundly different', 'vital moment', etc. (all from Weeks, 1991). As far as I am concerned, 'watersheds', 'shifts' and 'ruptures' have very little to do with queers themselves, and much to do with the education of heterosexuals, who gradually became less naive as sexologists and the more outrageous queens made clear what queers have always known. The trials of Oscar Wilde in 1895 and Prince Philipp Fürst zu Eulenburg-Hertefeld in 1907 were more important for revealing the truth about homosexuals than for creating false stereotypes about them. In the former, the inescapable link between platonic love and stained bedclothes was made plain for all to see. In the latter, as Eulenburg lamented,

> At the moment when the freshest example of the modern age, a Harden [who published the scandal in his newspaper], criticized our nature, stripped our ideal friendship, laid bare the form of our thinking and feeling which we had justifiably regarded all our lives as something obvious and natural, in that moment, the modern age, laughing cold-bloodedly, broke our necks. (Cited by Miller, 1995)

In the history of camp, including camp in public and in the movies, we can see that naivety is the only possible explanation for why such things were not immediately understood the moment they were uttered or imagined. There was a thriving American queer/fairy subculture in the 1910s and 1920s, quite safe and secure due, as one man said, to 'the ignorance and naïveté of the American public' (Chauncey, 1994). Skinner (1978) recalls that in the 1930s 'most people were incredibly ignorant about the gay world'. I cannot help but agree with Edmund Gosse's interpretation of Walt Whitman, in a letter written to Bliss Perry on 6 March 1907: 'The real psychology of W. W. would be enormously interesting. I think the keynote to it would be found to be a staggering ignorance, a perhaps wilful non-perception, of the real truth about him; the innermost truth escapes from almost every page for those who can read' (cited in Legg, 1994).

Virtually everyone today perceives von Gloeden's photographs for what they really are – queer signifiers – and von Gloeden's contemporary queers *also* perceived them in the same way, whereas contemporary heterosexuals were blind to the nature of neo-Hellenic 'pastoralism'. The main difference in historical changes of perception is that the heterosexual public at large has gradually become more sophisticated in recognizing queer semiotics. It is not that 'modern perception' has changed, but that modern straight perception has belatedly incorporated queer perception. This is not a conceptual 'rupture', merely straight time-lag. Not even the time-lag itself is modern: for many centuries queers have felt themselves to be sophisticated and cosmopolitan, in contrast to provincial rustics. In Vanbrugh's play *The Relapse* (1696), the character Coupler, an obvious homosexual, makes a pass at a young man who rebuffs him – 'Stand off, old Sodom' – and Coupler retorts, 'Has thou been a year in Italy, and brought home a fool at last? By my conscience, the young fellows of this age profit no more by their going abroad, than they do by their going to church.'

Sexuality

Social constructionism violates common-sense in its insistence that 'sexuality' did not exist until modern times. Of course sexuality has cultural meaning, but it does not therefore follow that sexuality 'represents the *appropriation* of the human body and of its physiological capacities by an ideological discourse', nor does it follow that '"sexuality" seems indeed to be a uniquely modern, Western, even bourgeois production' (Halperin, 1993). Note Halperin's pre-emptive use of the Marxist term 'production' rather than something more neutral such as 'phenomenon'. Halperin's employment of concepts such as 'the production of desire' obviously mirrors the Marxist theory of production and distribution:

> Instead of concentrating our attention specifically on the history of sexuality, then, we need to define and refine a new, and radical, historical sociology of psychology, an intellectual discipline designed to analyze the cultural poetics of desire, by which I mean the processes whereby sexual desires are constructed, mass-produced,

and distributed among the various members of human living-
groups.

His theory of 'modes of construction' is an echo of 'means of production',
part of the socialist subtext of nearly all social constructionist theory.
Theorists who adopt the cultural emphasis of the theory often seem
unaware of its fundamental premise that a sexual construct is an economic
product.

Halperin's interpretation of Greek and Roman 'sexuality' has been
imposed upon the data rather than arising from it. His argument that
sexuality 'did not express inward dispositions or inclinations so much as
it served to position social actors in the places assigned to them, by virtue
of their political standing' is based largely upon Athenian definitions of
citizenship (adult free males) and their monopoly of power on one side
of a great divide between them and women, children, foreigners, slaves.
He finds within this body of mostly legalistic discourse concerning
legitimate sexual relations 'a cultural definition of sex as an activity that
generally occurred only between a citizen and a non-citizen, between a
person invested with full civil status and a statutory minor'. The bizarre
inference would have to be that among themselves non-citizens had no
sexuality. The mutual love of peasants and shepherds in the homoerotic
pastoral tradition popularized by Virgil would exist in a limbo outside
of Halperin's theory.

It may be perfectly reasonable to analyse the structures of power and
status to which sexual relations – heterosexual and homosexual – are
linked, but that is not all there is to be said about sexual relations: we
still need to deal with precisely what makes them specifically *sexual* and
distinguishes them from non-sexual power relations. The history of
homosexuality as power is not coterminous with the history of
homosexuality as desire. It is entirely possible to read modern sexuality
as 'gendered power relations' very similar to ancient sexuality.

The problem is not so much Halperin's reading of the Hellenic world,
but his misreading of the modern world. While it is true that modern,
specifically Freudian, psychology views sexuality as the key to the secrets
of personality, Halperin ridiculously exaggerates the alleged 'obsessions
of bourgeois Westerners'. 'In the Hellenic world, by contrast, the measure
of a free male was most often taken by observing how he fared when
tested in public competition against other free males, not by scrutinizing
his sexual constitution.' Since when have university exams or employment
interviews scrutinized sexual constitutions? Surely most intelligent modern

people believe that things other than sexuality are the measure of the man; in fact they usually espouse the view that the sexual life is a private matter that should not affect our judgement of the public man or woman.

Although Halperin is a classicist, and I would not wish to challenge the accuracy of his examples, the inferences he draws from them are not clear-cut. His important example drawn from Dio Chrysostom, of the late first century AD, seems not to prove his point that the ancients were indifferent to the sex of their partners:

> In a speech denouncing the corrupt morals of city life, Dio asserts that even respectable women are so easy to seduce nowadays that men will soon tire of them and will turn their attention to boys instead – just as addicts progress inexorably from wine to hard drugs.

Surely Dio cites this to make the point that heterosexual or ordinary relations have become so unexciting that men will turn to homosexual or extraordinary relations; in other words, Dio is drawing the lines of a dichotomy which is crossed by the corrupt.

Halperin discusses the important fifth-century medical treatise *De morbis chronicis* (a Latin translation by Caelius Aurelianus of a Greek work on chronic diseases by Soranus who practised in Rome in the second century), specifically the passage on *molles* (*malthakoi*), 'soft' or unmasculine men, 'men who depart from the cultural norm of manliness in so far as they actively desire to be subjected by other men to a "feminine" (that is, receptive) role in sexual intercourse'. Caelius attributes this 'mental disease' to excessive desire, which leads to shamelessness and even to the adoption of the clothes and mannerisms of women. This 'defect' has a parallel among women 'called *tribades* [who] are more eager to have sexual intercourse with women than with men and pursue women with an almost masculine jealousy'. Halperin explicitly rejects the common-sense interpretation of these passages as a perception of male and female homosexuality. Instead, he maintains that what is being problematized is not 'desire for sex with the same sex' but 'sex-role reversal, or gender-deviance'. This is largely true, but beside the point. It is precisely 'gender deviance' that has been seen as the problem of 'homosexuality' in the modern conception. How can we say that Caelius's view widely differs from a modern conception? Even Caelius's apparent belief that old men who tried but failed to have penetrative sex with women become *molles* is a common theme of modern conceptions of homosexuality – it is certainly the theme of innumerable satires on enervated 'mollies' during the eighteenth and nineteenth centuries, and at least until the 1950s it was commonly believed that men who could not get it up for women turned to boys or offered themselves to other men.

Halperin's view that only sexual *acts* are evaluated and categorized in classical texts, that 'there was no conceptual apparatus available for identifying a person's fixed and determined sexual *orientation*', is contradicted by his own quotation from Caelius: 'But in the case of old men who have lost their virile powers, all their sexual desire is turned in the opposite direction and consequently exerts a stronger demand for the feminine role in love.' This is a perfectly understandable – and modern – apparatus for assessing and classifying sexual desire as an *orientation*: 'turned in the opposite direction'. Halperin acknowledges that in this text *molles* are conceived to have 'a constitutional tendency to gender-deviance': how, then, can he claim that this does not resemble the modern view that (homo)sexuality is 'a positive, distinct, and constitutive feature of individual human beings'? Ah – 'but they are not homosexuals: being a womanish man, or a mannish woman, after all, is not the same thing as being a homosexual'. But this is *precisely* the concept of 'the third sex' in nineteenth- and early twentieth-century discourse, and this is *precisely* how the modern queer is still perceived by the modern unwashed public. Has Halperin never read any tabloid newspapers? These contain as much 'ideology' and 'discourse' as Freud and Foucault.

To support the theory that in the ancient world boys and women were functionally interchangeable (he rejects out of hand the ethos of 'bisexuality' in favour of the ethos of domination/penetration), Halperin mentions fewer than a dozen examples, though he claims many more could be cited. But buried in his notes he acknowledges numerous exceptions, which it seems to me fatally undermine his position: 'I am *not* claiming that all Greek men must have felt such indifference: on the contrary, plenty of ancient evidence testifies to the strength of individual preferences for a sexual object of one sex rather than another.' He cites *thirty* 'attestations to the strength of individual preferences (even to the point of exclusivity) on the part of Greek males for a sexual partner of one sex rather than another', in works by Seneca, Theognis, Euripides, Xenophon, Antigonus of Carystus, Athenaeus, Seleucis, Plutarch, Achilles Tatius, pseudo-Lucian, Firmicus Maternus and the *Palatine Anthology*.

Halperin could have cited many more examples illustrating ancient concepts of 'sexuality', 'constitutionality' and 'homosexual orientation'. The idea that pederasty, for example, is solely a matter of sex acts rather than an attendant set of feelings and culture is contradicted by a super-abundance of pederastic poetry by Rhianus of Crete (fl. c. 275 BC),

Aristides of Miletus (c. 100 BC), Apollonius of Rhodes (c. 295 BC), Diotimus (third century BC), Moschus (150 BC), Meleager of Gadara (c. 100 BC) and Phanocles (c. 250 BC). One has to be unbelievably insensitive to read Bion's (c. 100 BC) 'Lament for Adonis' as nothing more than an elegy for the loss of a sex object, callously exchangeable for another object of a different sex.

We must bear in mind that most of the commentary on homosexual relations during the medieval and Renaissance periods arises within the context of the Roman Catholic belief that the sin is separate from the sinner, that everyone is morally responsible for succumbing to rather than resisting sinful behaviour, which is held to exist in a realm into which people occasionally stray. During the visit of the Holy Office to Bahia in 1591–2, the Inquisitors brought to light several long-standing loving pairs, such as two young men who had 'sinned' together more than two hundred times (Trevisan, 1986). The social constructionist focus on acts is the modern secular equivalent to the Inquisition's counting of the frequency of sins: both approaches are blind to the reality of queer identities. This bifurcated view seldom prevailed outside the West. In ancient Chinese culture male pair-bonding was 'an integral part of Zhou and Han homosexuality, which celebrated male couples for their deep affections' (Hinsch, 1990); two thousand years of Chinese homosexual history belie the social constructionist emphasis upon random sexual acts. In ancient India, medical texts from the first century contain queer typologies of the third sex that are strikingly similar to modern views, and demonstrate that 'medicalization is not an exclusively Western or modern phenomenon' (Sweet and Zwilling, 1993, 1996).

Uses and abuses of theory

A theory that is politically useful may be either true or false: its political value does not depend upon its accuracy, but upon its power of persuasion or coercion. Social constructionism is politically useful for undermining mechanisms of social control and oppression. Essentialism is politically useful for empowering minority groups by a sense of solidarity grounded upon an awareness of identity. An effective gay rights movement might well employ strategies suggested by both schools of thought, exploiting each approach according to circumstances, without regard to consistency; the fundamental contradiction between them can be mitigated by arguing that homophobia is a construct while homosexuality is innate.

It is naive to think that one theory or the other will inevitably affect the predominantly negative attitudes of modern Western society, and societies influenced by the West:

the idea that *any* particular political posture or strategy would guarantee success in eradicating homophobia is probably wishful thinking. As others of the dispossessed have discovered, where the dominant culture is hostile, it can transform *any* minority self-presentation into a reinforcement for hostility. (Duberman, 1991)

A major problem with social constructionism is its foundation upon behaviourism, which has been used to defend attempts to change or convert homosexuals. On the other hand, an essentialist view can also be used to justify genetic research, and if a 'gay gene' is discovered society will no doubt attempt to eliminate or modify it.

It does not really matter *what* view queer historians take, biological scientists will pursue their endeavours: lobotomies have been performed and have fallen out of favour but no apologies have been issued; hormonal theory remains somewhat current and chemical castration is still performed; the latest and perhaps most serious development is genetic research, which is inevitably linked to eugenics. The Richard Dadd research centre at Broadmoor prison in England, opened in 1995, at the time of writing is co-ordinating a study of the brain structures and genetic make-up of murderers and violent sex offenders in top-security prison hospitals. According to a report in the *Sunday Times* (24 December 1995), 'The specialist psychiatrists involved hope the knowledge gained from the group of "criminally insane" patients will revolutionise the treatment of mental illness, allowing children at risk to be identified early and given preventive drugs.' Similar studies are being conducted in Holland, where researchers believe they have discovered a gene connected to aggression and 'inappropriate sexual behaviour' (a standard way of referring to homosexuality). The search for genes that predispose one towards 'antisocial behaviour' is in vogue, and homosexuality is a popular text model precisely because the majority of scientists believe it to be self-evident that same-sex relations are 'antisocial' (that is, non-procreative, unnatural) and 'inappropriate' (namely, directed to the 'wrong' sex). By the end of the millennium the Forensic Science Service DNA database in Birmingham, England, will have gathered the genetic profiles of four million persons not only convicted of crimes but *suspected* of sex offences.

Moderate arguments from gay activists will have little effect upon how this information may be used. The main opponents of genetic studies are those who espouse the equally unproven dogmas of social constructionism – for example, Anne Fausto-Sterling in *Myths of Gender* (1992) and Ruth Hubbard and Elijah Wald in *Exploding the Gene Myth* (1993) – and it is not likely that such genetic research is going to be abandoned. In the late nineteenth and early twentieth centuries Magnus Hirschfeld and his colleagues developed the idea that homosexuality was innate and congenital and therefore *impossible* to change, but tomorrow people will argue that it is genetic and therefore *possible* to alter:

> If LeVay is right, it will no longer be tenable to regard homosexuality as freely chosen and therefore 'sinful'. However, it might instead be seen as a biological defect, which can be diagnosed prenatally and 'cured'. One researcher in the field, Günther Dorner, director of the Institute of Experimental Endocrinology at Humbolt University in what was East Berlin, already suggests that women bearing male fetuses should have hormone injections to guard against the risk of having a homosexual son. (Vines, 1992)

Investigations into the 'causes' of homosexuality (or homosexualities) are almost invariably hostile, and are almost invariably premised upon a concept of abnormality or physical defect rather than mere difference. It is difficult to envisage a time when scientists will regard homosexuality as a variety rather than an anomaly. I have much sympathy with the gay liberationist resistance to the investigation into etiology, and perhaps queers are morally bound not to participate in such research. But to put a stop to such research seems like an admission of defeat. Surely it is better to put our weight behind the argument in favour of the strict regulation of genetic research, and to make the point that if a 'gay gene' is found to exist, then genetic intervention would be literally equivalent to genocide.

2

Queer BC (Before Constructionism)

Identity

In fashionable postmodernist deconstruction, identity is trivialized as a detachable signifier, rather like a baseball cap. The current dogma is that culture is a commodity. But few of us, unless we are very rich, buy a complete new wardrobe each season; rather, we settle for an accessory that matches our god-given complexion. The 'style' we adopt is not picked off the rail at random, but carefully chosen to suit us. 'Identity' is a politically loaded word which is too often used with linguistic carelessness. Chauncey (1994), for example, asserts that in large urban centres gay men constructed

> the multiple public identities necessary for them to participate in the gay world without losing the privileges of the straight: assuming one identity at work, another in leisure; one identity before biological kin, another with gay friends. ... their segregation from one another allowed men to assume a different identity in each of them, without having to reveal the full range of their identities in any one of them.

My own view is that people who genuinely possess 'multiple identities' are schizophrenics. What Chauncey describes as identity is what I would call situational role-playing, which we understand well enough through 1970s consciousness-raising groups or 1990s management seminars. Chauncey takes the position that work identities, ethnic identities, kinship identities and sexual identities are all relative and more or less equal, with no centrally organizing identity. But the gay men he interviewed about their lives in the 1930s and 1940s often refer to 'my type'. Clearly, what they mean by this is not 'we Italians' or 'we bus drivers' or 'we mutual insurers': they are talking about their basic, intrinsic or core identity, which is their queer identity.

Many public identities are really masks, which can be changed to suit the occasion, while the inner identity remains stable. A look at diaries written by queer men (for example, Parker Tyler and Carl Van Vechten) rarely reveals their work identity, but demonstrates instead that the subject upon which they reflect is a single, coherent queer identity. The fact that gay men and women frequented queer restaurants and clubs where they could 'let their hair down' suggests that their 'public identities' were superficial and artificial in comparison with their natural, personal identity. This is what I refer to when I use the word 'identity' – the rest are personae projected for public consumption.

Many practising counsellors and therapists who help people manage identity problems have misgivings about social constructionism because it is their experience that a damaged identity is healed by rediscovering an identity that was distorted by negative labelling; usually the label has to be reused in a more positive manner – thus coloured people became Blacks, queers and fairies became gays, and deaf people become Deaf people:

> As I learn more about deaf people through their own eyes, I can see how the social constructionist emphasis on the processes of 'identification' and the development of 'social identity' can act as a barrier to self-understanding and the achievement of personal identity in exactly the same way that a pathological view of deafness can, because the direction that these processes takes may be at odds with the person's structure of meaning. But there is a second view of society or community as a place where we, as individual deaf people, feel comfortable and 'at home' with ourselves and which to a large extent reflects who we are and embraces our fundamental values. (Corker, 1996)

The problem about labelling is not *difference* itself – even when it is used as the defining characteristic of a person – but the condemnation of that difference. Viewing difference in a negative light leads to isolation, but labels can also be used to establish commonality, albeit a marginalized community. Stereotypes hinder self-esteem when they are promoted as universal truths or norms against which people are judged and found wanting, but if this normative function can be resisted, 'stereotypes and labels can be powerful "reservoirs of meaning"' (Corker, 1996).

The major problem for young gay people is that the *straight* label doesn't fit, and they struggle to adopt a system of values and desires that contradicts their fundamental sense of self; the eventual adoption of the queer label, even with its stigma, comes with a sense of relief, and the process of integration begins. The classic labelling theory that a person branded as a queer is likely to fulfil the expectations of the label and become a queer is contradicted by the nearly universal experience of modern queers who felt that their queer identity was unique until they discovered the label later in life. There are literally hundreds of testimonies from people who on hearing 'lesbian' or 'homosexual' for the first time rushed to their local library to find out about themselves, to confirm and make greater sense of an identity that they already possessed.

The social constructionist position that sexuality could not have become a defining characteristic of identity until the medical/sexological discourse of modern times is simply incorrect. The 'demon' of desire has been part of the psychodynamics of identity for many centuries. Take, for example, the writings of a twelfth-century monk about his feelings for a 10-year-old boy left in his care whom he has raised as a son:

> I was tortured and overwhelmed by an obscene desire, and the beast of impure lust and a desire for pleasure burned in my soul. ... I was a changed person and completely in the grip of this unclean passion, and I wanted to have sex with the boy and to be with him, to my shame. ... [After the boy was returned to the father] I never saw the boy again, but the enemy, knowing this, came after me more fiercely, more hotly, more sharply, and put the boy's form into my mind and glued his likeness and image and appearance into my heart. (Boswell, 1995)

This man is dominated by homosexual lust, to the extent that he has become utterly *identified* with his desire.

At the opposite end of this same continuum we find the archetypal features of 'platonic love', notably the *identification* of the lover and the beloved ('another myself'). For a non-Western example, take the case of Persian mystic poet Rumi (1207–73) who fell in love and identified himself with the wandering dervish Shams al-Din (c. 1185–1248). Rumi's wife forced the two men to separate, but when they reunited, contemporaries acknowledged that their love was so mutual that no one could determine who was 'the lover' and who was 'the beloved'. Rumi's jealous pupils murdered Shams, and Rumi's subsequent abundant poetry of lamentation transcended grief through identification with Shams, as Rumi became the moon or mirror to Shams's sun. This may not be 'homosexual', because Sufism had a platonic view of love/friendship, but 'homosocial' inadequately describes it; it was obviously passionate and special (that is, beyond Rumi's friendships with his other pupils), and the only adequate term I can find for it is 'queer'.

Between these two extremes of lust and idealism we find a sense of identity based upon ordinary and unremarkable same-sex love. The records of the Inquisition in Spain, Portugal and Brazil; the police archives of early eighteenth-century Paris; the records of the Officers of the Night of sixteenth-century Venice – all clearly document a preponderance of bachelor men who prefer their own sex. Statistical analysis of the particularly full and detailed Florentine records

> of the marital status of the men incriminated for sodomy from 1478 to 1483 reveals that fully three-fourths of all such men aged nineteen to seventy were unmarried. The proportion of single men is even higher (81 per cent) among men who voluntarily turned themselves in to the sodomy officials to take advantage of an immunity clause in the office's statutes. (Rocke, 1989)

Such men had a substantially lower rate of marriage than in the general population. Many repeat offenders were arrested by the Officers of the Night over periods of several years, sometimes as the active partners and sometimes in the passive role.

Nearly all records from these sources also document cases of long-term relationships including men who lived together in 'sodomitical sin' that involved intimacy and tenderness. Saslow (1989) cites the instance of two Venetian boatmen, arrested in 1357, who had been together for several years. The sodomy court in fifteenth-century Tuscany heard cases in which youths were 'kept' (*si tiene*) by men in ongoing relationships, and men claimed that their *fanciullo* cost them as much as fifty florins each year. In some cases the men lived together, as this example from the court records for 1495 shows: 'Niccolò, son of Brunetto, shoemaker ... retains Bastiano his apprentice, about sixteen years old. He keeps him at home like a wife. And in fact he isn't married, so that his wife is Bastiano' (Rocke, 1989). Several men investigated by the Paris police claimed that they sought 'a relationship which might last', perhaps like that of the Abbé Candor and the young man who lived with him passing for his cousin. According to a police report of 1748 two men had lived and slept together intimately for two years: 'It was even almost always necessary for Duquesnel to have his arm extended along the headboard, under Dumaine's head. Without that Dumaine could not rest' (cited by Rey, 1985).

In Foucault's (1978) famous statement: 'Homosexuality appeared as one of the forms of sexuality when it was transposed from the practice of sodomy onto a kind of superior androgyny, a hermaphroditism of the soul. The sodomite had been a temporary aberration; the homosexual was now a species.' But the men discussed in the preceding paragraph had a sense of themselves that transcended both 'the practice of sodomy' and 'temporary aberration'. In fact Dutch sodomites in 1734 were described by contemporaries as 'hermaphrodites in their minds' (Boon, 1989), an exact match for Foucault's 'hermaphroditism of the soul'. The concepts of masculine homosexual women and effeminate homosexual men dominated the premodern world. The homosexual was considered an androgynous species in Aristophanes, in Juvenal and in all the ancient literature about the transgendered priests of Cybele.

The truth is that a homosexual category existed many centuries before the nineteenth century. There are literally scores of fifteenth-century Italian authors who portray homosexual *characters* rather than homosexual incidents (G. Dall'Orto, 'Italian Renaissance', *EH*), and it is a nonsense to label such sodomites 'temporary aberrations' rather than members of a species. In real life there is the famous example of the painter Giovanni Antonio Bazzi (1477–1549) who was proud of his nickname 'Il Sodoma'; according to his contemporary Vasari 'he did not take [it] with annoyance or disdain, but rather gloried in it, making jingles and verses on the subject, which he pleasantly sang to the accompaniment of the lute' (*Lives*, 1550). He even signed his tax returns 'Il Sodoma'.

Queers were perceived as 'the third sex' well before Hirschfeld and the sexologists popularized the concept: witness Lady Montague's observation in the early eighteenth century that the world consisted of three sexes: 'men, women, and Herveys', a reference to John, Lord Hervey, the archetypal pansy (Halsband, 1973). Madame d'Orleans used distinctively 'modern' sexual taxonomies to classify the men she knew in the court of Louis XIV: 'some prefer women, some like both men and women, some prefer men, some prefer children, and some have little interest in sex at all' (Boswell, 1992). Even earlier, in the twelfth century, Bishop Etienne de Fougères 'divides the women of his world into three categories: virtuous, adulterous, and lesbian' (Boswell, 1992). One cannot help but feel that Foucault has wilfully suppressed the fact that since the 1730s the favoured and most common French term for homosexual has been *pédérast* rather than *sodomite*, a clear indication that it was recognized as a secular cultural identity rather than biblical sinful behaviour (Rey, 1985).

Passive roles

The social constructionists argue that where no words exist, no concepts exist, and that indigenous societies revealed by anthropology have no word for 'the homosexual' and therefore no option for choosing such a state. The degree to which language exactly mirrors reality is debatable, but it is quite proper and accurate for a modern historian to investigate a past society using a concept which was given a name after that society disappeared. John Boswell points out that the ancient Romans had no abstract word for 'religion', though they obviously had religions, including Christianity itself. There is no classical Latin word equivalent to the modern concept of 'family', yet the Romans had families of various sorts and we can appreciate the differences between ancient and modern families without abandoning the word itself.

But the fact of the matter is that a great many indigenous societies *did* have words for 'the homosexual'. By this I do not mean terms that could match the sexological psychopathological personality disorder (which undoubtedly *is* a modern social construct), but rather words roughly equivalent to modern queers – words which demonstrate a consciousness (albeit often contemptuous) of a queer stereotype or gay identity. Here are just a few examples: in the Middle East the *xanitha*, who plays the receptive role with older or richer men; in Nicaragua *el cochon*; in Italy the *arruso* and *ricchione*, and *femmenella* ('little female') for the transvestite; *loca* and *maricón* in Latin America; the *teresita* in Argentina; *bicha* and *veado* in Brazil; *masisi* in Haiti; *zamel* in North Africa. In many languages the generic term for a male homosexual is derived from a female name: Spanish *maricón* and *mariquita* derive from María; Italian *checca* comes from Francesca; Flemish *janet* from the French Jeannette; a Portuguese queer is an *Adelaida*; while in England queer men have called themselves Marys, Mary-Annes, mollies, nancy boys and nellies.

Most – but not all – of these labels apply a derogatory stigma to the fucked rather than the fucker: this is also true of most modern non-scientific words for homosexuals. The following sentence runs as a *leitmotif* throughout Greenberg's *The Construction of Homosexuality* (1988): 'Though there was neither a word for, nor a concept of, a homosexual person, an adult man who took pleasure in the anal-receptive role was scorned and thought to require an explanation.' Of course the ancients lacked the benefits of modern science, poor things; but to say that ancient or indigenous peoples had no conceptual word for homosexuals in general is incorrect: it is just that their concept of the homosexual was primarily limited to the receiver – in exactly the same way that most modern words for homosexuals have that connotation (queer, fairy, pansy, faggot, cocksucker, gay, queen and homo). When 'Cocksucker!' or 'Wanker!' is spit out at someone – whether in ancient or modern times – it implies a great deal more than a literal sex role, hence the frequency of the contradiction-in-terms, 'You fucking cocksucker!'

Many social constructionists maintain that in ancient Rome, for example, homosexuality in itself was not a problem; rather, the issue given greatest consideration concerned the adoption of the 'passive' role in male–male sexual relations (namely, being penetrated). Thus, there is no term for the active (i.e. penetrating) partner in this relationship; he is simply a man, whereas his passive partner is a *catamitus*. Those who argue that before modern times (be it the early eighteenth or late nineteenth century) there were only homosexual roles rather than homosexual personality types contend that roles are determined by acts whereas personalities are characterized by orientation towards the gender of one's partners. Most periods and cultures have words for homosexuals, but the significance of these is dismissed by noting that the stigmatizing label is almost invariably applied only to the man who takes the passive role, and the passive role is determined by an act rather than orientation or object choice. But I would argue that the passive sexual role arises precisely because it formally requires a male–male gender relationship. The passive partner invariably needs a male penetrator, whereas the active partner is not stigmatized because the active sex act does not require a specific gender, that is he can penetrate male or female, and is always a man himself. The passive role necessitates a sexual relationship between two men: the catamite is a man-desiring-man, which is the basic definition of the modern male homosexual. Thus, the social constructionist argument that premodern and indigenous cultures have no word for the more abstract concept of the homosexual, but only a word for the effeminate/passive male, entirely misses the point. To say that 'catamite' is *not* a name for a 'homosexual person' is wildly misleading: the homosexual is a politically correct catamite.

In other words, the supposed line between *role* and *orientation* is not so hard and fast as the social constructionists pretend it to be. From a strictly formal point of view, the passive role is determined just as much by an emphasis upon sexual object choice and orientation as the personality type that is supposed to have arisen in modern times. This (premodern) passivity, in particular non-masculinity, is central to the stigmatization of the 'deviant' homosexual identity of more modern times. We are playing a semantic game (rather than genuine epistemology) if we insist that the catamite is a problem only because he assumes a female sexual role, and that the modern homosexual is an entirely different proposition because of his sexual object choice. The 'homosexual' is a rather over-refined, supposedly neutral 'scientific' concept: surely we all know that the homosexual is a problem because he is a queer, a fairy, a pansy, a molly – precisely because he plays an effeminate role. To be a cocksucker is to be oriented towards a specific gender.

The key feature of any relationship involving a receptive male is its homosexuality rather than its receptivity; to say that the hundreds of labels that denote this role/personality have arisen solely because of sex/gender role rather than homosexual orientation is wide of the mark. The social constructionist analysis of ancient and indigenous words-for-queers is characterized by muddle-headed double-think. A typical example is Greenberg's (1988) commentary on the temple inscriptions at Edfu, in Memphis, which proclaim that it is forbidden 'to couple with a *nkk* or *hmw*':

> The latter terms, though probably not exact synonyms, have been taken to refer to someone who acts as a receptive male homosexual. Elsewhere, the word *hmw* means coward; since it is derived from the word for 'woman,' it might better be translated as an 'effeminate poltroon.' It would be difficult to say whether this was a term of opprobrium applied stereotypically to anyone who preferred a receptive role in homosexual anal intercourse, or only to a distinct, socially recognized homosexual role. ... As far as we can tell, homosexuality per se was not a category in Egyptian thought. There was no distinctive word for a homosexual person, only composite terms suggesting that gender was the critical category. ... The negative confessions and temple inscriptions refer to acts, not inclinations or states of being.

It is perverse of Greenberg to cite this example as evidence that the ancient Egyptians had no concept of a homosexual person; rather, it states precisely that there *was* an ancient concept of the homosexual person, as an effeminate coward, a queer. Greenberg begs many questions of definition and his conclusion is patently incorrect. The temple inscription refers not merely to the act of copulation, but to copulation with a *nkk* or *hmw*, words for the homosexual person which are derived from the word for coward. A coward is a personality type, and cowardice a personality trait and state of being. Greenberg fails to note the important distinction between fucking an ass-hole (emphasis upon the act) and fucking a queer ass-hole (emphasis upon a person).

Terms of contempt for homosexuals are common throughout history and across cultures. In Old Norse and Icelandic sagas, and in Finnish and Estonian languages, the most powerful terms of abuse are the words *argr*, *ragr* and *ergi*, which all connote cowardice, effeminacy, sorcery and (receptive) male homosexuality, and probably derive from the archetype of the queer sorcerer (often a religious functionary acting as a scapegoat) found in many ancient societies and indigenous cultures. In modern Germanic languages *arg* just means 'bad', in the same way that the modern English word for criminal, *felon*, comes from medieval Latin *felo/fello* meaning 'evildoer', but this is derived from *fellare* ('to fellate') – thus, the primal felon is a cocksucker. Similarly, the modern term 'bad' derives from the Anglo-Saxon term *baedling* ('effeminate/receptive male'). In countless languages the basic pattern for the most contemptuous terms of abuse is practically the same: the archetypal bad man is one who performs a shameful receptive/feminine role in sex, i.e. a queer, cocksucker or cunt. They are all reducible to the single paradigm of the man who takes 'the woman's role' in sex, hence the affinity of homophobia and sexism.

Orientation

Even aside from this kind of formal analysis, the view that there are no premodern terms or concepts for sexual orientation is, quite simply, mistaken. Aristotle believed that some people were 'naturally inclined' to homosexual behaviour (*Nichomachean Ethics*); in a work attributed to him (*Problems*), Aristotle speculates on the origin of the 'orientation' of adult men who prefer to be anally penetrated. Dall'Orto (1989) notes the seventeenth-century Italian confessor who told a sodomite, 'That is a sin against nature', and was told in reply, 'Oh father, but it is very natural to me.' Other scholars cite conversations recorded by the Paris police in the 1720s that contain such statements as 'He had this taste all his life', or 'From an early age he did not do anything else but amuse himself with men; these pleasures were in his blood.'

The negative conceptualization of the homosexual as a class of person who was not erotically interested in the other sex is not limited to modern eras. An early chronicler of the life of the Emperor Ai (reigned 6 BC to AD 1) observed, 'By nature Emperor Ai did not care for women'; his love for his favourite Dong Xian gave rise to the 'cut sleeve' metaphor that became virtually a symbol for exclusive homosexuality in China. In England the broadside ballad 'The Women-Hater's Lamentation' was rushed out following the arrest of a group of forty sodomites in 1707, after which several men killed themselves while awaiting trial. In the term 'women-hater', the attitude is a metonym for the act, but it nevertheless clearly points to one of the features regarded as being central to an *orientation in relation to gender* rather than a specific sexual act. Among seventeenth-century Japanese merchants known as *shojin zuki* ('connoisseurs of boys' – married men who preferred youths), there was a subgroup of exclusively homosexual men called *onna girai* ('woman-haters'). Misogyny is also a characteristic feature of the boy-lovers in Ihara Saikaku's (1990) work in the seventeenth century, even though they are supposedly bisexual and married, and it is clear that Ihara's intended audience is exclusively homosexual.

The equivalent to 'woman-hater' is common in many ancient languages, where terms denoting attraction to the same sex are complemented by others that suggest orientation away from the opposite sex. Throughout the medieval period men who have sex with men are often perceived as being misogynist, or at least as having no desire for women. The social constructionist emphasis upon sodomitical acts fails to account for the fact that premodern homosexuals of many types were characterized by an orientation away from a specific gender, often accompanied by the same sort of unaccountable antipathy ascribed to homosexuals by modern sexologists. One of the boy-lovers in *The Greek Anthology* makes it clear that 'My heart feels no love for women, but burns with an unquenchable flame for males' (trans. Boswell, 1992). A woman in the *Arabian Nights* tells a man that she perceives him to be 'among those who prefer men to women'. In the twelfth-century *Roman d'Eneas*, Aeneas loves men rather than Dido: 'This wretch is of the sort who have hardly any interest in women. He prefers the opposite trade. ... He does not know how to play with women, and would not parley at the wicket-gate; but he loves very much the breech of a young man' (trans. Boswell, 1992). Bernardino of Siena in 1424 preached against letting young men appear in public all spruced up, and warned mothers: 'Send your girls out instead, who aren't in any danger at all if you let them out among such people' (Rocke, 1989). Sarah Churchill in 1708 said that Queen Anne had 'noe inclination for any but one's own sex', and throughout history women who have 'no inclination to marry' have been perceived as lesbians. The history of lesbians in particular shows that the determination not to marry (which is an attitude rather than an act) is regarded as characteristic of a lesbian type.

Discussions of 'predilections' and 'propensities' and the call to embrace rather than struggle against one's sexual 'temperament' are central to French Enlightenment and pre-Revolutionary literature (which prominently features characters with homosexual 'sensual appetites'). The very popular and representative *Thérèse philosophe* (c. 1748) cites the example of three brothers who have the same upbringing but widely divergent passions (for example, one prefers books to women) to illustrate the proto-essentialist case for capricious nature and determinism, and rejects religious and moral scruples as artificial social constructs (Darnton, 1996). A footnote in a 1798 English translation of the works of Sappho refers to the rumours of her 'unhappy deviation from the natural inclinations', which demonstrates that the 'modern' concept of deviant orientation was well in place in England by the end of the eighteenth century. *Inclination* was similarly used in French nearly two centuries earlier: in the early seventeenth century François Callon, the head of a Dutch trading company at Nagasaki, gave an account of the third Shogun, Lemitsu (1604–51): 'the low opinion in which he holds women and the shameful inclination he has towards boys have always kept him from marriage' (Spencer, 1995), which clearly sums up the concept of orientation. Giordano Bruno in 1584 described Socrates – though continent – as having a 'natural drive towards the filthy love of boys' (Dall'Orto, 1989).

Clearly these examples fit the definition of the modern homosexual as a desiring person rather than a single-act sinner. Most ancient and indigenous languages also use the term 'inclination' to describe queer desires, and preferential inclinations are often commented upon. Sex-positive societies regularly defend sexual variety by reference to natural inclination. The Hindu manual of love, the *Kamasutra*, prescribed 'mouth congress' for eunuchs, and defended oral and anal sex: 'in all things connected with love, everybody should act according to the custom of his country, and his own inclination ... [considering only whether the act] is agreeable to his nature and himself' (cited by Nanda, 1993).

The History of the Life ... of Edward II, written between 1625 and 1628 by someone whom we know only by the initials E. F., 'offers an early example of a pathological model for homosexuality, two hundred and fifty years before Richard von Krafft-Ebing's *Psychopathia Sexualis*' (Miller, 1996). E. F. describes Edward's 'masculine affections' as unbridled, a 'passionate humour, so predominant in him' that 'alter them he cannot'.

This homosexual 'humour' is clearly seen as a mental disposition or orientation. Similarly, Marston says of a sodomitical gallant with his Ganymede at his heels: 'his clothes do sympathize, / And with his inward spirit humorize. / An open ass, that is not yet so wise / As his derided fondness to disguise.' This gallant is clearly conceived of as an openly gay 'type', all of whose features and behaviour have been constructed to correspond with his 'inward spirit' or queer core identity.

Because the term 'orientation' is now common in legal and psychiatric discourse, we think it is a scientific word. But of course it is merely a directional metaphor drawn from magnetism and navigation, which has gradually superseded the directional metaphors used prior to the 1970s: inclination, deviant, pervert, invert, preference, taste, tendency, bent, drive. Sexual love is often expressed in terms of directional metonyms: the flight of Cupid's darts towards the object of desire is as common a feature in classical homoerotic poetry as in heterosexual poetry. The man who 'has eyes for' good-looking youths frequently appears in classical Arabic poetry, and the direction of his gaze clearly establishes his sexual orientation as an integral part of his basic personality. Ancient peoples speculated about sexual orientation just as we do: 'A character in the Hellenistic novel *Affairs of the Heart* claims that it is possible to discern the sexual preference of a friend by noting the gender of his servants' (Boswell, 1995). Hellenic literature is full of references to the heterosexual and homosexual dichotomy, even attributing different sources to each orientation. Meleager in *Mousa Paidikē* describes how 'The Cyprian queen, a woman, hurls the fire that maddens men for females; but Eros himself sways the love of males for males.' And Plutarch in *Eroticus* refers to 'Eros, where Aphrodite is not; Eros apart from Aphrodite.'

The modern debate about identity has created a false dichotomy between role and orientation that has no historical validity. Most of the graffiti on the ruined walls of Pompeii are homosexual and bisexual, to the effect 'I want to fuck a boy' and sometimes even 'I love a boy'. The common graffito *volo piidicarii* is often mistranslated as 'I want to fuck someone', so as to humorously suggest urgent and undifferentiated horniness, but in fact it means 'I want to fuck a male'. Ancient people had special verbs indicating gender object choice for intercourse: Greek *pugizein*, Latin *pedico* and Arabic *lâta* mean 'fuck a male' (while Greek *binein* and Latin *futuo* mean 'fuck a female'). *Pedico* is usually mistranslated as 'sodomize', but in fact it is *never* used for anal intercourse with women; it is a specifically queer verb. The writers of this queer graffiti were active (penetrative) men, which in my view provides evidence that a homosexual 'role', and in particular a homosexual 'identity', was not limited to passive homosexuals; in this graffiti it seems to me that self-conscious queers are expressing themselves *as* self-conscious queers.

Just as the queers' antagonism for the fairies is the antagonism of the middle class for the working class (Chauncey, 1994), so the argument about 'identity' versus 'role' is a class issue. It is the middle-class queers wanting to be 'assimilated' who have ironically developed a more self-conscious gay 'identity' (partly by setting themselves in opposition to fairies and in legitimating their behaviour by reference to gay culture), while the working-class fairies who are better assimilated into their ethnic class have an effeminate 'role' rather than an identity. The fairy places himself along the male/female gender axis, while the queer places himself along the homosexual/heterosexual behaviour axis; 'role' is used to describe the former, and 'identity' the latter. But behaviour is the determining factor in both cases, and in both cases the participants 'see themselves' as something – and 'seeing oneself' is a characteristic of a self-conscious identity. We are simply playing class-based linguistic games when we further try to differentiate between sexual role and gender role in relation to identity. Chauncey acknowledges that 'gender role' is too simplistic a way to perceive the behaviour and self-understanding of fairies: they do not see themselves as women in general, but as tough street prostitutes in particular, and most of their mannerisms and argot are borrowed from subcultural female prostitution. In my view this is essentially a sexual role rather than a gender role: fairies act in such a way as to attract men; they offer their sexual services to men in the manner that is most readily recognized by their punters. The limp wrist, the swivel-hipped swish and the widespread use of rouge and powder are all markers to signal sexual availability rather than gender identity. 'Effeminacy' is undoubtedly a matter of *sexual* presentation. An anecdote Chauncey cites to demonstrate the use of the word 'gay' as a camp/gender term in fact shows that effeminate fairies conceived of themselves in terms of a sexual role as well as a gender role, and the whole point of the anecdote is to illustrate the naiveté of the gender-role conception of the fairy. A hairdresser who was a 'flaming faggot' recalls an occasion in the Bronx in 1937 when a boy who was hanging out with a group of gay men got picked up, only to return a short time later,

> crying, saying the boy he'd left with wanted him to suck his thing.
> 'I don't want to do *that*!' he cried. 'But why are you hanging out
> with us if you aren't gay?' we asked him. 'Oh, I'm *gay*,' he

exclaimed, throwing his hands in the air like an hysterical queen, 'but I don't want to do *that*.' This boy liked the gay life – the clothes, the way people talked and walked and held themselves – but, if you can believe it, he didn't realize there was more to being gay than that!

I think Chauncey (1985) has similarly misread the evidence concerning the queer sailors investigated at the Newport Naval Training Station in 1919. The members of this tightly knit group, calling themselves 'the gang', often wore lipstick and make-up, walked with their hands on their hips in the street, called one another 'the girls' and went to 'fagott parties' organized by 'queens' who wore 'drags' and had ladies' nicknames. They were 'fairies' and 'queers', and effeminacy permeated the subculture, but I think it is nevertheless inaccurate to say that gender was 'the determining factor' in the label 'queer'. The queers among themselves used *sexual* rather than gender labels: 'fairies' (active fellators), 'cocksuckers', 'pogues' and 'Brownies' (those who liked to be 'browned' or anally penetrated), 'two-way artists' and 'French artists'. It can just as well be argued that gender was simply the facilitating mode of behaviour chosen to satisfy the determining factor of sexual orientation. Gender and sexuality are inextricable in the queer subculture.

Exclusive homosexuality

One of the basic tenets of social constructionism is that exclusive homosexuality was not possible until the late nineteenth century. The claim is that before this period only homosexual *acts* existed, and these acts could be and were enjoyed alternately with heterosexual practices. Such acts were fairly randomly distributed and did not add up to an identity; to exclusively choose homosexual acts, which would imply an orientation, became available only in modern times. The words 'homosexual' and 'gay' generally imply that one prefers sexual intercourse predominantly if not exclusively with the same gender, so to apply these terms to premodern individuals is held to be anachronistic. But in fact there are *plenty* of examples of exclusive or preferential homosexual desire in ancient and indigenous cultures, and *plenty* of evidence of the existence of a concept of the predominant/exclusive homosexual.

Athens was ruled for a century by 'pederasts' in the classical bisexual mould, but at least one, Hipparchus – the tyrant assassinated by the famous lovers Harmodius and Aristogeiton (who also married) – was exclusively homosexual, and interested in adult (albeit young) men rather than boys. Other figures from the ancient world who were noted for being exclusively homosexual include Zeno, Bion, Alexander the Great, Virgil and Plato.

The *locus classicus* for the concepts of exclusive homosexuality and bisexuality is not a Victorian sexological text, but appears in Plato's *Symposium*, in Aristophanes's description of the famous theory that all people derive from three primordial dual ancestors who were cut in half by Zeus and forever try to reunite with their other half: male–male halves, female–female halves and male–female halves; according to this myth, then, heterosexuals derive from a primal hermaphrodite. To 'seek one's other half' is the goal of all lovers, whether male homosexual, lesbian or heterosexual, to use the modern terms, and none of these categories has priority over another. Aristophanes's theory may not be representative of the time, but it does nevertheless establish that an ancient Greek could deal with concepts of exclusive homosexuality, innate homosexuality and homosexual orientation. Agathon, who hosted the *Symposium*, was an effeminate 'aesthetic' queen, whom Aristophanes called 'wide-arsed'.

For many centuries, going back to Ptolemaeus, astrologers have suggested astrological configurations which are essentially homoerotic. For example, men with 'Venus in Aquarius in the fourth house, with the moon either squaring or in conjunction with Venus' are said never to marry or to 'always be lovers of boys'. Numerous astrological texts – the science of the ancient world – demonstrate beyond doubt that the ancient world had a scientific conception of homosexual orientation:

> In all charts, if the Moon is found in the Tail of Leo, it will produce homosexuals who serve as tympany players to the mother of the gods [*cinaedos efficiet, matris deorum tympanis servientes*]. The writings of Firmicus Maternus [fl. fourth century] and other astrologers clearly demonstrate that many individuals, especially those living in late antiquity, reckoned that to become a *gallus* was to live out a preordained destiny which, like the shaman's, could be ignored or rejected only if one were willing to accept divine retribution. (Conner *et al.*, 1997)

Juvenal in his *Satires* (second century) portrays half a dozen recognizable queers, queens and dykes. The key feature of Lucian's works – the satirical *Golden Ass*, the 'science fiction' *True Histories* about an all-male society on the moon where men marry and give birth from the thigh, his *Life of Alexander of Abonuteichos*, the biography of the philosopher/mystic who kept a harem of young priests – is that they satirize *personalities* rather than sexual behaviour *per se*. Martial and Lucian both portray exclusive lesbians, examples that are famous *topoi* in the literature of lesbianism. James Boswell has discussed a romantic novel of late antiquity, *Ephesiaca*, in which such categories (though defining words are not used) play an important role in the intrigues of the narrative: one man is exclusively heterosexual; the character Hippothoos is attracted to a man but marries a woman out of duty, subsequently leaving both to pursue two other men, and at the end of the story is united with a fourth man. Presumably readers easily recognized this character type of the predominant homosexual.

Most of the queer-specific words in classical civilizations relate to males who actively seduced other males in order to be fucked by them. The mythological archetype was Ganymede, from which was derived the mundane term *catamitus* and the modern word 'catamite'. Although Ganymede was raped (literally snatched up to serve Zeus in heaven), he is almost always portrayed not as a victim but as a boy who chooses men by preference, and to a nearly exclusive degree. He is not passive with men and active with women (which is the kind of paradigm that social constructionists would prefer), but vociferously despises women and actively sets out to seduce men. *Catamitus* was applied only to exclusively passive (young) men. From at least the thirteenth to the eighteenth centuries the 'bugger' and the 'catamite' formed a reciprocal pair whose decided preferences were well matched. Ganymede frequently appears in the debate dialogues popular in the medieval period, as both a misogynist and a misogamist. From the medieval to the Renaissance periods a genre existed that debated the respective merits of (a man's) love for (young) men or love for women, and occasionally a woman's love for women; in this tradition words and concepts of *choice* and *inclination* are abundant. In classical art and literature Ganymede, far from being just a part of a polymorphous *ménage*, was a provoker of marital discord and, as in a late Greek work by Achilles Tatius, served 'as a divine justification for men who preferred boys to women as sexual partners' (Saslow, 1986).

Exclusive lesbianism

Although the social constructionists deal only/primarily with men, they believe their theories apply to all genders (the concept of which they also regard as a social construct), so let us look at female homosexuality in premodern cultures. The Italian Catherine Vizzani (1718/19–44) was an exclusive lesbian, long before that personality 'type' supposedly became possible. By the age of 13 she already preferred girls to boys, 'and some she caressed with all the Eagerness and transports of a Male Lover' according to (John Cleland's 1751 English translation of) her 1744 biography. She courted a girl called Margaret for two years, even serenading her. She was not a tomboy, but when her father threatened to report her for her passions she left home disguised as a young man. Her mother remained loyal, and helped her 'Giovanni' to get jobs. Her father eventually accepted his 'son', commenting that 'since such was the Case, and the Vigour of his Constitution not to be repressed by Words or Blows, Nature must e'en take its Course'. This demonstrates a full awareness, around 1740, of the concept of lesbianism as a constitution that cannot be repressed but must follow its natural course – all ideas supposedly limited to the concept of the 'modern' homosexual. Vizzani gained fame as a promiscuous youth, having affairs with many women. She used a home-made strap-on leather dildo, with which it is difficult to believe that she was able to fool all of her partners all of the time. She was exclusively devoted to women even though, as a man, she would share a bed with male servants. She died of gangrene, aged 24. Her real sex was thereupon discovered and an autopsy was performed, which failed to find any genital abnormalities and revealed that her hymen was intact. She was buried in accordance with a ceremony reserved for the death of virgins.

Her biographer was Professor Giovanni Bianchi of the University of Siena, who also performed the autopsy; his account contains no exaggeration or titillation or fictionalization. John Cleland's translation, however, interjects moral condemnation and a theory that her anomaly was caused either by the warm Italian climate or that she 'had her Imagination corrupted early in her Youth' by hearing the maids (who are naturally corrupt) telling obscene tales, which led to masturbation and thence tribadism. There is very little in this relatively full biography which would 'date' it to 1740 rather than 1890: Catherine Vizzani exhibits features and characteristics of an exclusive lesbian type which social constructionists teach us to expect only in the medical case histories of a century and a half later.

The history of lesbianism is rich in examples of exclusive homosexuality; pair-bonding is a notable feature of lesbian culture, and many lesbians seem to have established female marriages. There is abundant historical material about women living together in marital-style relationships in seventeenth-century Holland, and innumerable examples of female husbands in seventeenth- and eighteenth-century Britain. These female husbands often had several wives in a kind of serial monogamy, but they seldom united with men once they began their career as female husbands. Contrary to the unsubstantiated claim of Trumbach (1994) that before the end of the eighteenth century women cross-dressed primarily for reasons of financial security and safety, and contrary to the view of Lotte van de Pol and Rudolph Dekker that women 'passed' so as to think of themselves as men in order to love women, Emma Donoghue (1993) presents a good case that cross-dressers assumed a disguise for the world that facilitated their marital relationship with a woman: 'Marriage was a refuge that seemed to offer so much: social status, domestic privacy, economic convenience, a sense of emotional stability, a "No Trespassers" sign for any man casting an eye at the female husband's wife.'

In around 1730 Mary East and her girlfriend tossed a coin to decide which one of them would play the public role of husband in their marriage (which lasted for thirty-six years), thus demonstrating that the masculine role need not precede a lesbian relationship or even be integral to it. There are many cases, particularly in the late seventeenth century, in which the motivation is a fraudulent attempt to obtain a bride's dowry or a widow's money, and perhaps these pseudo-lesbian 'conmen' are not properly considered as part of lesbian culture. The cases that came to the attention of the public, and to historians, would tend to be those in which the wife was not satisfied with the relationship; female marriages in which both partners were fully content would generally remain secret, and perhaps only come to light, as did the case of Mary East, as the result of blackmail. But quite aside from cases of fraud, Donoghue has demonstrated that in Britain 'female marriage seems to have flourished in the mid-eighteenth century. ... the female husband is not a one-off freak but quite a common social phenomenon'. Of course, we cannot automatically assume that all these women identified themselves as 'lesbians', but we can certainly postulate that women living in a marriage that is secretly homosexual must have operated with an identity of some sort, an identity that has some relationship to conscious role-playing, and one that is quite different from the random sexual acts to which the social constructionists would restrict them.

The bisexual myth

The social constructionists believe, as did Freud, that the ancient world experienced sexuality or sensuality rather than specific types of sexuality. That is, the instinct of sexual pleasure itself was far more important than specific gendered objects of that pleasure. Modern homosexuals identify themselves with reference to the gender of the object of their sexual desires, that is, an 'orientation', and supposedly few ancient people thought of themselves that way or were so viewed by others. Robert Padgug supports this view by citing the example of Plutarch's *Moralia* in which a series of love stories are provided in *pairs*: one concerning male–male love, followed by another about male–female love. He seems to think that the fact that they are accorded equal weight somehow proves that Plutarch believed there was just one single sexual passion. However, his example surely proves just the opposite: that Plutarch recognized there were two different sorts of passions, for which the gender of the beloved object was important. This formalistic pairing of straight and queer is very common in Hellenistic literature: for example, Philostratus (c. 170–245) wrote a series of rhetorical love letters, about half of which were addressed to boys, half to girls, and the medieval debate dialogues provide the same sort of indication that an awareness of opposing orientations is not anachronistic.

Demosthenes's wife complained bitterly when her husband shared his own bed with his boyfriend Cnossia – until, that is, she seduced him herself. Classical literature is full of jokes about men who like boys as well as women. Humorous literature from ancient China to medieval Europe is littered with tales about wives who are anxious or jealous about their husbands' boyfriends. In a very large body of satirical literature bisexuality is not so much the norm as a subject for humour. The key feature of 'bisexuality' is invariably its homosexual component.

Much has been made about the coexistence of institutionalized homosexuality and heterosexuality, as if to suggest that a dichotomy between them was not recognized in the ancient world. The representative model used to illustrate the difference between ancient and modern conceptions is that of Crete, where a 22-year-old youth 'mock abducts' a 12-year-old boy, gives him bride-gifts and effectively marries him, after which they live together for ten years. Subsequently the older man marries a woman and the younger man, now an adult, 'mock-abducts' his own younger companion, and so the cycle begins again. It is held that the transition from ten years of homosexuality to 'a life of heterosexuality' is possible only because the homosexual/heterosexual binarism did not exist, and there is no real transition because the erotic relationship remains structured along the same lines of gender/power. But the Cretan model is more problematical than that. After marrying a woman, the Cretan man nevertheless continued to live in the male barracks: 'It is thus most likely that even if an adult male had both a male "partner" and a wife, he would actually *live with* the former rather than the latter, at least until he was relatively old' (Boswell, 1995). It is quite possible to consider the Cretan model as evidence for predominant homosexual relationships with temporary and minor heterosexual interludes. Several studies of institutionalized homosexuality in Melanesia have also found that the transition from homosexual youth to heterosexual adult is not as straightforward as it is often portrayed; for example, among the Marind once the youth achieves adult status and becomes the dominant inseminator of a younger partner 'he is in no hurry to marry as he finds much gratification in his status', and even after marriage Marind men continue to engage in homosexual affairs throughout their lives (Creed, 1994).

It is not strictly true that the ancient Greeks assumed that all men were bisexual. It is more accurate to say that they assumed that all men were capable of homosexual desire. Philosophically these may add up to the same thing, but the focus is significantly different. In individuals, and often in groups, preference rather than capacity is the key issue. It might be correct to say that the Etruscans were bisexual, as they did have wives and courtesans, but according to the fourth-century Greek philosopher Theopompus, 'They certainly have commerce with women, but they always enjoy themselves much better with boys and young men.' In Rome in the second century it seems 'that *most* young men had male lovers' (Greenberg, 1988). However, Greenberg really overstates the case when he says that 'Indifference to the sex of a sexual partner' is manifest in the works of Martial, Catullus, Philostratus, Horace, Plautus, Tibullus and Meleager. Virtually all readers, scholarly and ordinary, straight and gay, agree that the love poetry addressed to women by Horace and Philostratus is artificial, whereas their love poetry to boys and young men has the ring of sincerity; their works have formal bisexual balance but passionate queer content. The social constructionist claim that 'bisexuality was the norm' in ancient and indigenous cultures is a careless use of language: bisexuality has never been a *normative* category in any culture.

It is an overgeneralization to say that 'the Greeks assumed that ordinarily sexual choices were not mutually exclusive, but rather that people were generally capable of responding erotically to beauty in both sexes', but in any case a so-called 'ambisexual capability' (a term Greenberg borrows from Freud) does not disprove preference. In fact *a passion for boys* is common in the satiric literature and lyrical poetry of ancient Greek, Roman and Arabic civilizations. Throughout history men who are technically labelled bisexual are noted for preferring boys; George Turberville on a diplomatic mission to Moscow in 1568 recorded that

'Perhaps the muzhik hath a gay and gallant wife / To serve his beastly lust, yet he will lead a bugger's life. / The monster more desires a boy within his bed / Than any wench'.

In indigenous cultures where institutional homosexuality has been documented, ethnographers point out the usual fact that these relations are integrated within larger heterosexual relations and then conclude that they are both part of a larger non-specific category of sexuality. But a closer look at such societies often reveals not only the existence of the hetero/homo dichotomy but a preference for homosexual relations: 'Lower-class women and female prostitutes are readily available to the men of the Swat Pukhtun of Northwest Pakistan, but they consider the most satisfying form of sexual gratification to be anal intercourse with a *bedagh* (passive male partner).' Among the Swat, pederasty has declined mainly because they can no longer afford to have several *bedaghs* in their retinue, though adult men nevertheless continue to have young male lovers (Greenberg, 1988). The bisexual net is similarly cast over the ancient Celts because they had boys as well as wives, but what Diodorus Siculus actually said, in the first century BC, is that 'the men are much keener on their own sex'.

Since the 1970s bisexuality has been held up as a 'liberating' goal, a 'pan-sexual' state to be achieved. But throughout queer history it has appeared not so much a status as a transitional phase from confused heterosexuality to confirmed homosexuality. Show me a man who before the 1970s 'aims for bisexuality' – as D. H. Lawrence is said to have done – and I will show you a tormented figure who is unable to admit his homosexuality to himself. The black American writer James Baldwin is a classic example of the modern so-called 'bisexual' type. Homosexuality was his natural bent. Baldwin nevertheless was unclear about his sexual identity until about the age of 17. He told his friend Sol Stein that he contracted gonorrhoea from a girl in his late teens, but Stein nevertheless said, 'I assumed from day one of knowing him that Jimmy's preferences were gay.' His first gay experience was with a Harlem racketeer soon after he turned 16, which he referred to many times in his life: 'I will be grateful to that man until the day I die.' By the age of 20 he had decided he was definitely a homosexual: according to his friend Emile Capouya, 'I thought he was a man who had flirted with homosexuality, but I had it the wrong way round' (Weatherby, 1989). Baldwin is still classified as 'a bisexual', but that is true in only the most unenlightening technical sense.

The nearly universal requirement that people get married has led to the assumption that married people who engage in homosexual relations are bisexual. But to apply the term 'bisexual' to many of these cases is to use the term so strictly and in such a minimalist sense that it ceases to be useful for the social historian. In many cases it is more accurate and more informative to employ the term 'married homosexuals'. Heterosexual marriage is so much a part of life in India that most lesbians are married; as lesbianism becomes slightly more visible, the direct result of the activities of the group Sakhi (*sakhiyana* means 'woman-to-woman bonding'), it is important to note that virtually none of these women call themselves 'bisexual' but use instead the phrase 'married lesbians' (Thadani, 1996). The concept of a bisexual lesbian is not too difficult to grasp, partly because it is a very frequent phenomenon – from Djuna Barnes and the chic women of the Left Bank in 1920s Paris to the black female singers of 1930s Harlem – and partly because there is no obvious linguistic conflict between 'bisexual' as a sexual term and 'lesbian' as a cultural term. The phrase 'bisexual homosexual', though it would be perceived as linguistically contradictory, accurately describes a phenomenon that certainly exists.

Oscar Wilde was married and had two children. That does not mean he was bisexual. As far as we can determine he had sex with more than a hundred young men, and only one woman, his wife. Even putting aside the issue of self-identity (and Wilde clearly identified with the love that dare not speak its name), it is obviously more accurate to call him a married homosexual than a bisexual. The Right Reverend Derek Rawcliffe, retired Bishop of Glasgow, first became involved in the Church at the age of 14 through his first boyfriend, and during his thirty-two years in the South Pacific from 1947 fell in love with a young Solomon Islander when he was 50. He became a bishop in 1974, and fell in love with an invalid woman on leave to England, to whom he was happily married for ten years until her death in 1987. During his marriage he felt he was no longer gay, but looking back realizes that this was not true: 'I have never been attracted to a woman before or since then. I remember when I was with her, walking down the street, I wouldn't look at the pretty girls but at the men passing by.' He finally realized that he had these feelings when he retired, and subsequently came out as gay in 1991 at the age of 70: 'I have always been a gay man' (interview in *Gay Times*, December 1995).

Questionnaires filled in by 388 homophile men for ONE Institute in 1961 revealed a high ratio of significance between homosexuals in heterosexual marriage and homosexuals in upper-level careers, the obvious conclusion being that marriage is vital to a conventional career structure even for homosexuals (Legg, 1994). It was very common in mid-twentieth-century Western societies for queer men to get married as a cover or as an attempt at cure, a trend which was becoming popular in the later nineteenth century. John Addington Symonds (1840–93) was a queer and knew it, but early in life was distressed by it: he consulted a doctor, who advised marriage as a cure. He married and had two children, enjoying sexual relations with his wife (though she did not, and eventually they ceased having intercourse). But his wife was the only woman he had sex with, while he had relations with a great many men and sometimes even brought them to live with him in the matrimonial home. It makes no sense to call him bisexual: he was a married queer. William Beckford (1760–1844), who married primarily as cover to mitigate the scandal over his affair with William Courteney, had two children, but never again engaged in sexual relations with a woman after the early death of his wife. He characterized himself as a *Barzaba*, the Arabic word for 'pederast': it is not meaningful to call Beckford 'bisexual'. The notoriously effeminate 'Monsieur', Philippe de France, duc d'Orléans (1647–1701), married twice and had three children, yet surely we have to agree with his wife Sophie that he was a 'pederast' not a 'bisexual'. The composer Jean-Baptiste Lully (1632–87) got married and had ten children specifically to avoid the scandals of his homosexual liaisons, but after becoming director of the Paris Opera and achieving a secure financial position he again publicly flaunted his relationship with his page Brunet; contemporaries who called him a sodomite were more accurate than we moderns who label him a bisexual libertine.

Well before the medicalization of homosexuality it was relatively common for queer men to get married as cover, or for other social advantages. In 1870 (just as 'the homosexual' was supposedly being constructed) John Fiske wrote from Edinburgh to his lover and 'darling angel' Ernest Boulton:

> Let me ask your advice. A young lady, whose family are friends of mine, is coming here. She is a charmingly-dressed beautiful fool with £30,000 a year. I have reason to believe that if I go in for her I can marry her. You know I never should care for her; but is the bait tempting enough for me to make this further sacrifice to respectability? Of course, after we were married I could do pretty much as I pleased. People don't mind what one does on £30,000 a year.

Paris police archives reveal the declaration of a lawyer in 1724 that 'he had a wife but hardly ever made use of her, that his marriage was a stratagem, cover-up, and that he had no taste for women, that he preferred an arse to a cunt'; he tried to persuade a young man – unfortunately a police decoy – to live with him, 'that we would live together like two brothers' (cited by Rey, 1985). A Dutchman investigated in 1730 for having seduced more than a hundred men, and who had lived with another man for two years, avoided conviction, but after repeated allegations he contracted a (childless) marriage to avoid further prosecution (Noordam, 1989). A satire published in 1707 purporting to be written by Abigail Hill Masham, Queen Anne's bedchamberwoman and almost certainly her lover, establishes an early awareness of the use of marriage as a strategy for avoiding lesbian stigma: Abigail confesses to being

> rather addicted to another Sort of Passion, of having too great a Regard for my own Sex, insomuch that few People thought I would ever have Married; but to free my self from that Aspersion some of our Sex labour under, for being too fond of one another, I was resolv'd to Marry as soon as I cou'd fix to my Advantage or Inclination.

There is hardly any period in history for which we can safely say that being married is a clear indicator of sexual identity. Quite a few wives were virtually abandoned or cruelly ignored by their queer husbands, and 'lavender' marriages were usually unhappy affairs unless some compensation could be found. In the fourteenth century, we read in Boccaccio's *Decameron* the story of a man who marries in order to dispel rumours that he is queer; the inevitably unsatisfying nature of his marriage is resolved when he makes love to a young man, who then makes love to his wife. The young man is the bisexual in this relationship, not the husband.

Vita Sackville-West and Harold Nicolson present the not-uncommon phenomenon of a lesbian married to a gay man: they are called 'bisexual' but in fact their sexual relations with one another ceased after a year or two, while remaining quite lively with others of the same sex. The 'lavender' marriage of Natacha Rambova and Rudolph Valentino was unconsummated (Rambova's lover was Alla Nazimova). Like perhaps most lesbians, Mercedes De Acosta married as she was expected to do, and she remained married for fifteen years, but her husband was the only man she ever had sex with, and they spent hardly any time together (Collis, 1994).

China, both ancient and modern, is a kinship-based society in which marriage and children are important at all levels, from the use of children as agricultural labourers to the dynastic linking of families in the courts.

Men we now call 'bisexual' usually married a woman simply to bond two lineage groups. *Nearly all* the rulers of ancient China were 'bisexual' in this sense, but homosexual favouritism was nevertheless almost universal and in very many cases was the primary love relationship of the ruler: for example, the emperor would have sex with his concubines in their quarters, but his favourite would sleep in his room every night and would be his most intimate companion. (But despite this norm, homosexual monogamy was not inconceivable; exclusive homosexual relationships between students are documented as early as the third century BC.) The ancient Chinese saw no contradiction in maintaining a heterosexual marriage and a homosexual romance:

> Since this seeming sexual dichotomy between duty and pleasure resulted from the kinship-based tradition, it would survive for as long as kinship continued to provide the foundation for social structure. ... Some men undoubtedly had sexual intercourse with women because they were expected to do so, not because they desired it. (Hinsch, 1990)

Spencer's (1995) history of homosexuality is a good corrective for those of us who too glibly subsume people who are more or less bisexual under the category homosexual and who fail to mention the fact that many people we call queer also had relations with the opposite sex:

> It is clear that we are discussing bisexuality, though writers constantly fall into the trap of talking about 'homosexual' Renaissance artists. Although Benvenuto Cellini was charged with sodomy three times, he also had affairs with women and eventually married. ... Caravaggio openly painted his boy models for a patron, Cardinal Francesco del Monte, who himself had homosexual interests. Caravaggio was notorious in his passion for boys but also had relationships with women. Aretino seduced a married woman but also chased boys.

But neither Leonardo da Vinci nor Michelangelo had sexual relationships with women. Greenberg (1988), determined that gay identity and gay subculture cannot arise except in the context of exclusive homosexuality, misleadingly claims that Renaissance 'sodomites' were also 'actively heterosexual', but, as with Spencer, the examples he cites seem to be men who were predominantly homosexual but who had either some limited affairs with women or who married for convenience: e.g. Cellini suppressed knowledge of his homosexual affairs and married, Caravaggio had an affair with one woman but 'lived for years with one of his male models', Pietro Aretino seduced women but really seems to have preferred boys, whom he actively chased. Greenberg also emphasizes that during Elizabethan and Jacobean eras homosexuality was seldom exclusive, but he cites as an example the marriage of Francis Bacon – which was a late marriage, and it is clear from letters by Bacon's mother that he preferred his menservants. While it is true to say that many of the so-called 'great queens of history' in fact were seldom exclusively homosexual, the lists are nevertheless full of rulers such as Grand Prince Vasily II (father of Ivan the Terrible), who got married for reasons of state and was able to fulfil his conjugal duties only when a naked guardsman joined the royal couple in bed. Most public figures – virtually all rulers and ministers – have to marry for reasons of state, and such marriages hardly indicate bisexuality except in the most arid academic sense. To then go on to maintain that 'This lack of exclusivity was an obstacle to the formation of a homosexual personal identity, or the creation of a subculture organized around homosexual choice' is utterly without foundation.

Bray (1982) characterizes the typical libertine of the seventeenth century, John Wilmot, Earl of Rochester, as having 'his mistress on one arm and his "catamite" on the other' – a phrase repeated *verbatim* in all social constructionist homosexual histories. But it is characteristic of libertine literature to express *the superiority of homosexual relations*, not the equality of heterosexual and homosexual relations, nor even to praise bisexuality as such. A satirical poem of 1703 describes James Stanhope as one 'who thinks no Pleasure like Italian Joy, / And to a Venus Arms prefers a Pathick Boy'. The libertines deliberately provoked and shocked the public not by expressing bisexual inclinations, but by exhibiting a preference for homosexual tastes; for example, a character in the anonymous *Wandering Whore* (1660) says he would 'fayn be buggering some of our wenches, if the Matron could get their consent, but had rather be dealing with smooth-fac'd prentices.' Like many historians of homosexuality, Spencer (1995) quotes some famous lines by Rochester as evidence of libertine bisexuality: 'There's a sweet, soft page of mine / Does the trick worth forty wenches.' Spencer says that this demonstrates the view that going with a boy is 'more or less like going with a girl'. On the contrary; what these lines explicitly claim is *a forty-to-one preference in favour of queer sex* – which by any standards, such as Kinsey's seven-point scale, must characterize the author as being almost exclusively homosexual by inclination!

Spencer also emphasizes, for example, the well-documented phenomenon of the younger receptive boy in a homosexual relationship being the active partner in heterosexual relationships, as with male servants in ancient Chinese households. Nevertheless he misleads us when he speaks of young Chinese male prostitutes as being part of 'a bisexual tradition', for that implies that the prostitutes as well as their clients were bisexual, when in fact we know that male prostitutes were almost exclusively homosexual in ancient China and Japan and this should therefore be called 'a queer tradition'.

It is indicative that Spencer, like most theorists, almost always sees the bisexual man as active, namely as a libertine who penetrates girls and boys fairly indiscriminately. The passive male bisexual hardly exists as a concept, which points up the extent to which the word 'bisexual' is really a code word for 'non-passive homosexual'. Some evidence of bisexuality, however limited, provides the saving grace for men who would otherwise be labelled with the same term used to stigmatize passive catamites. Trumbach's influential theory about the 'gender revolution', which he supposes took place around 1700, depends heavily upon the stereotype of the 'bisexual libertine'; but the libertines chosen to illustrate the case are not meaningfully bisexual by my reckoning, and most of the quotations cited to illustrate 'indifferent bisexuality' in fact, like the quotation from Rochester, are prima facie evidence of preferential homosexuality.

3

The Myth of the Modern Homosexual

Assertions that the modern homosexual and modern gay subculture are significantly different from the past are based primarily upon ignorance of that past. In his discussion about the gay press, for example, Bronski (1984) argues that 'The marketing of gay culture was possible only to gay people and then only after a gay movement had emerged and given the community a more visible and national presence.' This betrays great historical ignorance about the existence of gay publishing before the 1950s. What about the marketing of the Fortune Press in the 1940s, or the slim volumes of Uranian verse in the 1910s? What about the marketing and distribution of nude photographs of boys by von Gloeden and others? During the late nineteenth century many art magazines and poetry journals were owned by and sold to culturally identified queers; they were not blatantly queer – in the same sense that the New York magazine *After Dark* was not blatantly queer – but they were very easily 'read' as queer, and formed as much a part of the marketing of gay culture as anything in the 1990s. Even distinctive queer 'lifestyles' were promoted long before the development of commercial gay subculture and the periodicals that promoted it: culture, opera, theatre, music, interior decoration and art have notably fed queer consumers for many decades, and even today more of 'the pink pound' goes towards these activities than towards discos and drugs.

An astonishingly parochial American viewpoint informs most of the social constructionist arguments:

> Of all the national histories being investigated, that of the United States most clearly confirms the argument of Weeks and Foucault concerning the emergence of a distinctive gay identity. The peculiarities of North American development meant that only after the American Civil War did the market relations of industrial capitalism finally triumph; only in the late nineteenth century did the United States unmistakably become a nation of cities. These changes coincided with the professionalization of medicine, its seizure of sexuality as a specialized domain of knowledge, and its

reconceptualization of homosexuality as a condition. (D'Emilio, 1992)

America is a colonial construct; to draw conclusions from such a society about how a gay identity might emerge in an indigenous or premodern society is ludicrous. America developed in a peculiar way, as D'Emilio acknowledges, and it really cannot be used as an ideal model in the essentialist/constructionist debate – it simply did not develop as a society until the modern period, and its features are modern by definition. To claim that features that arose in this modern society are *by nature* modern is to beg many questions.

Katz's (1994) straightforward Marxist analysis is similarly based solely upon the American experience. Early colonial documents often mention 'sodomy' but rarely mention 'sodomite' (fitting nicely with Foucault's thesis), but this is quite the opposite of the case in all European countries, and arises because the early colonists brought with them to the New World the old laws and jurisprudence of the Old World, but not the queer subculture of the Old World. At the same time Katz nevertheless admits that even in the early colonies 'sodomy included feeling as well as act', and early colonial documents refer to it as a 'propensity' and 'habit', which suggests it was an inborn impulse (requiring restraint); in fact single acts of sodomy were not prosecuted: prosecutions were made against those who habitually committed sodomy – namely persons who acquired the character of being sodomites. When one is trying to determine the 'origins' of homophobia or the homosexual subculture, the American experience is largely irrelevant.

Social control

Foucault (1978) argues that a strict heterosexual/homosexual dichotomy (or 'binarism') was established in the nineteenth century, mainly by scientists in the medical and paramedical professions, so as to promote and constitute 'a sexuality that is economically useful and politically conservative'. The control of sexuality is intimately tied to the rise of capitalism, and is thus subject to an economic-political analysis (as social constructionism is founded upon Marxist, specifically Maoist, principles). In other words, the social establishment wished to control sexuality in order to promote the reproductive capacity of the labour force and to discourage 'fruitless pleasures'. In parallel with this, doctors increased their power by categorizing and introducing mechanisms of surveillance of 'peripheral sexualities' – the more perversions they could classify and treat, the greater the prestige of their profession. As an analysis of the self-enhancement of the medical profession in the late nineteenth century, this seems reasonable. I would contend, however, that this concerns a fairly sophisticated type of social control, which achieves its aim only within an environment that is already highly controlled: outside of hospitals and prisons – where measures more forceful than linguistics are employed – medical labelling is far less effective. The idea that the label created that which was labelled has little historical evidence to support it.

Even within these controlled environments, the medical literature is full of reports of clinical interviews in which doctors are astonished by how often the 'inverts' reject their 'help'; a typical case concerns the doctor who lamented that the working-class 'fags' he interviewed in New York's city jail in the early 1920s actually claimed they were *'proud* to be degenerates, [and] do not want nor care to be cured' (Chauncey, 1994). My basic argument is not that this medicalization of the homosexual did not take place (and a range of homosexual stereotypes constructed to match various physiological and psychiatric theories prominent at the time), but that homosexuals already existed before they were forcibly laid upon this procrustean bed. In other words, the genuine social construct is paramedical homophobia.

As an analysis of the mechanisms of control and power, social constructionism provides a useful basis for deconstructing the various medical, educational and familial agencies of oppression which serve the economic interests of bourgeois capitalism. A concept shown to be based upon fictions, artefacts and cultural relativism can be undermined more readily than a concept based upon fact and observation, and this is part of the strategy of Foucault's school. But as an analysis of the *origins of identity* – for either heterosexuals or homosexuals – the social constructionist analysis is woefully inadequate.

The simple-minded notion that one must create homosexuals in order to have a boundary which establishes heterosexuals completely ignores the long history of the suppression and censorship of knowledge concerning the *crimen nefandum* or *peccatum mutum*, the mute sin. The legal practice in early eighteenth-century Amsterdam is typical of many periods and cultures: trials for sodomites were secret affairs; when sodomites were executed the trial documents were sometimes destroyed so that no record would remain (Noordam, 1989); most sodomites were executed in secret, rather than in public, as with other criminals; sodomites who were imprisoned were kept hidden in solitary confinement in the cellars of prisons, and were not allowed to mix with other prisoners or to take part in prison labour: Jan Jansz, convicted in 1741 at the age of 17, spent his remaining fifty-seven years alone in his cell, his existence virtually unknown except to modern scholars (Meer, 1989). How did Jan Jansz serve as a 'negative example' to define or enforce normality? There is hardly any era where the social authorities were not desperate to keep the love that dare not speak its name a secret from the masses of people rather than display it as a public warning. Fear that ordinary people would be tempted by homosexuality after learning of its existence is the overriding concern of the agents of social control.

What Foucault regards as the *formation* of non-procreative sexualities is in reality the *warping* of pre-existing identities: natural-born queers were turned into perverts. The subsequent rigidification of such identities into modern, remembered, times – for example, the terrible 1950s – should not blind us to the historical and archaeological evidence of these identities well before the onslaught of medicalization. The reason why the homosexual identity was so easily consolidated was precisely because it already existed. In contrast, many of the other 'perversions' never really emerged as identities, for example, the foot-fetishist is not a very clearly conceived personality type that goes beyond the incongruous images of foot fetishization; only the masturbator, the 'wanker' in modern British slang, became a personality type, though with a range of characteristics much more limited than the homosexual.

The 'homosexual'

The one person most responsible for the creation of the labels that would be used in the discourse about homosexuality was Karl Heinrich Ulrichs (1825–95), a law student, secretary to various civil servants and diplomats, and a journalist – he was not a medical doctor. In May 1862 his acquaintance Johann Baptist von Schweitzer, active in the Social Democracy workers' movement, was arrested for 'public indecency'. Ulrichs wrote a defence and sent it to Schweitzer, but it was confiscated by the authorities. Ulrichs, who had been sexually attracted to men since his early teens, decided that now was the time to solve this 'riddle'. In November 1862 he told his relatives of his intention to publish a study of 'The Race of Uranian Hermaphrodites, i.e., the Man-Loving Half-Men'. He had finished most of it by 1863, and it was published in 1864, as *Forschungen über das Rätsel der mannmännlichen Liebe* (*Researches on the Riddle of Male–Male [Man-to-Man] Love*). He used the pseudonym Numa

Numantius in deference to his shocked relatives, but acknowledged his identity in 1868. By 1879 he had published twelve volumes on this subject.

His 'scientific' inspiration was contemporary embryology, which had discovered that the sex organs are undifferentiated in the earliest stages of the development of the foetus. By analogy, homosexual desire was just as 'natural' as this containment of the opposite sex within the developing embryo. He believed that the 'germ' of the female sex could be retained in the fully developed male, creating a kind of psychic hermaphrodite or half-man: a feminine direction of the sex drive within a masculine sex. (This direct linking of sex organs to direction of sex drive is a common *non sequitur*.) After some refinements he settled on the phrase *anima muliebris virili corpore inclusa* – a feminine soul or mentality confined by a masculine body.

The substantive source for Ulrichs's theory was not heterosexualist medicine, but Plato's *Symposium*, in which Pausanius declares that love for males is the offspring of Heavenly Love (Aphrodite Urania) who is the daughter of Uranus, while love for females is the offspring of Common Love (Aphrodite Pandeumia) who is the daughter of Zeus and Dione. Ulrichs modified the Platonic/Pausanian terms in accordance with German linguistic usage and came up with *Urning* for homosexual male, *Dioning* for heterosexual male, *Urningin* for lesbian and *Dioningin* for heterosexual female. As Ulrichs became more widely acquainted with other homosexuals, he realized there were many varieties, and he expanded his system of classification thus:

- *Urningthum*, male homosexuality (or *urnische Liebe*, homosexual love);

- *Urning*, male homosexual:
  - *Mannlinge*, very masculine except for feminine soul and sex drive towards effeminate men;
  - *Weiblinge*, feminine in appearance and behaviour as well as soul, and sex drive towards manly men; with variations between these extremes, such as the *Zwischen-Urning* who prefers adolescents;

- *Uranodioning*, male bisexual:
  - Conjunctive, with tender and passionate feelings for men;
  - Disjunctive, with tender feelings for men but passionate feelings for women;

- *Virilisierte Mannlinge*, homosexual men who have learned to act like heterosexual men, through force or habit;

- *Uraniaster* or *uranisierter Mann*, heterosexual man who acts like a homosexual (often due to lack of women, for example in prisons or military environments).

All of these were matched by female counterparts for the *Urningin*.

Kennedy (1985) observes that 'the theory seems ready to collapse under the weight of its own complexities', and the terminology of *Uranismus* was gradually dropped, although it lived on in England for almost half a century as 'Uranian love' (and the modern gay tourist agency Uranian Travel). But let us honestly acknowledge that the system of descriptive classification used today is nearly the same as Ulrichs's, even if the terminology does seem less absurd:

- homosexual:
  - active/masculine or
  - receptive/effeminate;

- bisexual;

- closet or latent gay;

- situational homosexual.

The main difference between the two systems is that the concept of the 'feminine soul' has been dropped since the 1960s, though in the 1990s it is being revived in the term 'transgender'. Many (perhaps most) folk cultures have a concept of a natural (biological) third sex in addition to male and female, and the most recent anthropological theorists are coming round once again to the possibility that there really is – physiologically and psychologically – a third sex or third gender (Herdt, 1994). The motivating source or etiology of homosexuality has been debated ever since, and the 'cause' of homosexuality or specific categories such as effeminacy are as hotly disputed as they were in the 1890s.

The basic emancipationist argument was (and often still is) that homosexual desire is congenital and therefore it is inhumane for the law to punish homosexual acts as if they were crimes wilfully chosen. Ulrichs was not scientifically disinterested: he was politically motivated by a fear that the Prussians would invade Hanover and impose the anti-homosexual statute of the Prussian Penal Code (which had no equivalent in Hanover) – which is precisely what happened when Prussia annexed Hanover in

1866. Ulrichs was briefly imprisoned for expressing outspoken Social Democrat views, and in 1867 the police confiscated his collection of homosexual research material. He was ridiculed in the press, and forced to leave Hanover on his release from prison. He moved to Bavaria and in August 1867 at the Congress of German Jurists in Munich gave a speech for homosexual rights which Kennedy (1985) says 'mark[s] the beginning of the public homosexual emancipation movement in Germany'. But by 1872 Prussia's anti-homosexual legislation was extended to all of unified Germany. In 1880 Ulrichs felt compelled to leave his country, and he settled in Italy for the remaining fifteen years of his life.

The word *Homosexualität* was invented by the German-Hungarian Károly Mária Kertbeny (born Karl Maria Benkert, 1824–82). It is a compound of Greek *homo* ('same'), and medieval Latin *sexualis* ('sexual'), and was coined along the lines of the late eighteenth-century French botanical terms *unisexuel* and *bisexuel*. There are no grounds for rejecting it as a 'bastard' term, any more than innumerable Greek/Latin hybrids such as *petroleum* and *automobile* and *television*. It occurs first in a letter to Karl Heinrich Ulrichs, dated 6 May 1868, and then in two pamphlets published in 1869 in Leipzig arguing for reform of Paragraph 143 of the Prussian Penal Code penalizing sexual relations between men. Kertbeny's noun for the male homosexual was *Homosexualisten*, and *Homosexualistinnen* for the female homosexual; the term 'homosexualist' is used even today, representing a kind of provincial survival. These terms were not used again until 1880, when a text written by Kertbeny was published in a popular-science book (*Entdeckung der Seele*) by Gustav Jaeger, a zoologist and anthropologist at the University of Stuttgart, at which time the word *Heterosexualität* first appeared, also taken from a paper by Kertbeny, here attributed to 'Dr M'. Thus heterosexuals were invented eleven years later than homosexuals.

This pseudonym and title helped to promote the mistaken belief that Kertbeny was a doctor or scientist. The wholly incorrect view that he was a physician is asserted, for example, by Lauritsen and Thorstad (1974), Bullough (1976), Bronski (1984), Spencer (1995) and others too numerous to cite. Kertbeny was in fact a writer, a translator, a journalist and a polemicist: he engaged in no medical or scientific profession, and did not even write in these fields except in the limited area of homosexual law reform. We know little about his life (he seems to have died of syphilis): although he claimed to be a *Normalsexualer*, his long-term anonymous and pseudonymous campaign for gay rights suggests that he was secretly homosexual.

'Homosexuality' thus originated not as a medical term, but rather as a neutral, legal, scientific term. The 1950s 'homophile' and 1970s 'gay and lesbian' communities have rejected the term because of its medical and clinical connotations, but such connotations were not integral to the word and did not originate in the clinic. It was coined precisely in order to serve the emancipationist needs of a network of gay-identified German men who for a dozen years at least had been advocating the reform of laws against them and the education of society regarding their modes of behaviour. Contrary to the labelling theory paradigm, the label clearly followed rather than preceded the identity; it was not something 'constructed' by society in order to identify and thereby control a deviant group; on the contrary, it was for the sake of achieving public tolerance of the behaviour of an identifiable group that the label was invented, by that group themselves. The discourse about '*homosexualität/* homosexuality' came towards the end rather than at the beginning of the development of a gay consciousness.

An examination of the history of the term 'homosexual' very clearly demonstrates the exact reverse of what is required by labelling and social control theory. The label 'homosexual', instead of being generated by society to control people, was self-generated by gay (or gay-friendly) men to empower individuals and set them on the road to freedom rather than enslavement. By retrospective analysis Ulrichs did claim to have discovered feminine traits within himself *after* he developed the third-sex theory, which would accord with classic labelling theory: 'not everyone arrives at a consciousness of this female element. I myself ... became aware of it only very late, and I might never have arrived at it had I not pondered the riddle of Uranian love or become acquainted with other Urnings.' However, even if this assertion were true, the label nevertheless arose from within Ulrichs's struggle to solve a riddle about himself – it was not imposed from without, by society, in order to control him. (In any case we are not compelled to believe Ulrichs on this point: it sounds like a rationalization to defend the absence of self-interest in his theory and hence its scientific objectivity.)

Ulrichs promoted his theory by analogy to the emerging science of embryology, but his labels themselves are rooted in the queer philosophy of Plato's *Symposium*. To some extent Ulrichs became entrapped by the purely formal or logical requirements of classification, but his motivation and stated purpose were always queer-political: to resist the imposition of Prussian legal strictures on homosexual acts upon Hanover. In other words, the label used most often in the modern discourse on homosexuality originated from queer men, drawing upon queer culture, whose stated aim was queer liberation. So much for social control.

Ulrichs's and Benkert's theories were subverted by Richard von Krafft-Ebing (1840–1902), to whom Ulrichs had sent his publications in 1866. They inspired Krafft-Ebing's own researches and he extracted from them some of the classifications – but not the basic premise. Ulrichs's theory that homosexuality was natural and congenital was significantly modified in accordance with a criminal/medical model which emphasized perversion, sickness and deficiency. A theory that began as an effort to legitimate homosexuality was expropriated by theories used to justify a long tradition of repression and legal punishment. Ulrichs summed it up:

> My scientific opponents are mostly doctors of the insane. Thus, for example, Westphal, v. Krafft-Ebing, Stark. They have observed Urnings in lunatic asylums. They have apparently never seen mentally healthy Urnings. The published views of the doctors for the insane are accepted by the others (cited in Kennedy, 1980).

Unfortunately Ulrichs's term 'half-man', though he did not use it for his final classification system, easily fell in with the view of homosexual men as being incomplete or defective.

Several writers have carefully examined the process and linguistic developments by which homosexuality came to be 'medicalized' in the very late nineteenth century (notably Bleys, 1996), but the issue I wish to focus upon here is the date at which social control of the masses of ordinary gay people became possible. Karl Friedrich Otto Westphal (1833–1890) used the term 'Die Konträre Sexualempfindung' ('contrary sexual feeling'), in an article in *Archiv für Psychiatrie und Nerven-krankheiten* in 1869, thus defining homosexuality as a contradiction between desire and anatomy. In 1870 an American psychiatrist abstracted Westphal's article, using the phrase 'inverted sexual feeling', and in 1878 Arrigo Tamassia invented *inversione dell'istinto sessuale* in an article in an Italian medical journal: his phrase was subsequently simplified to 'inversion', which remained the standard medical term. Westphal, who helped to popularize the views of Ulrichs and Kertbeny in his 1869 article, concentrated in particular on the phrase *drittes Geschlecht* or 'third sex', which Ulrichs had coined in 1864 and which gained widespread popularity outside scientific circles. Magnus Hirschfeld's book on the homosexual subculture of Berlin is entitled *Berlins drittes Geschlecht*. However, this is by no means a new term of alleged social control: the Emperor Alexander Severus in the third century is supposed to have characterized

eunuchs as the *tertium genus hominum* on the basis of Latin grammar
(i.e. masculine, feminine, and neuter), and Balzac in *Splendeur et misère
des courtisanes* (1847) calls the *tante* (homosexual 'auntie') 'le troisième
sexe'. In any case the English phrase 'the third sex' was not used before
the 1950s, when it was usually aligned with 'the twilight world'. It was
never a 'medical' term.

Homosexualität was a very useful neutral way to refer to 'same-sex
love', 'scientifically' defusing such highly charged words as 'bugger',
'sodomite' or 'degenerate'; but it was not taken up very quickly by the
scientifically minded community of physicians and anthropologists. For
nearly twenty years it circulated almost entirely within a gay
emancipationist discourse. The word 'homosexual' did not appear in
English until 1891, in John Addington Symonds's *A Problem in Modern
Ethics*, where he used the phrase 'homosexual instincts'. No one seems
to have remarked on the irony that the first English person to write the
word 'homosexual' *was a homosexual long before he put pen to paper*.
Symonds was one of the very few men familiar with the so-called scientific
writings on this subject, which he sought out to support his already well-
developed sense of homosexual identity. Havelock Ellis and John
Addington Symonds tried to revive some of Ulrichs's theory in the 1880s.
Symonds frequently corresponded with Ulrichs about 'the slave-cause of
the Urnings'. He knew himself to be an *Urning* when he wrote *A Problem
in Greek Ethics* in 1883, and the footnotes to his *Modern Ethics* (1891)
demonstrate that he did not discover most of the medical literature until
after 1883. The 1891 book was privately printed in an edition of ten
copies: it hardly popularized the word, although pirated editions were
published from about 1900. In *Sexual Inversion* (1897) Havelock Ellis
(together with Symonds, whose name was removed from the title page
after the first edition) popularized the idea of 'inversion' as an inborn
non-pathological gender anomaly. Symonds privately despised the
'authorities' on the subject:

> The ignorance of men like Casper-Liman, Tardieu, Carlier, Taxil,
> Moreau, Tarnowsky, Krafft-Ebing, Richard Burton is incalculable,
> and is only equalled to their presumption. They not only do not
> know Ancient Greece, but they do not know their own cousins and
> club-mates. (Letter to Havelock Ellis, 20 June 1892)

Symonds felt strongly that homosexuals should be considered as a
'minority' group, but he gave way to Ellis's preference for viewing

homosexuality as a neurosis and congenital abnormality in the hope, proven vain, that this would gain sympathy and tolerance from the public.

The 1869 watershed

The word 'homosexual' has acquired such a powerful mystique that Neil Miller's (1995) anthology *Out of the Past* is subtitled *Gay and Lesbian History from 1869 to the Present*, farcically suggesting that the year 1869 marks a specific watershed. This is one of those shifts of which the social constructionists are so fond – the queer moment slovenly posited by Foucault (1978): 'Westphal's famous article of 1870 [*sic*] on "contrary sexual sensations" can stand as its date of birth.' If the homosexual was born in 1869 (the actual date of Westphal's article), his parent was queer rather than straight: 1869 is the year that Edward Carpenter (1844–1929) first read Walt Whitman: 'It was not till (at the age of twenty five) I read Whitman – and then with a great leap of joy – that I met with the treatment of sex which accorded with my own sentiments.' (Miller, 1995.) Carpenter wrote to Whitman in 1874 thanking him for legitimizing the 'love of men'. Neither Whitman nor Carpenter at this time, and hardly anyone else in the English-speaking world, had heard of the words 'homosexual' or *Urning* or 'third sex' or 'invert'. It is inconceivable that a gay consciousness so well developed as Carpenter's was in 1874 was not already firmly established before the homosexual labels were invented. It is not credible that only five years after a concept is created Carpenter can say to Whitman, 'You have made men to be not ashamed of the noblest instinct of their nature. Women are beautiful; but, to some, there is that which passes the love of women.' It is argued that 'Whitman himself stubbornly resisted the notion of a distinctive homosexual sensibility' (D'Emilio, 1992), but it might be more accurate to say that he resisted the stigma that he knew would be attached to this sensibility. Contemporary queers who read Whitman immediately *identified* with the sensibility that he clearly suggested in his works. He himself talks about 'adhesiveness' as a special sensibility intimately connected to one's self-conception, male-bonding and generalized eroticism. Symonds noted the testimony of a young German man who visited North America in 1871:

> There the unnatural vice in question is more ordinary than it is here; and I was able to indulge my passions with less fear of punishment or persecution. The Americans' tastes in this matter

resemble my own; and I discovered, in the United States, that I was always immediately recognized as a member of the confraternity.

The epiphanic moment of reading Walt Whitman is recorded in the diaries and memoirs of countless gay men (his English admirers were called 'Calamites', a pun on 'catamites') from the 1860s to the 1960s, and was passed on through intermediaries such as Carpenter. Countee Cullen was only 19 when he experienced self-recognition after reading Carpenter's (1906) pioneering anthology of gay love, *Iolaüs*, at the suggestion of gay Harvard professor Alain Locke:

> I read it through at one sitting, and steeped myself in its charming and comprehending atmosphere. It opened up for me Soul windows which had been closed; it threw a noble and evident light on what I had begun to believe, because of what the world believes, ignoble and unnatural. I loved myself in it, and thanked you a thousand times as many delightful examples appeared, for recommending it to me. (Cited in Norton, 1997)

Carpenter's more polemical book *The Intermediate Sex* also had a profound impact, upon women as well as men. The second-generation feminist Frances Wilder in 1912 was advocating self-restraint and abstinence in the radical *Freewoman*, but only three years later Carpenter's book had helped her to realize that she was not simply a feminist, but a lesbian feminist, as she wrote to him:

> I have recently read with much interest your book entitled The Intermediate Sex & it has lately dawned on me that I myself belong to that class & I write to ask if there is any way of getting in touch with others of the same temperament. (Cited by Newton, 1984)

Plato and Whitman and Carpenter and Wilde – the fountainheads of queer wisdom – have had a more profound impact upon the queer self-image than Krafft-Ebing and Westphal. That was still true for my own generation, and true for working-class people as well as intellectuals. Gay liberationist historian John D'Emilio (1992), who was brought up in Jesuit schools and was full of guilt and self-doubt, recalls how a Catholic Cuban emigré, Luis,

> saw straight through to the heart of my interior struggle and found a way to help. Getting up from bed, after we'd had sex and had talked for a time, he went to his bookshelf and reached for a well-thumbed copy of Oscar Wilde's *De Profundis*, which he gave to

me. Later, alone in my room, I read it through in a single sitting.
... I think it fair to say that it saved my life.

Camille Paglia (1994), as an adolescent, found a second-hand copy of
The Epigrams of Oscar Wilde: 'It became my bible. I memorized its phrases
and repeated them until they became part of my brain chemistry.'

Social constructionists are so obsessed with abstract categories that
they seldom pause to examine the lives of real people. If 'homosexuals'
did not exist until they were invented in the late nineteenth century, then
it would be a very useful exercise to look at the biographies of people
whose lives spanned the watershed or 'shift' that is supposed to have
occurred in 1869. One quickly discovers that such men and women were
demonstrably as queer before 1869 as afterwards. In 1868 Ethel Smyth
– at the age of 10 – began compiling her 'Book of Passions', 'which
included names of over a hundred girls and women to whom, had she
been a man, she would have proposed. Ethel admitted, "From the first
my most ardent sentiments were bestowed on members of my own sex"'
(Collis, 1994). Verlaine had numerous homosexual affairs from his teens,
consciously defying society's taboos: he more or less lived with Rimbaud
from 1871 to 1873, despite being married, and was a self-conscious queer,
in the French pederastic mode, before any sexological label could be
applied to him.

In the year 1870 Ernest Boulton and Frederick William Park, otherwise
known as Lady Stella Clinton and Miss Fanny Winifred Park, were
arrested in London after a year-long surveillance by the police of their
practice of soliciting men in the Burlington Arcade and outside theatres
while wearing women's clothes. It transpired that they and their associates
stored vast quantities of dresses, petticoats, gloves and make-up at an
accommodation address. A small network of their non-effeminate
boyfriends was subsequently discovered, in Edinburgh as well as in
London. Lord Arthur Pelham Clinton, MP, third son of the Duke of
Newcastle, lodged near Boulton, and there are posters showing both men
in their theatrical performances in male and female roles. Boulton was
accustomed to dressing in girls' clothes from the age of six; now 20, as
Stella, he became Clinton's 'wife' and wore his wedding ring. (Witnesses
gave evidence that Lord Arthur paid for a hairdresser to go to Stella every
morning, and had ordered from the stationers a seal engraved 'Stella' and
even visiting cards printed 'Lady Arthur Clinton'.) Lord Arthur, aged only
30, died allegedly of scarlet fever (that is, he killed himself) before the
case came to court.

Two years earlier Boulton had lived with a young Post Office surveyor in Edinburgh. Some two thousand love letters and photographs were discovered during the police search of their home, and many of the letters were read out in court. These contained references to 'going about in drag', 'getting screwed' and a great deal of camp behaviour that is reminiscent of the behaviour of drag queens in the 1990s. But to the court and members of the jury, the letters were insufficient to convict for conspiracy to commit a felony (i.e. sodomy) and everyone was acquitted. It is clear from the trial 'that neither the police nor the court were familiar either with male homosexuality or prostitution' (Weeks, 1985). The doctor who examined them, and was criticized for it by the judge, 'had not heard of the work of Tardieu, who had investigated over two hundred cases of sodomy for purposes of legal proof, until an anonymous letter informed him of its existence'. In other words, not only were queer identities and a queer subculture well established several years before Foucault's 'queer moment', but society's 'construct' or conception of 'the homosexual' had not yet been formed.

The painter Simeon Solomon (1840–1905) sums up his own pre-watershed gay life:

> As an infant he ... developed a tendency toward designing. ... He was hated by all of his family before he was eighteen. He was eighteen at the time he was sent to Paris. His behaviour there was so disgraceful that his family – the Nathans, Solomons, Moses, Cohens, etc., et hoc genus homo – would have nothing to do with him. He returned to London to pursue his disgraceful course of Art ... His 'Vision of Love Revealed in Sleep' is too well known. After the publication of this [in 1871] his family repudiated him forever. (Quoted by Conner *et al.*, 1997)

We think of Solomon as a figure of the 1890s, broken by his arrest in a urinal in 1872, but he had been branded as a queer long before this. And clearly he identified as queer from an early date: his lover from 1868 was the Eton schoolmaster Oscar Browning. Homoerotic love and the androgynous male – all evidence of his culturally queer identification – run throughout his work even in the 1860s: *The Bride, the Bridegroom and Sad Love* (1865; 'Sad Love' being a personification of homosexual love); *Spartan Boys about to Be Scourged at the Altar of Diana* (1865); *Heliogabalus, High Priest of the Sun* (1866).

It is highly unlikely that Edith Simcox, who began writing her *Autobiography* in 1876, was conversant with the sexological discourse on homosexuality, yet she seems to have been aware of her own sexuality in very much the same terms – and using the same labels – that were popularized for 'the lesbian' in the 1890s and later: 'It *is* a blessing that what was abnormal in my passion caused no pain or grief to her [i.e. George Eliot] – bore nothing worse than mere denial for me.' She analyses her own 'development', including characteristic features such as a tomboy stage, lack of sympathy for girlish pursuits – 'I didn't care for dolls or dresses or any sort of needlework' – and attachments to older girls whom she used to caress. She felt a 'constitutional want of charm for men' and that her love for women indicated that she was 'half a man'. She is using a common concept that was being reified by sexologists, but it is too early for her to have 'internalized' the sexological construct. She may not have applied the 'lesbian' label to herself, but she *does* seem to be aware of her sexual feelings for women and that *these feelings place her in a class*. In her wooing of George Eliot she even tried to persuade the author that she also belonged to that class of women euphemistically described as those who 'did not like men' (Johnson, 1989).

The slowness of 'medicalization'

The third-sex or intermediate sex theory (*sexuelle Zwischenstufen*) was not used in any popular publications until 1907–8 when Maximilian Harden in his political weekly *Die Zukunft* exposed Prince Philipp Fürst zu Eulenburg-Hertefeld as the central figure of a circle of homosexuals at the court of Wilhelm II; as a result of the series of trials and scandals that followed, the word 'homosexual' firmly found its place as *the* word of choice in the European languages. The term does not seem to have been used in American newspapers until 1914, in reports of a scandal in Long Beach when a group of homosexual men resisted arrest (Legg, 1994). The term was used not by physicians or even 'sexologists', but by journalists and apologists for homosexual law reform. Nor did it gain much headway in psychiatric and medical literature until just before and after the First World War. The 'medicalization' of 'homosexuality' certainly did occur, but it dates from the 1910s and 1920s, when it was relatively unconnected with the specific label 'homosexual' and was unknown to the queer man in the street:

> Much of the degeneracy-theory/evolutionary-theory literature on homosexuality appeared in medical journals or in books that were not readily accessible to the public. The more salacious passages

of *Psychopathia Sexualis* were printed in Latin. The first English edition of Ellis's *Sexual Inversion* was suppressed, and retail sales of the American edition were at first restricted to doctors and lawyers. Newspaper and magazine coverage was virtually nonexistent. ... The *Lancet*, England's leading medical journal, refused to review *Sexual Inversion* lest lay people read it. (Greenberg, 1988)

In other words, the 'new' medical concept could have had hardly any influence on the queer subcultures which had already existed for decades. Whatever effect homosexual labels might have had upon the formation of the homosexual identity, it could not have taken place until the 1920s, two generations *later* than the social constructionists have argued. J. R. Ackerley, who was by no means uneducated, did not hear the word 'homosexual' until during the First World War. After being taken prisoner during the war he was interned in Switzerland, where in 1918 a fellow internee asked him if he were 'homo or hetero'; the words had to be explained to him, after which he knew immediately and exactly where he stood. His compatriot, the 'hetero' Arthur Lunn, was better read and recommended several books for him to read, including Plutarch and Edward Carpenter. The label helped a light to dawn, but Ackerley's queer identity very quickly sorted itself out with the help of queer sources, not medical ones. Studying at Cambridge University following the war, Ackerley remembered being

> very romantic and talkative; chatty about the Classical Greeks and their ways, inclining to Bohemia, busily acquiring the usual pictures by Flandrin, Tuke, Praxiteles and Glyn Philpot for decorating my room, and ready to respond to understanding and sympathy from any quarter. (Parker, 1989)

Chauncey's (1985) study of the working-class homosexual (sub)culture investigated at the Newport (Rhode Island) Naval Training Station in 1919 demonstrates that the 'medical discourse still played little or no role in the shaping of working-class homosexual identities and categories by the First World War, more than thirty years after the discourse had begun'. Only one fairy used the word 'invert', which he had heard in theatre circles merely as a synonym for 'queer'; only one person – the man who supervised the training of decoys – read any of the medical literature, and then only after his methods were being called into question; no 'medical expert' was invited to testify during the two years of hearings.

The very people who helped consolidate the image of the 'invert' were the lesbians and gay men who contributed their case histories to Ellis's *Sexual Inversion*, people who had well-developed queer identities long before its publication in 1897, often from their early childhood. The major queer readers of sexological literature were such 'educated inverts' as Symonds, Oscar Wilde, Marcel Proust and Radclyffe Hall, who all read Krafft-Ebing and were influenced by the 'third sex' theory. But even here we should note that Radclyffe Hall was influenced not so much by Krafft-Ebing himself as by *the testimony of lesbian women* such as Countess Sarolta that he included in his book. *Psychopathia Sexualis* is one of the books, including several by Karl Heinrich Ulrichs, which are shown to be in the library of Stephen Gordon's father in *The Well of Loneliness*. It is typical of the social constructionists to arrogantly dismiss case history testimonies as 'the eruption into print of the speaking pervert' (Weeks, 1991).

In any case, educated queers did not create the queer subculture, which is largely a working-class phenomenon, and their educated self-labelling is not relevant to the 'construction' of the homosexual identity to be found, for example, in the forty queer brothels (or bars) in Berlin noted by George Bernard Shaw in 1914 (W. H. Auden, probably more assiduous than Shaw, identified 170 such brothels in 1928). Chauncey's (1994) impressive collection of historical data documents the fact that doctors did *not* play a major role in the regulation of homosexuality, as they did in the regulation of abortion, prostitution and venereal disease, until after the Second World War, and demonstrates the truth of the common-sense view that preceded Foucault's muddying of the waters:

> The writings of doctors ... represent little more than an (often unsuccessful) effort to make sense of the male sexual culture they had observed or of which they were a part. The medical analysis of the different character of 'inverts,' 'perverts,' and 'normal people' reflected a set of classificatory distinctions already widely recognized in the broader culture. The fairy, regarded as a 'third-sexer,' more womanly than manly, was a pivotal cultural figure in the streets of New York before he appeared in the pages of medical journals. ... The fairy and the queer, not the medical profession, forced middle-class men to consider the possibility of a sexual element in their relations with other men.

Like the doctors, a great many historians have sought a single 'explanation' to account for the very existence of homosexuality, rather than concentrate on the more genuinely historical task of chronicling and analysing the growth and development of homosexual customs and folklore and the historical experience of homosexual peoples. This psychological/sociological/political focus has resulted in the construction of a series of models – I will call them social constructs – of homosexuality, many of which do not stand up to historical analysis. In the remainder of this chapter I will review the weakness of several of the most common models.

The myth of internalized homophobia

I do not think that queer historians have appreciated the limitations of the concept of 'internalized homophobia' (in some circumstances called internalized oppression, self-oppression, internalized lesbophobia), especially as a historical tool. It is true that, historically, queers have feared capture, or public humiliation, but these are reasonable fears, and prompt ways of evading discovery rather than self-hate. Gay liberation theorists seized upon the concept of internalized homophobia to account for everything which they considered to be bad in the 'pre-Stonewall' subculture – that is, virtually anything to do with gender inversion, power roles or 'aping' heterosexuality – irrespective of the fact that the very same gender inversions were found in cultures which were not significantly homophobic, such as ancient China and Japan. The concepts of psychoanalysis were employed to argue that anything considered bad could be accounted for as the product of a tool of repression: sublimation, projection, displacement, splitting or repetition compulsion. The theory has become more sophisticated since the early 1970s, and has even been turned on its head. Today, some theorists are reclaiming aspects of the subculture that gay libbers found repellent by claiming that they are 'tactics for negotiating space' in the supra-culture. So the transsexual is no longer a sorry victim of gender hegemony, but its radical challenger. This political use of psychoanalysis, however, is not a great deal more informative than psychoanalysis by itself: both operate within a purely theoretical framework and ignore historical evidence that does not support it.

The precursor to the theory of internalized homophobia is the Freudian theory of homosexual masochism, which was held to be integral to homosexual neurosis *vis-à-vis* the Oedipus complex. Internalized homophobia is basically a psychoanalytical concept taken over by sociologists; it purports to explain how the view of one's self as being generally 'sick' is the result of 'conditioning' and acceptance of the psychiatric view that homosexuals are abnormal and pathological. It is difficult to show precisely how it comes to be internalized to such an extent that it is no longer recognized as an alien judgement, but this is one aspect of the development of the ego according to Freudian theory. Within the black community it is rather easier to show how feelings of inadequacy – as demonstrated, for example, by black children drawing pictures of their fathers with no arms – develop, by simply citing figures of black unemployment. But lesbians and gay men whose novels in the 1950s ended in suicide or despair now tell us that they did not personally believe in such feelings nor were they integral to the works; they were simply tacked on in accordance with the requirements of the discourse of fiction current at the time. Such novels are admittedly clear examples of 'self-oppression' in so far as they connive with the oppressor, but they do not demonstrate the actual existence of internalized homophobia in their authors.

Self-oppression can be seen more in literature and other forms of queer public presentation than in actual queer life or culture. In this respect it should really be called rationalization rather than internalization. Many gay people, particularly writers and intellectuals, happily seize upon a theory that helps them account for themselves, but far fewer actually adopt a theory that does not already 'feel right' to them, which is what a full internalization theory would require. Empirical research into self-esteem in the late 1980s and early 1990s has demonstrated that the self-esteem of gay men is no lower than that of heterosexual men, and that the self-esteem of lesbians is often *higher* than in heterosexual women; theoretical speculations about the influence of negative sanctions upon one's self-image are not only not substantiated by the research: they are contradicted by the research (R. Savin-Williams, 'Self-Esteem', *EH*).

Suicide is regarded as the ultimate act of self-loathing, but historically homosexuals have committed suicide from fear of arrest and public humiliation rather than self-loathing. Suicide is seen as a typically romantic solution to an identity problem, and it has been claimed that Heinrich von Kleist was the first person whose suicide (in 1811) was linked to homosexual guilt. It seems to me that Kleist was born to kill himself (his writings are full of suicidal imagery), and his personality is too complex for simple analysis. In any case, queer suicides are recorded much earlier. In 1707, following the arrest of more than forty mollies as part of a systematic series of raids and entrapments, three mollies hanged themselves in prison while awaiting trial, and one cut his throat with a razor (Norton, 1992). An identical pattern is found in the records of early eighteenth-century Amsterdam and Paris. Shame at public dishonour was the motivation for suicide rather than internalized guilt. In the early nineteenth century the suicides of prominent public figures were linked to blackmail (for example, Lord Castlereagh in 1822). In the late nineteenth and early twentieth centuries Hirschfeld collected the life histories of 10,000 homosexual men and women, claiming that 25 per cent had attempted suicide, and many others had contemplated it, due primarily to the threat of legal prosecution; he even found that many men carried poison with them to use at the moment of their arrest. In the 1970s, when 40 per cent of gay men and lesbians had attempted or seriously considered suicide, the motivation had allegedly changed from fear of arrest to unease with one's orientation (W. Johansson, 'Suicide', *EH*). The non-act of 'seriously considering suicide' is impossible to measure or assess adequately. As for the act itself, it is still demonstrably true today that men kill themselves *after* being arrested for committing 'gross indecency' in a urinal: whatever their inner self-image may be, it is the *public* disgrace that triggers the suicide. Men do not kill themselves out of disgust at a secret habit of picking up youths at the local cottage – they kill themselves after being discovered by the police use of video cameras and thirteen-year-old rent boys ('Two gay men die after Scottish cottaging crackdown', *Gay Times*, January 1997).

In so far as any significant degree of self-loathing can be demonstrated in queer lives, it is limited to the period 1940–70, when a panoply of oppressive regulations was systematically enforced to a degree perhaps sufficient to prompt internal guilt and shame. Chauncey (1994) has shown that the psychopathological self-image was still far from commonplace in the 1930s or earlier, when men interviewed by psychiatrists were still rejecting the pathology concept. He provides abundant evid :nce to demolish the myth 'that gay men uncritically internalized the dominant culture's view of them as sick, perverted, and immoral, and that their self-hatred led them to accept the policing of their lives rather than resist it'. Queers interviewed by doctors in the 1930s regarded their 'abnormality' not as an internal failing but as a stigmatizing label. One man told a doctor he wanted to 'overcome' his homosexuality because 'it had made me more nervous [and made] ... me a social outcast. At work I try to act as a normal person. I don't think the double life is good.'

Far from being a successful tool of social control, the medical literature shows that men 'stubbornly' resisted the doctors' views about homosexuality. One doctor in 1917 recalled how he interviewed a 'loquacious, foul-mouthed and foul-minded "fairy" [who was] lost to every sense of shame; believing himself designed by nature to play the very part he is playing in life'. Another doctor in 1912 interviewed a 26-year-old chorus boy called Rose who had to flee his hometown to avoid persecution and was 'very busy in arraigning society for its attitude toward those of his type, and was prepared to ethically justify his characteristics and practices'. Many men interviewed by doctors in the 1930s said they considered their homosexuality 'natural'. The only truly accurate part of the medical literature was the 'artistic type' paradigm promoted by John Addington Symonds – an artistic queer – in the list of great homosexuals he contributed to Ellis's *Sexual Inversion*, and by Carpenter – an intellectual queer – in his queer anthology *Ioläus*. A noted birth-control doctor in the mid-1920s revealed that many homosexual men and women who presented their case to him (as he was a prominent sex reformer) not only claimed they were not degenerate, but that 'they stand on a *higher* level than those normally sexed, that they are the *specially favored* of the muses of poetry and the arts'.

The conspicuous visibility of the gay life in the 1930s provoked a reaction, and during the 1940s and 1950s gays were forced into hiding by numerous new laws and local regulations used to suppress them following the repeal of Prohibition. Only then did the gay world become invisible, and Chauncey (1994) argues that:

> gay life in New York was *less* tolerated, *less* visible to outsiders, and *more* rigidly segregated in the second third of the century than the first, and … the very severity of the postwar reaction has tended to blind us to the relative tolerance of the prewar years.

Gay activist Pat Bond remembers being in the WACS when the purge began in the 1950s: 'They started an incredible witch hunt in Tokyo. Unbelievable! Sending 500 women home for dishonorable discharges. Practically every woman I knew who was in the army has a dishonorable discharge. Every day there were court martials and trials' (Bronski, 1984). But even the self-regulation created by this tremendous fear cannot be called internalized homophobia.

To the extent that self-contempt ever existed, it was probably most characteristic of men who were born in America in the 1920s. Such men were forming their sexual identity just at the time when psychiatry's homophobic stereotypes were becoming popularized. It was these men, aged 30 to 40 in the late 1950s, who predominated in the gay subculture. Men born just after the Second World War, who were tasting their sexual freedom in the 1960s, were desperate not to grow up to be like their fathers – especially their queer role models. Gay activists in the late 1960s knew only the experience of the immediate past, upon which 'we constructed a myth of silence, invisibility, and isolation as the essential characteristics of gay life in the past as well as the present' (D'Emilio, 1992). Many of the theorists of the gay liberation generation, who lacked a sense of history and in any case who were refused access to the gay past because of censorship, saw that emotions such as guilt had constructed these queer personality types, and some tended towards a theory that ascribed all negative features entirely to the oppressive culture. American society in the 1950s was so insistent in its unitary view of life that gay liberationists saw their status as outsiders in relation to 'straight' society rather than as insiders in relation to queer culture. The mood was ripe for social constructionism, and gay theorists were the first to extensively employ such strategies in the mid-1970s; a decade later social constructionism had conquered. In the early 1970s I thought self-oppression and internalized homophobia explained a great many things; now I realize that they were used, crudely, to explain too much.

The distorting/subverting mirror

The greatest impediment to the accurate history of gay and lesbian people is the dogma that queer culture is an inversion of straight culture and that all of its features arise solely in relation to straight culture. This parallels the sexological/psychiatric view of the homosexual as always and necessarily an 'invert' of the heterosexual. The view that homosexuality is a mirror in which heterosexuality is distorted is a widespread myth: none of the reaction/compensation/inversion theories stands up to critical historical scrutiny. In the 1970s and 1980s many theorists shared Bronski's (1984) view that:

> Much of gay sensibility (and the whole range of interests it encompasses) aims to gain entry into, some acceptance by the mainstream culture. ... The most common version of this legitimization plea is the argument that gay men excel in the innovation and promotion of the arts. ... Because high culture (opera, classical music) carries with it respectability by definition, many gay men are drawn to it in order to cash in on that respectability.

This is stuff and nonsense. To be known as an opera buff is to be an outsider in most City offices, let alone blue-collar environments! Any man in northern Europe or North America who affects an interest in opera or interior decoration is marked as a pansy, even among gay men themselves. To be interested in classical music is to set oneself outside the boundaries of normal masculine and lower-middle-class interests, not to enter the mainstream. I cannot believe that anyone would seriously think this was a road to acceptance by straights.

Although Chauncey (1994) demolishes the internalized homophobia model for explaining features of the queer subculture, he sets up a 'strategy model' for which there is no real historical evidence. For example, he asserts that the flamboyant antics in fairy cafeterias and other public spaces where the fairies 'put on a show' for the normals comprise 'one of the central strategies deployed by gay men for claiming space in the city':

> They regularly sought to emphasize the theatricality of everyday interactions and to use their style to turn the Life [name of a cafeteria] and other such locales into the equivalent of a stage, where their flouting of gender conventions seemed less objectionable because it was less threatening. It lets slummers experience the thrill of seeing the 'perverts,' while letting gay men themselves adopt a style that mocked the conventions of heterosexuality.

The notion that fairies behaved in an objectionable manner in order to make themselves seem less objectionable is filled with contradictions, and in any case Chauncey offers no first-hand evidence from the fairies as to what their motivation was. In my own experience of watching fairies 'put on a show' for straights in the early 1970s, their motivation may be summed up in the line: 'So you want to see a pervert? Well, I'll *show* you a pervert!' Flamboyant antics are a mixture of defiance and exhibitionism. Far from being a strategy of assimilation, they comprise a procedure of separation, the performer's expression of enjoyment at being quite noticeably different from the viewer. It may well be a 'strategy for claiming space', but it is the display strategy characteristic of all territorial occupations: this is *my* territory, plentifully marked with my fairy scent – you keep off!

The psycho/sociological position that the 'self' creates the 'other' in order to define itself may well be broadly true, but exactly how this works in relation to 'the homosexual question' is problematical. The view that normal people defined themselves in relation to queer people is a theoretical assertion without historical evidence. Although Chauncey (1994) claims that 'in its policing of the gay subculture the dominant culture sought above all to police its own boundaries', in fact his whole book is ample testimony to the fact that the vast majority of ordinary people were either indifferent to or merely curious about queers. Most of the policing he cites had hardly any effect upon queers, much less upon straights. Court records and the early medical literature demonstrate time and time again that the existence of queers comes as a great revelation to most people – especially to the ordinary members of the juries for whose benefit this 'other' has supposedly been constructed. Newspaper exposés of scandalous queer networks or the queer subculture are precisely that – astonishing exposures of matters that would remain unknown to us but for the activities of our intrepid reporter. In fact, rather than exploit the 'other'-defining potential of queer scandals, the authorities often attempted to hush them up when they realized how many people, some prominent, would be implicated. The 'policing of the boundaries' consists mainly of sporadic crackdowns on vice when it threatens to tarnish the public image of a city. Queer people and subcultures are actively hidden from view so as not to jeopardize the definition of normal people and cultures.

The queer subculture was not created as a boundary by a dominant culture: in the first place many of its features were modelled upon other subcultures, for example the customs of working-class Afro-American, Italian and Irish immigrant neighbourhoods (Chauncey, 1994); and in the second place it was created by queers themselves as a community or a private area where they could be themselves in relative privacy and safety without attracting the notice of the dominant community; for example, at the turn of the century gay 'sisters' socialized and danced together and had drag shows in privately rented rooms connected to working-class saloons in New York, and there were secret drag queen societies such as the Circle Hermaphroditus, none of which were set up or meant to be seen as a defining 'mirror' by ordinary society.

The key theme of the 1990s is that characteristics of queer culture previously considered products of internalized homophobia, notably drag and cross-dressing, are really 'subversive'. This is a product of the social constructionist view that nothing is inherently queer, that queer culture and identity are constructed entirely in reaction to straight culture. I would say that since the early 1970s certain queer stances such as radical drag *are* subversive, both in fact and in intention, and interviews with some of the founders of the radical drag movement such as Bette Bourne (Power, 1996) clearly document that it was *intended* to be subversive of straight society. But when we look at transvestism in the eighteenth century we can demonstrate that it neither subverts nor reinforces straight culture, because not only did it arise from within queer culture but it was also practised and expressed almost entirely within queer culture. It is only because of the infiltration and raids on the molly-houses in the 1720s that we know drag existed. And within the molly subculture its primary function was to cement feelings of solidarity among the mollies. Straight society was completely excluded from viewing the 'lying-in' ritual, carnivalesque mock-birth pantomimes which are documented sporadically from the early 1700s to about 1840 in England. It was subversive only in the limited sense that it may have fostered a contemptuous attitude to the heterosexual rituals of childbirth, but this is to deprive the word 'subversive' of any meaningful political sense.

The issue of female cross-dressing is somewhat different, but again the historical evidence does not document 'subversion'. For the most part, women donned men's clothes in order to gain the independence normally granted only to men: by trying to prevent discovery they reinforced rather than subverted the common expectations of male and female behaviour. They were in a sense 'secret infiltrators' in their male disguise, but they did not 'subvert' the system itself, they only exploited it for their own personal benefit. The political metaphor of 'subversion' really does not illuminate the history of cross-dressing.

'Intergenerational' and 'egalitarian' models

Most overviews of homosexual history claim that there is a clear line of development from ancient pederastic relationships through early/modern patron/protégé relationships to modern egalitarian relationships. It is no accident that this resembles the alleged dialectic leading from feudalism through capitalism to a classless society. All three paradigms have been simplified and exaggerated, and the supposed shift from one period to another cannot be supported without ignoring a host of exceptions.

The basic premise that the dominant model of male homosexuality has shifted from the ancient and premodern model, in which the partners were significantly separated by age (transgenerational, intergenerational, cross-age), to the modern model, in which the partners are roughly the same age (egalitarian, androphilia), is challenged by the fact that egalitarian models also existed in ancient times and transgenerational models also exist in modern times. An outstanding exception to the supposed rule, dating from around 2600 BC, is the tomb of Niankhkhnum and Khnumhotep discovered at the necropolis of Saqqara in 1964. It is a joint tomb built for two men to cohabit through eternity: on the two pillars flanking the entrance both men are given the identical title 'Manicurist and Overseer of the Manicurists in the Palace, King's Acquaintance and Royal Confident'; above the entrance the two men's names are combined into one name, with a play on words signifying 'Joined in life and joined in death'. The men were given the tomb by King Niusere of the Fifth Dynasty. Although both men were married and had children, a series of bas-reliefs nevertheless depict them embracing virtually as lovers. Illustrations can be viewed on one of the best World Wide Web sites on the Internet, designed by Greg Reeder (see References). Reeder describes the culminating image as

> the most intimate embrace possible within the canons of ancient Egyptian art. Niankhkhnum on the right grasping his companion's right forearm; Khnumhotep, on the left, has his left arm across the other man's back, tightly clasping his shoulder. Again the tips of the men's noses are touching and this time their torsos are so close together that the knots on the belts of their kilts appear to be touching, perhaps even tied together.

The large relief of a banquet scene curiously has a space behind Niankhkhnum once occupied by an image of his wife, but this was effaced apparently before the tomb was sealed, so as to suggest that only he and Khnumhotep are present at the eternal banquet. The earliest visual evidence from the ancient world concerning two men who loved one another intimately thus depicts two adult men. The earliest written evidence of specifically homosexual relations also shows the love of two adult men, though from different classes: the love of King Pepy II Neferkare (Phiops II; 2246–2152 BC) for his general Sisinne.

The love of Achilles and Patroclus, described by Homer during the seventh or sixth century BC, is clearly an example of egalitarian love rather than institutional pederasty. But authors after Homer imposed a pederastic model upon the egalitarian pair, to accord with the *paiderastia* common in Greece at their own time (they oddly portrayed Patroclus as the catamite, though he was perhaps a year older than Achilles). It has become so commonplace to view ancient homosexual relationships as examples of pederasty that we even think of Alexander and Hephaestion as a case in point, when in fact Hephaestion was a nobleman of Macedonia, and the same age as Alexander. Many pairs in lists of famous lovers that feature prominently in the homosexual literary tradition are egalitarian, in marked contrast to the modern attempt to force the pederastic model upon them.

'Intergenerational' is commonly used as a synonym for 'pederastic' or 'adult/adolescent' relationships, but the younger partner is by no means always adolescent. Euripides at the age of 72 fell in love with 40-year-old Agathon: 'A fine Autumn is a beautiful thing indeed!' Demosthenes is supposed to have fallen in love with Plutarch, who was never young. In the institutionalized homosexual marriages among the indigenous South African Thonga, the *nkhonsthana*, the 'boy-wife', is often more than 20 years old. Just as age inequality is a cultural ideal of romantic love (gay or straight) which does not necessarily mirror reality, so the 'beautiful boy' is an icon of the homosexual imagination. Love letters between gay men regularly begin 'My Dear Boy' – but Marcus Aurelius was 18 years old at the time Marcus Fronto addressed him as 'Beloved Boy'; the Earl of Sunderland's 'dearest Boy' Captain Wilson was 22; Whitman's 'Dear Boy and Comrade' Peter Doyle was 18; Henry Greville's 'dear boy' Frederic Leighton was 26; Henry James's 'dearest Boy' Hendrik Andersen was 27; and Lord Alfred Douglas was 23 when Oscar Wilde wrote his infamous letter to 'My own Boy' (Norton, 1997). Historians of homosexuality recognize that the transgenerational relationship was idealized, but they seldom go one step further to note that the age difference itself is part of an ideal fiction rather than reality. Ihara Saikaku's work in the seventeenth century 'makes it clear that the strict formulation of male love as a relationship between an adult man and a youth is frequently maintained only in the form of fictive role-playing' (Schalow, 1996a). In one tale the samurai youth and his boy lover are both nine years old; in another the samurai is 66 years old and his lover is also 63 years old but still sports the hairstyle of the 'youth'; in another, a 14-year-old samurai, in order to establish his new manhood, goes out and gets a 'youth' – a 24-year-old kabuki actor/prostitute.

Greenberg (1988) may be the person most responsible for promoting the conceptual category of the 'intergenerational' or 'transgenerational' relationship, which he regularly conflates with 'pederastic'. He states, as if it were a matter of fact, that

> Many of the male homosexual relations of the time [the Renaissance] were pederastic. Salai was ten when he began living with the thirty-eight-year-old da Vinci [there is no evidence that their affair actually commenced at that stage]; Michelangelo was fifty-eight when he took up with the young Roman nobleman Tommaso Cavalieri [whose age Greenberg does not mention: Cavalieri was *not* a young boy but a young man].

Greenberg seems almost intent on deliberately misleading us: 'Homosexual relations within the male aristocracy were generally pederastic, in congruity with the explicit inequalities that constitute an aristocratic order. George Villiers, Duke of Buckingham, who shared James I's bed, was twenty-five years his junior.' This would correctly be called 'transgenerational', but Villiers was a 21-year-old adult at the time James fell in love with him. Greenberg, and others in his steps, use their terms indiscriminately, and quite regularly call relationships involving an adult and a child 'transgenerational' even though there is very little age difference between them, and relationships involving adults 'pederastic' even when both partners are over 18 or even over 21. Such a practice seriously distorts the meaning of both words, rendering them not very useful for queer history.

It should be emphasized that the extensive friendship literature of Latin classicism and the Renaissance all focused upon love between men of about the same age. Montaigne in his essay 'On Friendship', inspired by his love for Etienne de la Boétie, pointedly contrasts this masculine love with the inequalities of pederasty. Sir Francis Bacon explicitly holds up 'equality' as a key feature differentiating friendship between men from heterosexual marriage. A major theme of this tradition is that 'my friend is another myself', which erases all inequalities. Virtually no 'adjustments' have to be made in combining sixteenth-century friendship literature with the 'manly love of comrades' advocated by Walt Whitman in the nineteenth century – often cited as the *locus classicus* of egalitarian homosexual love. The ideology of egalitarian homosexual relationships is not a product of capitalism or the modern age, but is directly traceable to the classical and Renaissance homosexual literary tradition (Norton, 1974a). Boswell (1995) has similarly pointed out that the ideology of earlier medieval same-sex unions emphasizes their mutuality and equality, in marked contrast to the ideology of heterosexual unions which always emphasize subordination and possession of the woman by the man. Ceremonies of same-sex union closely follow heterosexual marriage ceremonies but notably omit the section about one partner 'yielding control' to the other. The rise of 'companionate marriage' itself draws upon several centuries of the philosophy of same-sex friendship. For many hundreds of years 'brotherly' comradeship has been emblematic of queer relationships, to such a degree that it was perceived as a threat to the hierarchical structures of straight society, from the time of Harmodius and Aristogeiton to Oscar Wilde and his panthers. The view that all homosexual relationships in the ancient world were temporary and age-related is exaggerated even for Athens, and homosexual relationships in the rest of ancient Europe were certainly far more varied and flexible than this, probably not very different from their heterosexual counterparts. ... Most ancient writers ... generally entertained higher expectations of the fidelity and permanence of homosexual passions than of heterosexual feelings. (Boswell, 1995)

A focus upon youth is characteristic of classical discourse about *paiderastia* not because it is pederastic but because romantic love and desire always presuppose an age difference, and romantic love for the Greeks was homosexual rather than heterosexual. *All* romantic desire, heterosexual as well as homosexual, is presumed directed towards the young, and 'most Athenian males married women considerably younger than themselves' (Boswell, 1992). As far as cross-cultural evidence is concerned, many interpreters misleadingly apply the inaccurate term 'intergenerational sex' to relationships that typically entail a difference in age of only a half or a third of a generation. The usual and only valid meaning of a 'generation' is the difference in age between parent and child, hence the 'generation gap'. In historical and anthropological studies it is usually defined with reference to the average age at which a male marries and produces offspring, namely the difference in age between a father and his first-born child. A generation thus equals twenty to thirty years, and in most historical writing it denotes a period of twenty-five years (in other words, four generations per century). But the average difference in age in so-called 'intergenerational' homosexual relationships is usually seven years, rarely fifteen years, scarcely ever a full generation. The classic relationship of institutional military pederasty in Sparta/Crete is between a 12-year-old 'listener' and a 22-year-old 'inspirer'. Heterosexual relationships in ancient and indigenous societies, in contrast, are invariably 'intergenerational' by this standard; in fact usually the age difference between men and women at marriage is significantly greater than between homosexual partners. In the Spartan/Cretan model, the 30-year-old man would marry an 18-year-old woman. And Aristotle recommended that men marry at the age of 37 and women at the age of 18 (Boswell, 1995).

To assert that the 'modern' homosexual was invented in the late nineteenth century, and then go on to say that 'modern' homosexuality is characteristically egalitarian rather than pederastic or transgenerational, is to completely ignore the fact that pederasty was still the major and perhaps even dominant model for homosexual relations at least until the

Second World War. The strongly pederastic *Der Eigene* was published in Germany from 1898 to 1930. Late Victorian and Edwardian homosexual literature is dominated by pederastic themes (Reade, 1970). Young rough trade is a common feature of homosexuality in England at least until the 1930s. In France *pédérasts* were the archetypal homosexual roles up to the 1950s. In southern Europe today it is common to find significant age differences between partners, and even in France the *pédérast* is still an important queer cultural paradigm.

It is really not until the late 1960s, and specifically in America, that androphilia or egalitarian homosexuality came to be held up as the ideal model for a modern queer democracy and the pederastic model was characterized as being exploitative. But early gay liberation collections of poetry, such as Winston Leyland's *Angels of the Lyre*, Ian Young's *The Male Muse* or Paul Mariah's *Manroot* journal, contain a superabundance of pederastic verse. Homosexual photographic magazines in London were dominated by the slim adolescent male during most of the 1970s; chunky rough types and 'older men' were not common objects of desire until the 1980s. The view that a 'fundamental transition' has taken place is hardly tenable for the period since 1969, and demonstrably untrue as an indicator of the 'modern' period in general. Those who think that equal-age 'androphilia' rules the day ought to peruse 1990s personal ads and porn videos, a typical title of which is *Just Eighteen*. In the ancient world the ideal beloved was not a 'boy' but an 'ephebe' just below 17 years old; to judge by modern gay literature and videos the 17-year-old boy is still the primary object of desire. Late adolescence is the classical ideal, as in *The Greek Anthology* (third century):

> I delight in the prime of a boy of twelve, but one of thirteen is much more desirable. He who is fourteen is a still sweeter flower of the Loves, and one who is just beginning his fifteenth year is yet more delightful. The sixteenth year is that of the gods, and as for the seventeenth it is not for me, but for Zeus, to seek it. But if one has a desire for those still older, he no longer plays, but now seeks 'And answering him back'. (Beurdeley, 1994)

The ideal Renaissance ephebe is of course Michelangelo's statue of *David*, a classic queer icon. Such ephebes feature prominently in the photographs of Bruce Weber and Herbert List.

I am astonished whenever I hear it said that age-asymmetrical relationships are a thing of the past. One look at a photograph of Christopher Isherwood with his lover Don Bachardy ought to dispel the

notion that 'pederasty' is purely an ancient paradigm. In 1996 Mr Gay
UK was 20 and his lover was 36; he has taken his older spouse's last
name, a not uncommon practice. In heterosexual culture May/December
relationships are nearly as common today as they used to be in the Middle
Ages. Photographs of couples on the 'social pages' of contemporary
newspapers and magazines make it obvious that wealthy and important
men have wives noticeably younger than themselves: the higher a man's
status in 'high society', the younger his wife is likely to be. It was ever
thus. Scholars and critics who would castigate the 45-year-old
Winckelmann for falling in love with 26-year-old Friedrich Reinhold von
Berg would barely raise their eyebrows to learn that in 1996 the London
nightclub owner Peter Stringfellow, age 55, lived with his girlfriend Helen
Benoist, age 17; when he took her to New York in 1995 and stayed at
the Hilton, 'I kept it quiet that Helen was only 16. ... Remember, in New
York you've got to be 21 to drink and 17 to have sex – wonderful
American hypocrisy' (*Sunday Times*, 26 May 1996).

The alleged evolutionary progression from intergenerational to
egalitarian paradigms is too inaccurately conceived, and too
undifferentiated from a common heterosexual paradigm to be a useful
tool for queer history.

Capitalism and the family

By recognizing that there are historic contexts for the homosexual well
before 1800, the queer historian avoids the truly anachronistic
interpretations of the social constructionist. The essentialist points out,
for example, that certain queer phenomena operate in many contexts and
therefore cannot be said to be determined by nineteenth-century family
values and economic structures. Since a queer subculture existed in
sixteenth-century Venice, the industrial revolution can hardly be said to
be necessary for the emergence of a queer subculture. Since men married
one another and lived together as couples during the early Roman Empire,
free-labour capitalism and the breakdown of the self-sufficient household
economy can hardly be sufficient or necessary explanations of the
emergence of modern queers. Contrary to the view that gay subcultures
emerge when feudalism gives way to capitalism, the traditional gay peasant-
based subcultures of Spain and Italy are breaking up in the more heavily
industrialized areas of these countries (G. Dall'Orto, 'Mediterranean
Homosexuality', *EH*). Until very recent times, homosexual guilt and

homophobia have been notably absent in Asian cultures where the family is paramount, so 'the family' is insufficient to account for homophobia.

Within the field of lesbian history,

> all the usual criteria used by historians to explain social change do not seem sufficient. A lesbian identity did not result from economic independence or from an ideology of individualism or from the formation of women's communities, although all these elements were important for enhancing women's personal choices. (Vicinus, 1993)

It is very interesting to chart the progress of the American ideal of manhood and the denigration of effeminization, but Chauncey (1994) does not seem to recognize that the ridicule of 'namby-pambies' was as common in the early eighteenth century – and used exactly the same terms. This feature of homophobia is not specific to a set of circumstances in twentieth-century America. Whether or not anyone could ever gather the kind of statistical evidence that would prove that 'sissy, pussy-foot, and other gender-based terms of derision became *increasingly* prominent in late-nineteenth-century American culture' (my italics) is impossible to say, but it is completely untrue to identify this era as the time when men *first* 'began to define themselves in opposition to all that was "soft" and womanlike'. Criticism of softies – mollies and molly-coddles – was very prominent in the 1720s, when pamphlets about the dangers of boys being softened by their effeminate upbringing were commonplace. Chauncey admits that:

> The fairy was not invented as a cultural type by fin de siècle male angst, but that angst – as well as the growth of the gay subculture – made the fairy a much more potent cultural figure, and one so prominent that it could serve to mark the boundaries of acceptable male behavior. As Rotundo has noted [in *American Manhood*, 1993], the sexual implications of 'Miss Nancy,' 'she-men,' and other epithets became more pronounced around the turn of the century.

All these terms of degree – 'increasingly', 'much more', 'so prominent', 'more pronounced' – require rigorous numerical evidence rather than impressions. Perhaps this 'increase' is true for America, but literally the same kind of attack on 'Miss Nancy' and 'he-whores' was a commonplace in England by 1700, and sporadically documented half a century earlier. There may well have been a crisis in middle-class American masculinity after the First World War, but the same 'crisis' has occurred re throughout the centuries, in different cultures.

The discussion of the relationship between homosexuality capitalism restricts homosexuality and homosexuals entirely to log categories rather than people with experiences. A homosexual is conceptualized as a non-procreative individual and that is deemed to be sufficient to explain capitalism's rejection of him, as he does not increase the market. That does not explain why capitalism fails to reject with similar virulence nuns and spinsters. Real homosexuals spend more money on fashions and furnishings and decorations than heterosexuals, and this seems to have been true in the past when sumptuary laws had to be passed to prevent fops from spending so much money on their clothes. Supposedly the family is promoted as the agent of consumption, necessary for the market. From an early date it was argued that (large) families encourage men to work harder in order to consume more for their family: 'consumerism became the machine which activated the whole of society' (Spencer, 1995). But how can a consumerist society reject the sodomite – who is a veritable symbol of conspicuous consumption? The portrayal of sodomites as big spenders and buyers of luxury goods is commonplace in Western history. 'Bachelors were warned to take care not to deck themselves out in too opulent a manner: "rolling in foreign silks and linens" is likened to "blind sodomites groping after their filthy pleasures"' (Spencer, 1995, citing a work of 1680). The queer has always been conceived as the consumer of luxury goods *par excellence*.

Even if capitalism rejects homosexuals as being non-productive, it is not clear why it would *create* the concept of homosexual. If we want one word to explain homophobia, it is not capitalism, but religious puritanism. It is beyond doubt that canon law is the direct source of medieval/ Renaissance secular statutes regulating 'sodomy', using Christian phraseology that underwent few changes for six centuries. Virtually all specific pogroms against homosexuals can be traced to the initiative of a fundamentalist Christian (or Islamic) group or person: moral reform is motivated by religion, not by economics.

In any case there is no evidence that the persecution of homosexuals rose concurrently with the emergence of the bourgeois family. Many reviewers of Weeks's (1977) *Coming Out* remarked upon the author's failure to support his central thesis with satisfactory evidence, and even noted that, on the contrary, homophobia declined during the nineteenth century (Licata and Petersen, 1985):

Why is Weeks so intent on clinging to the hypothesis that persecution of homosexual males and sodomites grew in the nineteenth century? As far as I can determine, the answer lies in the author's ideological predilections: the conviction that persecution of homosexuality had something to do with the rise of capitalism in the nineteenth century and, in particular, the growth of what the author calls the 'capitalist family.' ... Weeks' ideological biases seem to have overwhelmed his judgment. (Gilbert, 1985b)

The capitalist family model does not really account for why sex outside of marriage should be disparaged, as bastards will also be consumers. The fact that the sodomite does not procreate is but a very tiny part in the mechanism of consumption; in fact asceticism was still revered in some quarters, and late marriages were common. And although marriage was promoted, spinsters and bachelors nevertheless were not reviled. The argument that homosexuality is condemned in inverse proportion to the promotion of procreation is not borne out by, for example, the mid-eleventh-century enforcement of celibacy for the secular clergy, who were forced to abandon not only their wives and concubines but also sodomy. Peter Damian's *Liber Gomorrhianus* (1059), a *locus classicus* for homophobia, was a call for clerical chastity. Protestants in general and Puritans in particular rejected the Roman Catholic view that sex should be engaged in during marriage only for the purpose of procreation, and yet the Puritans, when they were in the ascendancy, were more fanatical than Catholics in rooting out the evil of homosexual intercourse, even while they celebrated the domestic joys of conjugal intercourse. Moral purity is the key to homophobia, not anything so rational as a biological principle given an economic gloss.

In the higher 'discourse' of churchmen and jurists, the ideology of procreation played its role in condemning homosexuals, but the expression of homophobia among the populace, for example, throughout the eighteenth century, took the less rational – and more ethnic-based – forms of hatred such as xenophobia (queers are usually rejected as practitioners of a foreign vice), expressions of disgust at effeminacy and the castigation of sinfulness and blasphemy. The most commonly expressed economic view was the accusation that mollies 'take the bread from much more honest whores' – amply demonstrated by the female prostitutes who gathered in great numbers to torment gay men in the pillory (Norton, 1992).

The relationship between homophobia and specific political regimes is fortuitous. Homosexuals fared reasonably well under Italian fascism, but were persecuted under English, American and French democracies during the same period. The right-wing paramilitary groups in Weimar Germany seem to have attracted a significant number of homosexuals, but the fully organized National Socialists attempted to exterminate homosexuals, and the Falangists in Spain murdered Lorca by firing bullets up his arse. From the mid-1920s homosexuality was denounced by Stalinist Communists as bourgeois decadence or as fascist perversion. You pays your money and you takes your choice. Or rather the choice is made for you. In 1933–5 the German homosexual emancipation movement was exterminated 'by both the fascists and the Stalinists' (Lauritsen and Thorstad, 1974).

The widespread modern view that institutionalized pederasty is characteristic of cultures which degrade women is traceable to Engels's statement in *The Origin of the Family, Private Property and the State* that 'this degradation of women was avenged on the men and degraded them also, till they fell into the abominable practice of sodomy and degraded alike their gods and themselves with the myth of Ganymede' (cited by Hallam, 1993). Women have been degraded and subjugated in many (most) societies – more notably in Christian Europe than in ancient Greece – but nevertheless pederasty is *not* institutionalized in all such societies. The supposed link between egalitarian relationships and the rise of industrial society founders upon the continuance of 'intergenerational' relationships in Mediterranean industrial capitalist societies today. Any simple equation of a certain type of relationship with a certain 'stage' in the development of capitalism is refuted by innumerable exceptions. D'Emilio's (1992) theory about the relationship between free-labour capitalism and homosexuality has never been developed further than as a working hypothesis (limited to the American context), and is so simplistic and lacking in a historical ground as to be ludicrous:

> Only when individuals began to make their living through wage labor, instead of as parts of an interdependent family unit, was it possible for homosexual desire to coalesce into a personal identity – an identity based on the ability to remain outside the heterosexual family and to construct a personal life based on attraction to one's own sex. ... These patterns of living [gay networks, lesbian couples, etc.] could evolve because capitalism allowed individuals to survive beyond the confines of the family. ... The decisive shift in the nineteenth century to industrial capitalism provided the conditions for a homosexual and lesbian identity to emerge. As a free-labor system, capitalism pulled men and women out of the home and

into the market-place. ... Free labor and the expansion of
commodity production created the context in which an autonomous
personal life could develop.

What D'Emilio is theorizing is at most a facilitating factor rather than a
constructing factor; the rise of large urban conurbations seems to be linked
to the rise of gay subcultures, and the social opportunities offered by large
populations are more important than how one earns one's living. The
mercantile centres of medieval and Renaissance European cities were
sufficient to facilitate the growth of thriving queer subcultures. It is true
enough that capitalism simultaneously weakens and idealizes the nuclear
family; but that such a situation is sufficient to promote a gay identity I
find incomprehensible.

That capitalism is universally and intrinsically homophobic I also find
difficult to comprehend. For social constructionists such as D'Emilio,
capitalism and homophobia are inextricable: 'The elevation of the family
to ideological preeminence guarantees that a capitalist society will reproduce
not just children, but heterosexism and homophobia.' Allegedly the worker
required by capitalism will postpone pleasure because of the work ethic
and will be subservient to his wage masters, generally avoiding male–male
intimacy, much less male–male sex. But there is no inherent reason why
the structures of capitalism should not foster male bonds and homosexual
relations. In eighteenth- and nineteenth-century Russia the Skoptsy sect
of Old Believers who engaged in commerce 'had an institutionalized practice
of an older merchant adopting a younger assistant–lover as his son and
heir. After the older man's death this heir would repeat the process with
a still younger man, thus giving rise to a mercantile dynasty' (S. Karlinsky,
'Russia', *EH*). Innumerable assistant/apprentice systems since the fourteenth
century have had homoerotic parameters.

It seems perverse to talk about secular capitalism rather than the
Christian right as a major factor in the hatred of homosexuals. No one
has seriously tried to dispute the fact that homophobia predates capitalism
by at least a thousand years – if hanging sodomites and burning lesbians
at the stake are not homophobic, what is? This raises a philosophical
conundrum: if homophobia and homosexual identities are inherently
linked – 'identity and oppression are bound together' says D'Emilio (1992)
– how is it possible for homophobia to thrive in the absence of homosexual identities?

Victorian repression of course had a tremendous impact upon the
expression of homosexuality, but this is not attributable to capitalism *per*

se. It is more an accident of the time and place in which capitalism flourished, namely the rise of religious fundamentalism and revival which emerged to counter the materialistic values of capitalism. The Marxist interpretation of prostitution during the Victorian period has been applied over-simplistically to the homosexual model. Something labelled 'prostitution' is often incorrectly inferred in the case of sex between men. Paul D. Hardman in a 1992 ONE Institute lecture on his experience among the Zapotecas, Mixtecas and Chatinos of Mexico advised that

> confusion may arise regarding requests for gifts or money by an Indian lad when sex is offered. [These boys] are not necessarily hustlers, especially in the villages. They may well be when they are in the big cities, but that is a different phenomenon. The whole question of asking for things along with sex requires more study to determine if the phenomenon is based on ancient culture, as it appears to be, or merely an adaptation to meet modern needs. (Legg, 1994)

To some extent accepting money may be a face-saving ritual for macho lads. In modern Western societies the exchange of gifts is part of working-class sexual culture. Although Weeks (1985) acknowledges that a wide range of meanings can be attached to the concept of 'prostitution', he nevertheless promotes the widespread (socialist) myth that prostitution is characteristic of the homosexual subculture, that prostitution provides the links between the aristocratic world and the subculture, and that with 'the great disparities of wealth and social position among the participants, the cash nexus inevitably dominated'. On the contrary, throughout the eighteenth century the molly subculture was uniformly working class (aristocrats and gentlemen never went to molly-houses), and – despite the epithets of 'he-strumpets' and 'he-whores' that were thrown at the mollies – an abundance of records can provide no more than two or three instances of the exchange of cash for sex, although many instances of blackmail; male 'prostitution' in any recognizable modern sense of the term was virtually non-existent until the 1780s (Norton, 1992). Mutual pleasure rather than financial benefit is characteristic of male prostitution throughout history; modern hustlers and sex performers clearly enjoy their job more than female prostitutes. Male prostitution in ports is commonplace, but generally very small amounts of money are required by the sailors, which suggests that such 'nominal sums [are] an excuse for a desired sexual contact' (S. Donaldson, 'Seafaring', *EH*). Imposing the Marxist analysis of the 'cash nexus' and class war upon such circumstances can only lead us wildly astray.

4

It's Just a Phrase We're Going Through

Social constructionists argue that labels must be rejected (or deconstructed) because they are allegedly the tools of external social control. Some modern gay apologists fondly believe that there was once a golden age when no one was labelled and everyone enjoyed fluid sexuality (or even polymorphous perversity). Thus Cowan (1988) maintains that

> Throughout much of human history it seems that people – both gay and straight – could live comfortably without a name for the 'love that dare not speak its name'. In biblical times it was enough for David to simply say that his love for Jonathan 'was wonderful, passing the love of women'.

What an extraordinary example to choose: it means precisely the opposite of what Cowan says. The whole point about this famous biblical passage is that the lack of a name for David's love made it difficult to speak about it: far from demonstrating a 'simple', 'comfortable' acceptance of something common, it vividly illustrates the struggle to describe something 'wonderful' that lay beyond the common conceptions available at the time. Contrary to this being a commonplace occurrence, David loved Jonathan 'as he loved his own soul' – a phrase that has 'no parallel anywhere else in the Jewish Scriptures' (Boswell, 1995). In biblical times it became the archetype for true, lasting love, pointedly set against the transitoriness of heterosexual passion.

The relationship between language and experience has been one of the central problems of philosophy for centuries; in more recent times the issue has been the complex relationship between language and identity. The social constructionist school maintains the omnipotence of words: I label you, therefore you are. The school is rooted in structuralism, a linguistic/semantic approach to literature in which text rather than context is the final arbiter of meaning. The sociological development of the theory maintains that the homosexual did not exist as a personality type or identity until he (or she) was labelled. According to this theory, the labelling occurred in the work of the sexologists in the late nineteenth century, and therefore homosexuals did not exist until they were created, that is constructed, in the late nineteenth century. The essentialist rejects the philosophical presumption that meaning precedes experience, and adopts the common-sense view that homosexual identity precedes labelling. Despite the sophistication with which social constructionists deal with epistemes and semiotext(e)s, they are profoundly ignorant of historical linguistics.

Generic queers

In the search for specific words about homosexuality we should not ignore the fact that most people use euphemisms or phrases made up of ordinary words to describe what they do; even today most people do not use a specific word to describe themselves when engaged in intercrural intercourse, although slang words are available. When General Kuno Count von Moltke explained in court his sexual relations with Prince Philipp Fürst zu Eulenburg-Hertefeld, in the first decade of the twentieth century, all he could say was this: 'Fooling around. I don't know of no real name for it. When we went rowing we just did it in the boat.' (Spencer, 1995.) 'Fooling around' was perhaps the most frequently used euphemism from the 1920s to the 1940s, and is probably still the term used by adolescents engaging in their first 'experiments'. In the early 1930s British gay men referred to each other as 'so' and 'musical', terms gradually supplanted by 'queer', which may have been used earlier by the Irish and were popularized in theatrical circles (Skinner, 1978). To say that such words show a lack of scientific refinement is quite true, but everyone knows exactly what they mean. The absence of language does not necessarily indicate the absence of conceptual thought. The concept of lesbian sex existed even when no particular term was used to identify it; Donoghue (1993) documents the use of generic terms such as 'kind', 'species' and 'genius' (i.e. genus) in mid-eighteenth-century discussions of lesbians, abstract phrases such as 'feminine congression' or 'accompanying with other women', and abundant euphemisms: 'irregular', 'uncommon', 'unaccountable' and 'unnatural', 'vicious Irregularities', 'unaccountable intimacies', 'uncommon and preternatural Lust', 'unnatural Appetites in both Sexes', 'unnatural affections', 'abominable and unnatural pollutions'. There is much evidence to suggest that the earlier use of the word 'hermaphrodite' was as much a euphemism for 'homosexual' as the modern term 'bisexual'. There is ever-increasing pressure towards abstraction: in many circles today, gay men are called 'men-who-have-sex-with-men (MSM)', while lesbians are regularly called 'women-loving-women'. (Though abstract, these phrases reflect a binary prejudice: men

99

fuck, women love.) On the Internet, all groups are now embraced within the acronym MOTSS (members of the same sex) or LGBT (lesbian gay bisexual transgender).

In any case, the social constructionists are quite incorrect in their assertion that in ancient and indigenous cultures there are no words for homosexuality as a general concept, and that it was not until the modern age that abstract, generic, 'scientific' terms were invented to describe it. Ancient cuneiform texts have been found describing male homosexuality as a generalized concept, 'the love of a man for a man', and one document mentions lesbians. As early as the third century BC Hellenic writers coined the word *gynerastia* to denote sexual relations between women: this is as scientific a term as one could wish, less euphemistic than 'lesbian', more economical than 'sex between women', and devoid of value judgements. There were many ancient terms for abstract concepts or categories of homosexual. In the Byzantine Empire there were several words for homosexuality in general (rather than words for effeminate or receptive homosexuality in particular): *paiderastia* ('pederasty'); *arrhenomixia* ('mingling with males'); *arrhenokoitia* ('coitus with males'). The two latter terms are perfect behaviourist equivalents to 'homosexuality'. *Paiderastia*, from Classical Greek *paiderastes* ('boy-lover'), is itself a general concept, strictly speaking no narrower than the modern 'man-lover'. Boswell (1995) points out that 'the most common words for "child" in both Greek (*pais*) and Latin (*puer*) also mean "slave," so in many cases when an adult is said to be having sex with someone designated by these terms it could simply be with his slave or servant'; in other words *paiderastia* is not necessarily narrowly confined to boys, but may be closer to 'homosexuality' than modern historians acknowledge. The pederastic pair consists of the *erastes* and the *eromenos* ('lover' and 'beloved'); we can infer an active/passive division, but strictly speaking these are not examples of inserter/receptor terminology, and the term 'boyfriend' was not used in a particularly derogatory fashion. The modern Greeks, under the influence of (American) English usage, have abandoned these terms, and use the awkward *omophylophilia*.

Metaphors and tropes are as important for understanding homosexual culture as more precise 'scientific' terms. Among the ancient Toltecs (conquered by the Aztecs), queers worshipped the transgender god/goddess of non-procreative sexuality and flowers, Xochiquetzal, and sodomy was called the 'Dance of the Flowers'. In China, metaphors such as 'the passion of the cut sleeve' or 'the southern custom' encompassed queer-cultural values of love and loyalty for some two thousand years. The earliest Chinese word referring to homosexual relations dates from the sixth century: *nanfeng*, literally 'male wind' (still used today as a literary expression for male homosexuality), perhaps more accurately translated as 'male custom' or 'male practice' (Hinsch, 1990). Another term from this period is *nanse*, male lust or male eroticism, *se* denoting sexual attraction or passion. These words are as abstract (hence 'scientific') as the word 'homosexuality' coined thirteen hundred years later. *Nanfeng* actually has two sets of characters pronounced the same, one meaning 'male custom' and the other 'southern custom' ('man' and 'south' are both pronounced *nan*). Homosexuality is believed to have been especially popular in Fujian and Guangdong, the southern regions of China, and 'southern custom' was the term for homosexuality during the Ming period; *nanfeng shu*, the southern custom tree, which consists of two trees, one larger than the other, entwined with one another to become one, was a standard icon of homosexuality in Chinese literature (Ng, 1989; Hinsch, 1990).

The Chinese language is particularly rich in queer metaphors that do not relate directly to sex/gender roles, but to a larger complex of queer culture, with an emphasis upon desires, tendencies, preferences and emotional commitments rather than sexual acts. The two main terms for male homosexual relations, 'passion of the cut sleeve' (*duanxiu pi* or *pian*) and 'joy of the shared peach' (*fen tao zhi ai*) both derive from ancient stories of specific emperors and their favourites dating back to the sixth century BC, a literary tradition kept alive for more than two thousand years. 'Emperor Ai [reigned 6 BC–1 AD] was sleeping in the daytime with Dong Xian stretched out across his sleeve. When the emperor wanted to get up, Dong Xian was still asleep. Because he did not want to disturb him, the emperor cut off his own sleeve and got up.' This story

> was alluded to repeatedly in later literature and gave men of subsequent ages a means for situating their own desires within an ancient tradition. By seeing their feelings as passions of the 'cut sleeve,' they gained a consciousness of the place of male love in the history of their society. (Hinsch, 1990)

The story of the fickle emperor Duke Ling of Wei (534–493 BC) and his devoted favourite Mizi Xia was so famous that his very name became a catchword for homosexuality, and 'the joy of the half-eaten peach' became one of the most frequently used phrases to denote homosexuality in general for more than two thousand years:

Another day Mizi Xia was strolling with the ruler in an orchard and, biting into a peach and finding it sweet, he stopped eating and gave the remaining half to the ruler to enjoy. 'How sincere is your love for me!' exclaimed the ruler. 'You forgot your own appetite and think only of giving me good things to eat!' (Hinsch, 1990)

However, later, when the ruler's ardour cooled, Mizi Xia was executed for committing some crime against Duke Ling, who professed not to believe his innocence. '"After all", said the ruler, "he once stole my carriage, and another time he gave me a half-eaten peach to eat!"' This is obviously a poetic symbol, and it seems to me that like all symbols it encapsulates an essence, in this case the essence of homosexual love. The metonym of the half-eaten peach connotes a generalized eroticism rather than any specifically active or receptive sexual role, emphasizing the mutual sharing of the fruits of that love.

The male prostitutes who flourished in late Imperial China were called *xiaochang* ('little singers'). By the time laws were promulgated to regulate homosexuality during the Ming dynasty, the legal term for homosexuality was *jijian*, a derogatory word meaning 'chicken lewdness', from *ji* ('chicken'), and *jian* ('private', 'secret'), which may reflect a popular belief about the behaviour of domesticated fowl. By 1985, in Taiwan, a long and noble history of poetic metaphors had been replaced by an exact translation of the most notorious Western euphemism: *Bugan shuo chu kou de ai* – 'The love that dare not speak its name'!

The 'sodomite'

The social constructionists are convinced that 'the sodomite' is a modern concept, that until relatively recent times 'sodomy' was simply a collection of sexual acts. The theory that 'sodomy' precedes 'the sodomite' is a major tenet of all the classic social constructionist texts, which insist that homosexual identity is preceded and determined by the active or receptive role taken during anal intercourse, or female role identification. As with so much social constructionist theory, the view that acts rather than persons were the important features of discussions of homosexuality until modern times is historically and linguistically unsound. In virtually every society and period of history nouns relating to persons have been more important than terms for disembodied acts. It is only in the English language that there has ever been a debate whether 'homosexual' is a noun as well as an adjective; in all other languages it is always both. The view that 'homosexual' and equivalent terms are valid only as adjectives rather than nouns is a political/philosophical position, not historical observation.

Many such terms were originally nouns applied to persons long before they came to be adjectives applied to behaviour. In the Latin language the word 'sodomite' (*sodomita*) existed earlier than the word 'sodomy' (*sodomia*). In linguistic terms the concept of the homosexual person preceded the concept of the homosexual act. The ecclesiastical phrases *peccatum sodomitae* or *crimen sodomitae* are not properly translated as the sin or crime 'of sodomy' but as the sin or crime 'of the sodomites'. Long before the term 'sodomy' became the word of choice, there were a large number of Latin-based words which relate to a generalized conception of homosexuality rather than to specific acts: for example, Saint Jerome employs the forms *Sodoman, in Sodomis, Sodomorum, Sodomæ, Sodomitæ* (Hallam, 1993). Florio in an English–Italian dictionary of 1598 cites the following:

Sodomia, the naturall sin of Sodomie.

Sodomita, a sodomite, a buggrer.

Sodomitare, to commit the sinne of Sodomie.

Sodomitarie, sodomiticall tricks.

Sodomitico, sodomiticall.

Florio uses 'Sodometrie' as an English word; Thomas Nashe referred to 'the art of sodomitry' in 1594. Today, *sodomia* and *sodomitia* and their equivalents in various romance languages are usually but inaccurately translated as 'sodomy', which is simply a specific sexual act, but the more accurate (albeit infelicitous) translation is 'sodomiticalness', a collection of characteristics encompassing licentious behaviour: that is a generalized (albeit negative) concept equivalent to 'homosexuality', not anal intercourse. Even Aquinas defined 'the vice of sodomy' as 'male with male and female with female' – which is a *relational* concept rather than descriptive of a specific act (Gilbert, 1985a).

Sodom of course is the name of a town (apparently from *Sadeh Adom*, 'red field' or 'field of blood', origin and derivation obscure). A Sodomite is a person who comes from Sodom, or who exhibits the characteristics of the inhabitants of Sodom. Thus, the primary Christian and Jewish term for a queer is a national–cultural term rather than a sexual signifier. In the Middle Ages the term 'sodomy' could be used to describe anal intercourse, even heterosexual anal intercourse, but the word 'sodomite' invariably meant male homosexual, whether the sex he enjoyed was anal or otherwise. 'Sodomite' from the very earliest times conjured up an identity, an identity linked to the idea of same-sexuality and a panoply of identity characteristics rather than anal sex. The Christians viewed the sodomite as a complete personality type whose whole being endangered the community, whose homosexual *behaviour* was symptomatic of his antisocial *attitudes*. The basic theme of anti-sodomitic literature is that the sodomite indulges in sodomy because that is the worst thing he can think of to express his fundamental perversity and his contempt for God and nature. Greenberg's (1988) statement that 'medieval inquisitors were not concerned with homosexuals, but with sodomites' not only sets up a false distinction, but is founded upon bad history; surviving records of the Inquisitions of sodomites (and lesbians) show that the Church was very interested in such issues as their background, when they first experienced their homosexual feelings, what their general moral and religious attitudes were – in other words, what their *character* was. Sodomy is merely one symptom of the sodomite's *essential nature*.

The 'active' homosexual

Social constructionists claim that there are no words for the active homosexual in ancient societies or indigenous cultures, that queer labels are always reserved for those who take the receptive role in anal intercourse, that those who take the active role are not stigmatized or labelled by their society, and that all of this demonstrates how the homosexual identity is culturally constructed as either the receptive *sexual role* or the female *gender role*. The classic example of this kind of role-playing is the 'Mediterranean model', in which, allegedly, the man who fucks youths has no homosexual identity or identity crisis differentiating himself from men who fuck women, and it is only the youth who gets fucked whose role is stigmatized and who consequently develops a queer identity in accordance with this label. Many social constructionists take this as a kind of universal paradigm, though it is specifically characteristic of the sexual peasant cultures of southern Italy and Spain, supported by the Roman Catholic dogma that there are no homosexuals, only homosexual acts (sins).

The view that in ancient and indigenous cultures only the receptive rather than the active homosexual was labelled is grossly inaccurate, for there are scores of exceptions. For example, a great many terms come in pairs, one of which defines the active partner: thus *bugger* and *berdache*, or *bugger* and *catamite*, or *paedico* and *pathicus*; in Arabic *Al-Fá'il* (the 'doer'), and *Al-Mafúl* (the 'done'); in Nicaragua the *machista* and the *cochón*; in Greek *erastes* and *eromenos*. In the pedagogic pederasty of ancient Sparta the partners were the older 'inspirer' and the younger 'listener' (these are certainly role labels, but they are not sex/gender roles except by inference and in accordance with a modern theory about the ritual ingestion of semen, which is by no means proven with regard to the Spartans); in tenth-century China courting male couples consisted of the older *ch'i hsung* and the younger *ch'i ti*. In eastern Java where man/boy relationships nearly took the form of marriage, the teenage (effeminate) youth was a *gemblakan*, and his masculine adult (but still young) partner was a *warok*. In England the *ingle*, documented from 1532 in a translation of Rabelais, more frequently from the 1590s, was a catamite, or kept boy (from Latin *inguen*, 'groin'), but the keeper of such a boy was also given a separate term, the *ingler*, recorded from 1598. In Spain, in Andalusia, effeminate queers are *maricas*, but there were also masculine queers, called *guarrones*, who were feared, and *amaricados*. In the famous Sacred Band of Thebes, the 300 pairs of male lovers consisted of the older *heniochoi* ('charioteers') and the younger *paraibatai* ('companions'). In ancient Rome male prostitutes were sometimes classified according to the roles they played and the image they projected: *exoleti* ('active'), and *cinaedi* ('receptive'); but the latter term was often used with the broader generic meaning of 'hustler' and the *cinaedus* was frequently considered to be active rather than receptive despite the fact that the term derives from Greek *kinein* ('buttocks'). This usage of the 'tough' *cinaedus* paired with the effeminate *catamitus* survived in several Romance languages, for example in sixteenth-century French. He is not often discussed by the social constructionists, because the Roman citizen who likes to be penetrated by young men does not fit in well with their theory about status and roles.

Sir Richard Burton in his famous essay on the Sotadic Zone cites several indigenous Hindu words for the active homosexual role in the 1840s, including *Gánd-márá* ('anus-beater') and *Gándú* ('anuser'). The Albanian active homosexual or pederast is called the *büthar* ('butt man'). In Latin the *pullus* ('chicken') was chased by the *pullarius* ('kidnapper of boys', literally 'poulterer'), the modern equivalent being 'chicken hawk'. The ancient Greeks had other specialized active terms, such as *philephebos* ('fond of young men') and *philoboupais* ('fond of hunky young men', literally 'bull-boys'). Although the majority of modern slang terms imply a receptive/effeminate sex/gender role, there nevertheless are many words for men taking the active role, for example arse-bandit, shitten prick (Irish), backgammoner and hock (Australian rhyming slang for cock). In French the word of choice for homosexual, *pédérast*, denotes the active partner. The English pederast is also the active partner, though today the term more narrowly means lover of boys. French *pédé* ('queer') can be either active or receptive. The *bugger* is the active partner; like *sodomite*, also active, it has a racial/geographical origin, derived from French *bougre* (and the sin of *bougrerie*), from the medieval Latin *bulgarus* in reference to the Albigensian/Cathar heresy of southern France in the early thirteenth century that was supposedly similar to the Bogomils in Bulgaria. The same word is the origin of the Spanish *bujarrón*, the Italian *buggerone* and the German *puseran(t)*, a word which survives in Eastern Europe: when Allen Ginsberg visited Prague in 1965 the Communist police called him a *buzerant*.

Cultural queer-words

Many words which have evolved into a (usually receptive) sexual meaning can be traced back to non-sexual origins. The Nicaraguan word for passive homosexual is *cochón*, derived from *colchón* ('mattress'); to argue that power and dominance and the penetrative ethos is *intrinsic* to the metaphorical mattress is to stretch credulity. A very large group of words for the receptive male began life as 'favourite servant', such as *girsequ*, meaning chamber palace servant or charioteer (in the Code of Hammurabi, c. 1725 BC). Greenberg (1988) describes these men as the receptive partners, but in the Sacred Band of Thebes the charioteer was the active partner; charioteers are high-status persons, and it is odd to think of the astrological charioteer, *girsequ*, as a catamite rather than a hero. The Chinese *xianggong* was originally the title of a high government minister, then became a polite term for addressing young men, then was applied to male actors who impersonated women, and today is a synonym for a receptive homosexual male; in modern editions of ancient Chinese joke books this word is mistranslated as 'catamite' when it should be translated as 'favourite' (Hinsch, 1990), and it is only by inference that the original *xianggong* were receptive rather than active (or both). I believe that many words which we now say *only* describe receptive homosexuals followed this line of evolution and once described *all* homosexuals irrespective of sex/gender role. Terms which we see as stigmatic may have begun as straightforward accurate labels, which then became stigmatized by the prevailing prejudice. Nor should we ignore the occasional appropriation of words for use in a positive heterosexual context. Chinese 'favourites' – essentially favoured male concubines – 'were called *ai ren*, literally "lover" or "beloved", the term used in modern China for "spouse"' (Hinsch, 1990).

The Greek term *bryallicha* (or *brydalicha*) came to mean 'male transvestite', but originally it denoted the ancient Greek dance performed by women as well as men in honour of Artemis and Apollo, in which 'The male dancer's costume included stag antlers, padded buttocks, and feminine masks and attire, while the female dancer's costume included a large, artificial phallus' (Conner *et al.*, 1997). The transgender aspect of a religious ritual now dominates the meaning of the term, but we do not know its literal meaning. A similar word possibly linked to the role of music in ancient ritual is the German slang term *Schwuchtel* ('queen', 'fairy'), which 'originally meant a player of comic dame roles, and the cultural historian Gisela Bleibtreu-Ehrenburg links it with the Latin *vetula*, a frivolous music maker' (L. Senelick, 'Theatrical Transvestism', *EH*). Conner *et al.* (1997) cite abundant evidence linking gay, lesbian, bisexual and transgendered persons and ancient musical rituals.

There is an immense body of literature concerning whether the word *qdesh* (*Kadesh*) is more accurately rendered by the terms 'holy or consecrated person', 'sacred temple prostitute', 'male cult prostitute or hierodule' or 'sodomite'. The *qdeshah* or female temple prostitute is customarily translated as 'harlot', and there is indisputable evidence that her male equivalent in the service of ancient Near Eastern mother goddesses serviced the male worshippers (Greenberg, 1988; W. Johansson, 'Kadesh' and 'Kadesh Barnea', *EH*). Such religious functionaries in the service of Ishtar, noted particularly for their ritual music, were called *assinu*, which has the same root as *assinutu*, meaning 'to practise sodomy'; and the various titles of the chanter-priests can be literally translated as 'womb', 'penis-anus' and 'anus-womb'. Best known to us (that is, there are ancient biographies of named individuals) are the *galli*, the castrated transvestite priests of Asian Cybele, who by the fourth century had become troupes of itinerant beggars, characterized by effeminate homosexuals, who no longer served any religious function, as famously portrayed in Lucian's *Golden Ass*. The modern *hijra*, castrated transvestite (or transsexual) prostitutes and worshippers of Parvati and other mother goddesses of India, similarly originated in cultic ritual, as still seen in their music and dance performances to bless the birth of males.

Among the numerous indigenous terms denoting what anthropologists have called the *berdache*, for example Native American Indian males who dress (partly) as women, who marry men and who serve as religious officials for foretelling the future, etc., and the similar group of *shamans*, there are a variety of terms connoting sexual roles, gender roles and religious roles, though there is a tendency to subsume them all under the term 'transgender'. *Berdache* itself is a French word derived from the Persian root *bardag* or *bardaj* ('young male slave'), metaphorically 'buggered boy' or catamite, and is wholly inappropriate as a name for the phenomenon; modern Native Americans have opted for the more accurate (though sanitizing) term 'two-spirit' which is now coming into usage (Conner *et al.*, 1997). The word *berdache* was first employed in 1575 by André Thevet, chaplain to Catherine de Medici, to describe native Brazilian Indian two-spirit persons (queers) who used the word *tivira* or *tibira* to describe themselves: its literal meaning is 'man with broken behind'. Some terms for these functional queers (almost all of them engage in homosexual relationships) range from the 'man–woman' to 'neither man nor woman', but the literal meaning of native terms cannot always be teased out, for example the *alyhā* of the Navaho. Many terms seem to be linked specifically to such personages' religious/ritual role: thus the *mahūs* of Tahiti, who acted as wives to the principal chiefs, are 'healers', from Maori *mahū* ('to heal'); in Mangaian, *mau* ('to be healed'); in Samoan, *mafu* can mean either 'to heal a wound' or 'a male homosexual' (Greenberg, 1988). Similarly, a Bantu word for homosexual anal intercourse is *bian nku'ma* ('a medicine for wealth'). Among the Navaho the *nadle* is 'that which changes', which partly suggests gender change, but also relates to the transforming power of this spiritual functionary. There is a host of native terms for the *berdache – wintka* among the Santee Dakota, *manang bali* of Borneo, *fakaleiti* of Tonga, *wakawawine* in Pukapuka – most of which have not received adequate linguistic study.

In the Philippines, whose native culture seems always to have had a positive attitude towards homosexuality, homosexual men are usually called *bakla* or *bayot*; these are as abstract and general as the word 'homosexual', for they are used whether the men are masculine or effeminate, whether transvestite or not; they may derive from *bayoguin*, recorded by the first Europeans to arrive in the Philippines in 1589, the early indigenous term for their two-spirit religious functionaries. The indigenous Philippine term for lesbian, *lakin-on*, has been superseded by the borrowed Western term *tomboy*.

Among the group of terms which do not originally denote an act or specific sex/gender role are many queer-words which have no literal meaning other than the name of a person (or deity) associated with homosexuality. The best-known examples are *sapphist* from Sappho and *lesbian* from the island of Lesbos. In India some homosexuals are called *Sambali* ('eunuch'), named after Krishna's son Samba, a notorious cross-dressing homosexual. There are amusing French verbs meaning 'to sodomize': *socratiser* from Socrates and *engider* from André Gide! Some English terms recall queer scandals, such as 'Tilden' from the tennis star, and 'Wildeman' from Oscar Wilde; the case of the Bishop of Clogher, caught *in flagrante delicto* with a soldier in 1822 (his name rhymes with 'bugger', exploited by limericks during the period) was followed with interest and amusement in France, where 'Clogher' came to be a sobriquet for a British sodomite. 'The Biblical/Midrashic tale of Potiphar and Joseph [Potiphar purchased Joseph for the pharaoh of Egypt because of the young man's beauty] was remembered in nineteenth-century French bohemian circles, where to *putiphariser*, or "potipharize", a young man was to reach inside his trousers and grab his genitals' (Conner *et al.*, 1997).

Geographical regions often give their names to queer-words. Homosexuality is often castigated as 'the English vice', 'the Spanish vice', 'the French vice' or 'the Italian vice', depending on one's own home country. Because of the prevalence of homosexuality in fifteenth-century Florence, 'to sodomize' was termed *florenzen* in Middle High German. *Chian*, from the island of Chios was synonymous with *pedicatio* in Rome because the men of Chios were so fond of receptive anal intercourse (Conner *et al.*, 1997). In Arabic, homosexuals are called *ahl Lūt*, 'the people of Lot'; in other words, throughout Islam the words for homosexual sex, *liwat*, and homosexual (effeminate and corrupt) persons, *luti*, do not denote an act, but a racial characteristic.

The 'lesbian'

The social constructionist linguistic argument cannot account for the fact that the modern lesbian identity had the label 'lesbian' well before the 'queer moment' in 1869. In fact, in English at least, the term had exactly the same meaning in the early eighteenth century as in the late twentieth. In Western cultures, women-loving-women have been called 'lesbians' and sometimes 'sapphists' for hundreds of years. These are generic terms for 'female homosexual' rather than specific sexual acts or sex/gender roles, for lesbian sexuality generally is not perceived in binary penetrative terms, but as a matter of mutual genital rubbing. Most lesbian terms indicate female–female sexuality rather than specific sexual acts. There are of course words denoting sex/gender roles: for example, Spanish *mal-flor*, *manflora* ('tomboy'); *marimacho* ('masculine Mary'); *pantalonuda* ('tomboy', 'trouser-wearer'). But there are also many words, like *lesbian* and *sapphist*, that are linked to orientation and gender object choice (namely, homosexual orientation) rather than to specific sex/gender roles: for example, Spanish *Donna con Donna* ('woman with woman'); German *mädchen Schmeker* ('girl-taste'); the Klamath tribe's *sawa linaa* ('to live as partners'); Mexican slang, *tortillera* ('tortilla maker'); French *vrille* ('a gimlet') (Richards, 1990). The Chinese term for female homosexual couples is *dui shi* ('paired eating'); it was used to denote the bonding of two palace women as husband and wife in ancient China, and may suggest (mutual?) cunnilingus – but that is an inference rather than a known fact.

Sometimes a specific sex act is indicated, other times it has to be inferred, and at other times unspecified same-sex desire is the fundamental meaning. There is no particular pattern of 'shifts' in meaning beloved by the social constructionist. The *tribas* ('lesbian'), from Greek *tribein* ('to rub', i.e. rubbing the pudenda together, or clitoris upon pubic bone, etc.), appears in Greek and Latin satires from the late first century. The *tribade* was the most common (vulgar) lesbian in European texts for many centuries. 'Tribade' occurs in English texts from at least as early as 1601 to at least as late as the mid-nineteenth century before it became self-consciously old-fashioned – thus, it was in current use for nearly three centuries.

The argument that there is no language for erotic love between women is based on the authority of the *Oxford English Dictionary*, 'which traces "lesbianism" back to 1870, "lesbic" to 1892, and "lesbian" as an adjective to 1890 and as a noun to 1925. Similarly, the entries for "Sapphism" start in 1890, with 1902 given as the first date for "Sapphist"' (Donoghue, 1993). Historians in this field seem to be quite unaware that the editors of the *OED* specifically excluded sexual slang from their remit, and relied mostly upon 'literature'; only today is this omission gradually being rectified. Unlike those who trust overmuch in the *OED*, Donoghue has established beyond doubt that throughout the seventeenth and eighteenth centuries the word 'lesbian' was used in the same sense as today, and that lesbians were viewed as a distinct sexual and social group. To cite an example from a literary work that was excluded from the *OED* survey (either because it was libellous, or because it was published in Dublin), sexual relationships between women are described as 'Lesbian Loves' by William King in *The Toast* in 1732, where he explains 'she loved Women in the same Manner as Men love them; she was a Tribad'; in the 1736 edition such women are called

'Tribades or Lesbians': 'So "Lesbian" could be used both as an adjective and a noun to describe women who desired and pleasured each other more than a century and a half before the OED's first entry for that meaning' (Donoghue, 1993). A 1762 translation of Plato's *Symposium* uses the phrase 'Sapphic Lovers' to describe women-lovers. In 1773 a London magazine refers to sex between women as 'Sapphic passion'. Hester Thrale in her diary in the 1790s describes a 'Sapphist' as a woman who likes 'her own sex in a criminal way', leaving no room for doubt about its sexual usage. In France the terms *fricarelle* and *fricatrice* (from 'friction', sex-by-rubbing) were common, and were also used in English from the seventeenth to the nineteenth centuries.

There are also many indigenous words not derived from classical literature or language: in England, from the mid-eighteenth century, sex between women was called 'The Game of Flats', a metaphor derived from a card game (Norton, 1992), and from the late eighteenth century to the late nineteenth century lesbians were called Tommies: '"Tom(my)" is just one example of how an unbroken slang tradition can go unrecorded by the OED' (Donoghue, 1993). Lesbian sexuality was neither silent nor invisible, it simply went unrecorded by compilers of those social constructs we call dictionaries. To base whole theories about the historical development of sexual identity upon the dates of 'first citations' given in dictionaries demonstrates only how far removed from empirical history and experience the intellectual academic 'discourse' has become.

Queer language

The theory that queer culture is determined by the structures and labels imposed upon it by an external mainstream culture is belied by the existence of queer language. Historical evidence shows that a significantly large proportion of labels arise from within or from the margins surrounding a queer subculture – that they are terms indigenous to queer culture, self-generated and self-cultivated. Perhaps one reason why scientists scrupulously avoid using this slang is because they realize that the language arises at least partly from within the minority group and to some extent empowers it. Homosexuals have not found it very difficult to call themselves fairies, queers or faggots, whereas they do not generally call themselves perverts, sexual psychopaths or homosexuals (though they have used the term 'homos'). To suggest that homosexuals do not constitute an ethnic group because they lack a distinctive language is to blind oneself to a great deal of evidence to the contrary.

Unfortunately most analyses of camp are based upon the compensation model: 'camp changes the real, hostile world into a new one which is controllable and safe. ... Camp was and is a way for gay men to re-imagine the world around them. It exaggerates and therefore diffuses real threats' (Bronski, 1984). Frankly, I hardly think that Ronald Firbank was concerned to make the world safe for homosexuals, or that the decorator Elsie de Wolfe was diffusing the threat of the Parthenon when she first saw it and exclaimed, 'It's beige! *My* colour!' Many theorists uncritically echo Bronski's analysis that

> 'camp talk' – especially gay men referring to one another with women's names or pronouns – evolved as a coded, protected way of speaking about one's personal or sexual life. If one man were to be overheard at a public dinner table saying to another, 'You'll never guess what Mary said on our date last night,' nothing would be thought of it.

A moment's thought ought to dispel this theory of the origins of camp talk: queers camped it up and referred to each other with women's names *almost entirely within a queer context in which no heterosexuals were present*. It operated primarily *within queer culture* and functioned to cement the relations therein. Far too many theorists interpret gay culture as a strategy for coping with or undermining straight culture rather than having cultural values *for its own sake*.

The vast bulk of queer slang is created by queers to communicate with one another. When a queer says, 'That queen over there is camping for jam' (making a play for a young boy, cited by Duberman, 1991), he is not employing a language imposed upon him by heterosexuals. The free and unselfconscious use of obscenity and slang is characteristic of working-class men and prostitutes, and the queer subculture often borrows terms from the cant of the criminal underworld, such as 'bent'. In American prisons, a 'pitcher' (macho man) 'hooks up' ('gets married') with a 'catcher', usually the 'punk' rather than the 'queen', who is often 'turned out' by rape or the threat of rape. In female prisons the 'femme' or 'mommy' 'make it' ('pair off') with the 'stud broad' or 'daddy' (S. Donaldson, 'Prisons, Jails, and Reformatories', *EH*). In memoirs of German queers imprisoned in the concentration camps we find not only *Homos* and *175-ers* (referring to Paragraph 175 which criminalized homosexuality) but also indigenous queer-terms such as *warmer Bruder* ('queer'), *Sittenstrolch* ('faggot'), *schwules Arschloch* ('queer arsehole') and *Arschficker* ('arse-fucker') (Lautmann, 1985).

Queer language is not something that is new to modern times. In ancient times the transgendered priests of the Thracian goddess Cotytto spoke an obscene lingo of their own. Many people recognize that Juvenal's portrait of the priests of Cybele is virtually indistinguishable from a gaggle of outrageous queens in the 1940s or even 1970s, but even writers lacking Juvenal's satirical bite document the existence of certain gestures and speech characteristics – queer language – among the *galli*:

> One such gesture involved rolling the eyes and raising them toward the heavens. ... Another consisted of holding the neck in a lilting or tilted manner. ... The *galli*, like female hierodules and courtesans, were said to converse with the palms of their hands turned upward, a gesture depicted on figurines portraying female deities. They were also said to speak in shrill tones, to lisp, to giggle and whisper, to use obscene language, to employ women's oaths, and to address each other in the feminine gender. Finally, the *galli* and other transgendered males were said to employ a verbal signal peculiar to them, the *regkeis* ... commonly translated as 'snort'. From Clement of Alexandria, who also suggests that the *regkeis* signal was nasal in character, we learn that the men employing this signal 'make a sound in their nose like a frog'. The *regkeis* signal may have actually sounded more like heavy breathing or hissing. ... Dio Chrysostom describes the *regkeis* as 'a sort of password of their own.' ... The *regkeis*, while apparently inciting laughter in hostile males, was clearly employed with the intention of announcing to the listener one's erotic desires. ... Dio Chrysostom insists that, even more than appearance, the *regkeis* may reveal a man to be a *cinaedus*, a gender variant male engaging in same-sex eroticism. (Conner *et al.*, 1997)

It is worth noting the possible continuity of this tradition in the speech mannerisms of modern queens, too readily dismissed by the anti-essentialists. The speech of gay men has a broad range of pitch and animation, more like that of women than the monotone of straight men, 'But there is also an aggressive, "bitchy" form of gay male intonation that has no precise equivalent among women', and older gay men remember using certain 'tunes' or special intonations to convey meaning when they told gay jokes (W. R. Dynes, 'Language and Linguistics', *EH*).

In the molly subculture of early eighteenth-century London, queer slang was a modification of thieves' cant and prostitute slang (Norton, 1992); as today, the mollies would 'make Love to one another', and they used other euphemisms such as 'the pleasant Deed' and 'to do the Story'. They 'swived', as did heterosexuals, but also had more specific verbs for anal intercourse, such as 'to *indorse*', from contemporary boxing slang, and 'caudle-making' or 'giving caudle', from the Latin *cauda* ('a tail'); later in the century, sodomites were called 'backgammon players' and 'gentlemen of the back door'. Gay cruising grounds were called 'the markets', where the mollies went 'strolling and caterwauling'; if they were lucky, they 'picked up' partners, or 'trade' (both terms are still in common use today); if luckier still, they would 'make a bargain' or agree to have sex (this derives from a rather obscure game known as 'selling a bargain'). Another variation is 'bit a blow', equivalent to the modern phrase 'score a trick'. To 'put the bite' on someone was to arrange for sex, possibly sex for money, derived from a contemporary phrase implying some sort of trickery, usually financial. Other recorded terms include 'Battersea'd' (probably a synonym for 'clapped'), 'brother' with a special meaning, 'cull', 'festival night', 'Gany-boy', 'husband', 'madge culls', 'mameluke', 'Margery', 'marrying', 'Mary-Ann', 'molly cull', 'patapouf', 'pullet', 'queen/quean', 'queer', 'tail quarters' and 'wedding night'.

The most striking feature of the 'Female Dialect' was that gay men christened one another with 'Maiden Names': Madam Blackwell, Miss Kitten, Miss Fanny Knight, Miss Irons, Moll Irons, Flying Horse Moll, Pomegranate Molly, Black Moll, China Mary, Primrose Mary, Orange Mary, Garter Mary, Pippin Mary (alias Queen Irons), Dip-Candle Mary, Small Coal Mary, Aunt Greer, Aunt May, Aunt England, Princess Seraphina the butcher, the Countess of Camomile, Lady Godiva, the Duchess of Gloucester, Orange Deb, Tub Nan, Hardware Nan, Old Fish Hannah and Johannah the Ox-Cheek Woman. The Maiden Names which the mollies assumed bore little relation to specific male–female role-playing in terms of sexual behaviour. Fanny Murray was 'an athletic Bargeman', Lucy Cooper was 'an Herculean Coal-heaver', Kitty Fisher was 'a deaf tyre Smith', 'Kitty Cambric is a Coal Merchant; Miss Selina, a Runner at a Police office; Black-eyed Leonora, a Drummer [of the Guards]; Pretty Harriet, a Butcher; ... and Miss Sweet Lips, a Country Grocer'. Similar lists can be found in the queer subcultures of sixteenth-century Italy, seventeenth-century Portugal, Spain and France, and elsewhere.

Dutchmen in the 1730s had a special way of speaking to one another which they called *op zijn janmeisjes* ('John girlish') (Noordam, 1989). Campy 'queen talk' can be found in the early eighteenth century (perhaps even earlier, though the subtleties of humour make it hard to detect). The mollies in London would enquire of one another, 'Where have you been you saucy Queen?' and engage in banter: 'O, Fie, Sir! — Pray, Sir. — Dear Sir. Lord, how can you serve me so? — I swear I'll cry out. — You're a wicked Devil. — And you're a bold Face. — Eh ye little dear Toad! Come, buss!' And the queens of Paris were camp in a recognizably modern mode: says one to another while cruising in the Luxembourg gardens in 1737, 'There's somebody who looks like one. Let's split up and see what this sister is all about' (Rey, 1985). Or again, when a young man did not respond to their advances, 'they said to each other: Let him go, he doesn't understand Latin.'

British camp language – polari – was very popular during the 1950s, and has been recorded by Peter Burton (1977):

> As feely homies, when we launched ourselves onto the gay scene, polari was all the rage. We would zhoosh our riahs, powder our eeks, climb into our bona new drag, don our batts and troll off to some bona bijou bar. In the bar we could stand around polarying with our sisters, varda the bona carts on the butch hom[m]e ajax who, if we fluttered our ogle riahs at him sweetly, might just troll over to offer a light for the unlit vogue clenched between our teeth. If we had enough bona measures, we might buy a handful of dubes to zhoosh down our screechs – enabling us to get blocked out of our minds.

A translation can be made with the glossary overleaf.

Polari contains mostly nouns, and some adjectives, but there were a few verbs, such as *blag* ('to make a pick-up'). Contrary to the social constructionist view that a secret gay language develops in order to allow homosexuals to communicate with one another without being understood or recognized by straights, polari was never designed to escape notice, but was often confrontative:

> Even when travelling in the singular, we weren't averse to shrieking a quick *get you, girl* at some menacing naff. ... We flaunted our homosexuality. We were pleased to be different. We were proud and secretly longed to broadcast our difference to the world: *when we were in a crowd.* (*Naff*, dreary and dull, especially heterosexuals, purportedly derives from Normal As Fuck.)

The origins of most gay argot, in other languages as well as English, can be traced to a core of faggots who couldn't give a damn about being overheard by respectable people: they used queer language for the purposes

Polari: A brief lexicon

acqua	water
ajax	adjacent
batts	shoes
bijou	small
blocked	get high on pills ('Purple Hearts')
bold	darling
bona	very good, splendid
brandy	bum ('brandy and rum')
butch	masculine
carts/cartes/cartso	crotch, cock, penis
cod	awful
dolly	nice, pleasant
drag	clothes
dubes	pills
duckie	mate
eek	face
esong	nose
feely/feele	young
fruit	queen
homme/omi, homies	man, men
lallies	legs
lilly	police (Lilly Law)
measures	money
nanti/nante	not, no/nothing
ogle riahs	eye-lashes
omi-polone	effeminate man, gay
on the team	gay
park	give
piece	he/she
polari	homosexual slang
polone	woman
riah	hair
screech	mouth, throat
shush	bag, holdall
sister	close friend
slap	make up
trade	sexual partner
troll	walk, look for trade
varda/vada	look (at), see
vogue	cigarette
zhoosh	comb, fix (also shoplift)
zhoosh off	go away
zhooshed up	dressed up

of cultural solidarity, not to convey secret messages past the ears of unwitting straights.

As with the mollies two centuries earlier, many 1950s gay men and *pollones* ('women'), and especially *homie pollones* ('effeminate queens'), used camp nicknames, such as 'Dobbin Clit, the Slender Slinky, Monica Christmas Tree, Terry the Pill, Pussycat Michael, ... the Antique Pam, Bambi, Twizzle, Samantha (a transvestite cat burglar who lived on a diet of black boot polish, cold cream and sniffed wig cleaning fluid)'. If it was not clear from the list of molly names, it should now be clear that 'female' nicknames is a misnomer: these are *queer* nicknames.

Many polari terms come from the working-class East End of London, as Burton explains: in East End backslang the order of the letters are reversed, hence 'hair' becomes *riah*, 'face' becomes *e-caff* and is then shortened to *eek*. 'A considerable amount of the East End slang itself is derived from foreign words which were brought to this country by the various influxes of refugees'; for example, *jarrying the cartes* ('eating cock' or 'cocksucking'), from Italian *mangiare* ('to eat'):

> Such polari as survives is that which is handed down from one generation of queans to another (incidentally, giving us at least one 'living' link with our homosexual past). ... There was something deeply reassuring about polari – it gave those of us who used it an additional sense of corporate identity.

Among queers this language is almost universally called polari: Burton derives it from *palaver*; Eric Partridge calls it *parlyaree*; the *Oxford Companion to the English Language* says it comes from the eighteenth-century Italian *parlare* ('to talk'), and is sometimes spelled *palarie*, *parlyaree*, *parlary*, etc. It was once an

> extensive argot or cant in Britain and elsewhere, among sailors, itinerants, people in show business (especially the theatre and circuses), and some homosexual groups. ... A composite of different Romance sources, it was first taken to England by sailors, may derive ultimately from Lingua Franca [seventeenth-century Italian, the language of the Franks], a mixed language based on Italian and Occitan (Southern French), used for trading and military purposes in the Mediterranean in the Middle Ages.

Polari seems to have survived only in Britain (perhaps specifically England), with a vocabulary of about one hundred words, some of which have

THE MYTH OF THE MODERN HOMOSEXUAL

entered general British slang, for example *ponce* ('effeminate man'), from *poonce* (Yiddish for 'cunt'), and Spanish *pu(n)to* ('male prostitute').

Modern Greek homosexual argot, called *Kaliardá*, is used more specifically by the receptive homosexual, the *kinaidhos* or, pejoratively, the *poustis* (the active partner is the *kolombarás*). This argot is sometimes called *Latinika* Latin, and a more secret subdivision of it is known as *Vathia Latinika*, Deep Latin, or *Etrouska*, Etruscan. In 1971 the folklorist Elias Petropoulos privately printed his book *Kaliardá: An Etymological Dictionary of Greek Homosexual Slang*, for which he served a seven-month prison term in 1972. He suggests it may originate from the French word *gailliard*; others have suggested it comes from a Romany term meaning 'gypsy'. It uses words derived from modern Greek, English, French, Italian, Turkish and Romany, and presumably is another example of queer Lingua Franca disseminated by sailors and immigrants landing in major seaports:

> A Kaliardá compound can indeed be an alloy of two or three roots from two or three different languages. … Among the grammatical curiosities of the argot is the fact that nearly all nouns and adjectives are used in the feminine form. As opposed to other Greek argots (such as underworld slang) which grammatically are Modern Greek but with slang terms inserted, Kaliardá is nearly a language in itself: only a few Greek words are necessary, along with two particles required in the construction of verbal tenses. … Kaliardá nicknames, proverbs, curses, and place-names also exist. (J. Taylor, 'Kaliardá', *EH*)

Obscure origins

Bill Bryson's humorous writings on the English–American language have demonstrated that (a) the first time a word is recorded in print, the context usually demonstrates that it was already widely used and understood, and (b) the origins of many words are entirely obscure. The notion that labels are used by the ruling society to control minority cultures is contradicted by the existence of queer labels whose origin is completely unknown to either the straight culture or queer culture. The Japanese slang for homosexuality is *xia zhuan* ('intimacy with a brick'); no one knows its origin. Many of the queer words which we take for granted today have an obscure history. To 'camp' it up might come from the French verb *se camper* ('to posture or flaunt'); or it might come from the polari/Lingua Franca word *kaemp*, also meaning to display transgendered behaviour (Conner *et al.*, 1997); or neither. No one quite knows the literal meaning or origin of the British term for pansy, *poof* – or even how it should be spelled (pouf, poove, pooff, puff) or pronounced. Everyone assumes that *fairy* comes from the word for the supernatural creature of folklore, but this is by no means certain; the queer term, first used to describe the participants in New York drag balls in the 1890s was *fary* – it always meant effeminate, but 'fairy' mythology/lore was seldom an explicit part of the context, and may be a retrospective interpretation. The origins of some of the most frequently used modern slang words for homosexual are unknown, which has given rise to queer folk etymology.

Dyke

No one quite knows why 'dyke' is used to refer to a butch lesbian. It can be traced back to 1920s black American slang, 'bull-diker' or 'bull-dagger', but the meaning of 'diker/dagger' is unclear. Some speculate that it is connected to 'to be diked out', traceable back to the 1850s, meaning 'faultlessly dressed', as in the modern American phrase 'all decked out'. Conceivably, therefore, it might mean all dressed up like a man, a bull (or presenting a butch image). It might also be related to *tyke*, an old Germanic term meaning 'bitch', and the concept of a 'bull-bitch' seems apt. But no historical link between the two terms can be found. But that has not prevented speculation.

Unfortunately all of Judy Grahn's (1984) insights (*Another Mother Tongue: Gay Words, Gay Worlds*) into gay 'offices' and ceremonial functions, and the transmission of gay culture via a 'core' of queens and dykes, are seriously marred by the worst sort of folk etymology. Because Grahn has heard someone pronounce *bull* as *boa*, and because certain Celtic rites were performed, supposedly, on *dykes*, *bulldyke* is said to derive from Queen *Boudicca*, who is taken as an Amazon model (the lack of any lesbian references to this married queen with daughters is conveniently passed over):

> Her name was Boudicca and came to be pronounced 'Boo-uh-*dike*-ay'. Or, as we would say (those of us who say such things) in modern American English: *bulldike*, or *bulldiker*. ... Queen Boudicca's name could very well have been a title rather than an individual queen's name: *bulldike* and *bulldagger* may mean bull-

slayer-priestess. As high priestess of her people, perhaps the queen performed the ceremonial killing of the bull (who was also the god) on the sacred altar-embankment, or dyke.

Grahn never stops to consider how a word can pass straight from Celtic Norfolk to modern black America without leaving any linguistic trace in Britain during the intervening centuries. I do not say that only professional linguists are entitled to address such issues, but an etymology that is not firmly based upon the historical principles of etymology is worse than useless.

Faggot

No one knows the literal meaning of 'faggot'. As a queer term it dates only from 1914, in America, when 'fagots', meaning 'sissies', are reported as going to a 'drag ball'. 'Fagott parties' were described in 1919 (Chauncey, 1985). 'Fagot' was soon abbreviated to 'fag'; Nels Anderson in *The Hobo* (1923), defines it thus: 'Fairies or Fags are men or boys who exploit sex for profit.' Presumably – but not necessarily, for the significant spelling difference was maintained for many years by writers who were otherwise literate – it comes from *faggot*, slang for 'slovenly woman, slut, whore', which dates back to the thirteenth century, but why it should have taken so long to be applied to queer men is a problem, and no direct link to American usage can be established. The term has no connection with the nineteenth-century British term 'fagging' ('beating'), or the 'fag' system in public schools. Undoubtedly fags were also fucked, but they were more frequently beaten, which is the salient point in this term's linguistic history (which produces related words such as 'all fagged out').

Nor does the term have anything to do with the bundle of sticks called 'faggots', though queer folk etymologists like to link the term with the supposed burning of sodomites at the stake, using them as the very faggots to burn witches! This never happened. Arthur Evans (*Witchcraft and the Gay Counterculture: A Radical View of Western Civilization and Some of the People It Has Tried to Destroy*, 1978), the main proponent of this line of enquiry, properly points out that men sentenced to be burned at the stake as sodomites wore robes on which were depicted burning faggots, so the metaphorical link theoretically could arise between burning faggots and homosexuals. But faggot in its queer sense is an English word, and in England neither homosexuals nor witches were ever burned at the stake, but were hanged, so even the metaphorical link would not arise.

Presumably 'faggot' is simply a variation on 'baggage' or prostitute (derived from *bagasse* and *bagascia*, French and Italian for 'prostitute' – the 'f', 'v' and 'b' commonly interchanged), which was colloquially applied to a not-yet-enlisted soldier or sailor (probably by analogy to *faggot-master*, whoremaster), a nineteenth-century usage picked up by the hobo/tramp subculture. That 'faggot' should mean 'male-whore' seems likely – but not proven.

Gay

'Gay' in its ordinary sense comes from Old Provençal *gai* ('high spirited, mirthful'). The French gay publication *Gai saber* took its name from the Troubadour expression for 'gay knowledge', but *gai* in its queer sense was imported into France from American gay slang. In England *gay blades* (libertines) date from the seventeenth century, but were not specifically homosexual. A famous slang dictionary by Captain F. Grose in 1811 defines 'gaying instrument' as 'penis'. During the nineteenth century a 'gay woman' was 'a prostitute, a whore', and 'gay' meant 'on the game', i.e. prostitution. According to Dynes,

> it has not been found in print before 1933 (when it appears in Noel Ersine's *Dictionary of Underworld Slang* as *gay cat*, 'a homosexual boy'). ... As Jack London explains in *The Road* of 1907, gay cat [also recorded as 'gey cat'] originally meant – or so he thought – an apprentice hobo, without reference to sexual orientation. ... Despite ill-informed speculations, thus far not one unambiguous attestation of the word to refer specifically to homosexual men is known from the nineteenth century. The word (and its equivalents in other European languages) is attested in the sense of 'belonging to the demi-monde' or 'given to illicit sexual pleasures,' even specifically to prostitution, but nowhere with the special homosexual sense that is reinforced by the antonym *straight*. (W. R. Dynes, 'Gay', *EH*)

Several gay men writing in the 1950s (for example, Peter Wildeblood) assert that 'gay' was a term imported from America that was just becoming popular on the scene. However, words are used long before they get recorded in print. Lew Levenson in his 1934 gay autobiography *Butterfly Man* wrote, 'I'm lush. I'm gay. I'm wicked. I'm everything that flames.' It is hardly likely that Levenson could employ this term if it had not already had that meaning for at least a generation. There is in fact one early nineteenth-century use of the word 'gay' in a homosexual context. The lawyer Robert Holloway, in *The Phoenix of Sodom, or the Vere Street Coterie, Being an Exhibition of the Gambols Practised by the Ancient Lechers of Sodom and Gomorrah, Embellished and Improved with the Modern Refinements in Sodomitical Practices, by the Members of the Vere Street Coterie, of Detestable Memory* (published in London in 1813), relates that when James Cook, the keeper of the homosexual brothel The Swan, was released from prison on 21 September 1812, 'In the course of a few days after, he accidentally met John Church, and recognised him as the *gay parson*, whom he had formerly seen at a certain house in the London Road, and at his own house in Vere Street.' The Reverend John Church blessed homosexual marriages at The Swan, not entirely as a joke: he also performed the funeral services for Richard Oakden, a bank clerk who was hanged for sodomy at Tyburn in 1809; Reverend Church was a gay-identified Christian active in the gay subculture, and was eventually imprisoned himself (Norton, 1992). The italics are Holloway's own, which seem to me to make it likely that he intended *gay* to have a specific sodomitical meaning.

Miller (1996) believes that an even earlier use can be documented. In Mary Pix's 1706 play *The Adventures in Madrid* a girl dressed as a boy is pursued by a man named 'Gaylove', who calls her his little 'Ganymede' and 'fairy':

> This may be the first recorded use of 'gay' and 'fairy' in the context of male homosexuality. If so, it reverses the etymology of 'gay', usually described as a development from describing prostitutes as 'gay women', for which the earliest references are in the nineteenth century, over one hundred and twenty years after Pix's play was seen.

Queer

'Queer' has been the most frequently used queer-term in twentieth-century English, by both queers and homophobes, but no one really knows for certain how its homosexual meaning arose. The term was common in the Rogues' Lexicon of the early eighteenth century in phrases such as *queer-ken* ('prison house'); *queer booze* ('bad drink'); *to cut queer whids* ('to use foul language'); *queer-bird* ('man lately released from prison'); and *queer cull* ('a fop or fool') – used concurrently with *molly cull* ('homosexual'). Back in the seventeenth century and late sixteenth century the term 'queer' is basically the criminal underworld's antonym for 'straight, respectable', sometimes in the literal sense of 'counterfeit', sometimes in the sense of 'queasy', and frequently in the sense of 'odd, eccentric, strange'. There are some 'queer fellows' in early texts who are also (or seem to be) sodomitical, but it is difficult to show that the term was specifically used in a queer sense earlier than the nineteenth century. It seems to be essentially a metaphorical term, and it is not always easy to demonstrate that the metaphor was queerly intended. One instance in which this usage seems intentional occurred in Canada in 1838: George Markland, Inspector General of Upper Canada, was observed making evening assignations with young soldiers in the Toronto government building. A cleaning lady overheard noises from his room that convinced her he was having sexual connections with a woman, but was surprised to see a drummer boy emerge; when Markland appeared she said to him, 'Well Sir these are queer doings from the bottom to the top.' (Burns, 1976.) An inquiry was begun, and Markland resigned and left town.

Dyke, faggot, gay, queer: these are queer-words. When straights heard them for the first time in the 1930s or 1950s they did not know what they meant. Because they had not created them – queers had. When the mollies were tried in the early eighteenth century, the judges and juries heard words they had never heard before and phrases they did not understand. In a homosexual trial in Britain in the 1950s the jury had to be handed a glossary of queer terms so that they could comprehend the testimony they were about to hear (Higgins, 1996). These are not words of social control; these are words indigenous to an ethnic culture. The fact that they happen to be fairly modern queer-words does not mean that queer culture is a modern invention: these particular words have simply superseded earlier queer epithets such as molly and tribade, both of which have had a longer history than dyke, faggot, gay and queer.

Part II

The Nature of Queer History

5

What Is Queer History?

Queer historians

The compilation of queer biographies was felt to be an important feature of the early homosexual emancipation movement in the late nineteenth and early twentieth centuries, particularly in Germany, not because of their apologetic motive but because the nineteenth century conceived of history as the acts of great men. What should really be appreciated about the early queer historians is the cultural breadth of their focus, from ethnographic studies to contemporary accounts of queer subcultures in large cities. The pioneering antiquarian, literary and historical pioneering studies of homosexuality in the late nineteenth century were gradually superseded by interest in Darwinian evolution, whereby historical investigation was replaced by the biological approach. From the 1830s to the 1920s we can observe that the 'natural' and 'cultural' model of the third sex was steadily replaced by the medical model of the homosexual. The specifically historical approach was gradually superseded by a focus upon individual persons, as psychology and psychiatry rejected the cultural model. By the 1970s the traditional historical–cultural model was replaced by the political analysis of the homosexual as victim of the ideological discourse of homophobia. The idea of 'gay history' that emerged in the 1980s focused almost exclusively upon the history of homophobia and the 'contemporary history' of the gay liberation movement. The concept of a queer cultural heritage was thus 'deconstructed'.

The pioneering queer historical research was conducted by Heinrich Hoessli (1784–1864), an effeminate amateur scholar who earned his living as a milliner and interior decorator. His book *Eros: Die Männerliebe der Griechen: Ihre Beziehungen zur Geschichte, Erziehung, Literatur und Gesetzgebung aller Zeiten* (*Eros: The Male Love of the Greeks: Its Relationship to the History, Education, Literature and Legislation of All Ages*; two volumes, 1836 and 1838; material for a third volume was not published) assembled mostly literary examples from ancient Greece and medieval Islam. It was partly an 'answer' to issues raised by Heinrich

Zschokke in *Eros oder über die Liebe* (1821), perhaps the first example of gay 'apologetics', in which Hoessli appears as a Socratic character arguing his case. Zschokke and Hoessli (their personal relationship to one another has not been investigated) were both roused to public debate by the execution in 1817 of Franz Desgouttes in Bern for killing his lover in a fit of jealousy.

Their work was followed by Karl Heinrich Ulrichs's more erudite and far-reaching *Forschungen zur mannmännlichen Liebe (Researches on Love between Males*; several volumes published between 1864 and 1870). A vast amount of material was published by Magnus Hirschfeld in his book *Die Homosexualität des Mannes und des Weibes* (1914) and in the journal of his Wissenschaftlich-humanitäre Komitee (Scientific-Humanitarian Committee), the *Jahrbuch für sexuelle Zwischenstufen unter besonderer Berücksichtigung der Homosexualität (Yearbook of Sexual Intergrades*; twenty-three volumes, 1899–1923) (this included major articles on queer history by the Dutch writer L. S. A. M. von Römer). Other important works include Carlo Mantegazza's *Gli amori degli uomini (The Sexual Relations of Mankind*, 1885); Marc-André Raffalovich's *Uranisme et unisexualité (Uranism and Unisexuality*, 1896); Havelock Ellis's *Sexual Inversion* (German 1896, English 1897; most of the historical material was contributed by his co-author John Addington Symonds); Ivan Bloch's *Beiträge der Psychopathia sexualis (Contributions to the Etiology of Psychopathia Sexualis*, 1902) and *Das Geschlechtsleben in England* (three vols, 1901–3; one volume translated by M. Eden Paul as *The Sexual Life of Our Time*, 1908); Xavier Mayne's (pseudonym of Edward Irenaeus Prime-Stevenson) *The Intersexes* (1908); and Edward Carpenter's *The Intermediate Sex* (1908). Queer apologetics outside of the Anglo-Germanic movement have not been much studied. Very little seems to be known about possibly gay apologists in Portugal between the wars, such as Dr Arlindo Camillo Monteiro, who published a massive history of homosexuality, *Amor Sáfico e Socrático* (1922), or Dr Asdrúbal de Aguiar's *Evolução da Pederastia e do Lesbismo na Europa* (1926) and *Medicina Legal: A Homosexualidade masculine através dos tempos* (1934). 'The world Depression and the rise of Nazism put a stop to most serious homosexual research' (W. R. Dynes, 'History', *EH*).

Queer history did not get under way again until the 1950s, but many works have basically recycled this earlier scholarship, and modern research has seldom matched the scale or depth of the work published before the 1930s. In 1891 Dr F. C. Müller published the transcript of the 1721 trial of Catharina Margaretha Linck because of its unique lesbian interest, but he observed that in the Prussian Secret State Archives there were records of more than one hundred sodomy trials – it is significant that none of these have been investigated to this day.

In terms of queer anthologies, a direct line of descent can be traced back from Alistair Sutherland and Patrick Anderson's *Eros: An Anthology of Friendship* (1961) to Edward Carpenter's *Ioläus: An Anthology of Friendship* (1902) – dubbed the 'bugger's bible' (it went through two editions and numerous reprints) – and thence to Elisàr von Kupffer's *Lieblingminne und Freundesliebe in der Weltliteratur* (*Love of Comrades and Friends in World Literature*, 1900), which in turn was inspired by Hoessli's *Eros: Die Männerliebe der Griechen*. One of the more recent contributions to this tradition, Cecile Beurdeley's *L'Amour bleu* (originally published in 1979), is a large-format illustrated book which is especially interesting for the many colour reproductions of the pederastic frescos with which Kupffer decorated his Sanctuarium Artis Elisarion at Minusio, near Locarno, Switzerland. Kupffer began his anthology partly in response to the trials of Oscar Wilde; Kupffer was himself a playwright (and homosexual), as well as a painter; in 1908 he published a monograph on the Renaissance homosexual painter Sodoma; he and his lover Eduard von Mayer founded the Klaristiche movement, a kind of aesthetic/socialist/homoerotic/Christian emancipationist movement.

Social constructionists do a great disservice to these scholars by suggesting that the 'central purpose of the project of gay historical reclamation' was merely fabricated:

> Having no access to a formal body of scholarship, gay men needed to invent – and constantly reinvent – a tradition on the basis of innumerable individual and idiosyncratic readings of texts. ... By constructing historical traditions of their own, gay men defined themselves as a distinct community. By imagining they had collective roots in the past, they asserted a collective identity in the present. (Chauncey, 1994)

It is patently unfair to belittle the achievement of these men as mere propaganda. Symonds nearly worked himself to death *discovering facts* rather than inventing fictions. Many 'idiosyncratic readings' – for example, of Michelangelo, Whitman, Thomas Mann, E. M. Forster *et al.* – have been proven correct by recent publication of diaries and letters (though the Shakespeare controversy still rages). Though Carpenter was more of a journalist than a scholar, he nevertheless travelled to India to gather evidence of queer culture. These men did not 'construct' gay history: they succeeded in uncovering it. It was important for them to recognize that they had common ancestors and they were determined to share this tradition with their fellow queers by making their researches public. Queer scholarship of the late nineteenth and early twentieth centuries is no more deficient or eccentric than the scholarship of other ethnic and ethnographic historians of the period. The vast majority of queer scholars were scrupulously accurate – and produced far more reliable texts than the straight scholars who had buried queer history.

Culturally identified queers have made the most significant contributions to the study of queer history. They have been responsible for uncensored translations of material into English, German and French which many would like to see remain in the original languages or put into Latin; and they have made this material accessible to the non-specialist public in a large number of anthologies. Were it not for modern culturally identified queers, the evidence of ancient queer culture would be even less than what survives now. For example, many Greek vases depicting homosexual relations in the collections of various museums around the world were collected from 1885 to 1910 by Edward Perry Warren (1860–1928); though his collection in Boston's Museum of Fine Arts was not publicly exhibited until 1964, it nevertheless has contributed to the more forthright study of the subject in works such as Kenneth Dover's (1978) ground-breaking *Greek Homosexuality*. Warren was an American art connoisseur who came to Oxford University, where he met his lover John Marshall in 1884, and who rejected the American ideals of democracy and feminism. He was specifically a pederastic apologist, and under the pseudonym of Arthur Lyon Raile wrote several volumes of pederastic poetry as well as a novel, *A Tale of Pausanian Love* (1927), and *The Defence of Uranian Love* (1928–30) (d'Arch Smith, 1970).

Queer scholarship is not limited to the West, however. The anthology of Japanese gay literature *Partings at Dawn* (ed. Miller, 1996) includes a selection from the remarkable correspondence between Minakata Kumagusu (1867–1941) and Iwata Jun'ichi (1900–45), from a total of 120 letters that began in 1931 and continued for thirty years (though Iwata burned many of the letters before he died). Both men were deeply interested in the history of homosexuality in Japan and the details of the homosexual subculture from the 'Golden Period' to cruising the parks in modern Tokyo, from the poetic 'Way of Prince Lung-yang' (a legendary icon of homosexuality in China) to the 'way to proceed when a handsome boy is spread out beneath you'. Minakata was a naturalist and a scholar of Japanese folklore and folk history, and Iwata was an illustrator and artist. In 1930 Iwata contributed a series of articles, *Nanshoku-kō* ('On Man-Love/Lust'), to a journal of criminology, which caught the attention of Minakata and prompted the correspondence. Iwata's great project was a complete 'History of Man-Love' and he engaged in an enormous amount of research on literary and historical sources related to homosexuality, publishing a draft bibliography during the Second World War. The letters between the two men are a treasure-house of sources and linguistics. They are, above all, written by culturally identified queers concerned to establish the cultural unity of queer history.

Minakata assembled a large collection of queer studies, and was the proud owner of numbered editions of John Addington Symonds's privately printed *A Problem in Greek Ethics* and *A Problem in Modern Ethics*. Like many gay men, Minakata was concerned to be part of a living link with the ancient queer past. Like Alain Daniélou in India, he travelled around Japan studying visual representations of sacred boy-princes, in whose cult he believed homosexuality to have originated. The ancient monastery on Mount Kōya was legendary for the homosexual tradition carried on by its priests. He regularly visited the monastery in the early 1880s, where he interviewed old men who had been 'acolytes' in their youth, when they wore triangular cushions of velvet pressed down on their genitals to keep their penises limp; they received the attentions of their older monk-partners in the standard frontal position, and Minakata records a host of slang terms that were in common use in the queer culture of the monasteries in the 1840s. Iwata confirmed that in modern Tokyo the chest-to-chest position was preferred, and a wad of bleached cotton was used as a sexual restraint during intercourse. Minakata visited the Kōya monastery once again in 1920 at the invitation of its abbot, a friend he had met in London, together with a painter friend. During the visit the abbot produced from storage several paintings brought back from China by Kōbō Daishi (774–835), reputed to have 'introduced' homosexual love into Japan, including a remarkable thousand-year-old painting using powdered coral to depict a beautiful 25-year-old eunuch, an ancient queer icon.

Minakata's letters began appearing in 1951, Iwata's in 1991; English translations of a limited selection began in 1996; other letters are rumoured to exist and are expected to appear in due course. It hardly needs to be said that only culturally identified queers feel that these letters are profoundly important and merit detailed study; heterosexual historians will not touch the subject and institutions are not likely to fund extensive translation and commentary. Ancient queer culture is taboo.

Queer culture versus homophobic discourse

Queer historians need to widen the definition of 'homosexuality' so as to encompass queer culture rather than just queer sex and the laws against it, and then to engage in the task of verifying the authentic features of queer culture. Many aspects of our heritage have been misinterpreted or unjustifiably rejected as being alien. Queer history should use the techniques of the post-colonial analysis. Queers can be trapped by a historical straitjacket unless we believe that not all of the forms of our past behaviour are products of colonization, but that some constitute part of a genuine authentic self or core. Determining which is which is a central problem for the queer historian. If we focus entirely on the oppression of queer history we will not find the threads necessary to reweave the suit of clothes most appropriate for us.

Queer history is essentially the history of queer culture. It is not the history of specific sexual acts, nor should it be a history of social attitudes towards homosexuality. Queer history is still too much part of the 'history of sexuality' and needs to be resituated within the history of non-sexual culture and ethnic customs. Similarly, although it is important to recognize the (often hostile) environment in which queers fashion their culture, a history of heterosexual prejudice is not *central* to a history of homosexuality. Queer history is about queer experience, not about straight attitudes; queer history is about love among queers, not about laws against queers; queer history relies more on information *from* queers than information *about* queers. We need more of what anthropologists call 'thick description' as opposed to grand narratives. Personal authentic testimony from a queer during a trial for sodomy is worth more than any statistical analysis of executions for sodomy during a given century, and worth far more than the opinions of jurists. The testimony of the oppressed must always be granted primacy.

Social constructionism has its roots in literary criticism associated with linguistic theory (structuralism and post-structuralism), which emphasizes that the meaning of a text is dependent upon those who interpret it. It is felt that nothing can be known about what precedes the text (for example, the author's intention), but whoever reads it will interpret it in their own way in the light of their own prejudices. The professional body that interprets the text establishes the 'discourse' within whose terms the text is discussed. There is of course some truth in this, especially when applied to literature, and especially when applied to the body of interpretation assigned to it. Because of this bias, social constructionists do not look at phenomena which precede the text – hence the view that homosexuality did not exist until it was created in the discourse about it. Social constructionists do not allow for the fact that queer culture is not simply a text and is not fully enveloped by the discourse about homosexuality.

Within the medical and legal discourses insufficient attention has been given to the testimony of queer witnesses, either as defence evidence submitted in court or as case studies provided by the queers themselves in their own words. Homophobic discourse may well give an overriding shape to this testimony, but very often we hear authentic testimony that does not directly answer the question and therefore provides information about the reality that lay outside the discourse, or testimony that refutes the conclusions drawn by the discourse. Deconstruction of the discourse is not enough: recovery of what lay outside the discourse must also be an important part of political action. Queer people's understanding of themselves is shaped by many things *outside* the psychiatrists' and sexologists' counselling rooms and lecture halls:

> Events come wrapped in meanings, so we cannot separate action from interpretation or strip history down to pure events. But it does not follow that events are construed exclusively through philosophic discourse or that ordinary people depend on philosophers to find meaning in their lives. The making of public opinion takes place in markets and taverns as well as in *sociétés de pensée*. To understand how publics made sense of events, one must extend the inquiry beyond the works of philosophers and into the communication networks of everyday life. (Darnton, 1996)

The life of the eighteenth-century molly butcher John Cooper, for example, existed outside of this discourse, and only came to the attention of the courts when in 1732 he unwisely decided to bring charges against an unemployed servant who had robbed him and stolen his clothes. This servant, in his defence, claimed that Cooper had wanted to sodomize him, for which purpose he had removed his clothes, and defence witnesses were called who revealed that Cooper was what we now call a drag queen who earned money by delivering messages between sodomites. As the landlady of his favourite pub revealed, 'he's one of them as you call *Molly Culls*, he gets his Bread that way; to my certain Knowledge he has got many a Crown under some Gentlemen, for going of sodomiting Errands' (Norton, 1992). A washerwoman who had overheard Cooper demanding that the servant return his clothes ended her testimony with the startling revelation that John Cooper was commonly known in the district as the

Princess Seraphina. The judge was so taken aback by this turn of events that he required the witness to repeat what she had just said. Her story was confirmed by Mary Poplet, the keeper of the Two Sugar Loaves public house in Drury Lane, who astonished the court with her testimony:

> I have known her Highness a pretty while, she us'd to come to my House from Mr. Tull, to enquire after some Gentlemen of no very good Character; I have seen her several times in Women's Cloaths, she commonly us'd to wear a white Gown, and a scarlet Cloak, with her Hair frizzled and curl'd all round her Forehead; and then she would so flutter her Fan, and make such fine Curt'sies, that you would not have known her from a Woman: She takes great Delight in Balls and Masquerades, and always chuses to appear at them in a Female Dress, that she may have the Satisfaction of dancing with fine Gentlemen. ... I never heard that she had any other Name than the Princess Seraphina.

Additional testimony revealed that Princess Seraphina was widely known and liked by all the women in her neighbourhood, some of whom loaned her their clothes so that she could attend masquerade balls, and that nearly everyone referred to the butcher unselfconsciously as 'her' even when 'she' was not wearing women's clothes. This trial for robbery lies outside the homosexual discourse and would not figure in any statistical analysis of sodomy cases, but I cannot help but feel that it describes the cultural reality that will later be characterized as a homophobic stereotype.

Most historians of homosexuality fail to distinguish adequately between homosexuality and homophobia, and rather than researching queer experience, take the easier route of studying laws against queers, thus shifting the focus from queers to queerbashers. This represents a useful political strategy rather than a proper historical endeavour. Theories about queer identity or homophobia in the general populace cannot be founded upon a study of legislation, which as an approach to queer history should be relegated to a minor niche or even abandoned. Although Duberman (1991) feels it is important to document the history of repression, he wryly acknowledges that 'The initial determination of historians to document repression has sometimes led them to obscure the actual gay/lesbian experience being repressed.' Duberman rightly feels it is more important in this area to study the history of resistance to oppression, in order to 'begin to restore the historical agency of gay men and lesbians themselves'.

Attitudes to homosexuality should not be altogether ignored, but in most of the literature they are given a disproportionate amount of space. Such histories amount to little more than an account of homophobia in the heterosexual population; often they do not even differentiate between attitudes in general and the attitudes of queers towards themselves – of which the latter is by far the more interesting. Far too often homosexuality and homophobia are discussed in the same breath, which either fails to note that they are separate entities or all too easily assumes that there is a direct and inevitable link between the two. In fact the spotlight has to be focused in two opposite directions in order to illuminate these two subjects adequately. Homophobia has a direct link to *heterosexual* needs, fears and ideology; social constructionists have quite properly turned their attention to this subject, and have concluded that the image of the homosexual that is projected by homophobia is a silhouette originating in heterosexual ideology. The deconstruction of this subject has proved so interesting, and so useful for undermining heterosexual hegemony, that they have failed to turn the spotlight around to the other direction; they have simply posited the non-existence of homosexuals as an independent entity.

The law

In his introduction to *The Construction of Homosexuality*, Greenberg acknowledges that 'the scope of our project ... is to understand perceptions of homosexuality, not homosexuality itself', but throughout the book he conflates the two phenomena. For some writers the equation of homophobia with homosexuality is part of a political strategy, but the fact that homosexuality has become totally subsumed within the field of homophobia is also partly the result of an accident arising from the way that the history of homosexuality has been structured. Most historians of homosexuality have been gay men who wanted to reform the law that repressed them; their lines of research and their findings were determined by this goal. Thus *The Gay Past*, a collection of essays written in the late 1970s, edited by Licata and Petersen (1985), is introduced with the statement that 'the history of homosexuality is largely a chronicle of how society has made the homosexual option unbelievably difficult and dangerous for those who exercised it'.

But the inference that antihomosexual legislation has a significant impact upon queers and that it reflects commonly held views are unfounded assumptions. The deterrent effect of the law is often a subject of argument; in cases involving actions inspired by instinct rather than conscious choice such laws serve merely to punish rather than to deter. Andrew Hallidie Smith, Secretary of the Reform Society in the 1960s, corresponded with several hundred homosexuals, of whom 'not one has admitted to be deterred by the law' (Spencer, 1995). The long 'history of homosexuality' of Licata and Petersen's definition is a history of anti-gay laws that were not rigorously enforced – in fact they were enforced so rarely that we may well doubt that they had any influence upon behaviour *at all* for several centuries. This is patently *not* a 'history of homosexuality'. If the only 'evidence' we have for a certain period comes from anti-gay laws and satires, then I say that we know *virtually nothing at all* about queer history for the period in question.

The paucity of evidence concerning homosexuals is partly why historians have taken the easier option of studying laws against homosexuality. The social constructionists, being interested in mechanisms of social control, naturally focus upon laws designed to control sexuality. A study of law easily supports their pet theories: thus Weeks (1977) says that 'the central point [of the 1533 Act of Henry VIII outlawing buggery] was that the law was directed against a series of sexual acts, not a particular type of person. There was no concept of the homosexual in law.' But surely this is characteristic of all legal capital statutes: *acts* are invariably regulated rather than persons. All laws cite capital *crimes* rather than capital *criminals*: felonies rather than felons are always the subject of legislation. The only practicable way to control people is to regulate their *actions*. Foucault (1978) in his history of sexuality regularly makes the mistake of treating legalistic definitions as if they were exactly equivalent to social definitions. *Of course* the ancient and canonical codes deal with sodomy as a category of forbidden acts: legal texts are always scrupulous to identify acts because only acts can be regulated. This in itself is neither surprising nor significant: in no sense does it provide evidence that types of persons susceptible to crime were not recognized in society – indeed society, lacking the fine discrimination of ecclesiastics and lawyers, quite regularly refers to criminal *types of persons*. Virtually all ancient and medieval satires were invariably aimed against sodomites and catamites as persons rather than sodomy and anal intercourse *per se*.

Theories about queer identity or homophobia in the general populace cannot be founded upon a study of legislation, for there are few demonstrable links between them. It is difficult to judge the effect of the anti-homosexual laws of early Christian Europe because there are so very few known prosecutions. A popular charioteer in Thessalonika was arrested in 390 on homosexual charges, but his fellow Thessalonikans rioted in protest at the arrest and killed a Gothic officer; clearly the indigenous population felt more anti-Goth sentiment than anti-homosexual sentiment.

Michael Goodich's (1979) *The Unmentionable Vice* is an exhaustive and systematic study of official documents – penitential manuals, papal decrees, canon law, scriptural commentary and secular statutes – from the later medieval period. Although he provides a fascinating legal history of anti-homosexual attitudes in canonical, conciliar and secular legislation, Goodich can offer no evidence that these laws were ever applied, and we never see queers or queer subcultures in these documents. Either there are no trial records because there were no trials, or, possibly, the trial records have not been discovered and researched. Goodich prints an amazing appendix – documenting the record of the trial of Arnold Verniolle before the Inquisition in 1323 (to be discussed in a later chapter) – and reveals that the Inquisition's records are full of such trials, but there has been no attempt to uncover all these documents. I would suggest that the reading of court records is no more tedious than the reading of scholastic summae – and would gather more material about queer history.

Anti-gay laws are seldom enforced. It is not really true to say, for example, that in thirteenth-century France sodomites had their testicles amputated on the first offence, their penis amputated on the second, and were burned for a third offence, or that lesbians suffered similar penalties – because no one was prosecuted under this law. Medieval prosecutions are exceedingly rare, though there are exceptional cases: a knifemaker was burned to death in Ghent in 1292; a man was castrated in mid-fourteenth-century France. There were some fifty prosecutions in Florence from the mid-fourteenth century to the mid-fifteenth century, with the death sentence passed in perhaps a dozen cases. But by the mid-sixteenth century, when Benvenuto Cellini was convicted of sodomy, he was merely fined; subsequently convicted a second time, he was sentenced to four years' imprisonment, commuted by Duke Cosimo de' Medici to house arrest (Saslow, 1986).

Generally it is not until the fifteenth century that we find evidence of prosecutions. But the laws were applied neither consistently nor vigorously, and the cases are so sporadic that no patterns can be inferred and few conclusions drawn. An eyewitness in 1495 recalled seeing the corpses of two convicted Spanish sodomites hanged with their genitals strung around their necks (though the law officially required that they be castrated and stoned to death). Spain was particularly repressive, but prosecutions varied widely from city to city: from the late sixteenth century to the early seventeenth century there were fifty-two executions for sodomy in Seville, seventeen in Valencia, thirty-four in Zaragoza and only two in Barcelona; several lesbians in Granada were whipped and sent to the galleys. In France, between the mid-sixteenth and mid-seventeenth centuries in Paris there were 121 appeals against death sentences in sodomy cases; in 1533 two women were tried for tribadism but acquitted; in the sixteenth century several women who disguised themselves as men and married women were burned to death; in 1691 a sodomite was confined to the General Hospital for life; in 1750 an 18-year-old journeyman joiner and his consenting partner, a 24-year-old butcher, were burned at the stake. During a 120-year period in Geneva, from the mid-sixteenth century on, there were sixty-two prosecutions and thirty executions for sodomy. Two dozen monks from Ghent and Bruges were burned to death in the sixteenth century, but only three men were executed in the seventeenth century. Two women were flogged and banished for lesbianism and transvestism in Leiden before 1700. These details are horrendous – but they do not add up to a pattern of 'genocide' as claimed by Crompton (1978).

The kind of statistical analysis favoured by the Annales school of historical research simply will not work in the field of queer history. A good attempt at this method was made by Monter (1985), who has exhaustively uncovered the homosexual prosecutions in the law archives of Geneva (and Fribourg). He examines the distribution and clusters of prosecutions and relates that to contemporary religious and political events in order to draw some conclusions. His analysis of individual 'clumps' is excellent, but a close look at Monter's appendix listing seventy-five trials in Geneva from 1400 to 1800 illustrates the dangers of quantitative analysis. Monter counts the number of individual defendants rather than the number of cases or incidents. The seventy-five trials in fact relate to only thirty-eight cases: in eleven cases the *pair* of men caught in the act were tried separately. Monter maintains that 'The relative frequency of sodomy trials in the period 1555–1570 exactly coincides with the greatest activity of Geneva's famous morals tribunal, the Consistory' – but that 'relative frequency' consists of only ten cases (involving thirteen people). We can in fact establish a relationship between religious zeal and these prosecutions, but only because we know the exact circumstances of each individual case, not because of any estimation of 'relative frequency'. What after all do the Genevan prosecutions amount to in the seventeenth century? A pair of men in 1600; a group of twelve men arising from one incident ten years later; one three years later; one

WHAT IS QUEER HISTORY?

four years after that; one four years later; a pair two years later; a pair ten years later; a pair the next year; a pair ten years later which brings us to 1647; then a pair fifteen years later; one ten years later which brings us to 1672 – then none until 113 years later, in 1785. I submit that no patterns can be inferred from these figures.

It was not until the early eighteenth century, in the Netherlands and in England, that sodomy was prosecuted with systematic vigour. Very large numbers of sodomites were brought to trial and executed in eighteenth-century Amsterdam, but Theo van der Meer (1989) has demonstrated beyond doubt that this was not the result of long-term systematic persecution, but that each of the three main sequences of trials that took place (in 1730, 1764 and 1776) 'were the result of a snowball effect. It always started with the more or less accidental arrest of a sodomite and his subsequent confessions.' The same snowball effect arose from raids on molly-houses in England, though nets were deliberately cast to catch sodomitical fish.

In England the gap between legislation and enforcement is very wide indeed. The death penalty for buggery was instituted in 1533, and the first prosecution occurred in 1540, when Walter, Lord Hungerford, was beheaded on charges of sodomy and harbouring a traitor. The second prosecution took place in 1541, when Nicholas Udall was convicted in the Privy Council but merely lost his position as headmaster of Eton. The third prosecution occurred in 1631 – *almost a century later* – when the Earl of Castlehaven was convicted of sodomy and the rape of his wife. This hardly adds up to a history of persecution. Burg (1985) easily demonstrates that the earliest sodomy trials prosecuted men not for sodomy alone but only when compounded with religious heresy, political offences, gross violation of class distinctions or violence; even the efforts of the Puritans to crack down on cardplaying, bearbaiting, drunkenness and homosexuality do not provide hard and fast evidence of widespread social abhorrence of homosexuality during the reigns of James I and Charles I. Admittedly one execution is sufficient to strike fear into the heart of anyone contemplating sodomy – but one execution is hardly enough to terrify three or four generations of potential queers.

In America, a conviction for sodomy in 1861 was the first such conviction for almost two hundred years, despite the presence of severe statutes during those centuries. A survey of the various seventeenth- and eighteenth-century anti-homosexual statutes passed in the various states, ably done by Jonathan Katz (1976), does not lead to any significant conclusions, because the penalties were not supported by prosecutions.

It may be interesting to survey the various legal methods of expressing abhorrence of the sin of Sodom, and to show how this could be in conflict with humanistic and rationalistic ideals of the emerging Republic, but it is more properly a subject of legal history rather than queer history.

It has been argued, but I do not think the statistics are sufficient to prove the case, that there was an 'upsurge' of prosecutions for sodomy in England from the 1780s. Technically this may be accurate, but a single raid on a molly-house that results in the prosecution of fifteen offenders does not signify more of an 'upsurge' than two raids that lead to the prosecution of only six offenders. It has not been shown that there was a significant increase in legal harassment in general, because there has been no comparative study of arrests that did not lead to prosecution.

Laws against homosexuality have never been enforced with full vigour systematically in any country: prosecution always proceeds by fits and starts. For example, in Belgium there were no executions for sodomy until the last decade of the thirteenth century; there were perhaps one hundred executions in the fourteenth century, and the same in the fifteenth century, with only a few in the sixteenth and seventeenth centuries, and then hardly any at all in the eighteenth century. This is in comparison with very marked persecutions in the Netherlands (formerly part of Belgium), and despite the growth of a visible queer subculture in the major Belgian cities; homosexuality was decriminalized by the *Code Pénal* when the French took over at the very end of the eighteenth century. Even for this one single country it is enormously difficult to find a satisfactory explanation for why the law was more harshly enforced in some centuries than in others.

Notable increases in prosecution/persecution are virtually always linked to specific prosecutors (be they specific judges, or police chiefs or moral-reform groups) rather than to a general rise of popular prejudice; there is rarely any link to the growth of anti-gay attitude throughout the populace at large, at least until the mid-twentieth century, and even then public sentiment is usually deliberately stirred up by newspaper proprietors wishing to increase their circulation or politicians eager for votes. The supposed increase in intolerance during the rise of market capitalism (as posited by the social constructionists) is refuted by an actual *decrease* in the severity of the laws: homosexual acts were decriminalized by the French Penal Code of 1791 and the Napoleonic Code; the death penalty was dropped in late eighteenth-century Russia, Prussia, Austria and Tuscany; penalties were reduced in all the Latin American countries; homosexuality was decriminalized in Brazil in 1830; and penalties for homosexual acts steadily declined in Britain as imperialism advanced. If harsh penalties are adduced as evidence of greater intolerance, then lenient penalties must be similarly taken as evidence of greater tolerance.

The very narrow legalistic approach to the history of homosexuality has produced a host of fallacies about the punishment and regulation of homosexuality. It is often stated, for example, that, in Britain, hanging for a conviction of the felony of sodomy was not abolished until 1861, that the misdemeanour of homosexual intercourse (excluding anal intercourse) was first created in the same year, and that all homosexual acts, even kissing in private, were first criminalized in 1885. All of these misconceptions rest upon the recodification of the laws in the 1861 Offences against the Person Act, as amended in 1885 (the Labouchère Amendment), which was a consolidating Act that simply gathered together and restated in Victorian terms the very same felonies and misdemeanours that had existed in English law since 1533.

The single most-often repeated fallacy of homosexual history is the claim that the Labouchère Amendment made all homosexual behaviour illegal 'for the first time'. In fact, the laws against homosexuality throughout the eighteenth and early nineteenth centuries, though *narrowly defined* (sodomy in the sense of anal intercourse punishable severely, often by death), were *broadly applied* (sodomy as anything other than provable anal intercourse, punishable by a fine, the pillory and two years' imprisonment). Before 1885 most of the men prosecuted under the anti-gay law were convicted of 'attempted sodomy', a misdemeanour covering behaviour such as oral intercourse, mutual masturbation, frottage, groping and soliciting. Though the Amendment contains the phrase 'in public or in private', it was always the case that sex between men in private was a criminal offence: men were regularly convicted solely upon the testimony of the other consenting adult party, and 'in private' was never raised as a possible defence. The Amendment's phrase 'gross indecency' is simply the late-Victorian phrase which *exactly replaces* the eighteenth-century phrase 'attempted sodomy'. It is nothing more than a typically reticent Victorian reworking of something unacceptably coarse.

The Amendment had no effect whatsoever upon queers' own conception of what was legal or illegal. The Amendment was not debated, nor was there any contemporary discussion of its meaning or effect after it was introduced. Not only was Oscar Wilde not its 'first victim', but under legislation existing for the previous two centuries he would have received the same sentence, two years' imprisonment. It has not been established that prosecutions increased because of this Amendment, or indeed that there was any significant increase in homosexual prosecutions throughout the nineteenth century, as claimed by Weeks (1977) (Gilbert, review of *Coming Out*, 1985b). The effect of the trials of Oscar Wilde has also been exaggerated. Frank Harris's anecdote that homosexual men fled across the Channel in droves the day of Wilde's conviction was made up by him, and is wholly false. Members of the Cambridge Apostles – a secret society whose members preached the 'higher sodomy' while practising the lower – such as E. M. Forster, Lytton Strachey, Leonard Woolf and John Maynard Keynes, and the Bloomsbury Group in general, in the early years of this century pursued numerous liaisons unhampered by any fears supposedly instilled in queer society by the prosecution of Oscar Wilde only a decade earlier.

The fallacy of 'anachronism'

Anachronism is a double-edged sword. Errors in historical interpretation arise not only from projecting modern views and concepts upon the past but from drawing general conclusions solely from modern circumstances without a historical perspective. In earlier chapters I have challenged the social constructionist position that it is anachronistic to regard anyone as being 'homosexual' before the nineteenth century, by illustrating premodern conceptualizations of various people and categories that in my view are patently queer. Here I wish to approach the problem of anachronism – admittedly an important issue in all historical analysis – by showing how censorship and suppression (to be discussed in detail in the following chapter) have helped to create the false view that modern queer interpretations of premodern lives are anachronistic. In a great many cases queer interpretations were expressed by contemporaries of the persons or events in question, but they have been suppressed; in other words, queer readings do not have to be projected backwards – they only have to be rediscovered.

Modern queer readings of Renaissance art and literature are usually dismissed as 'anachronistic' – but there are no grounds for this misjudgement. Donatello's statues of *David* and *St George* became homoerotic icons of the young boyfriend figure during his own lifetime, and there are various contemporary stories about Donatello's homosexuality in the court of Cosimo de' Medici. A classic modern 'anachronistic' reading of Dante holds that because Dante treats Brunetto Latini and the sodomites noticeably sympathetically in the *Inferno*, we can infer that Dante shared their homosexual feelings; but this same conclusion was drawn by an anonymous commentator in the fourteenth century and therefore cannot be called anachronistic.

The classic example is the case of Michelangelo. His male nudes, whether in paintings (the *ignudi* in the Sistine Chapel) or sculpture (notably *David* and the *Dying Captive*) for centuries have inspired homoerotic sensibilities (for example, in one of Robert Mapplethorpe's homoerotic photographs a young man assumes the pose of the *Dying Captive*) – something again dismissed as anachronistic. But when the queer art historian John Addington Symonds was granted access to the Buonarroti family archives in Florence in 1863 he discovered a note written in the margin of the poems by Michelangelo's grand-nephew (called Michelangelo the Younger) to the effect that the poems must not be published in their original form because they expressed '*amor ... virile*', literally 'masculine love', a polite Renaissance euphemism for *paiderastia*, better translated as 'male–male desire'. Symonds thus was able to make public the fact that when Michelangelo the Younger prepared his great-uncle's poetry for posthumous publication in 1623 he had changed all the masculine pronouns in the love poems to feminine pronouns, thus ensuring that any sentiments in the poems that could not be interpreted as being merely platonic would at least be interpreted as being normal, i.e. heterosexual.

Many of Michelangelo's contemporaries were also aware that he was 'different', and a queer contemporary, Varchi, recognized his work as being homosexual. Michelangelo's contemporaries Leonardo da Vinci, Sandro Botticelli, Benvenuto Cellini and Giovanni Antonio Bazzi ('Il Sodoma') were publicly charged with sodomy, and Michelangelo, like them, was offered 'services' by the *ragazzi* who worked as apprentices in the art studios. Whether his love-gift to Tommaso Cavalieri of a drawing of the rape of Ganymede is an emblem of neo-platonic sublimation or an invitation to bed, there cannot be too much doubt that he had homosexual relations with his model Gherardo Perini and his assistant Febo di Poggio. In any case, regardless of all this contextual evidence, Michelangelo the Younger's censorship provides as much evidence as is needed to prove that Michelangelo's sonnets were *perceived as homosexual during his own time*, and the inclusion of them in *The Penguin Book of Homosexual Verse* is not the least bit anachronistic.

A combination of camp and boy-beauty can be found in many seventeenth-century Venetian paintings. Perhaps we are 'anachronistically reading into' the male pairs shown in paintings such as Johann Carlloth's *Mercury Piping to Argus* or Antonio Zanchi's *Seneca and Nero* or

Bernardo Strozzi's *The Baptism of Christ*, but the full-bottomed shepherd being carried away by the eagle in Damiano Mazza's *The Rape of Ganymede* is unmistakably the object of queer desire. That may equally be true of the paintings of Saint Sebastian by Antonio Belluci and Niccolò Renieri. And the models for many paintings by Caravaggio are patently hustlers and the boyfriends of his queer patrons. Frankly I cannot see how any definition of queer or homosexual that excluded Caravaggio would be complete or useful. Nor do I see how his paintings can be misread or anachronistically 'appropriated' by modern queer people.

The 'friendship tradition' is a homosexual literary tradition whose key texts were created by men who loved men. The ideology was created for the classical world in the *Symposium* and *Phaedrus* by Plato, whose boyfriends included Agathon and Aster, and in *De Amicitia* by Cicero, who freed his lover Tiro from slavery. These texts were revived for medieval Christians by *De spirituali amicitia* by St Aelred of Rievaulx, who admitted that during his adolescence 'the sweetness of love and the impurity of lust combined to take advantage of the inexperience of my youth', and revived yet again for the Renaissance in *De Amore* by Marsilio Ficino who loved Giovanni Calvacanti. Many of Ficino's contemporaries hinted at his homosexual inclinations after his death, rumours that his biographers succeeded in refuting, though some followers, such as Benedetto Varchi, were openly suspected of sodomy, and several were brought to court. Two of his followers, Giovanni Pico della Mirandola and Girolamo Benivieni were buried together, with an inscription acknowledging that 'their souls were joined by Love while living'.

From the mid-sixteenth century the concept of platonic love was carefully heterosexualized by philosophers because it was recognized that socratic love, *amor socraticus*, had been a disguise for homosexual love and was now openly identified with sodomy (Dall'Orto, 1989). When Edmund Spenser revived the pastoral friendship tradition by imitating Virgil's description of Corydon's love for Alexis in *The Shepheardes Calender* (1579) it was immediately recognized by his contemporary, the learned pedant known only by the initials E. K., that some would interpret it homosexually:

> In thys place seemeth to be some sauour of disorderly loue, which the learned call paederastice: but it is gathered beside his meaning. For who that hath red Plato his dialogue called Alcybiades, Xenophon and Maximum Tyrius of Socrates opinions, may easily perceiue, that such loue is much to be alowed and liked of, specially

so meant, as Socrates vsed it: who sayth, that in deed he loued Alcybiades extremely, yet not Alcybiades owne selfe. And so is paederastice much to be praeferred before gynerastice, that is the loue which enflameth men with lust toward woman kind. But yet let no man thinke, that herein I stand with Lucian or hys deuelish disciple Vnico Aretino, in defence of execrable and horrible sinnes of forbidden and vnlawful fleshlinesse.

This is not a post-Freudian reading that violates the temper of Spenser's times. Sir Philip Sidney in his *Defense of Poesy* (probably written at almost the same time as Spenser's *Calender*) says that Plato in his *Phaedrus* and *Symposium*, and Plutarch in his *Discourse on Love*, both 'authorize abhominable filthiness'. William Webbe in *A Discourse of English Poetrie* (1586) describes how his circle of literary acquaintances had debated the problem raised by E. K.'s commentary, and he concludes that critics have no right to prescribe a poet's morality. He even speculates upon Spenser's non-literary behaviour: 'perhaps he learned it from the Italians' (Norton, Website). Francis Palgrave in the nineteenth century summed up the complacent view that Spenser's allusion to Virgil's second eclogue was an 'anachronistic impropriety. ... Spenser is here, of course, only obeying the literary impulse of the age towards classical reproduction.'

Any attempt to dismiss the importance of romantic friendship in real life by saying that it is 'typical' of certain periods must come up against contemporary views that it comprises a special category that is markedly different from ordinary friendship. For 'special' I read 'queer' as being the nearest modern equivalent term. When reading passionate expressions of endearment between men, I submit that it is relatively easy for queer readers to recognize the difference between sycophancy and love, between rhetoric and passion, and that most of the writers of what I would call 'gay love letters' themselves knew what side of the division they were on. Lord Hervey says of his letters to Stephen Fox in 1730, 'I have often thought, if any very idle Body had Curiosity enough to intercept & examine my Letters, they would certainly conclude they came rather from a Mistress than a Friend' (Norton, 1997). Queer historians *do* have that curiosity, and *do* come to that conclusion – and rightly so.

Domenico Fusco in his 1953 biography of Pietro Aretino (1492–1556) dismisses the abundant contemporary accusations that Aretino was a sodomite as merely unfounded gossip. A playful letter written by Aretino to Giovanni de' Medici in which he explains that he has decided to give up sodomy temporarily because he has fallen in love with a woman, but will return to it soon – 'and if I escape with my honour from this madness, will bugger as much and as much for me as for my friends' – has been dismissed as a joke. Letters to Aretino from Federico Gonzaga in 1528, who was acting as a pimp to obtain boys for Aretino, have been generally ignored. The accusations need to be re-examined more fully by non-censorious gay-friendly scholars, but whatever our final conclusions may be, a queer reading would certainly *not* be anachronistic.

It is a commonplace for historians eager to dismiss the taint of homo-sexuality to point out that the sharing of beds was a very common practice until quite recent times 'and no one ever thought anything of it'. It *is* true that it was a very common practice, but it is also the case that people *did* think about it. Ellen Nussey and Charlotte Brontë always shared a bed at the vicarage at Haworth. Ellen tried to persuade Charlotte not to leave for Brussels to open a school, but to remain at home, to which Charlotte replied on 20 January 1842: 'You tantalise me to death with talking of conversations by the fireside and between the blankets' (Miller, 1989). The words 'and between the blankets' were omitted from the official biography by Elizabeth Gaskell, who had become Charlotte's friend only at the very end of her life. Since Mrs Gaskell (and Brontë's husband) were sensitive to this issue in 1857, two years after Charlotte's death, a queer view about sharing a bed must have been a *contemporary* possibility, and not an anachronistic reading imposed by modern queer historians.

The period of 'romantic friendship' between men in the mid-nineteenth century has also been unfairly dismissed as being in no way homoerotic. Tennyson's *In Memoriam* (1850) – an elegy for his beloved Arthur Hallam who died young – is the high point and archetype of 'manly love' in Victorian literature. However, Tennyson himself was aware of its problematic homoerotic nature, and homosexuality was not something that was beyond his ken (for example, he had read the Marquis de Sade's *120 Days of Sodom*). Two of Tennyson's friends, William Butler and Richard Monckton Milnes, certainly had sexual relations with men as well as women. Milnes was notorious as a collector of homosexual pornography, and Hallam acknowledged to Milnes that 'I have been the creature of impulse, … the basest passions have roused themselves in the deep caverns of my nature and swept like storm winds over me' (Spencer, 1995). In an essay 'On Cicero' Hallam called 'Greek love' 'the noblest kind of love'. His letters show an idealization of 'manly love' that modern readers will recognize as obvious sublimation. There were rumours that he had slashed his wrist, though it was claimed that a doctor had opened the vein to determine that he was dead (of an ague), a highly unusual practice. In the late 1870s Tennyson began revising his elegy for republication, during which he systematically removed indicators of its homoeroticism, for example by omitting masculine pronouns. Again, this is clear evidence that a homoerotic reading of something written in the 1850s is *not* anachronistic, but was in fact a possibility clearly recognized by the author himself.

The inversion of pronouns (and avoidance of gendered reference) is common in homosexual poetry, from John Addington Symonds who gave his lover, the gondolier Angelo Fusato, the name Stella and called him 'she' in the 1890s, to May Sarton who 'bearded the pronouns' in her 1961 sonnet sequence 'A Divorce of Lovers' (Faderman, 1994). Few writers had the audacity of Baron Corvo, whose *Desire and Pursuit of the Whole* (1934) concerns a man's pursuit of the 16-year-old girl Zilda who dresses as a boy and takes the name Zildo at the beginning of the novel; 'she' never resumes 'her' female identity, but respectable readers perhaps never realized the hoax that was being played upon them.

American literature of the Victorian period is full of romantic friendship of a very passionate nature. Whitman was dismissed from his job as a clerk in the Interior Department's Office of Indian Affairs when it was discovered he had written an 'indecent' book; this seems to me to suggest – contrary to the modern view – that Whitman's contemporaries did not think that *Leaves of Grass* illustrated merely romantic friendship. Whitman himself took pains to disguise the intensity and nature of his love for the young bus conductor Peter Doyle, which would have been unnecessary if he and his contemporaries had classified it as mere camaraderie. Not only did he use a code when writing about Peter in his diary – '16.4', being the sixteenth and fourth letters of the alphabet – but he even replaced the word 'him' with 'her': for example, 'pursue her no more ... avoid seeing her, or meeting her' (15 July 1870). Surely this falsification of sex object indicates a consciousness that his love was homosexual rather than heterosexual. Whitman acknowledged to Carpenter that what lay behind *Leaves of Grass* was 'concealed, studiedly concealed; some passages left purposely obscure. ... I think there are truths which it is necessary to envelop or wrap up' (Miller, 1995).

6

The Evidence of Things Not Seen

What are the main sources of queer history and what is the nature of the evidence? There are a limited number of archaeological artefacts, and for the very recent period we have recordings of interviews and radio, television and cinematic documentaries. But the vast bulk of evidence for queer history comes from written records whose nature is highly problematical. Legal records – laws, trial records, police reports, records ranging from the Inquisition to twentieth-century moral reform societies – are officially anti-gay, or at least records of anti-gay prosecutions. Sermons and other types of polemic, be it religious, humanistic, medical or legalistic, pamphlets or full-length diatribes, are usually anti-gay. Imaginative literary and artistic (and cinematic) sources are usually satiric and stereotypical. Newspapers generally report anti-gay prosecutions and promote anti-gay polemics. The only sources that are potentially free from homophobia are letters and memoirs/diaries by queers, but those are often destroyed, censored or self-censored. In other words, the vast majority of sources upon which any ethnic history has to rely are markedly prejudiced against the objective documentation of queer culture. By far the largest category is the indirect evidence provided by suppression and censorship: far from erasing the evidence from memory, acts of suppression, by providing so much smoke, point the historian in the direction of the fire, though when we reach it we may find only ashes.

Trials

The fullest and most trustworthy sources are the surviving records of trials for buggery, attempted buggery and solicitation, and blackmail for men; and trials for 'fraudulent' acts of cross-dressing and same-sex marriage, and occasionally 'sodomy' for women. In England at least, queers were given fair trials: the prosecutors made a genuine attempt to find out the truth, and defendants were allowed to have their say in the dock. For centuries these represent the rare occasions on which queers were allowed to speak for themselves: precious testimony that would otherwise never become part of the public record, because such people were hardly likely to record their 'crimes' in letters and diaries. Witnesses were often called to testify to the character (good or bad) of the accused, which ensures that the 'criminal' act is usually seen in a wider social context, with cultural value and no little amount of human interest. Circumstantial evidence was accorded great importance, because the actual commission of sexual penetration and emission were difficult to prove. Virtually every trial for the felony of sodomy or the misdemeanour of attempted sodomy throughout the eighteenth century attempts to determine whether or not the accused is a molly: although the specific act is the crime in question, it was invariably assumed (correctly, in my view) that such acts were performed by *homosexual people*. As a result, these records contain a great deal of information about the molly subculture, with a rich variety of details and many indicators of personal lifestyles. In more recent times judges would rule out such circumstantial evidence as strictly irrelevant to the commission of a criminal act.

The usefulness of trial records paradoxically declines as we move closer to recent history. From about 1800 queer trials were censored by the judges and the records become increasingly partial. In 1806 in a trial of five men sentenced to death for sodomy, the judge ordered that no notes be taken during the proceedings; the men called one another 'brother', so presumably queer culture rather than queer sex was what especially shocked the court. Regarding the trial of a queer publican, William Jackson, also in 1806, the compiler and publisher of most of the 'Newgate Calendars', noted that 'in such cases the judge generally forbids notes to be made' (Norton, 1992). No notes were recorded during the important trial of the soldiers Hepburn and White in 1811 (resulting from the famous raid on the Vere Street Coterie), presumably because important (royal) personages were implicated. From about this date the records of sodomy trials become so brief as to be nearly useless for recording queer culture, and one has to rely on newspaper reports.

It needs to be emphasized that historical evidence is not legal evidence: the historian builds up a case using information and speculation that would be rigorously excluded by the defence lawyer. Oscar Wilde (convicted even though he told a number of bold-faced lies) would not be convicted today for the technical reason that the amount of time that had passed between the acts and the report of the acts exceeded the statute of limitations. But whatever the fine points of the law, the queer historian would find him 'guilty'. It is fairly obvious that most people prosecuted for homosexuality were 'guilty', even when they were acquitted in specific cases. The nineteenth century is full of cases where men were arrested and acquitted for soliciting sex in a urinal – only to be tried and convicted for the same offence several years later. Back through the fifteenth century the records are full of repeat offenders who got off with a warning two or three occasions previously. Defendants have often hoodwinked the jury, whose members are too dim and straight to understand the evidence in front of them. Marianne Woods and Jane Pirie, who were accused of lesbianism around 1810 (the basis of Lillian Hellman's play *The Children's Hour*, 1934), sued for libel and won, mainly because the judge felt that it was 'preposterous' to suggest that middle-class women would have sex with one another (Faderman, 1985a).

The principal problem about using trial records for discovering queer history is the aura of criminality that hangs over them. Queer trials are only a small part of the record of theft, murder, sexual violence and poverty, and the queer world appears to be (and often is) part of the criminal and sexual underworlds. But it is relatively easy to demonstrate that most of the people convicted for homosexual offences have no record of being convicted of any other criminal offences, and that queer resorts are part of the working-class subculture rather than the criminal underworld (though they sometimes overlap). At the linguistic level, a commonplace pick-up will be encumbered with the prosecutor's attack on 'the horrible and detestable crime of buggery', which only obscures our perception of the matter. Social constructionists not only retain this vocabulary but even emphasize it so as to concentrate on the homophobic attitudes of society. The same approach is taken towards medical case records, that is they emphasize the anti-gay medical jargon rather than the words of the queer respondents.

In contrast, I believe that the queer historian should gently filter away this distracting vocabulary so that the gay life can stand out more clearly. I do not regard this as censorship, although it does involve selective use of the text of the records. I would never advocate the suppression of any *queer* text contained in such trials (even if it were politically incorrect, for example involving violent child abuse), but I do believe that the anti-gay discourse of the prosecution is part of an alien text that need not be the subject of our scrutiny always and for ever. The object of our study should be the queer life revealed by the trial, not the trial itself.

Ironically, lack of criminalization often results in lack of historical evidence of homosexuality. Just as the absence of legislation against lesbianism is largely responsible for the absence of lesbian history, there is no evidence of any queer subculture in Sweden until the 1880s. This lack of evidence almost certainly reflects the absence of court cases, because

Khnumhotep (left) and Niankhkhnum embrace: 'Joined in life and joined in death.' Bas-relief portrait in their joint tomb at Saqqara, c. 2600 BC. © 1991 Greg Reeder.

Hellenistic statue group, 1st century BC, possibly representing Orestes and Pylades. The head of the figure on the left was cut off and replaced by a bust of Antinous around AD 130. Hadrian may have re-used the group as a funeral monument to his lover, making it an early example of queer appropriation.

Bacchantes beating Orpheus, etching by Albrecht Dürer, 1494. The banderole in the tree bears the legend 'Orfeus der erst puseran' (Orpheus, the first bugger), making this an early explicit portrayal of 'the homosexual'. Kunsthalle, Hamburg.

Portuguese Delft tile, 17th century, discovered in London's Lambeth Road district among the ruins of Norfolk House. Dubbed 'The Bonking Cherubs' when it was unearthed by archaeologists in 1991, it may illustrate a children's guessing game – but the iconography suggests homosexual horseplay.
Photograph: Museum of London Archaeology Service.

Cartoon accompanying an *Evening Standard* comment on the teaching of classics in English schools, 1996. Courtesy Ron McTrusty. Author's collection.

Anne Lister's journal, 21 September 1825, a mixture of ordinary writing and code. At the bottom of the page she uses code to describe how she and Marianna prepare to exchange lockets containing each other's pubic hair. Courtesy Calderdale District Archives.

Photograph of a youth of Taormina by Baron Wilhelm von Gloeden, c. 1900, in the pose of Frederic Leighton's painting *The Bath of Psyche* (1890).

Actor in the Cambridge University Amateur Dramatic Society, playing a woman's role without a wig. From an 1890s photograph album. Collection Keith Cavers.

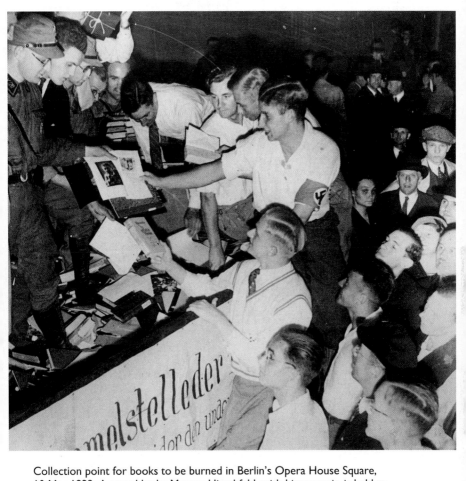

Collection point for books to be burned in Berlin's Opera House Square, 10 May 1933. A pamphlet by Magnus Hirschfeld, with his portrait, is held up for inspection by Nazi students. Photograph: Hulton Getty.

Right: Anna P., who lived for many years as a man.

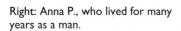

Below: Hedwig W. (left), accompanied by a friend with an even stronger butch identity. Hedwig was a friend of Magnus Hirschfeld, and lived for two years in Berlin under the name Herbert. From Hirschfeld's *Sexuelle Zwischenstufen* (*Sexual Intermediates*), 1922. By permission of the British Library, Cup 363.1.5/2.

Right: Photo-study of a hustler (?), by
Willinger, Hamburg, c. 1930.
Reprinted in the Swiss homophile
magazine *Der Kreis/Le Cercle*, January
1952. By permission of the British
Library, Cup 820.u.18.

Below: 'Shore-fisher': nude study by
Adolf Brand, in his Berlin homophile
magazine *Der Eigene*, 1921–2.
By permission of the British Library,
Cup 820.u.19.

Song cover, 1921, featuring the popular female impersonator Bert Errol. 'Hold me like a flower, For one little hour, And leave me with a smile.' Collection Keith Cavers.

Colin Ross (half of the female impersonation duo of Bartlett and Ross, famous in the 1930s–40s) performing a pantomime turn late in his career. This photograph is cryptically signed on the back, in two hands: 'Pour Mon Bon Ami – Frank / and the same to you – Happily Colin 13.5.52.' Collection Keith Cavers.

Sweden had no law clearly directed against homosexual relations. It was not until 1864 that they passed a law against 'unnatural' intercourse between persons. Evidence of the widespread use of parks and public places in Stockholm for homosexual assignation is to be found in records collected by the Swedish police in the 1880s. This is not evidence that a subculture and identity were socially constructed in the 1880s; it merely reflects the fact that evidence was not gathered until stimulated by the passing of anti-gay legislation.

Literature

Most queer historians (and social constructionists) are students and professors of literature rather than history (cf. Abelove *et al.*, 1993). We have not adequately come to grips with the problems of evaluating the historical nature of the evidence provided by imaginative literature. One of the problems of confusing the history of homosexuality with the history of attitudes towards homosexuals, or the idea of the homosexual, is that the evidence is treated as a single unitary discourse or text, whereas individual texts ought to be carefully differentiated and subjected to 'weighting'. For example, of any specific written source we ought to ask if it is by a queer, and, if so, does it express his or her own views or the views of society; if it is not written by a queer, is it written by a gay-friendly person, or is it obviously anti-gay, or is it pro- or anti-gay due perhaps to a hidden agenda? Is it a record of observations, or polemic? The structuralist and social constructionist position is that only the text exists and therefore no questions can be asked concerning the author, who is 'dead'. Whether or not this is arrant nonsense (I think it is), it incapacitates any textual queer history. The common-sense, and essentialist, view is that if we are examining fiction about lesbians we ought to establish a rating system which gives the greatest amount of 'truth-value' to works written by known lesbians on the one hand, and at the opposite end of the scale the least value to fiction written by known heterosexual men who hated lesbians. Much more meaning and relevance can be extracted from ostensibly autobiographical novels such as Sarah Scott's *Millennium Hall* (1762) than from Daniel Defoe's *Roxana* (1724) or even Samuel Richardson's *Pamela* (1740–1) (though this has an interesting, aggressive lesbian character, Mrs Jewkes). As autobiographical works are less likely to fall in with the 'ideological discourse' of the ruling classes, it becomes important for queer historians to establish such texts.

Fiction can be invaluable for articulating details of the intimate life and identity, but the study of lesbian and gay characters remains a literary rather than a historical study unless we carefully set out what we believe the links to be between literature and life. Donoghue's (1993) assumption that lesbians read such literature and were in some ways inspired by it as models is probably true, but still needs more underpinning than the few references that can be found, such as Anne Lister's record of the lesbian texts she read. In many ways literary texts are non-historical. Donoghue analyses the seventeenth- and eighteenth-century English translations of very important classical texts by Sappho, Ovid and Lucian – but it follows that these same texts can be used for the discussion of lesbianism in each and every century since they were written up through the twentieth century. The view that such texts were given subversive readings by lesbians, though probably correct, requires documentation by extra-literary sources such as diaries and letters or recorded conversations. Donoghue acknowledges that '*Passions Between Women* is a history not of facts but of texts, not of real women but of stories told about women, stories which reflected and formed both attitudes to lesbian culture and lesbian culture itself.' But it has to be said that lesbian texts were probably employed only by the book-reading classes. If we look at the male side of the coin, there is hardly any evidence that the mollies who formed the early eighteenth-century queer subculture ever read books, or that books played any role in the development of their markedly queer identities. Because literature has been subjected to so much censorship and self-censorship or distortion, ultimately it forms a very unreliable source for queer history:

> There is more truth about what it means to be gay packed into one of Hart Crane's letters about the 'kindness' of a twenty-year-old Bohemian athlete in a Cleveland park than can be found in all the fiction published during the decade [of the 1920s]. (Austen, 1977)

For the essentialist queer historian it is important to establish 'the queer text', but the problems of doing that are illustrated by the 3,000 lesbian pulp novels of the 1950s and 1960s cited in Gene Damon's bibliography of *The Lesbian in Literature* (1967 edition). Many of these were written by (straight) men for the consumption of (straight) men, but some were written by men for the consumption of lesbians, others by (straight or queer) women for the consumption of men, and some were written by lesbians for the consumption of lesbians. How can we determine which is which? Ann Bannon (pseudonym of Ann Thayer) and Valerie Taylor are real authors, but Sylvia Sharon is really Paul Little, who claims to have written 500 lesbian novels. Some of these novels contain distinctly different styles of writing, as if the sex scenes were inserted by the male editors to make a woman writer's novel of love into something more titillating for straight men. Before a historian can use these novels as a basis for understanding lesbian life in the 1950s, before we can determine when an image is a stereotyped prejudice or a reflection of experience, problems about the author and the audience need careful sorting out (Koski and Tilchen, 1975).

We must avoid interpreting evidence of homophobia as evidence of queer culture. It is very easy to document 'internalized homophobia' in literature written by queers from the 1930s to the 1960s: one can cite chapter and verse to show where Radclyffe Hall, to take the most famous example, picked up and duplicated allegedly anti-gay analyses in the sexological literature. But it is not strictly true, as Faderman (1985b) contends, that Hall and lesbians of her generation 'internalized this image' of the sick pervert. On the contrary, Radclyffe Hall and other feminists 'embraced, sometimes with ambivalence, the image of the mannish lesbian and the discourse of the sexologists about inversion primarily because they desperately wanted to break out of the asexual model of romantic friendship' (Newton, 1984). Hall presented herself as the mannish lesbian – tailored suit and monocle – that had been a reality, not a myth, since the 1890s or earlier, because it identified her as a sexual being. Several authors in the 1980s and 1990s revealed that they made the gay characters in their earlier novels commit suicide simply and solely because that was required by their editors and publishers. In the 1970s it was generally assumed (especially by gay liberationists) that the suicide of the gay character represented the internalized guilt and shame of the author. But we now know – what we should have known all along – that sad gay lives in fiction are the result of external censorship and oppression rather than internal self-oppression.

Censorship

The censorship and bowdlerization of erotic literature is of course an established fact, and I shall not belabour the point that queer erotic literature has been suppressed. What I wish to focus upon is the anti-queer substitution for the original texts. Heterosexualization is a very curious operation to which only queer history has been subjected. Not only are queer details deleted from the lives of notable people, but heterosexual details are gratuitously invented for them. In a comedy written two centuries after her death, Sappho was portrayed as the lover of the sailor Phaon, a figment of the heteroerotic imagination made popular by Ovid. Sappho's alleged marriage to Cercylas (*cercos*, 'penis') of Andros ('city of men') is a patent fabrication: 'Generations of classical scholars abused these bits of ancient wit to construct the preposterous image of a heterosexual Sappho whose unconventional [i.e. lesbian] love was a legend fabricated by slander or even by misogyny, and their falsehoods continue to be parroted in standard reference works' (Evelyn Gettone, 'Sappho', *EH*). In Vasco da Lucena's medieval French translation of the ancient Roman *History of Alexander the Great* by Quintus Curtius Rufus, Alexander's boyfriend, the eunuch Bagoas, appears in both text and illumination as Bagoas the beautiful young woman: Vasco says the change was made 'to avoid a bad example'. Saslow (1989) has traced the suppression of same-sex imagery in seventeenth-century art: for example Rubens's copy of a painting by Titian transforms embracing male *putti* into heterosexual couples, and Monteverdi's opera *Orfeo* omits the pederastic section of the life by Poliziano upon which it was based. The ancient story of the love of Polyeuct and Nearchos was transformed into a heterosexual triangle that included Polyeuct's wife 'Paulina', firstly by Corneille in the seventeenth century and then by Cammarano in the nineteenth century, a situation which 'is utterly wanting in the early texts' (Boswell, 1995). Horatio Alger (1834–99), the American novelist famous for his boys' stories promoting the American dream of success, early in his life was driven out of town for having sex with boys, evidence of which was suppressed and not rediscovered until 1971. Prior to that date, and even since that date, the biographies of 'the great American' simply created bogus relationships with women, complete with detailed episodes that were wholly fictitious. For domestic consumption Alger was a successful heterosexual, when in fact the great love of his life was a 10-year-old Chinese boy named Wing.

The suppression of queer themes in the most public art forms – the theatre, television and the cinema – has been amply demonstrated (Russo, 1987; Howes, 1993; Bourne, 1996). From about 1930 until 1961 the Hays Code, the voluntary self-censorship code of the American film industry, specifically forbade any representations of either male or female homosexuality. This resulted not only in indirection, subterfuge and camouflage, but in the rewriting of history:

> Hollywood rewrote original scripts, and even history, to ensure the exclusion of lesbian material – as witnessed, for example, by the

1950 *We Three* heterosexualized version of Lillian Hellman's play, *The Children's Hour*, or Garbo's portrayal of a heterosexual romance to explain the abdication of the Queen of Sweden in *Queen Christina*. (Kitzinger and Kitzinger, 1993)

Similarly for the Emperor of China:

> Although copious evidence exists to confirm the homosexuality of Puyi, final ruler of the Qing, the creative heterosexual love scenes in the acclaimed film *The Last Emperor* have created a lasting impression in both Asia and the West that Puyi zestfully took full advantage of his female concubines. (Hinsch, 1990)

Diaghilev's boyfriend Nijinsky is transformed into a woman, played by Moira Shearer, in the 1940s film *The Red Shoes*. Whenever a novel was adapted for the screen, the gay character was either straightened out or the gender was reversed. In 1952 Brian Desmond Hurst abandoned his dream of producing a film about Ludwig II because 'the (Bavarian) Royal Family didn't want any mention whatsoever of the King's homosexuality so it became pointless to continue with it' (cited by Bourne, 1996). Even theatrical and nightclub acts were censored through the 1920s and 1930s: female impersonation and pansy acts were prohibited, cabarets had their licences withdrawn if performers sang campy songs by Cole Porter, and theatre chains nationwide prohibited use of the words 'fairy' and 'pansy' in vaudeville routines (Chauncey, 1994). It is not really until the 1960s that film censorship ceases to be a serious problem, though film-makers had to proceed cautiously. John Trevelyan, Secretary of the British Board of Film Censors, in 1962 advised Bryan Forbes regarding Scene 404 of *The L-Shaped Room*:

> When Mavis talks about the love of her life, we learn from the photograph that this love was for another woman. ... I suggest that you shoot the scene in such a way as to make the omission of the photograph, if considered desirable, something which could be done without spoiling the scene. (Cited by Bourne, 1996)

'Obscenity'

The whole of queer history and culture, not merely queer sex, is frequently silenced. It is important to recognize that because of the common prejudice that male–male or female–female *love* is obscene *per se*, any texts that celebrate this love, despite being utterly devoid of explicit sexual details or even innuendo, are subject to suppression. When Christina Rossetti's brother edited her poetry for publication, he apparently destroyed some half-dozen of her poems, not because they were explicitly 'erotic', but simply because they were love poems addressed to women. The censorship of sexuality is seldom taken as seriously as the censorship of politics or religion, and because homosexuality is usually considered solely as a sexual 'problem' its censorship is rarely perceived as having racial or political overtones. The reason given for destroying Sappho's works was their 'immorality'. But the effects are the same as if the motivation were cultural imperialism, as it was when the English destroyed the archives of Ireland, or when Nazi newspapers described the destruction of Hirschfeld's Institute for Sexual Science as 'a deed of culture'. Some few examples of South American pottery depicting male anal intercourse and lesbian relations survive, but the vast majority of pottery illustrating sexual practices or representing sexual objects was destroyed by the Christian missionaries. Even in the twentieth century when a number of pre-Columbian pieces which showed same-sex images were unearthed in Peru, they were destroyed because they were regarded as 'insults to national honour'. There is much evidence suggesting widespread homosexual relationships among the Mayans during the sixteenth century, but the Spanish Jesuits destroyed the Aztec and Mayan libraries, so our knowledge about Aztec or Mayan queer culture does not predate the Conquest and does not come direct from the people themselves.

The censorship of queer history is the deliberate destruction of a culture, and it is no good making excuses for, say, early nineteenth-century historians by referring to their different sexual 'morals'. By regarding queers as people with dirty habits rather than people with a culture, sociologists and historians with more enlightened sexual 'morals' have connived at the obliteration of this culture. We must not lull ourselves into believing that this is merely a matter of distaste at obscenity. In India, from the 1920s to the 1940s,

> Gandhi decided to send squads of his devotees to destroy the erotic representations, particularly those depicting homoeroticism and lesbianism, carved into Hindu temples dating from the eleventh century, as part of a program to encourage both Indians and non-Indians to believe that such behaviors were the result of foreign, namely Euro-western, influence. (Conner et al., 1997)

This desecration was temporarily halted by Rabindranath Tagore, but renewed under Jawaharlal Nehru, who 'became extremely irritated with his friend Alain Daniélou when the latter, together with his lover, published photographs of the same-sex erotic and transgendered-themed sculptures.' Daniélou was no mere collector of obscene postcards; he was committed to making a photographic record of ancient queer culture before evidence of it was systematically effaced from Indian temples and monuments. Under Nehru the first law in Indian history was passed criminalizing homosexual relations, and most modern Indians firmly believe that homosexuality is a decadent Western import. This is the cultural equivalent of ethnic cleansing, and the battle is still under way. In 1993 Shivananda Khan, founder of London's Asian HIV health promotion agency the Naz Project, visited Daniélou in Rome to examine his collection of 10,000 photographs for 'proof that Asians have enjoyed gay sex for centuries', and subsequently showed pictures from Daniélou's archive to new members of the Naz male sexual health group in an effort to counter prejudice that homosexuality was a Western disease. In July 1996 Scotland Yard's child protection unit began investigating complaints that Shivananda Khan and his agency were distributing 'pornography'. He was suspended pending the outcome of inquiries; funding of the agency was discontinued and its staff were issued with redundancy notices (*Pink Paper*, 26 July 1996). The Naz Project, which has spread the safer-sex message among Asian, Turkish and Iranian communities in Britain and which has worked on similar projects in Bangladesh, Delhi and Calcutta, seems unlikely to survive this crisis. (Daniélou has since died, and donated his collection to a Berlin museum.)

The masculinization of feminine and lesbian iconography is current practice in Gujarat, and anti-gay cultural vandalism has been witnessed by Giti Thadani (1996):

> In Bhuveneshvar, at the Lingraj temple, I saw the breasts of a goddess being cut, then polished over with orange, and a new male divinity was born. At Tara Tarini, the temple of the lesbian twin goddesses, the original iconography of the goddesses in an embrace has been replaced by a heterosexual image.

Normative heterosexuality has been retrospectively imposed upon the history of India.

In China queer culture has received similar treatment. The 'Two Flower Temple', built near Guilin in southern China in the late seventeenth or early eighteenth century to honour the homosexual love of the handsome scholar Choy and a male actor, both murdered when they refused to submit sexually to a rogue named Wong, attracted pilgrims celebrating same-sex love until the nineteenth century – when it was rededicated as the 'Temple of Virtuous Female Ancestors', 'its earlier history purposely buried' (Conner *et al.*, 1997; it was subsequently destroyed by the Japanese in 1894).

Outright destruction

Research into queer history faces an insuperable problem – the outright total destruction of the queer record. Much of our knowledge about homosexuality in the ancient world comes from literary works featuring homosexual characters or incidents which are peripheral to the central action and hence contain only a limited amount of information. But many works which do not survive were devoted entirely to homosexuality, and presumably would have given us a much fuller picture: for example, Athenaeus, at the beginning of the third century, cites the titles of no-longer-extant works such as *The Pederasts* by Diphilus, a play called *Ganymede*, and *The Effeminates* by Cratinus. Four lost plays by Aeschylus were pederastic in theme, as was Euripides's tragedy *Chrysippus* and Sophocles's *Lovers of Achilles*. There seem to have been at least a dozen ancient comedies entitled *Sappho*; presumably they would have satirized a licentious lesbian and were full of realistic everyday details about queer life. Of course a vast amount of Greek literature in general has disappeared, and this is a problem common to all historical investigation. Nevertheless, the fact that not one single play dealing entirely with a homosexual theme has survived seems to suggest that queer works were deliberately suppressed and destroyed rather than merely lost during the passage of time.

As Christianity established its base in the remains of the crumbling Roman Empire, celebrations of 'pagan immorality' were systematically destroyed by monastic compilers busily engaged in rewriting history with a Christian slant. The destruction of the works of Sappho of Lesbos (c. 612–558 BC) is deemed by many, straight as well as gay, men as well as women, to be the greatest single loss in all literature. Although in her own day she was widely popular and there were even statues and coins in her honour, her works were burned in the late fourth century during the tenure of Gregory Nazianzen Bishop of Constantinople (c. 390), appointed by Emperor Theodosius's First Ecumenical Council of Constantinople, which outlawed paganism and declared homosexuality to be a crime punishable by death. In the Western Empire, only fragments survived the further destruction ordered by Pope Gregory VII during his reign (1073–85). These consist mostly of phrases quoted as examples in ancient books on rhetoric and poetic diction, and the archaeological discovery in 1897 of copies of a fourth-century Alexandrian edition on shreds of papyrus subsequently used as wadding material to stuff mummified sacred animals in Egypt – what survives typically consists of only one or two strips torn from a scroll, so that virtually every line has several gaps. In all, scholars have pieced together some 600 lines from a total output estimated at 12,000 lines – tantalizingly insufficient for the reconstruction of lesbian history, but precious for all that (Klaich, 1974). Only two complete (or nearly complete) poems of Sappho survived outright destruction, but did not survive censorship, at least in their English translations. Her 'Hymn to Aphrodite' in its last line indicates that the gender of the beloved is feminine, but translators regularly rendered this as 'he' until the twentieth century. 'Blest as the Immortal Gods Is He' is an ode addressed to Sappho's mistress, but its pronouns were transposed in the late eighteenth century. Many women also translated Sappho, but were as guilty of censorship as the men, sometimes even more so (Donoghue, 1993).

It is not solely Christians who are responsible. Homer's *Iliad* was subjected to censorship even in ancient times, for example by the Alexandrian editor Aristarchus, who omitted a line in Book XVI in which 'Achilles asks the gods to rid the world of all humanity except Patroclus and himself', and a line in Book XIV about Achilles mourning Patroclus's death, in which Thetis finds him 'Lying in the arms of Patroclus / crying shrill' (Spencer, 1995). If lines with homosexual import could be censored at such an early stage, it is quite possible that the oral tradition regarding the homosexual relationship between Achilles and Patroclus was modified by the time the epic was written down for posterity. Many modern homophile readers have sensed the homosexual relationship in the story, even without resorting to a psychoanalytical interpretation.

John Boswell, in his research into the ceremony of same-sex union that existed in the eastern Christian Church from the sixth to the sixteenth century, came across much evidence of the censorship of documents:

> folios from the ceremony have been ripped out of at least one Euchologion from the thirteenth century, ... and in two other Greek prayer books the folios immediately *following* the ceremony have been torn out, suggesting either that the censor was not good at reading Greek or that there was some additional text that could not be shared. Even Gerald of Wales' [late twelfth century or early

thirteenth century] description of the ceremony in Ireland has been defaced in one of its recensions and tampered with in others. ... [The title] has been cut out of the page, along with a drawing. This was obviously deliberate. (Boswell, 1995)

Thus visual evidence as well as textual evidence has been destroyed. In two twelfth-century liturgical texts that describe this ceremony, the phrase 'united together' is immediately followed by a lacuna in the manuscript; in another case the phrase is followed by the very rare word *euchlinus*, which seems to mean 'well in bed', so censorship of the homoerotic aspect seems likely. The office of same-sex union survives only in Greek and Old Church Slavonic texts, but Gerald of Wales's account proves that this homosexual marriage ceremony survived in Ireland, where Greek probably would have been unfamiliar (and Slavonic unknown), and where the service was almost certainly conducted in Latin. Boswell thinks that all of the liturgical Latin texts of the ceremony were destroyed rather than simply lost, the result of the fourteenth-century attack on homosexuality when such ceremonies were condemned in the West.

Destruction is not limited to the ancient or medieval world. The history of the early gay rights movement is hampered by the destruction of much material. On 6 May 1933 Nazi students from the Gymnastic Academy ransacked the library of Magnus Hirschfeld's Institute for Sexual Science in Berlin, and Hirschfeld's own apartment in the same building, seizing some 12,000 books and 35,000 photographs, plus thousands of irreplaceable original manuscripts. As two lorry-loads of books were removed, the students insultingly chanted out the names of such authors as Freud, Havelock Ellis, Wilde, Carpenter, Gide and Proust, and ended by singing a 'particularly vulgar song' and the Horst-Wessel song (Lauritsen and Thorstad, 1974). Everything was burned in a huge bonfire in Opera House Square on 10 May 1933. Photographs of this public book-burning, including a torchlight procession in which Hirschfeld's bust was waved aloft, appeared in international newspapers and became famous as a symbol of Nazi censorship and the destruction of culture; few people realize that it was queer culture specifically that was going up in flames.

Suppression

In 1993 85-year-old Elsie Duncan-Jones revealed to the *London Review of Books* that when she was helping Dame Helen Gardner compile her 1965 edition of *The Elegies and Songs and Sonnets of John Donne*, she suggested that the real 'marriage of souls' celebrated in 'The Anniversarie' was that of the poet and John King, chaplain to Sir Thomas Egerton, for whom Donne worked as a secretary. 'Helen said: "Forget it".'

When the ONE Institute of Homophile Studies gave its inaugural course on Homosexuality in History in 1957, the first thing they discovered when preparing the course was that ancient classical texts had been inaccurately translated, that names and genders were transposed, that behaviour had been deliberately obscured and unpleasant facts evaded through mistranslation, that even Plutarch was censored. After almost thirty years of offering such courses, the Institute still has to emphasize that the essential working tools for homophile studies are 'bias-free translations of texts from other languages and periods. ... Whether done consciously or through inability to believe that a text in question meant what it said, meanings have been subverted' (Legg, 1994); in particular, one has to reinstate the accurate meanings of words euphemistically translated as '*lewd, weak, dissolute, companion, favorite, friend, bohemian, decadent, fop, dandy, Arcadian, epicene, thigh, groin*' (Legg, 1994). Hinsch (1990) criticizes David Hawkes for a modern translation of *Long Yang zhi xing* as 'Lord Long-yang's vice' because the Chinese word *xing* is always a positive word, and denotes 'joy, merriment, passion, desire, and appetite' rather than 'vice'.

Protection of privacy

Much of queer history has gone up in flames, just like the records of sodomy trials in medieval Europe, which were burned together with the convicted queers, including some lesbians, because the information they contained was too shameful (or too threatening?) to become public knowledge. The register of bonfires makes sorry reading. Sir Richard Burton's wife destroyed the manuscript he was working on at his death, supposedly a massive study of homosexuality in the form of an annotated translation of Sheikh Nefzawi's *Perfumed Garden*. The wife of C. R. Ashbee, founder of the Guild of Handicrafts and promoter of the arts and crafts movement, after his death in 1942 burned his notebook *Confessio Amantis*, in which he probably described an affair with a young soldier named Chris. A box of 'secret papers' belonging to Thomas Lovell Beddoes, the poet and playwright who killed himself in 1849, found its way into the possession of Robert Browning, who told Edmund Gosse, who was editing Beddoes's works, that 'the particular fact about which you enquire is painful enough, and must remain a secret, at least for some time longer', whereupon 'the dismal box' disappeared for ever (Elliman and Roll, 1986). The papers of Edward Lear, who had many passionate friendships with men, were destroyed by his literary executor, presumably because they compromised his non-literary reputation.

John Addington Symonds – the father of queer history – wrote to his wife Catherine from his deathbed in Rome in 1893, asking her to give all his manuscripts, diaries, letters '& other matters found in my books cupboard' to his friend Horatio Forbes Brown (also queer): 'I do this because I have written things you could not like to read, but which I have always felt justified and useful for society. Brown will consult & publish nothing without your consent.' Catherine withheld her consent. Brown fully understood the importance Symonds attached to the memoirs – whose whole *raison d'être* was to chart the emotional and intellectual growth, the 'coming out', of a homosexual man, in the hopes of helping to liberate homosexuals of the future – and that they must be saved from destruction after his death, but forced to obey the wishes of Catherine, he totally suppressed all homosexual references in his biography of his friend; the strange gap sensed by most readers was inferred as an indication of a secret religious melancholy. Sir Charles Holmes, who was working at the publishers (Nimmo) at the time, recalled that Brown 'exercised little more than ordinary discretion in cutting out the most intimate self-revelations. But a straiter critic had then to take a hand'. That critic was almost certainly Edmund Gosse, who received the bowdlerized proofs of the biography and proceeded to completely emasculate them. Brown died in 1926, bequeathing Symonds's memoirs and papers to Gosse. Gosse and the librarian of the London Library made a bonfire in the garden and burned everything except the memoirs, which were deposited in the Library with injunctions that they were not to be made available or published for fifty years. The papers that were destroyed probably included Symonds's sexual diary and material collected for his project with Ellis on the history of sexual inversion, correspondence with fellow homosexuals across the world (including Gosse), and love letters. Symonds's granddaughter Janet Vaughan was nauseated by the 'smug gloating delight' with which Gosse informed her what he had done to preserve her grandfather's good name (Thwaite, 1984).

Women in particular have been brought up to value discretion, modesty and propriety, and families take special care to protect the unblemished reputation of their female members: this 'would have ensured that most passions between women were presented in letters and memoirs as harmless and innocent' (Donoghue, 1993). But at the same time, women tend to record more intimate personal details in their diaries and letters than men, possibly because they are urged to cultivate their sensibilities and express their feelings more, so it is not surprising that documents of possibly lesbian import are frequently suppressed. None of Ellen Nussey's letters to Charlotte Brontë survive: presumably they were destroyed, just as Nussey was asked by Brontë's husband Arthur Bell, soon after their marriage, to destroy those she had received because of their 'passionate language', though she refused. Her proposed biography of Brontë had to be suppressed because Bell refused to grant her copyright permission to quote any of the letters. A surviving letter from Charlotte to Ellen dated 20 October 1854 shows her husband's surveillance in action:

> Arthur has just been glancing over this note ... you must BURN it when read. Arthur says such letters as mine never ought to be kept, they are dangerous as Lucifer matches so be sure to follow the recommendation he has just given, 'fire them' or 'there will be no more,' such is his resolve ... he is bending over the desk with his eyes full of concern. I am now desired to have done with it ... (Miller, 1989)

George Eliot (Mary Ann or Marian Evans) formed intense friendships with women in her youth; in April 1849 she wrote to Sara Hennell, 'I have given you a sad excuse for flirtation, but I have not been beyond seas long enough to make it lawful for you to take a new husband – therefore I come back to you with all a husband's privileges and command you to love me' (Johnson, 1989). Such passages were omitted from the letters quoted by Eliot's husband when he wrote her biography in 1885. Sixteen lines of a letter by Mary Wollstonecraft describing her passion for Fanny Blood were obliterated by some 'well-meaning scholar', and are irrecoverable (Faderman, 1994). Willa Cather destroyed the letters she had written over a period of forty years to Isabelle McClung, with whom she fell in love, though McClung got married and denied her a passionate relationship, and after her death in 1947 most of her personal papers were burned in accordance with her instructions. Lorena Hickok, apparently Eleanor Roosevelt's lover, burned Roosevelt's letters after her death; the biographer Doris Faber tried to suppress the surviving letters between the women, for fear they would be 'misunderstood'. In the 1920s Emily Dickinson's niece censored Dickinson's passionate letters to her sister-in-law Sue Gilbert. Annie Fields, companion of the novelist Sarah Orne Jewett, wanted to publish Jewett's letters to her after the novelist's death in 1911, but was advised by the official biographer to omit most of the affectionate references for fear of 'all sorts of people reading them wrong' (Miller, 1995).

Many families continue to protect the family honour by refusing access to papers which would incriminate one of their members. When Henry Maas edited *The Letters of A. E. Housman* (1971) he was refused permission to include Housman's letters to Moses Jackson, the great love of Housman's life; Maas was permitted to see these letters, but he was not allowed even to summarize their content – all he could say was that they were 'of the greatest interest'. The family continues to refuse permission for publication.

Wives are understandably reticent concerning their husbands' papers. T. S. Eliot's widow in 1988 allowed the publication of a number of letters that had been written to him by Jean Jules Verdenal, with whom Eliot lodged in Paris in 1910–11 and to whom he dedicated *The Love Song of J. Alfred Prufrock*, recently interpreted as a gay love song; the letters are full of youthful enthusiasm and devotion to 'mon cher ami', but Eliot's replies have not been published, and there are said to be others that are franker. Although Yukio Mishima's autobiographical novels reveal his homosexual relations with complete frankness, his wife will not allow the publication of her husband's letters. Federico García Lorca, who was executed for leftist sympathies in 1936, has been subject 'to deliberate manipulation and "cleansing" of his image by surviving family members' (Eisenberg, 'Lorca', *EH*): his openly queer *The Public* was partly published in 1976 against his relatives' wishes; *Sonnets of Dark Love* were withheld by his family but published clandestinely in 1983; much other material is still suppressed and his intimate letters have not been published. When William Warren Bartley published a biography (1973) revealing that the philosopher Ludwig Wittgenstein (1889–1951) was homosexual, Bartley was vilified as a liar and mischief-maker by Wittgenstein's friends and admirers, even though Wittgenstein's literary heirs possess a coded diary detailing the philosopher's cruising for rough trade in Vienna. When Weatherby (1989) was preparing his biography of James Baldwin – who was quite open about his homosexuality – he discovered that

> Many of Baldwin's most intimate companions or lovers didn't wish to be interviewed. ... Several did talk providing they weren't identified. ... Others explained that they didn't trust American society's inconsistent attitude toward homosexual relations and thought they were safer remaining silent.

So even in the liberal 1980s it was not possible to write a full and frank biography of an openly gay man.

Sometimes family protectiveness is carried too far. Jean-Jacques Régis de Cambacérès (1753–1824), Napoleon's Arch-Chancellor, was openly homosexual and the object of prejudice. Though he is wrongly credited with being responsible for the decriminalization of homosexuality under the Napoleonic Code, his papers nevertheless ought to contain valuable material for the queer historian. But his memoirs remain unpublished, and his family has refused historians permission to examine their archives, according to Jean-Louis Bory who wrote his biography in 1979.

The protection of the reputation even of people long dead is still relatively common. Cole Porter's satiric song 'Farming' describes a bull as being 'beautiful, but he's gay', but Bronski (1984) was unable to say much more than that: 'The Cole Porter estate refused permission to reprint six lines of lyrics from "Farming" because they did not want them to appear in a "risque context".' For an even more absurd example, the South Caroliniana Library in 1978 tried to prevent the foremost gay scholar Martin Duberman (1991) from publishing a selection of gay love letters written in 1826 by Thomas Jefferson Withers, an important politician in the antebellum South. Withers wrote nostalgically to his former 'chum' James Hammond: 'I feel some inclination to learn whether you yet sleep in your Shirt-tail, and whether you yet have the extravagant delight of poking and punching a writhing Bedfellow with your long fleshen pole – the exquisite touches of which I have often had the honour of feeling.' Duberman went ahead and published the letters without permission, accompanied by an excellent essay on the dilemma of how gay historians can remain true to the ideals of their profession when confronted with such censorship. Lillian Faderman (1994) was refused permission to include poems by Edna St Vincent Millay in her anthology *Chloe Plus Olivia* because, according to Millay's literary executrix, 'These poems are not appropriate for your collection, as Millay did not write lesbian literature. She wrote poetry – pure and simple.' As possibly the most absurd example, the Fellowship of the School of Economic Science, London (not to be confused with the London School of Economics), and their publishers Shepheard-Walwyn, refused to grant me permission to include any selection from their modern English translation of the letters of Marsilio Ficino in an anthology of gay love letters (forthcoming). How preposterous that a modern academic institution would wish to prevent a sixteenth-century philosopher from appearing in a queer context.

Self-censorship

The intimate, private life is difficult to trace in the public pages of history. Public markers of private lives, such as marriage and children for heterosexuals, are not quite matched for homosexuals by non-marriage or lack of offspring. A natural prudence about one's personal life is exacerbated when certain revelations would subject one to ridicule or ostracism or criminal prosecution. Working-class people seldom have the leisure or inclination to record and examine their lives in diaries, and the middle classes are often too 'proper' to record details that are not quite 'respectable'. It is remarkable that revelatory queer diaries and letters get written at all, much less survive death. The fact that the lesbian sections of Anne Lister's journals in the early nineteenth century were written in a code using the Greek alphabet and special characters is ample testimony to the perceived need for secrecy. Countee Cullen, leading poet of the Harlem Renaissance, in the 1930s and 1940s used codes in letters to his friends recording his queer affairs, and even signed letters to his lover with a pseudonym. Tchaikovsky once said, 'To think that one day people will try to penetrate the intimate world of my feelings and thoughts, everything I have kept so carefully hidden throughout my life, is very depressing and hard to bear' (Norton, 1997). But when his brother Modest, who was actually more openly queer than he, compiled Tchaikovsky's *Life and Letters* in twenty-five volumes, not a word was mentioned about *gomoseksualiszm*, which the *Great Soviet Encyclopedia* in its 1952 edition defined as a symptom of the 'moral decay of the ruling classes'.

Anne Lister was always quite careful in the phrasing of the letters she wrote to her lover Mrs Barlow after returning to England in 1825; she even asked her to burn them and was rather disturbed that Mrs Barlow was not equally cautious. On one occasion Anne carefully studied a love letter she had composed the previous night, to determine if it was safe enough to send or if it should be modified:

> This ought not to be seen – not that there is anything in it flaming but some allusions to herself & others; telling her how much I am altered; to have no fear of me in future, etc., which might be ambiguous & turned against us. Yet there is nothing, I think, I could not manage to explain away to warm friendship if I had the letter before me & was obliged to defend myself. (Lister, 1992)

This journal entry constitutes important and incontrovertible evidence that lesbians modulated their writings so that their sentiments could be 'explained away' as part of a non-sexual 'friendship' tradition. If someone in 1825 can self-consciously avoid giving the appearance of being a 'flaming' lesbian ('flaming', as in 'flaming faggot', was a slang word for 'flagrant' from about 1780), then 'passing' must have been part of the lesbian repertoire for at least a generation or two earlier, well into the period for which we have 'no evidence' other than the literature of 'romantic love' between female friends. Surely we can no longer dismiss documents expressing 'warm friendship' without carefully considering the possibility of self-censorship.

There are probably a vast number of queer love letters which have not survived because (a) personal papers of unmarried persons without younger heirs are destroyed immediately when personal effects are cleared up; and (b) they are destroyed prior to marriage. Many such letters were brought to light in the 1950s as a result of police investigations and helped to convict many men of various homosexual offences (Higgins, 1996). John Reynolds, one of the RAF airmen involved in the prosecution of Lord Montague of Beaulieu, Peter Wildeblood (diplomatic correspondent to the *Daily Mail*) and Michael Pitt-Rivers in 1953–4, had written a letter describing one of his friends as 'my husband dear', which did not help when Lord Montague's letters to 'Dear Johnny' were read out in court. Upon conviction of these men for indecency (with boy scouts and RAF men), Michael Davidson, foreign correspondent for the *Observer* who was over-fond of young men, 'destroyed two suitcases of letters, diaries and photographs of friends. He was far from alone. Late-night burning of incriminating material occurred far and wide' (Spencer, 1995). In an unrelated case, Lieutenant Colonel Julius Caesar, sentenced to a year's imprisonment in 1954, had written to Private John Everton, 'I am dreadfully afraid that I am desperately in love with you. ... Please, please, try to make chances to meet me privately somewhere. I want you so much. ... Burn this without fail' (Higgins, 1996). I have no doubt that this closing injunction was obeyed by many persons, and that much documentation of queer love has been thrown upon the flames of prudence. One man who saw *Victim* in 1961 recorded in his diary (cited in Bourne, 1996):

> *Victim* – and for me a lesson in how not to become one. ... It was letters which exposed the Wilde–Douglas affair, and in this film it was the same. I'll never commit anything to paper in that aspect, and destroy all I may receive.

The dearth of material for British lesbian life in the 1930s (and the stigmatization of spinsters as lesbians) may be owing to the prosecution of *The Well of Loneliness* for obscenity in 1928. In that year the poet Charlotte Mew burned most of her work, almost certainly an attempt to destroy all evidence of her lesbianism, then killed herself. In the 1930s well-known lesbians wrote very circumspect autobiographies (for example, Viscountess Rhondda, Cicely Hamilton, Elizabeth Robins), and 'One of Constance Maynard's executrices apparently destroyed a particularly revealing portion of her intimate diaries' (Lesbian History Group, 1989). Ann Bannon, author of the *Beebo Brinker* series of lesbian novels in the 1950s, destroyed all the correspondence she received from women in response to her novels for fear that it would be discovered by her children.

Misconstruction

A serious problem for queer history is the deliberate effort by scholars to disguise the queer matter in historical documents. This has been a common practice since medieval times, when Latin translators of Arabic and Greek writings on ancient medicine simply deleted passages detailing homosexuality: for example, *Prose Salernitan Questions* (c. 1200) draws on the ancient *Problemata* but 'omits the passage dealing with pathic homosexuality' (Greenberg, 1988). Thomas Aquinas quoted a passage from Aristotle about homosexuality but deliberately suppressed the passage in which Aristotle says that some homosexual urges are determined 'by nature', which would have contradicted Aquinas's argument that sodomy is a (sinful) choice rather than something innate. Some medieval *lais* were edited, and homosexual references suppressed or turned around to become unfavourable references (Greenberg, 1988). Matteo Ricci was so distressed at the prevalence of male prostitution in Peking that when he translated the Ten Commandments for the Chinese in 1584, the commandment 'Thou shalt not commit adultery' was replaced by 'Thou shalt not do depraved, unnatural, or filthy things'. Boswell's (1995) survey of the nineteenth-century translations of the office of same-sex union is illuminating: Goar, a major scholar, translates the operative Greek term *adelphopoia* as *spiritualis fraternitas* despite the fact that 'the word for "spiritual" does not occur in a single manuscript title for the ceremony'; yet another prominent scholar, Frček, translated the Old Church Slavonic term as *fraternité adoptive*, 'though no word occurring in or relating to the ceremony in any version in any language justifies introducing the concept "adoptive"'. Boswell offers convincing evidence that 'soul mates' is a much more realistic translation than 'spiritual brotherhood', though mainstream scholars still find this view provocative.

Women's feelings for other women are regularly trivialized in biographies, while their feelings for men are exaggerated. To dismiss the love of Charlotte Brontë and Ellen Nussey as an 'adolescent crush', as has been done, is to define adolescence 'as a somewhat protracted period continuing until the age of 25 or so' (Miller, 1989). Similarly,

> Octavia Hill's passionate friendship with Sophia Jex-Blake was written out of mid-twentieth-century biographies, while a hasty engagement which lasted exactly one day was elevated into the romance of her life, with Hill holding the young man's memory 'sacred to her heart till the end of her life'. In fact she lived for the last 35 years of her life with another woman, Harriot Yorke. (Lesbian History Group, 1989)

We should also note that The Lesbian History Group attributes this 'normalizing' process to the negative associations of the word 'lesbian' – an insult, a label of abnormal perversion or pitiful handicap, a description solely of a sexual practice rather than a cultural universe. We should also recognize that there is a well-established economic market for heterosexual history.

The year 1996 marked the centenary of the death of Frederic Leighton. To celebrate, the Royal Academy of Arts – of which he was President from 1878–96 – held a major exhibition of his works between February and April. I suppose it was too much to expect the Royal Academy to endeavour to bring to light proof of Leighton's long-suspected homosexuality, but I burst into laughter when I read the catalogue entry describing his sculpture *The Sluggard*, which, while acknowledging the extraordinary languor and sensuous beauty of this young male nude, dismissed any suggestion that it might provide evidence of Leighton's 'suppressed homosexuality', because 'for Leighton this represented the ideal'! Can it really be possible that (heterosexual) critics do not recognize the link between the real and the ideal? Or do their mental faculties just seize up when faced by queer tangibility? Art historians are probably not really blind to the obvious – they just refuse to countenance it. Andrée Hayum in her 1976 biography of Giovanni Antonio Bazzi, 'Il Sodoma', claimed that 'speculations about his private personality' – including the source of his nickname – were 'essentially fruitless' and 'an extraneous issue'. It is for historians such as these that we require Saslow's (1986) excellent survey of *Ganymede in the Renaissance* to prove what is self-evident: that the image of Ganymede was 'an artistic vehicle' for the homoeroticism of artists or their patrons.

Mainstream critics and historians would rather do anything than call a queer spade a queer spade. Jason Wilson in the introduction to his 1995 translation of Alexander von Humboldt's *Personal Narrative of a Journey* has invented the curious term 'male-scientific friendships' to describe Humboldt's love of other men, so as to site it within the tradition of friendships among colleagues in scientific professions – but this hardly accounts for the fact that all of Humboldt's protégés and travelling companions were handsome young men. Wilson acknowledges that 'Humboldt deliberately suppressed his private life. He burned or destroyed many letters in order to further efface himself from biographers.' Many historians regularly refrain from reaching what seems to me to be the obvious conclusion: not that certain individuals have suppressed their homosexuality, but that they have suppressed *evidence* of their homosexuality. Humboldt died in 1859, one decade before 'the homosexual' was 'invented'; Hirschfeld gathered reminiscences about him from people still living in 1914, who recalled his participation in the gay subculture of Berlin.

Ethnography

George Catlin, who observed, described and painted the North American Indian *berdache* in the 1830s, concluded his account by saying, 'I should wish that it might be extinguished before it be more fully recorded' (Legg, 1994). Such a sentiment was not rare; surely many observers refrained from recording details that shocked their European sensibilities.

Greenberg (1988) includes an excellent appendix outlining the methodological problems in anthropological research on homosexuality, which amount to a conspiracy of censorship: anthropologists, fearful of being suspected as participants themselves, and of not being allowed to return to a research site, often simply remained obtuse and ignored it. As late as 1980 one anthropologist in New Guinea, despite published reports going back to the nineteenth century about ritualized sodomy in the area, and 'Even though he saw a good deal of same-sex physical contact, ... simply assumed that homosexuality could not be a part of the culture.' It is impossible to gather evidence of indigenous attitudes to homosexuality that has not been tainted by negative Western attitudes: 'For many cultures, sexual mores have been deeply affected by prolonged and extensive exposure to the sermons of missionaries, the lectures of school teachers, and the offhand comments of traders, tourists, and government agents.' An anthropologist in the 1950s found that among the Winnebago, 'the berdache was at one time a highly honored and respected person, but ... the Winnebago had become ashamed of the custom because the white people thought it was amusing or evil'. If homosexuality is unrecorded for some 60 per cent of known indigenous societies, we must ask if that is because contact with Western moral puritanism has exterminated it.

Bleys (1996) has established that the general tendency among nineteenth-century ethnographers was to focus exclusively on passive, effeminate roles and to dismiss the sexuality of their active or egalitarian partners as merely 'circumstantial'; indigenous behaviour that did not consolidate the Western preconception that homosexuality was a feature only of passive, cross-gender or age-structured roles was simply ignored: 'When these conditions were not fulfilled, observers were reluctant to acknowledge that, in these cases too, same-sex praxis may spring from an inborn drive or propensity.' Literally scores of native terms were translated indiscriminately as 'sodomite' or 'hermaphrodite' or 'catamite' depending on the anthropologists' prejudgement about what constitutes the homosexual, and without offering detailed observations that would help us sort out the semantics today; the Hawaiian *aikane* were literally 'man-fucking men' whose relations were neither age-structured nor gender-structured, yet they were grouped by early observers under the category of cross-gender roles.

When the 'pathological' discourse was being consolidated by the medical and criminological professions, the contrary views of anthropologists that 'uranism' could be found in quite normal and healthy peoples were suppressed. For example, when the Dutch criminal anthropologist Arnold Aletrino presented a paper sympathetic to homosexuals in Amsterdam in 1901, his colleagues and the President of the Congress prevented his views being publicized by the press. One of the reasons why social constructionists are able to assert that homosexuality did not become a subject of discourse until the later nineteenth century is because homosexual discourse preceding that date had been suppressed and censored.

Suppression of research

The increasing difficulty of maintaining effective censorship from the late nineteenth century has led to the illusion that the subject of homosexuality is 'modern'. But in fact homosexuality was certainly a subject of discourse from the mid-eighteenth century in Europe. Johann Matthias Gesner gave a scholarly lecture on Socrates's homosexuality in 1752, though the text, *Socrates Sanctus Paederasta*, was not published until 1769, eight years after his death, and not in Germany, but in Utrecht where there was greater freedom of the press. From the 1750s in Germany and from the 1780s in the Netherlands there were several studies of Greek pederasty, and theories about ancient Indo-European pederasty were developed in the early nineteenth century. Prior to this, the late-medieval and early Renaissance studies of platonic love and friendship are arguably self-censored or disguised studies of homosexuality. Homosexual apologetics existed centuries before the supposed 'invention' of homosexuality, but have never achieved a high profile precisely because they formed part of the 'secret history' tradition.

The Utilitarian philosopher and law reformer Jeremy Bentham (1748–1832) wrote some five hundred manuscript pages on the place of homosexuality in history, using common sense to counter the view that would dominate the nineteenth century:

> The Greeks knew the difference between love and friendship as well as we – they had distinct terms to signify them by: it seems reasonable therefore to suppose that when they say love they mean love, and when they say friendship only they mean friendship only. And with regard to Xenophon and his master, Socrates, and his fellow-scholar Plato, it seems more reasonable to believe them to have been addicted to this taste when they or any of them tell us so in express terms than to trust to the interpretations, however ingenious and however well-intended, of any men who write at this time of day, when they tell us it was no such thing. (Crompton, 1978b)

Bentham's extensive defence of homosexuality in 1785 – in which he argued that it is neither unnatural nor immoral – was never published because he feared being branded a queer; as he noted in marginal jottings: 'To other subjects it is expected that you sit down cool: but on this subject if you let it be seen that you have not sat down in a rage you have betrayed yourself at once'. Among Bentham's papers are 'fair copy', polished essays on this subject, obviously intended for circulation and perhaps sent to colleagues in France: his writings should therefore be treated as part of Enlightenment 'discourse'.

Historical research in southern Europe is still hampered by Mediter-ranean machismo: the censorship imposed during the seventeenth and eighteenth centuries is compounded in modern times by 'a certain reluctance by Italian historians to enter "obscure zones of a special character"' (G. Dall'Orto, 'Italy', *EH*). In Latin America anything that seems to legitimate homosexuality in print is censored as an apology for vice.

In America, Kinsey's findings on the widespread practice of homosexuality provoked a massive reaction from university professors, Congressmen and religious leaders, led particularly by Henry Van Dusen of the Union Theological Seminary, who was also on the board of the Rockefeller Foundation which funded Kinsey. Because of the outcry, the National Research Council requested the American Statistical Association to examine Kinsey's work. Though the ASA eventually praised Kinsey's methods and findings, the examination took many years, during which time Kinsey's financial backing disappeared. He had been effectively silenced, and never again has sexual research on this scale been attempted.

Public access to books dealing with homosexuality has been restricted until recent times, and the books themselves stigmatized so as to render them untouchable. When Judy Grahn (1984) in 1961, at the age of 21, tried to investigate the subject of homosexuals and lesbians in a library in Washington, DC,

> The books on such a subject, I was told by indignant, terrified librarians unable to say aloud the word *homosexual*, were locked away. They showed me a wire cage where the 'special' books were kept in a jail for books. Only professors, doctors, psychiatrists, and lawyers for the criminally insane could see them, check them out, hold them in their hands.

Secret history

A modern history of homosexuality published in Hong Kong in 1964 by Weixingshi Guanzhaizhu is appropriately titled *Zhongguo tongxinglian mishi* (*The Secret History of Chinese Homosexuality*). Secrecy has always been an important feature of queer history and culture, partly because sexual relations are usually very private affairs, whether they be the sexual rituals of religious mysteries that must be kept secret from the uninitiated, or the 'secret games' played between the Chinese Emperor Jing (reigned 156–141 BC) and his favourite Zhou Ren, to cite but one example from a thousand. Homosexual relations are frequently forbidden by a hostile society and therefore become especially secretive, even 'furtive'. When queer culture began to be driven underground in America in the 1930s, surreptitious communication networks were developed; for example, 'Science-fiction clubs attracted some, who corresponded with one another through the personal columns of the clubs' newsletters' (Licata, 1985). The Mattachine Foundation was formed in 1953 with secret cells along the Communist model so as to avoid widescale discovery in the case of penetration by outsiders, and an article in the *Mattachine Review* in 1955 explained that the society was named after late-medieval societies of 'unmarried townsmen who never performed in public unmasked'.

In premodern times queers were said to gather in 'secret synods' – which historians should not dismiss as homophobic rhetoric. In more recent times there have certainly been secret homosexual societies, such as the Order of Chaeronea (named after the spot where the Sacred Band of Thebes fell) organized by George Cecil Ives (Weeks, 1977). In America there were several semi-secret gay rights organizations about which little is known, such as the Sons of Hamidy around the turn of the century, which was reorganized in 1934; the Knights of the Clock, formed by the gay black man Merton Bird in 1949 to combat homophobia and racism; and the Cloistered Loyal Order of Conclaved Knights of Sophistacracy, established in 1951–2 (Licata, 1985). It is not widely known that in 1970 the largest homophile society in the world was the Society of Anubis, a semi-secret organization with a thousand members and a ten-acre club site in the San Gabriel Valley, interested primarily in social and community programmes (Legg, 1994).

The queer literary tradition employs not only strategies of camouflage and concealment that require decoding but has also used deliberately cryptographic language in order to convey secret messages. Giovanni Dall'Orto ('Bernesque Poetry', *EH*) has described a genre of early sixteenth-century Italian poetry created by Francesco Berni, a priest once imprisoned for a year and a half in a monastery because of a homosexual scandal, who composed ostensibly innocuous poems for boys which were actually obscene when decoded. Even in his private letters he employed a secret language so that seemingly quite ordinary correspondence secretly conveys a request that his friends send him boys. Many authors (presumably queer) wrote this 'Bernesque' poetry, employing double meanings in which, for example, a chamber pot symbolized the anus or a needle represented the penis; *asciutto*, meaning 'dry', stood for sodomy (often called the 'dry fuck'), *monte* ('mountain') signified the anus, and in a more convoluted manner *tagliare* ('to cut') meant 'to sodomize', from the *tagliere* or round chopping board symbolic of the anus. This secret language has not been the subject of any intensive scholarship, and no key has been worked out.

Writers during the sixteenth and seventeenth centuries took enormous delight in being clever, as illustrated by the complex allegories of Edmund Spenser and the metaphysical poetry of John Donne. I believe that the vast corpus of pastoral-mythological literature of the period has a homoerotic ambience not by the accident of imitating the ancients, but because the references to Corydon and Hylas are deliberately coded (Norton, 1974a). A vast corpus of late nineteenth-century pederastic poetry also employed code words, such as 'earnest' to mean boy-love, and used simple acrostic techniques to spell the names of their boyfriends in their verse (d'Arch Smith, 1970). Modern homosexual intellectuals have always rather enjoyed establishing contact with one another through the use of coded language. Henry James recognized that John Addington Symonds was *simpatico* and introduced himself by alluding to the love that dare not speak its name:

I sent [my article] to you because it was a constructive way of expressing the good will I felt for you in consequence of what you had written about the land of Italy – and of intimating to you, somewhat dumbly, that I am a sympathetic reader. I nourish for the said Italy an unspeakably tender passion, and your pages always seemed to say to me that you were one of the small number of people who love it as much as I do ... for it seemed to me that the victims of a common passion should exchange a look. (Summers, 1995)

Robert Martin, founder of the Gay Academic Union in America, in an interview in *Gay News* following the publication of his book *The Homosexual Tradition in American Poetry*, observed that

In the teaching of English literature there is a kind of accepted tradition that an author's gayness comes under the heading of gossip, that it has nothing to do with the work. It's this English thing that gayness is an amusing eccentricity, you chat about it over tea, *entre nous*, but otherwise it should be avoided. I see it, and resent it, in the works of someone like A. L. Rowse who treats it like telling tales. [Reference to the Cambridge historian's *Homosexuals in History*]

While I sympathize with Martin's dislike of the somewhat smutty contextualization of such knowledge, *thank goodness for gossips*, without whom queer historians would hardly get anywhere in our research. 'Secret history' – that long tradition of scandalous memoirs and political smears – is essential to the compilation of queer history. Classic examples include Suetonius's *Lives of the Caesars*; Luca Ombrosi's eighteenth-century *Vita dei Medici sodomiti*, biographical gossip about the last two rulers of the house of Medici; *The Private Life of the King of Prussia*, in which Voltaire reveals the homosexual relations of Frederick the Great (1712–86) and reprints Frederick's *Le Palladion*, a privately printed defence of homosexuality, which Voltaire successfully smuggled out of Prussia although Frederick's agents had his luggage searched. The *chroniques scandaleuses* of eighteenth-century France have many references to secret gay and lesbian scandals; such books are too often dismissed as libellous fictions, but they draw heavily upon contemporary gossip and insider information from court spies. Voluminous notes appended to the anonymous pederastic poem *Don Leon* (published sometime before 1853) help to document queer life in the early nineteenth century, while Henry Spencer Ashbee's po-faced *Bibliography of Prohibited Books* (1877–85) helps us do the same for the mid-nineteenth century. Books dealing with *curiosae* are invaluable for queer historians.

Lesbian clubs – the Order of Anandrynes – are supposed to have flourished in Paris in the 1780s and are well documented in several secret histories such as *Hic et Haec ou l'Eleve des RR.PP. Jesuites etc.* (Berlin, 1798), *La Cauchoise, etc.* (London, 1788), *Le Petit-Fils d'Hercule* (1788), *L'histoire de la secte anandryne*, Mairobet's *L'apologie de la Secte Anandryne* and his more notorious *L'espion Anglais* (1779). Members supposedly included even married women such as the Marquise Terracenes, the wife of the Attorney General, and several actresses such as Mlle Arnould. Such 'histories' are imaginatively embellished and salacious, but the real reason why the leads they contain have not been seriously followed up is because queer history is considered to be merely gossip not worth pursuing. To say that we know hardly anything about lesbian history, and then to say that gossip is not worth investigating, that it is pornographic 'literature' rather than history, is a dual bind that ensures that queers will always remain hidden from history.

Queer historians cannot afford to be as 'strict' as mainstream historians, who seldom allow much weight to anonymous works (as many secret histories are, if not pseudonymous), patently motivated by political animosity or private malice. But a good working hypothesis is that secret history is about 90 per cent accurate. The fact that defamatory accusations occur in the context of a political attack does not necessarily mean that the basic facts are untrue, only that they have been embellished so as to show the most negative aspect. Everyone who works in the news media knows a great many more facts than they are willing to publish, partly because of libel laws. When the British government failed to equalize the age of consent for homosexual men and lowered it only to 18, demonstrators outside the Houses of Parliament chanted the names of alleged queers in John Major's Cabinet; though done for the benefit of the television and newspaper reporters present, the chanting was neither reported nor broadcast. This kind of information is widely known and widely hinted at. A 1996 article by Peter Tatchell begins, 'At least 15 gay MPs, including two cabinet ministers, have voted against equality since 1994.'

The homosexuality of many celebrated people is an 'open secret' while they are living, though it may not reach print until after their death. As *The Observer* commented when reporting on the disposal of the '155 paintings, drawings, prints and sculptures of the male nude' from the estate of the late Rudolf Nureyev at the end of 1995, it 'tells us much about the dancer that was never made public while he was alive'. A kind of secret history finally becomes public knowledge when people not always widely known to have been queer meet a violent end: the suicide of Sir Hector MacDonald in 1903; the drowning, apparently as a lovers' pact of joint suicide, of Rupert Buxton and Michael Barrie in 1915 (one of the boys who influenced Peter Pan); the suicide of Alan Turing in 1954; the murder of Joe Orton by his lover in 1967; the murder of Marc Blitzstein by a hustler in 1968; the murder of Ramon Novarro by two hustlers in 1968; the hari-kari committed by Yukio Mishima in 1970; the suicides of Hart Crane, William Inge, Freidrich Alfred Krupp, F. O. Matthiessen, Charlotte Mew, Alfred Redl, Renée Vivien, James Whale, Virginia Woolf *et al*. And today many rumours are confirmed by death from AIDS.

A study of suicides (and murders disguised as suicide) in the past would no doubt turn up much queer material. A footman in the service of the Prince of Wales shot himself shortly after the Vere Street raid and trials in 1810, and a manservant of the Duke of Cumberland, the future King of Hanover, was discovered in the Duke's bedroom in St James's Palace with his throat cut. Cumberland said it was suicide, but the rumour was that he had killed the servant, who had discovered the Duke's homosexual relations with his valet, who in the meantime had vanished. Cumberland took a close interest in the Vere Street case, and was in the Newgate press-yard to witness the hanging of two of the convicted men in 1811. When the rumour about Cumberland was published in 1813 the journalist was sentenced to fifteen months in prison; when it was published again in 1832, another journalist was sentenced to six months (Norton, 1992). Further contemporary details of the affair appeared in 1861, in the gossipy *Autobiography of Miss Cornelia Knight, Lady Companion to the Princess Charlotte of Wales.*

To refuse to credit gossip and rumour merely on the grounds that they *are* gossip and rumour is to seriously undervalue the validity of any sexual information that is not allowed a place in the conventional public record. There is no legitimate reason why the historian of private lives should not rely upon private records, of which secret histories are a prime example. The more secret the life, the more secret will be the source that reveals that life. It is imperative for the queer historian not to succumb to the mainstream prejudice against secret history, for secret history *is* queer history.

Conclusion

It is odd that in the history of the love that dared not speak its name the authorities did not try to achieve social control by the widespread public naming of these crimes, which is what social constructionists propose they ought to have done. On the contrary they endeavoured to suppress all knowledge of such people and such acts, whether from fear that they would have the power to encourage similar behaviour or simply because they were felt to be too scandalous and shameful to be made public. This is a basic contradiction in Foucault's naming theory. The very high level of censorship applied to this field of study is sufficient indication that homosexual experience was not allowed to become part of this discourse. But to rest content with deconstructing the discourse, by revealing that it is wildly skewed and wacky, without endeavouring to recover what has been suppressed, is to conspire with the censors.

In so far as censorship is an incontrovertible fact, and the prejudicial rewriting of history/literature demonstrably evident, it seems to me that after we have recovered as much material as possible, the remaining gaps have to be filled in with a pro-queer interpretation rather than an apologetic admission of defeat. The 'nature of the evidence' is not so much that the sources are limited, but that the signs of suppression are plainly visible. What I want to suggest is that the queer historian should not despair when confronted by the charge that we really do not have the 'genital evidence' to prove incontrovertibly that someone was queer, for we often have *abundant* evidence of suppression *which in itself is sufficient confirmation of the likelihood of a queer interpretation.* Queer historians should never apologize for basing queer history on context rather than text, on ethnic culture rather than sexual behaviour, on 'queer' paradigms rather than 'homosexual' ones.

7

Lesbian Historiography

A separate herstory?

Should lesbian history and gay male history be separately considered? Male homosexuality and lesbianism are completely unrelated in Chinese eyes (Hinsch, 1990), and this seems to be the view of some modern queer historians. Lesbian history is usually presented as an appendage to gay history, which may be an inevitable consequence for the premodern period due to the paucity of material. Simply from a practical standpoint it is more satisfying to read a study devoted entirely to lesbian history than to intersperse lesbian evidence chronologically with male gay material. References to lesbianism throughout history are so sparse that it is difficult to incorporate them into any large overview of queer history without them being overwhelmed by the references to gay men's history.

Almost every theory about homosexuality is essentially a theory about male homosexuals, with a footnote containing a reverse-theory about lesbians, *mutatis mutandis*, in accordance with the requirements of abstract logic rather than observation. Lesbianism may be an altogether different matter from male homosexuality, and may require a separate line of enquiry which recognizes that gay and lesbian experiences are significantly dissimilar if not incompatible. Lesbian historiography may require a concept of sexuality more broadly based than narrow genital sexuality, a greater focus upon isolated pair-bonding than upon subcultural networking, and a greater necessity for employing hypothetical models in the face of the censorship of male indifference.

The claim that 'The differences between men's and women's power and the qualities ascribed to them in a male-dominated culture were so significant that the social and spatial organization of gay male and lesbian life inevitably took very different forms' (Chauncey, 1994) seems to me to be too broad. Whatever their differences, lesbians and gay men nevertheless share many social and cultural values. Particularly for the modern period, it is important to consider lesbian history and gay male history within the overarching field of queer history. It may be true that the gay male subculture is more visible and more extensive because men earn more money, act more independently from family life and have more freedom of movement than women. Alternatively, it may be that women are innately more drawn to pair-bonding and groups of small networks, which do not require a subculture. Whatever the case, modern queer historians do not seem to fully appreciate that there was a great deal of 'spatial' overlap between gay men and lesbians. For example, lesbian enclaves developed in Greenwich Village and Harlem in the 1920s for exactly the same reasons that these became gay male residential areas: because they were the major centres in New York for furnished-room housing for single men and single women. Many speakeasies were managed by lesbians and had lesbian performers, and many Harlem clubs attended by gay men were famous for performances by lesbian or bisexual artists such as Ma Rainey, Bessie Smith and Gladys Bentley. Culturally identified gay men like Leonard Bernstein – and countless others – constantly listened to records by these women. Modern studies of queer semiotics need to appreciate that there are queer signals as well as specifically gay or lesbian signals: for example, until very recently pinky rings and monocles were worn by both men and women who wished to signal their queer identity.

Lesbian entrepreneurs played an important role in the commercialization of queer culture in the 1940s: 'Spivy, an enormous lesbian famous in the elite gay world, sang for her gay following' in the back room at Tony's bar; in 1940 she opened her own penthouse nightclub, Spivy's Roof, and employed performers such as Mabel Mercer, Thelma Carpenter, Liberace and Paul Lynde (Chauncey, 1994). Eva Kotchever, a Polish Jewish émigré who used the pseudonym Eve Addams (alluding to Adam and Eve) and who was called the 'queen of the third sex' by a local newspaper, in 1925 opened a tearoom with a sign at the door announcing 'Men are admitted but not welcome'. In 1926 police raided her club and she was charged with writing an 'obscene' collection of short stories, entitled *Lesbian Love*, and disorderly conduct, for which she was sent to the workhouse and then deported the following year. She proceeded to open a lesbian club in Montmartre. She was fondly remembered in the Village, where in 1929 a theatrical group performed a play based upon *Lesbian Love*, which *Variety* reported drew 'mainly an audience of queers' (cited by Chauncey, 1994).

There is also an important overlap in the fields of queer literature and art by gay men and lesbians, which goes back at least to the late nineteenth century. The gay Victorian painter Simeon Solomon painted a large portrait of Sappho and Erinna – who actually were separated by centuries – as part of the lesbian community of Mytelene (exhibited for the first time in 1980, at Sotheby's). The intermingling of male and female homosexuality is a key element of Decadent literature. Djuna Barnes later imitated the style of Oscar Wilde and Aubrey Beardsley in her poems, plays and stories. Pierre Louÿs's *Les Chansons de Bilitis* (1894) created the archetypal lesbian Bilitis (an entirely fictional creation, falsely placed within the lesbian literary tradition), supposedly a Phoenician woman who settled on the isle of Lesbos where she became part of the circle around Sappho. It became a 'classic' of lesbian literature, lending its name, for example, to the first lesbian political organization in America, the Daughters of Bilitis, founded in San Francisco in 1955.

Marguerite Yourcenar (real name Crayencour, 1903–87), the first woman elected to the French Academy, who lived with Alice Frick for forty years, dealt with male homosexuality in many of her writings. Her first novel, *Alexis* (1929), consists of a letter from a gay musician to his wife explaining why he has to leave her; two men find self-fulfilment in *Coup de Grâce*; Zeno and his male lovers are the subject of *The Abyss*; Yukio Mishima and Masakatsu Morita are the central characters of her essay *Mishima: A Vision of the Void*; and the archetypal love relationship of Hadrian and Antinous is the subject of her masterpiece *Memoirs of Hadrian*. She also translated into French many works by queer novelists and poets, including James Baldwin, Constantine Cavafy, Henry James, Thomas Mann, Yukio Mishima and Virginia Woolf. Mary Renault (real name Mary Challans, 1905–83) similarly dealt with male homosexuality in numerous novels set in ancient history, notably portraying the love of Alexander and Hephaestion (in her historical work *The Life of Alexander* as well as the novel *Bagoas*). Male homosexuality is central to most of Carson McCullers's novels, not as lesbian encoding but because she liked gay men and went with them (dressed as a male) to their gay hangouts, in some genuine sense identifying herself as a gay man trapped in a female body (as have Camille Paglia and Poppy Z. Brite). All these novels are not indirect ways of dealing with lesbianism. Male homosexuality was no more easier to portray than lesbianism in the period when Yourcenar and Renault and McCullers were writing: it is just that many lesbians personally identified with the larger queer cultural tradition rather than a specifically lesbian tradition. Lesbians and gay men often take delight in one another's gender transgressions.

The standard of proof

Just as queer history in general often spends too much time trying to define 'homosexuality', so lesbian history in particular has been plagued by the problem of defining 'the lesbian'. Richards (1990) introduces her compilation of *Lesbian Lists* thus:

> Should I use a contemporary, twentieth-century definition? And if so, which one? Women who are sexually attracted to other women or women who became lesbians through feminism? Or should I use a much broader definition, one that includes the romantic friends movement – women who were women-identified, who had affectionate and loving relationships with other women but may not actually have had sex due to the repressive nature of the era? Should I include sworn sisters [as in China] and berdaches? Should I include transvestites? Should I include spinsters? ... My own bias is toward women-identified women, whether they call themselves lesbians or not, whether they had sex or not. To impose today's standards on earlier eras limits our vision and our history.

The problems raised by Richards are due partly to a social constructionist agenda that is happy to remain historically ignorant. She claims, for example, that the first time 'lesbian' was used to denote a woman-loving woman was in a medical journal in 1883, and the first time it was used this way in a newspaper was in 1892. In France, the modern theorist Joan DeJean has similarly been led by the nose of social constructionist dogma, arguing that the pornographic and scholarly views of Sappho were entirely separate, 'sapphic without being Sapphic', until the late nineteenth century. But *Saphao* was the most common French generic term for 'lesbian', and it is not likely that French literature was much different from English literature in this respect. Throughout the seventeenth and eighteenth centuries scholarly works often discuss Sappho's possible lesbianism or bisexuality, and fictional and biographical accounts of contemporary lesbians and bisexuals often refer to their foremother Sappho. In fact 'most British references I have found to the real Sappho at least mention rumours about her sexual deviance. There was, then, a long-standing Sapphic tradition of lesbian culture; this is not a twentieth-century invention' (Donoghue, 1993).

The Lesbian History Group (1989) calls attention to 'the standard of proof' which obstructs the identification of lesbians in history:

Because of society's reluctance to admit that lesbians exist, a high degree of certainty is expected before historians or biographers are allowed to use the label. Evidence that would suffice in any other situation is inadequate here. ... A woman who never married, who lived with another woman, whose friends were mostly women, or who moved in known lesbian or mixed gay circles, may well have been a lesbian. ... But this sort of evidence is not 'proof'. What our critics want is incontrovertible evidence of sexual activity between women. This is almost impossible to find.

Most historical figures and subjects of biographies are assumed to be heterosexual without the necessity of providing evidence of genital acts. The birth of children itself provides only limited evidence of heterosexual frequency or desire. Whole biographies have been written about bachelors and spinsters, even those who shared their lives with other bachelors or spinsters, without raising the suggestion that they might not be heterosexual. Only historians of homosexuality have been required to dig up the dirt:

The history of heterosexuality – and that is the only history we have been offered to date – does not rely on proof of genital contact. Men and women are assumed to be heterosexual unless there is 'genital' proof to the contrary. Women who have lived in the same house and slept in the same bed for thirty years have had their lesbianism strongly denied by historians. But men and women who simply take walks together are assumed to be involved in some sort of heterosexual relationship. (Jeffreys, 1989b)

A recent classic example of this was the outcry that occurred over Terry Castle's review of Jane Austen's letters to her sister Cassandra, in which she pointed out that Jane Austen and Cassandra, neither of whom showed much inclination for matrimony, shared the same bed for most of their adult lives, that Cassandra censored the letters, and that the relations between sisters in Austen's novels are more like the relations between lovers. The British press whipped this up into something rather less ambiguous – inviting academics to comment on Castle's view – and Castle was provoked into a reply:

Nowhere in my essay did I state that Jane Austen was a lesbian. ... I stand by what I *did* say in the piece, however: that Austen's relationship with Cassandra was unquestionably the most important emotional relationship of her life, that she lived with her sister on terms of considerable physical intimacy, and that the relationship – I believe – had its unconscious homoerotic dimensions. I am amazed, frankly, that in 1995 this should be considered so controversial and inflammatory a statement. (Castle, 1995)

In order to avoid this kind of genital-based debate, lesbian feminists in the 1970s constructed a political definition of the lesbian. In 1971 'The Woman Identified Woman' was published by the New York Radicalesbians, which identified the lesbian as a woman (politically) committed to women. In 1978 Adrienne Rich contended that there was a 'lesbian continuum' encompassing all woman-identified experience (Rich, 1993). This firmly brought lesbians into the mainstream feminist discourse. But a frequently observed corollary was the definition of lesbianism as not-heterosexuality. Dell Richards (1990), compiler of *Lesbian Lists*, not only includes as lesbians 'the women who have done everything in their power to escape heterosexual dominance', but defines her own lesbianism in these negative terms:

For me, becoming a lesbian was a conscious political decision, the logical extension of feminism. ... I decided to see what I would be like in a mirror that reflected me at my natural size. The only way I could think to do that was by ridding my life of men – or at least ridding my personal life of heterosexual men.

Sexuality is here being defined as power rather than desire, and it is revealing that far more feminists countenance the homosexual choice than men: for women this is a choice to become powerful, while for men it is a choice to become weak. This political definition has been perceived to diminish the lesbianism of lesbian-feminist discourse, and is now much disputed (Griffin, 1993a). Sheila Jeffreys (1989b) argues that

Lesbianism cannot be subsumed beneath the good feelings of hand-holding sisterhood. This leaves no space to talk about specifically lesbian oppression and gives us little chance to build up the history and culture of lesbianism which we need for our pride and our survival. In this context Adrienne Rich's idea of the lesbian continuum is problematic; her argument that all women's friendships with women are some shade or gradation of lesbianism inevitably confuses attempts to analyze lesbian oppression. Women who simply have 'best friends' who are women share neither lesbian oppression nor lesbian experience.

By the mid-1990s the lesbian aspect of lesbian feminism had reasserted itself. Bradby (1993) opines:

> I don't agree with Rich's 'lesbian continuum' for it seems to deny the sexual and erotic side of being a lesbian, to make what is a powerful identification for some women (myself included) virtually meaningless, and to deny the quite separate oppression which these women face.

Bradby prefers the straightforward definition put forward by the cultural theorist C. R. Stimpson in 1988: 'She is a woman who finds other women erotically attractive and gratifying. ... Lesbianism represents a commitment of skin, blood, breast and bone.' Donoghue, by choosing the term 'passions between women', re-emphasizes the erotic component of lesbian experience and identification, and highlights specific lesbian markers such as cross-dressing and 'mannish' behaviour.

The trend for the future will be to put the sex back into lesbian history – an essentialist position. The study of spinsters and the study of friendship networks among women have an uneasy place in lesbian history. There are economic reasons why women choose to be spinsters and to live with other spinsters, and emotional reasons why women enjoy friendship networks with other women. These are important fields within the feminist history of women-identified women, but they cannot occupy the foreground of lesbian history except in those instances where a case can be made for sexual expression (including sexual suppression and sublimation). We must be careful not to attribute romanticized desire to all female friendships, or we connive with the 'frustrated spinster' stereotype. But ways can be found to distinguish the sheep from the goats, the feminists from the lesbian feminists.

Evidence

In the field of lesbian history, the problem is not so much how to interpret the evidence, as finding the evidence to begin with. Until quite recent times 'history' was invariably chronicled by men, and women feature in historical sources 'either as property or as objects of sexual desire' of men (Boswell, 1995). Female same-sex unions do not fall into these categories and therefore go unrecorded. Activities of 'the weaker sex' are felt to be beneath serious notice by men; women, like children, are considered to be naturally affectionate toward one another, and even in the mid-eighteenth century it was recognized that this helped to obscure our perception of lesbianism: the author of *Satan's Harvest Home* (1749) condescendingly admits that 'Woman *Kissing* Woman, is more suitable to their natural Softness.' Men harbour surprisingly few suspicions about intimate relations between women: the idea that they might have sex with one another without a penis is regarded as laughable.

Although the lives of women in general have always been carefully regulated (and subordinated), specifically lesbian sexuality has been subject to very little social control, with the result that lesbian identities have arisen from within lesbian culture rather than been culturally determined by patriarchal society. Students of lesbian history constantly have to remind themselves that lesbian culture is more likely to be *ignored* than *absent*. Chinese literature was controlled by men, and lesbianism was never part of a sustained literary tradition in Imperial China – nevertheless, references to lesbian relations do exist from as early as the second century. According to Ying Shao (c. 140–206), 'When palace women attach themselves as husband and wife it is called *dui shi*', or 'paired eating'. Other ancient records document specific sexual practices such as pudendal rubbing, nicknamed 'grinding bean curd', and the use of double-headed olisboi, made of wood or ivory or silk stuffed with bean curd. Outside of court circles, lesbian group marriages are recorded, and in southern China 'Golden Orchid Associations' survived into the twentieth century, involving formal marriage ceremonies with an exchange of gifts between 'husband' and 'wife', female companions acting as witnesses and the marriage feast; women who married one another could even adopt female children, who could inherit property from the couple's parents' area. Clear evidence, then, that although lesbian relations were institutionalized and part of a culture they were seldom deemed important enough to be recorded.

Donoghue (1993) suggests that heterocentric critics and scholars are not careful readers of homosexual material: they 'miss th[e] quiet documentation of love between women'. She establishes cases in which data has been misread, through carelessness, or, rather, 'lack of interest in such things'. Passion between friends is generally treated as ordinary friendship, and 'Stories about women-only groups have not so much been ignored by scholars as under-read. Feminist historians often celebrate them as examples of solidarity and sisterhood, ignoring the eroticism that pervades them.' Twenty or thirty years ago it was common to categorically state that 'there is no evidence' of lesbian relations in a particular premodern period, but as the very idea of lesbianism becomes less 'inconceivable' and as more queer or gay-friendly historians pursue research into the subject, evidence has come to light and more evidence may yet be discovered:

> Since Faderman's study was published [1981], many texts have emerged from obscurity or been read with a new eye. Suspicions expressed in seventeenth- and eighteenth-century publications about the eroticism and threat to society posed by attachments between women have turned out to be neither 'slight' nor 'rare'. (Donoghue, 1993)

Trumbach (1994) has himself begun to revise the views he held in the late 1970s and early 1980s in the light of more research; in his most recent work the development of the lesbian 'third sex' role has been pushed back from the nineteenth century to the mid-eighteenth century. Nevertheless, Donoghue takes Trumbach to task for unsupported generalizations. What he still sees as a steady development from a sin to a psychological perversion, Donoghue sees as constant overlapping of the two ideas throughout the eighteenth and nineteenth centuries. Words suggesting special peculiarity occur quite early, for example 'genius' in 1709, 'singularity' of loving only women in 1714, an exceptional 'Cast' of personality in 'Lovers of their own Sex' in 1741. 'I can discern no point at which one explanation gave way to another' (Donoghue, 1993). As late as 1989 Dekker and van de Pol's study of female transvestism 'suffers from some startlingly unwarranted conclusions': for example, that most people were ignorant of the existence of tribady, that no women knew of any examples of sexual relations between women, that the common people had never heard of such things, that women who loved women logically thought themselves to be like men. Since the late seventeenth century there were in fact 'songs, court cases, pornographic pictures, medical and literary books and endlessly retold anecdotes about that very subject' (Donoghue, 1993). The evidence presented by Donoghue convincingly demolishes the social constructionist view that there is a datable 'profound shift' from a lesbian 'role' to a lesbian 'identity':

> When seventeenth- and eighteenth-century texts are full of women loving each other and playing a variety of roles, it makes no sense to try to track down the birth of a single 'lesbian role' ... it is nonsense to represent the variety of lesbian culture as a parade of types, each one replacing the last.

Ancient Amazons and other foremothers

Grahn (1984) points out that 'The earliest poetry signed by an individual in any literature' is by a lesbian, Enheduanna, who lived in present-day Iraq around 2300 BC. Enheduanna was a priestess and her hymn exalts the omnipotence of the goddess Inanna. Whether or not the poem bears evidence of a transition from 'matriarchy' to 'patriarchy', Grahn's inference about its lesbian nature seems just:

> Enheduanna's lushly sensual descriptions of Inanna's physical beauty, her unbridled love of her fierceness, the complete absence of heterosexual references, and her accounts of Inanna's undertaking of ceremonial Gay rituals – all make it highly probable that Enheduanna was a Lesbian. That she describes herself a 'spouse' of the goddess makes it nearly certain that she was a Lesbian, and expressing a Lesbian office.

Lesbian prehistory is even more speculative than the prehistory of proto-Indo-European pederasty. The nineteenth-century theory that a prehistoric 'matriarchy' preceded the historical establishment of 'patriarchy' is the cornerstone of much feminist history, but is unsupported by archaeological evidence. Palaeolithic cave paintings and rock carvings of men with erections dancing together (i.e. patriarchal virility rituals) precede Neolithic carvings of 'Venus' figures (i.e. matriarchal fertility rituals) by about ten thousand years (Greenberg, 1988): 'This fantasy – for little conclusive evidence has been offered for a universal horizon of matriarchy in humanity's past – has returned today among some anthropologists, who search for traces of a lost system of social organization which probably never existed' (W. R. Dynes, 'Anthropology', *EH*). In several ancient and modern non-Western cultures women are allowed to own property and wealth, and this independence from men can sometimes facilitate lesbian relationships. For example, among Mombasa women there are open social networks of lesbian patron/client couples. The existence of matrilineal inheritance of status and property in some indigenous societies certainly demonstrates that there is an alternative to patriarchal systems, but the modern use of such terms as 'matrifocal' and 'gynocratic' prejudges some very problematic issues. Lesbian-feminist prehistory is dominated by the construct of a proto-lesbian Amazon nation. Thus Susan Cavin in her book *Lesbian Origins*

> theorizes that all-women Amazon tribes evolved from the high-female/low-male ratio of primary kinship groups that are still seen

today in primates, our nearest relatives. These Amazon tribes spanned the globe and preceded the heterosexual, patriarchal society of equal female-to-male kinship groups that we know today. (Richards, 1990)

Advancing into history proper, lesbian relations are documented, however sparsely, for most historical periods, ranging from lesbian initiation rituals in ancient Greece (notably Sparta), through the visual representation of lesbian Tantric erotic positions on ancient Indian temples (Thadani, 1996) and lesbian relations in Eastern harems, to at least one example of lesbian Provençal troubadour verse. Erotic verse letters were written by one twelfth-century Bavarian nun to another, 'recall[ing] the kisses you gave me, / And how with tender words you caressed my little breasts' (trans. Boswell, 1980). Some medieval rules prescribed forty days' penance for nuns who 'rode' one another or caressed another's breasts, unless there was a 'flow', in which case two years' penance were required (Boswell, 1995); many penances seem to be logical categories rather than observations – the outcome of the intellectual hothouse of monasticism – but the slangy characterization of nuns 'riding' one another suggests the reality of lesbian intercourse. And there is the famous case of Sister Benedetta Carlini, fully documented by Brown (1986), an early seventeenth-century abbess of a convent near Florence who had sex with many nuns while impersonating an angel called 'Splenditello', until she was placed in solitary confinement for the remaining forty years of her life.

The lesbian and the law

Trial records, an otherwise rich repository of material about gay men, produce only fragmentary evidence about lesbians. It is often said that there are no legal records because there have never been any laws against lesbianism, but that is not true. There have been no laws against lesbians in England and America, but

> In Europe before the French revolution, however, notably in such countries as France, Spain, Italy, Germany, and Switzerland, lesbian acts were regarded as legally equivalent to acts of male sodomy and were, like them, punishable by the death penalty. On occasions, executions of women were carried out. (Crompton, 1985)

But such instances were rare, and laws which formally existed on the statute books were seldom enforced in practice.

The earliest legal reference to lesbians seems to be the French law code *Li Livres di Jostice et de plet* (c. 1270), which prescribed that a man who engages in homosexual relations shall, on the first offence, lose his testicles, shall lose his member (penis) on the second offence, and shall be burned to death on the third offence; and that a woman 'shall lose her member each time, and on the third must be burned'. It is not clear how a woman can 'lose her member' (*perdre membre*) twice – obviously the law is a purely formal example of *mutatis mutandis*. No prosecutions under this law are known, although Crompton calls attention to the fact that in an early fourteenth-century romance two women suspected of *bougrerie* are threatened with burning, so the possibility of such a punishment was part of the popular imagination. In Spain *Las Siete Partidas*, compiled in about 1265, provided for the death penalty for men; a gloss prepared in 1555 interpreted the law as applying equally to lesbians, but there is no indication that it was so applied during the intervening three centuries. A report of around 1645 revealed that in Russia women 'are burned alive' for sodomy, but it is not clear if this refers to an actual prosecution or just to a statute. Treviso, near Venice, had statutes providing for the burning of lesbians (*fregatores*) as well as buggers (*buzerones*), but there seem to have been no resulting prosecutions.

The earliest lesbian execution seems to have occurred in Speier in 1477 when a girl was drowned for lesbian love. Two nuns in Spain were executed in the sixteenth century for using 'material instruments' (i.e. dildos). In 1549 a woman was banished from Saragosa, in Aragon, for 'imperfect sodomy'. In Bordeaux in 1533 two women were tortured at their trial but acquitted for insufficient evidence. A woman from Fontaines was burned alive around 1535 for disguising herself as a man and marrying a woman. In his diary Montaigne records the hanging in 1580 of a weaver named Marie, convicted of dressing as a man and marrying a woman and using a device for intercourse. In the mid-sixteenth century in Granada a group of women were whipped and sent to the galleys for using sexual instruments, and in Geneva in 1568 a lesbian was put to death by drowning – the only case found after extensive search of the Genevan archives (Monter, 1985). The lesbian Isabel Galandre was burned as a witch at Neuchâtel in 1623. The Puritan settlers in New England made lesbianism a capital crime in the mid-seventeenth century, but there are no known capital prosecutions, and hardly any non-capital prosecutions. In March 1648–9 a woman was publicly chastised and given a warning to amend her lewd behaviour with another woman. In 1792 a Dutch woman was convicted for having murdered her girlfriend out of jealousy over her affair with a third woman. These are not 'representative' cases: they are practically the only cases we know.

English law ignores lesbianism, although women cross-dressers were sometimes prosecuted under laws penalizing vagrancy or fraud or other ambiguous misdemeanours (cross-dressing as such was not illegal). Anthony Wood in 1694 reported that a woman was tried at the King's Bench for impersonating a man and marrying a maid to obtain her dowry and was about to marry a second wife, noting that 'her love letters were read in court, which occasioned much laughter'; she was sentenced to be whipped and to serve at hard labour (Donoghue, 1993). The next earliest case was that of Mary Hamilton, who was discovered to have married a woman and used a dildo to have sexual relations with her; in 1746 she was prosecuted under a clause of the vagrancy act, 'for having by false and deceitful practices endeavoured to impose on some of his Majesty's subjects', for which she was publicly whipped in four market towns and sent to prison for six months. Ann Marrow was convicted of fraud in 1777 'for going in man's cloaths, and personating a man in marriage, with three different women, ... and defrauding them of their money and effects', for which she was sentenced to three months in prison, and to stand in the pillory at Charing Cross, where she was pelted so severely, primarily by the female spectators, that she was blinded in both eyes (Norton, 1992).

This is nearly a complete list of all known cases of prosecution. Some extensive research in French and Italian legal records has drawn a blank regarding lesbian trials, so although further research will undoubtedly make more discoveries, we can predict that these cases will be very localized and not representative of any national practice. It can readily be seen that there is no historical evidence of widespread systematic legal persecution of lesbians. It should also be appreciated that these sporadic instances of prosecution will not support any theories about lesbianism being perceived as a threat to the body politic, or lesbians being subjected to social control by state authorities. Certainly we should continue to search for lesbian prosecutions – not for statistical evidence of homophobia, but for the insight they offer into the daily lives and personalities of lesbians.

Catharina alias Anastasius

On 13 October 1721 in Halberstadt, Saxony, Catharina Margaretha Linck and Catharina Margaretha Mühlhahn were prosecuted for lesbian relations. A transcript of the trial from the Prussian Secret State Archives was published in 1891 by Dr F. C. Müller and translated into English by Brigitte Eriksson in 1980.

Catharina Linck (or Lincken) was a religious fanatic, a bit of a wife-beater, a member of the vagabond/religious underworld and one of life's losers. Linck was about 27 years old in 1721. For many years she had disguised herself in men's clothes 'In order to lead a life of chastity'. She became a member of a group of Inspirants, a wandering band resembling the Quakers, had ecstasies and delusions and professed to be a prophet for two years. She joined the army as Anastasius Lagrantinus Beuerlein, but deserted in 1708. She was captured and sentenced to hang, but was freed upon the discovery of her true sex:

> She had made a penis of stuffed leather with two stuffed testicles made from pig's bladder attached to it and had tied it to her pubes with a leather strap. ... She said that while she was a soldier she had hired many a woman whom she excited with the leather object. At times she ran for miles after a beautiful woman and spent all her earnings on her. Often when a woman touched her, even slightly, she became so full of passion that she did not know what to do. (Eriksson, 1980)

For the next few years Linck alternated between male and female clothing, and also had herself baptized alternately in the Catholic and Lutheran faiths. In 1717, pretending to be a man, she married, in church, Catharina Margaretha Mühlhahn (who was 22 in 1721). She used a leather-covered horn to urinate standing up like a man, but her wife noticed that 'Other men can piss quite a ways, but you always piss on your shoes.' Her wife found out her disguise, and Linck promised that henceforth they would live together as brother and sister, but soon they continued having sexual relations.

The two women lived as vagabond beggars for a time. Linck was able to make her 'leather sausage' 'stiff or limp'. The bride complained to her mother of soreness, especially after Linck forced her to take it in her mouth. The mother-in-law beat Linck and tore open her clothes to discover the false penis. Mühlhahn was too fearful of her 'husband' to bring any charges against her; instead her mother probably brought the irregularity to the attention of the authorities, not realizing that her daughter would also be prosecuted, but we do not know the exact circumstances of why this came to trial. Both women were convicted of sodomy, exacerbated by the circumstances of 'the abuse of holy baptism and the frequent apostatizing', which were also crimes, though not capital crimes. Linck was sentenced to be beheaded and then burned (rather than burned alive); Mühlhahn was sentenced to three years 'in the penitentiary or spinning room' and afterwards to be banished from the country.

Linck's own testimony does not suggest that she identified herself as a man, although she obviously took a male sexual role and even used her *olisbo* in a symbolic act not unknown in modern butch/femme relations. There seems no reason why we should not agree with the lawyers at the trial, who defined her as a *fricatrice*, a 'rubbing woman' – a lesbian.

Female husbands and cross-dressing

Male impersonation (women dressing as men and pretending to be men) is a major theme of lesbian history (cf. Richards, 1990). Cross-dressing has been a central feature of lesbian culture in Britain from the seventeenth century onwards (Donoghue, 1993). There is the very curious case, perhaps fiction (in *The Life and Adventures of Mrs Christian Davies, the British Amazon*, possibly by Daniel Defoe, 1741), of a woman who dresses as a man in order to follow her husband into the army, whose disguise is completed by a silver 'urinary instrument' that once belonged to a colonel who was herself a woman in disguise, which suggests a kind of secret tradition of cross-dressers. Many names could be cited, including the first English woman doctor James Miranda Barry (c. 1795–1865); the American doctor Mary Edward Walker (1823–1919) who wore her hair in curls to keep her gender visible; Dr Sara Josephine Baker (1873–1945); Jim McHarris (Annie Lee Grant, fl. 1940), a black short-order cook, gas station attendant and preacher discovered to be a passing woman when she was given a traffic ticket; and Dr Eugene C. Perkins, married to another woman for twenty-eight years, discovered to be a female only on her death in 1936. The numbers of passing women (and men) must be very much higher than the ones we know about, who have been discovered only because they became seriously ill (or died) and were subject to a medical examination and hence came to public attention. Billy Tipton the Big Band musician who married and adopted sons, was discovered to be a woman at her death in 1989. Presumably there are still such women who lead this kind of secret existence.

The tradition of female husbands, women who not only passed as men but who married women, existed in Europe from the seventeenth century; they are labelled after the famous case of 'George' Hamilton which was reported by Henry Fielding in *The Female Husband* (1746). There are innumerable other examples: James How (Mary East, fl. 1750) ran a pub with her wife; Nicholas de Raylan (d. 1906) fought in the Spanish–American war, and had two wives, the first of whom divorced her because of her affairs with chorus girls; Charley (Charlotte) Wilson (b. 1834) and her niece passed as man and wife until Charlotte had to enter the poorhouse; Katherine Vosbaugh (b. 1827), who married a woman, wasn't discovered until she entered hospital for pneumonia; Charles Winslow Hall (Caroline Hall, fl. 1901), according to her Italian wife, decided to live as a man after 'brooding over the disadvantages of being a woman'; Peter Stratford (Derestey Morton, d. 1929) emigrated from New Zealand to America where she married the screenwriter Beth Rouland. American medical journals from 1901–6 reported on several married men discovered to have been women upon their deaths, including George Greene, William C. Howard (she and her wife adopted two children) and Nicholas de Raylan, who had married twice and who at her death in 1906 was discovered to have had an 'elaborately-constructed artificial penis'. Joseph Lobdell (Lucy Ann Lobdell, b. 1829) wrote an autobiography, *The Female Hunter of Delaware and Sullivan Counties*. In fact a surprising number of cross-dressing women have written their autobiographies: Mary Frith (1662), Jean de Préchac (1713), Christian Davies (1740), Maria ter Meetelen (1743), Hannah Snell (1750), Maria van Antwerpen (1751), Charlotte Charke (1755), Mary Anne Talbot (1809), Renée Bordereau (1814), Françoise Després (1817) and Anne Jane Thornton (1835). The number of women who cross-dressed who are generally believed to have had lesbian relations is legion.

From about 1865 many Chinese women, gaining some measure of economic independence due to employment in silk factories, rejected heterosexuality, called themselves *tzu-shu nii* ('never to marry'), and established 'sister societies', communes of 'sworn sisters' (*shuang chieh*), of pairs or trios; the slang term for them was *sou-hei* ('self-combers'), because they adopted the married woman's hairstyle. These associations declined during the 1930s economic depression, and were put down by the Communists as examples of decadent feudalism. Many sworn sisters fled to Singapore, Malaya and Hong Kong, where some groups were still in existence in the 1980s. Similarly, in the early 1800s in Eastern Europe (parts of Albania and the former Yugoslavia) women could become 'sworn virgins', wear male clothing and take wives.

When dealing with romantic friendship we must not ignore the possibility that such women hid the sexual nature of their relationship, just as thousands of 'passing women' kept their real sex secret throughout the eighteenth and nineteenth centuries. During the American Civil War some four hundred women masqueraded as men and fought in the ranks (Miller, 1995). This necessarily involved very extensive secrecy of the most calculated sort. The New York politician Murray Hall (born Mary Anderson) impersonated a man for nearly thirty years. She married two women, one for three years and one for twenty years, and had an adopted daughter. 'According to neighbors, both her marriages broke up because Hall paid too much attention to other women' (Miller, 1995). Her adopted daughter did not realize (or claimed not to realize) that her father was really a woman. She died of breast cancer in 1901, when her true identity was discovered. The very many women who lived together as apparent man and wife and even married women in civil and church ceremonies throughout the eighteenth and nineteenth centuries provides ample evidence of deceit and 'lesbian survival'.

Anne Lister

If we need more evidence that the lesbian identity existed before 1869, we have only to investigate the life of Anne Lister (1791–1840). During the 1810s and 1820s she possessed a fully formed lesbian personality whose characteristics (except for the absence of a political consciousness) are easily recognizable to modern lesbians. In her remarkable journals, large parts of which are written in a secret code combining characters from Greek and algebra, she records her systematic seduction of several women, and her awareness of herself as a lesbian (though she did not use that word) situated within a lesbian culture. This is the authentic voice of lesbian experience, worth more than a dozen volumes of abstract theory. Virtually nothing in the social construction model can help us to analyse this important document or to account for the lesbian awareness that is so obviously revealed in it. The decipherment and publication of these journals by Helena Whitbread in 1988 and 1992 was a culture shock, and a malicious rumour was started that they were a hoax, but abundant documentary evidence quickly established their authenticity.

Not only is Anne Lister a self-conscious lesbian in the psychological sense ('I love and only love the fairer sex and thus beloved by them in turn, my heart revolts from any love but theirs'), she is also a self-conscious lesbian in the social/cultural sense and a careful observer of lesbian 'signs' among other women. She went to Paris in 1824 to master French and to find a cure for a venereal infection passed to her by her English lover

Marianna Lawton (who nicknamed her 'Fred') who, Anne believed, had caught it from her husband Charles, and which Anne had subsequently passed on to a Scottish woman she met in York. (The marriage of Marianna was a severe blow to Anne, but the two women renewed their sexual relationship a couple of years later.) The *pension* in which she stayed was a veritable hothouse of female friendship. She engaged in 'arrant flirting' with the young and frail Mlle de Sans, 'which she seems to like & understand well enough'. Her main object of desire was the older Mrs Barlow, whom she begins to seduce by passing off as foolish behaviour, kissing, touching of knees and playful 'nonsense'.

One of Anne Lister's techniques of seduction was to mention books which touched upon lesbianism or male homosexuality and then to observe her companion carefully to judge her reaction. In 1823 she remarks that 'Miss Pickford has read the Sixth Satyr of Juvenal. She understands these matters well enough.' Juvenal's satire was the *locus classicus* for the ancient world's description of both male and female homosexuals, often appropriated through allusion to become part of modern queer cultural unity. Lister's allusion to Suetonius being 'a little free' is not picked up by Mme Galvani, but in early October 1824, as Anne is flirting with Mrs Barlow, Miss Mackenzie, a visitor who is her match in the classics, passes her a confidential note:

> 'I have a question to ask you. Êtes-vous Achilles?' I laughed & said she made me blush. ... Brought Miss Mack into my room. Joked with her about her question. Said it was exceedingly well put. She said I was the only one in the house to whom she could have written it, because the only one who would have so soon understood it, that is, who would have understood the allusion to take it that way.

The very clever allusion is to the incident in which Achilles dresses as a girl in the court of Lycomedes in order to escape the oracle that says he is to die in the battle of Troy. This incident exhibits a high degree of consciousness of the lesbian type among sophisticated women. A few days later, Mrs Barlow

> began talking of that one of the things of which Marie Antoinette was accused of was being too fond of women. I, with perfect mastery of countenance, said I had never heard of it before and could not understand or believe it. ... I said I would not believe such a thing existed. Mrs Barlow said it was mentioned in scripture, not in the New Testament not Deuteronomy, nor Leviticus. I said

I believe that when reduced to the last extremity – I was going to mention the use of phalli but luckily Mrs Barlow said, 'You mean two men being fond of each other?' & I said 'Yes' ... I declared I was the most innocent person in the world concerning all I had seen & heard, for everybody told me things. She said she should not have mentioned it but she knew she was not telling me anything I did not know before. I said I read of women being too fond of each other in the Latin parts of the works of Sir William Jones. ... In fact, she suspected me and she was fishing to find it out but I think I was too deep for her. ... We agreed it was a scandal invented by the men, who were bad enough for anything.

Mrs Barlow is nearly as 'deep' as Anne, and both women relish this coy cultural seduction. By early November Mrs Barlow regularly sits on Anne's knee while Anne hugs and kisses her and rubs her through her petticoats until Anne's thighs shake and she experiences orgasm. Soon 'She begins to stand closer to me. I might easily press queer to queer. Our liking each other is now mutually understood and acknowledged.' Mrs Barlow regularly allows Anne to 'grubble' her 'queer' with her hand through a thin layer of petticoat while they lie in bed together and Anne presses herself against her and experiences orgasm. During the Christmas/New Year holiday they lie together naked and Anne is allowed to insert her finger and 'dawdle' Mrs Barlow until they both achieve orgasm.

Anne's generic euphemism for lesbianism was 'connection with the ladies', and for full sexual connection involving full commitment, 'going to Italy'. Mrs Barlow's euphemism for Anne's orgasms was that she 'will do yourself harm'. Anne's use of 'queer' to denote the female pudendum is nowhere else recorded. It has no demonstrable link to the slang 'quim' for 'cunt', literally 'cleft'. Scores of slang terms going back to the mid-sixteenth century use the term 'queer', whose exact origin is obscure, though it virtually always means 'inferior' – perhaps Anne's application of the term literally to the 'nether' regions is the original meaning of the word. It seems likely, though etymologically unproven, that the male homosexual is called a queer in the sense of a cunt.

It is difficult to entirely comprehend the sexual act covered by Anne's euphemism 'kiss' (which like the French *baisser* can mean 'fuck'): menstruation is sometimes a reason not to 'kiss'. 'Two good kisses at once last night & three this morning, after eight.' Presumably these are multiple orgasms: 'Three or four all at once last night & one more, a good one, at four this morning.' Anne joyfully discovers that Marianna is still a virgin because her husband is incompetent; Anne describes in detail how she uses her middle finger to break the membrane.

In sexual affairs Anne prefers not to be treated overtly as a woman. Anne does not like it when Mrs Barlow touches her queer and wishes to 'do to you as you do to me'. She is 'astonished' rather than angered, but unable to explain her feelings adequately:

> This is womanizing me too much ... she lets me see too much that she considers me too much as a woman. She talks to me about being unwell [i.e. menstruating]. I have aired napkins before her. She feels me, etc. All which I like not. Marianna never seems to know or notice these things. She suits me better.

She and Marianna 'talked of the management my temper required. Marianna knew it well. It had its peculiarities but she did not fear. Talked of ... my sensitiveness of anything that reminded me of my petticoats.' Anne seems to prefer a recognized gender division between giver and receiver, with herself as giver: in the 1940s and 1950s she would have been classified as a 'stone butch'.

Marianna was initially ashamed to be seen in public with Anne because the latter's masculine appearance was remarked upon by others. They are a butch/femme couple. A woman friend told Anne that Marianna is '"plus femme que moi" [more womanly than me]. I have the figure & nature of a man. Have not beauty but agreeable features tho' not those of a woman. I joked, pretended to be shocked.' Many people suspected things and talked about Anne's masculinity, but she and Marianna withstood it:

> For if we once got together the world might say what it pleased. She should never mind. ... She shrank from having the thing surmised now, but declared that if we were once fairly together, she should not care about it. I might tell our connection to all the world if I pleased.

Like many homosexuals of a later period, Anne realized she was different and tried to understand the nature of her sexuality. To Mrs Barlow she

> Said how it was all nature. Had it not been genuine the thing would have been different. [I] said I had thought much, studied anatomy, etc. Could not find it out. Could not understand myself. It was all the effect of the mind. No exterior formation accounted for it. Alluded to their being an internal correspondence or likeness of

some of the male or female organs of generation. Alluded to the stones not slipping thro' the ring till after birth, etc.

Anne is aware of, but rejects as deficient, the early proto-sexological literature regarding lesbians as hermaphrodites. Although she did consult anatomical works (including Latin works), she is the instigator of her own attempt to understand herself – she is not a dupe coerced by doctors into seeing herself on their terms. She already has a powerful sense of identity, but is nevertheless endeavouring to understand its nature:

> Got on the subject of Saffic regard. [I] said there was artifice in it. It was very different from mine & would be no pleasure to me. I liked to have those I loved near me as possible, etc. Asked if she understood. She said no. [I] told her I knew by her eyes she did & she did not deny it, therefore I know she understands all about the use of a —.

What Anne is talking about here is the use of a dildo, an artificial device which she feels is inferior to her own idea of natural lesbian intercourse. 'I mentioned the girl at a school in Dublin that had been obliged to have surgical aid to extract the thing.' (Horror stories of this nature are a feature of queer folk tales.) Nevertheless, in a later adventure when Anne seduces a coquette, she fantasizes about having a penis: 'Fancying I had a penis & was intriguing with her in the downstairs water-closet at Langton before breakfast, to which she would have made no objection.'

Anne is both secret and blatant; like many lesbians and homosexuals until relatively recent times, she openly assumes the liberties and manners of the opposite sex but is sufficiently clever to prevent a direct accusation, at least to her face. Her flirting with women is so open and gentleman-like that several women of her acquaintance wonder if she is a man in disguise. She is aware that her sexuality is an object of discussion among friends and relatives, and Mrs Barlow asks what her maidservant thinks of her behaviour: '"Oh, merely, that I have my own particular ways." I happened to say that my aunt often said I was the oddest person she ever knew. Mrs Barlow said, "But she knows all about it, does she not?" "Oh," said I, "she & my friends are all in a mist about it."'

Anne's journals document features of lesbian culture that have no conceivable relationship to any sort of social control imposed from without. Anne wears an engagement ring and a wedding ring given to her by Marianna, and they go through a little ceremony of kissing these and swearing their love for one another. More remarkably, we discover that there is a tradition of lesbian lovers exchanging pubic hair with one another, just as heterosexual lovers exchanged locks of hair. Anne has a collection of these love tokens in her cabinet of curiosities, which she shows to Marianna and asks her to guess whom they came from (one set even came from Marianna's sister). To celebrate their reunion,

> Marianna put me on a new watch riband & then cut the hair from her own queer & I that from mine, which she put each into each of the little lockets we got at Bright's this morning, twelve shillings each, for us always to wear under our clothes in mutual remembrance. We both of us kissed each bit of hair before it was put into the locket.

An economic analysis of the situation reveals mainly that financial independence allowed Anne Lister to follow her own instincts. Capitalism facilitates rather than inhibits lesbian relations. The rise of capitalism, if it has any direct effect on homosexuality, allows its freer expression because of increased mobility, more tolerance of unconventional behaviour for those whose status is achieved through wealth rather than birth, and greater independence through inheritance of moderate but adequate wealth without the necessity of marital or family alliances. Anne always knew that she could live practically in the open as a lesbian with a companion because her aunt and uncle were a spinster and bachelor sister and brother and she was destined to inherit the family estate and be independently well off. She drew quite a reasonable income from them, and discussed her affairs with them quite openly, barring the explicit sex, comparing the different merits of her potential female partners; they looked forward to the time when she would fix upon a suitable female companion to live with her and settle down. Anne became her own master at the age of 35, on the death of her uncle. But views such as that of Ann Ferguson that 'financial independence was a necessary precondition for the formation of a lesbian identity' (Vicinus, 1993) are brought up short by the fact that the women with whom Anne Lister had relations were themselves *dependent*, either upon men or upon her, and some of them were nevertheless lesbian-identified.

Anne was a member of the petit bourgeois, and most of her sexual partners had a lower social and financial status than she. Economic considerations were as important for Anne and her lovers as for heterosexuals. The affair with Mrs Barlow eventually failed partly because Mrs Barlow felt like a kept mistress rather than a wife. Marianna had originally left Anne to get married and thereby gain a higher income –

Anne regretted what she termed 'legal prostitution' but nevertheless encouraged the marriage because of its obvious financial prudence (Charles breaks off friendly relations with Anne when he discovers that she and his wife hope for his early death so they can live together); later Marianna reinstates her relationship with Anne when she realizes that she is not going to have a child by her husband (who seems to be infertile) and that he has not put her into his will, though she has signed her income over to him, which means she would be destitute at his death. Eventually Charles reconciles himself with Anne and resigns himself to her affair with his wife, facilitating their travelling together and feigning indifference when they share the same bed, even in his own house. Under pressure from Anne, Charles ensures that Marianna will receive a good annual income after his death. The two women often discuss the details of pooling their resources (including the anticipated annuity from Charles) during their passionate second honeymoon.

But Charles does not die soon, and after several years Anne tires of Marianna, especially after an affair with a sophisticated Frenchwoman in Paris. In 1832 she began an affair with a 29-year-old Ann Walker, a rich heiress who became her live-in companion, with whom she travelled widely and with whose money she reshaped her beloved Shibden Hall in Halifax, Yorkshire, which ought to be a place of lesbian pilgrimage. She caught a fever and died in 1840 in the foothills of the Caucasus Mountains in Georgia, and Ann Walker spent seven months bringing her lover's body back to England to be buried in the local parish church.

'Romantic friendships'

Anne Lister's diaries do not simply move the 'lesbian moment' back from the late nineteenth to the early nineteenth century. It is a very easy matter to push this back further, to the late eighteenth century. Anne Lister visited the famous Ladies of Llangollen in 1821 and recorded in her diary: 'I cannot help thinking that surely it was not Platonic. Heaven forgive me, but I look within myself & doubt.' I shall not rehearse the well-known story about how Lady Eleanor Butler (1739–1829) and Sarah Ponsonby (1755–1831) eloped together in 1778 and set up house at Plas Newydd, where they were visited by all the writers and celebrities of the Romantic age. A newspaper in 1790 described them in terms that implied they were indeed lesbian, and they took it seriously enough to ask their friend Edmund Burke, the famous orator and MP, whether or not they should sue for libel – he wisely advised them against such a course. Donoghue

(1993) has suggested that Elizabeth Mavor in her biography of the Ladies 'resurrected the phrase "romantic friendship" in 1971 specifically to shield the Ladies of Llangollen from being called lesbians. It has become a popular term among historians, often invoked to neutralise and de-sexualise textual evidence.' Lillian Faderman (1985b) followed Mavor's lead in her study of 'romantic friendship between women', *Surpassing the Love of Men*, arguing that their contemporaries all agreed they were merely female friends. But in 1992 Liz Stanley discovered an unpublished diary by Hester Thrale (whose daughter once visited the Ladies) which describes the Ladies as 'damned Sapphists' and which claims that women were reluctant to stay the night with them unless they were accompanied by men.

Of course none of these views establishes whether or not the Ladies of Llangollen enjoyed sex together. But the fact that two women – one of them a self-conscious lesbian – contemporaries of the Ladies felt that they probably were lesbians thoroughly demolishes the view that it is 'anachronistic' for us to view them as lesbians. The entire body of literature of female 'romantic friendship' has been too cavalierly dismissed as being 'homosocial' rather than homosexual. Unfortunately Faderman (1994) seems to have been unaware of the work of Donoghue or Stanley when she compiled her anthology of lesbian literature from the seventeenth century to the present, *Chloe Plus Olivia*, wherein she continues to base her non-sexual interpretation of romantic friendship specifically upon the error that Hester Thrale considered the Ladies to be *only* 'fair and noble recluses' and 'charming cottagers' rather than sapphists. (Faderman must have been aware of Lister's remark, but ignores it.)

Faderman's anthology exhibits enormous breadth and scholarship, but the material is arranged to reinforce the editor's theory that the sexologists called 'the lesbian' into being, undermining the earlier ideology of romantic friendship. In the section on 'The Literature of Sexual Inversion', extracts from Krafft-Ebing and Freud precede selections from Charlotte Charke, Maria Edgeworth, Anne Lister and others, allowing careless readers to form the mistaken impression that these women were influenced by the theories of the two men, when in fact the writings of these women predated Krafft-Ebing and Freud by a good many years. A strictly chronological arrangement of the entire anthology would tend to undermine the view that lesbians imitated male-generated models of themselves.

Jeffreys (1989b) also criticizes Faderman for devoting too much energy to proving in *The Scotch Verdict* that the two teachers accused of lesbianism in 1811 (who won their case for libel) did not have genital sex, and could not possibly have had sexual relations because that is an 'anachronistic' modern view. In fact, the study demonstrates 'that girls at "nice" boarding schools in 1811 seem to have been as keenly aware of and as likely to chatter about lesbians as they are today. They talked of lesbianism with maids and nannies who all seem to have known something about it.' Faderman treats merely as 'amusing' the memorandum prepared by the senior counsel citing the 'authorities' – with extensive quotations – to prove to the Lords of Council and Session that 'the practice of tribadism' exists. Faderman should have appreciated this as a substantial summing up of the lesbian cultural tradition – and a full awareness of it in 1811.

Early lesbian history seems to be made up largely of pair-bonding rather than larger networks, for example numerous female–female marriages can be documented back through the seventeenth century. Nevertheless, we occasionally find evidence of what might be called lesbian 'quasi-sub-cultures'. In the early 1730s, Lady Frances Brudenell, the bisexual widowed Duchess of Newburgh, is supposed to have ruled over a social circle of tribades in Dublin, her particular lover being Lady Allen, and there were 'small groups of tribades in 1790s Amsterdam' (Donoghue, 1993). In France, the lesbian Sect of Anandrynes was founded in 1770 by Thérèse de Fleury; it was mostly the subject of gossip and journalism but several documents survive. Apparently there was an internal dispute as to whether or not effeminate male homosexuals should be admitted as members, which brought about its dissolution in 1784. The leader of the group was the actress Raucourt (Françoise Marine Antoinette Joseph Saucerotte), who was imprisoned by the Jacobins in 1793 but released; Napoleon was an admirer. When she died in 1815 the curé of St Roch 'refused to admit her body to the church. A mob of over 15,000 persons broke in bearing her coffin, and an order of Louis XVIII assured her the last rites' and she was buried in Père Lachaise (L. Senelick, 'Raucourt', *EH*).

Johann Wilhelm von Archenholtz who travelled to England in the 1780s reveals that there was a club of lesbians or Anandrinic Society in London, one of its presidents being the famous actress Mrs Y, whom Donoghue identifies as the Drury Lane (bisexual) actress Mary Anne Yates (1728–87). Much earlier in England, Delarivière Manley in her *Secret Memoirs ... from the New Atalantis* (1709) describes the 'new Cabal' of lesbians, society ladies who met regularly to indulge their lesbian 'inclinations', who included: Margaret Sutton, Lady Lexington and her daughters Elenora-Margareta and Bridget; Anna Charlotte, Lady Frescheville, a founder member who fell in love with Mrs Pround, an attendant to Queen

Anne; Lady Anne Popham and her favourite Ann Gerard, Countess Macclesfield; Lucy Wharton, wife of a Whig minister, and her lover Catherine Tofts the opera singer; Catherine Colyear, Duchess of Portmore and Dorchester, and her favourite Catharine Trotter the playwright, who is described as having male lovers purely for financial security. Manley's work was a political attack, and therefore little effort has been expended upon proving or disproving her assertions concerning this lesbian 'Sodality' or network.

Romantic friendships between women are the more refined, middle-class versions of working-class sapphism and upper-class anandrynism. I suspect that the idealization of romantic female friendship was used to mask lesbian love in the same way that Oscar Wilde idealized 'Greek love' to defend himself in the dock. From the mid-eighteenth century genteel women began living together and pooling their resources. The rise of the women's movement in the later eighteenth century provided homosexually inclined women the opportunity to work together for a cause that helped to legitimate and refine their desires by channelling them towards intellectual and cultural goals, within a 'homosocial' environment. Most of the Bluestockings who set up all-female establishments were unmarried (usually spinsters by choice) or widowed or separated. By the late nineteenth/early twentieth century the contiguity of lesbianism and feminism was recognized by contemporary observers. This was the first-hand perception of Edward Carpenter (Miller, 1995): 'It is pretty certain that such comrade-alliances – of a quite devoted kind – are becoming increasingly common, and especially perhaps among the more cultured classes of women who are working out the great cause of their own sex's liberation.' This was also the view of the American temperance leader Frances Willard, who herself had romantic attachments with women:

> The loves of women for each other grow more numerous each day, and I have pondered much why these things were. That so little should be said about them surprises me, for they are everywhere. ... there is no village that has not its examples of 'two hearts in counsel' both of which are feminine. Oftentimes these joint-proprietors have been unfortunately married, and so have failed to 'better their condition' until, thus clasping hands, they have taken each other 'for better or worse.' These are the tokens of a transition age. (Cited by Miller, 1995)

They were the outgrowth of the nineteenth-century American institution called the 'Boston marriage', in which two financially independent women lived together and worked to further feminist, philanthropic or cultural causes. Henry James, himself homosexual, described the union between his lesbian sister Alice and Katharine Loring in his novel *The Bostonians* (1886), albeit with his usual coded allusions. Sarah Orne Jewett characterized her Boston marriage to Annie Fields as 'a union – there is no truer word for it' (Miller, 1995).

The non-genital aspects of such female friendships have been very much exaggerated. Many of these romances were certainly physical, if not strictly genital. For example, Louise Brackett in Boston wrote to Anna E. Dickinson, American actress and political activist in the 1870s:

> How much I want to see you: as your letter gave me such exquisite pleasures indeed! I will marry you – run off any where with you, for you are such a darling – I can feel your soul – if not your body sweet Anna – do I offend your delicacy?

Dickinson was also loved by Susan B. Anthony the suffrage leader, who wrote to her:

> Now when are you coming to New York – do let it be soon – I have plain quarters – at 44 Bond Street – double bed – and big enough and good enough to take you in – ... I do so long for the scolding & pinched ears & every thing I know awaits me – what worlds of experience since I last snuggled the wee child in my long arms. ... Your loving friend Susan.

Miller (1995) argues that to assume that such passages imply sexual unions 'is to impose the ideas of the late twentieth century on a far more reticent era'. I disagree: I think we should not be so condescending towards the past.

The butch

Masculine women dominate the history of lesbians even more noticeably than effeminate men dominate the history of gay men. Most of the women in Rose Collis's (1994) collection of lesbian portraits are mannish. In the 1920s Mercedes De Acosta (1900–68) frequented the Paris café Chez Fischer, which she described in her memoirs as being a club where the women tried to look masculine and the men tried to look feminine, 'Which after all proves once again that there is nothing new under the sun.' She had an affair with Greta Garbo from 1929: 'De Acosta claimed credit for introducing Dietrich to the sartorial style sported by her in the 1930s: white flannel trousers and silk shirts, cream polo-neck jumpers and berets, complete with short, boyish haircuts.' The artist Rosa Bonheur (1822–1899) claimed to wear trousers out of necessity rather than a desire to shock: 'Eventually, she was issued with police certificates – *permission de travestissement* – renewable every six months, which allowed her to wear male clothes in public places.' In 1943 when the composer Ethel Smyth (1858–1944) was old and deaf and had to go into a nursing home for the last year of her life, her nurse insisted on dressing her in 'most unbecoming lady-like clothes'. Eve Balfour (1889–1990), who lived on a farm with her companion Beryl 'Beb' Hearnden from 1919 to about 1951, and then lived with Kathleen Carnley until her death, 'discovered the freedom of breeches' in the First World War; Elizabeth Lutyens remembered, 'She had an Egyptian face of great strength and charm, with cropped hair and masculine manners, in spite of a feminine heart.' The mannish lesbian, the butch dyke, is found as a 'given' across many centuries. The great nelly queens of history are matched by the great Amazons of history, of which Queen Christina of Sweden (1626–89) was an example. As Leopold von Ranke observed, she was 'the greatest princely woman from the race of intermediate types'. She was big-boned, large-featured, masculine in deportment and temperament; even as a child she was often thought to be a handsome little boy. She was a classic lesbian type.

Butch/femme role-playing was a very common feature of lesbian culture in the 1950s. In the 1970s, under the influence of gay liberationist political ideals, butch/femme roles were rejected by lesbians as a retrogressive legacy of patriarchy and an aping of heterosexual relationships. In the late 1980s there began a revival of butch/femme role-playing that is still on the increase. Lesbian feminists such as Jeffreys (1989a) are shocked that

> They were not only adopting roles cheerfully but reclaiming roleplaying in lesbian history as well as the lesbian present as revolutionary and positive. ... Butch and femme identified lesbians today criticise feminists for having disapproved of roleplayers, and most importantly, for having distorted lesbian history by playing down the importance of roleplaying or recording it in a negative light. Some lesbian historians who are chronicling lesbian roleplaying in history treat roleplayers with unqualified admiration.

Lesbian feminist Merrill Mushroom is not untypical in simultaneously holding three contradictory attitudes towards butch/femme role-playing – that it is forced upon women, that it is freely chosen, that it is innate:

> Over the years, I have worn different tags and taken different images, and by now I can take them or leave them. But as I think back through all of the roles I have played and either kept or left behind, I know that deep down in my most secret heart of hearts ... I am still the butch.

Jeffreys may be justified in subjecting role-playing to a political analysis, but considered strictly from the historical view, the claim that butch/femme roles are part of lesbian heritage is well documented. Jeffreys's attack is marred by the lack of a historical perspective and by her dogmatic reliance on the social constructionist model. She claims quite incorrectly that Havelock Ellis's sexological depiction of the 'mannish' lesbian is based on such things as male erotica; in fact his case studies were provided by his lesbian wife Edith Lees, who had persuaded half a dozen of her lesbian friends to contribute their life histories – such self-selected material may be unrepresentative, but it is not 'mythological' as Jeffreys claims. Mannish lesbians were a commonplace reality throughout Europe and America by the 1820s, long before they were used as the model for the 'invert' by the sexologists, who 'did not so much define a lesbian identity as describe and categorize what they saw about them' (Vicinus, 1993). Jeffreys typically constructs a straw-man reductionist model of essentialism in order to knock it down:

> The recorded experience of 1950s roleplayers lends no support to a biological determinist explanation. The motivations mentioned are much more prosaic. ... [Ethel] Sawyer's informants [in Missouri] make it clear that stud and fish [the butch/femme terms among black lesbians] are social roles that were quite consciously chosen:
>
>> One fish expressed the desire to turn stud but had certain reservations. Her reasons for wanting to turn stud were that she wanted 'to be the aggressor, to pick and choose, and to do the protecting'. On the other hand, she felt that she could not live up to the idealised social role of a stud. 'I don't feel that I would be able to support someone. I feel that a stud should be the provider and protector and right now, I'm not able'.

This is the only example Jeffreys cites to prove that social roles are 'quite consciously chosen' – but notice that it presents a woman *who felt unable to choose the role of stud even though she wanted to*. Jeffreys's patent misreading of the evidence illustrates the kind of wish-fulfilment found in politically motivated history. It may be true, as Jeffreys argues, 'that both the butch and femme roles had serious disadvantages attached to them which make the revalidation of these roles today particularly difficult to understand'. But this in itself suggests that social roles are not consciously chosen. The evidence that Jeffreys cites and the argument she puts forward contradict the social-choice theory that she is advocating.

Many butch lesbians wore a breast band (some still do, and many now wear tight T-shirts) to preserve a masculine shape, and such devices (extending to strap-on dildos) are of course 'artificial' – but tomboy identities almost invariably precede the development of the breasts which threaten to weaken that identity: in other words, the butch identity in itself is not a construct. It is quite mistaken to see butches as simply aping men, and 'to recognize their masculinity and not their "queerness" is a distortion of their culture and their consciousness' (Kennedy and Davis, 1992). The acclaimed research of Kennedy and Davis into the lesbian community of Buffalo, New York, demonstrates that butch/femme role-playing is a case of authentic lesbian sexuality rather than internalized oppression or an imitation of heterosexual sexism. Jeffreys seems to deliberately misinterpret their use of the term 'authentic' as if they imply that role-playing is the only universally valid lesbian behaviour. It seems to me that Davis and Kennedy are using the word 'authentic' in its most valid meaning: indeed, it parallels the Marxist use of real as opposed to false consciousness.

Joan Nestle, in several essays, argues that upper- and middle-class feminist historians have exaggerated the importance of 'romantic friendship' while neglecting working-class lesbians. The earliest lesbian-feminist organizations, the Daughters of Bilitis in America and the Minorities Research Group in England, both debated the issue of 'trousers versus skirts'. Clearly diversity and flexibility of clothing were not the goal; the aim was to hide from public view the butch lesbian, just as gay male reformers wished to eliminate the fairy. This concern with image comes primarily from the middle classes, be they gay liberation activists or feminists. Jeffreys counters that Nestle's approach is bad because it

> could lead to the creation of false stereotypes of the working-class butch or femme. ... There has been an unfortunate tendency

amongst the detractors of feminism over the last few years to exploit the issue of class in inappropriate ways to support anti-feminist ideas and practice.

Jeffreys's argument is patently a case of the politically correct approach to history. She is so committed to the social constructionist dogma that homosexuality is entirely a reaction to heterosexuality (both being ideological phenomena) that she cannot intellectually comprehend Nestle's position that butch/femme relationships arise specifically from within queer culture.

In England, Skinner (1978) remembered that in the 1920s lesbians were described as 'horsey' or 'collar and tie girls'. In America, the very marked butch/femme dichotomy, and the use of the words themselves, first became noticeable in the 1930s, and then particularly apparent in the 1950s. It was very much a public gesture of proud defiance:

> In the fifties, butch women, dressed in slacks and shirts and flashing pinky rings, announced their sexual expertise in a public style that often opened their lives to ridicule and assault. Many adopted men's clothes and wore short 'DA' hair cuts to be comfortable and so that their sexual identity and preference would be clearly visible. (Joan Nestle, 'Butch–Fem Relationships', *EH*)

There are regional variations: in the black lesbian culture of New York the butch is more often called a 'bull dagger' and 'stud', while the femme is called 'my lady' or 'my family'. Although the word 'kiki' arose within the butch/femme culture, it could apply to either, and was essentially the equivalent of 'lesbian'; its exact origin and meaning are unclear. The most clearly marked features of the butch/femme are to be found in the working-class bar culture of the 1940s and 1950s, when women as well as men were called 'gay' and 'queer'.

Lesbian feminism in the early 1970s consciously and undisguisedly endeavoured to sever lesbians from their cultural roots (Case, 1993). *The Persistent Desire* (Nestle, 1992) amply documents the 'forced disinheritance' of the lesbians of the 1940s and 1950s by 'liberated' lesbian feminists; the experience of an entire generation of black and working-class lesbians was erased from politically correct lesbian history, and by 1975 butch/femme couples simply stopped going to the gay bars, and were wrongly thought to have 'disappeared' (MacCowan, 1992). This enforced silencing shows the true face of social constructionism. I am sure that Joan Nestle, who founded the New York Lesbian Herstory

Archives, is correct in her view that 'feminist writings have distorted lesbian history through their unwillingness to recognise the existence of roleplaying'. In their views of history, 'Passing women, Lesbian sex workers or working class Lesbian "married" couples were either completely missing or dismissed as examples of victimisation' or internalized oppression. For Nestle, butch/femme roles are 'complex erotic statements, not phony heterosexual replicas ... filled with a deeply Lesbian language of stance, dress, gesture, loving, courage, and autonomy'.

Amber Hollibaugh, a founding member of the San Francisco Lesbian and Gay History Project, similarly reclaims butch/femme role-playing as 'a developed, Lesbian, specific sexuality that has a historical setting and a cultural function' (Jeffreys, 1989a). That cultural function is almost certainly to establish the existence and visibility of lesbian cultural unity. Judy Grahn (1984) points out that in the 1950s,

> For all our boyish clothes and mannerisms ... we women did not pass as men or boys. ... our point was not to be men; our point was to be butch and get away with it. ... A dyke learns much of her social function from other dykes. ... Whether she ever has the chance to enter a Gay bar or not, she imitates dykes, not men. She may identify with traditionally dyke figures: Diana the Huntress, Beebo Brinker, Gertrude Stein, Bessie Smith, Natalie Barney, Queen Christina, Joan of Arc, Amy Lowell, Oya, St Barbara, modern athletes, and other leaders. ... the social message she bears and is delivering is not 'I am a man' but rather 'Here is another way to be a woman.'

Feminists like Jeffreys are trapped in the social constructionist model and cannot conceive how the butch/femme model could arise from within queer culture independently without being an inversion of heterosexual stereotypes. But as Grahn points out, the dyke cuts her hair short, 'shorter by far than any men are wearing it, because short hair is a dykish thing'. We may not agree with Grahn's theories about the dyke cosmology, or her view that butch/femme roles are closer to our tribal roots, but it is nevertheless true that the Eton crop is not a man's hairstyle, but part of the butch cultural heritage.

Part III

Queer Culture

8

The Great Queens of History

I am sometimes asked, 'But does it really matter that some historical figure, for example Tchaikovsky, was gay? Do we really need to assemble lists of the great queens of history?' I realize that I am expected to make the liberal answer, 'No, of course not. The important thing is that he composed great music, and his homosexuality is ultimately irrelevant.' But I like to pose some questions of my own in response: 'If it doesn't really matter, why has society taken such great pains to conceal Tchaikovsky's sexuality, maybe even murder him for it? If it doesn't really matter, why has such an inordinate amount of effort been put into the censorship and suppression of queer history?' Society is happy to benefit from outstanding gay and lesbian writers and artists and musicians, and then has the impertinence to evade the issue of what desire motivates their work.

When people say it really doesn't matter whether or not some great artist or hero was homosexual, they should consider the attacks upon the Brazilian anthropologist and historian Dr Luiz Mott, who

> had his house and car daubed with graffiti and his windows broken after publishing an article suggesting that a black anti-slavery leader was gay. Mott, who is white and his lover, who is black, were shocked but unhurt and have now asked for police protection. The attack was attributed to anti-gay activists in the Brazilian black movement. ... The subject of Mott's article, Zumbi dos Palmares, led a community of runaway slaves in the interior of Brazil in the 17th century. In modern Brazil he is a symbol of freedom and resistance for Afro-Brazilians and others. ... In the past, Luiz Mott has received death threats from elements linked to the military for claiming that the aviation pioneer, Santos Dumont, was gay. (*Gay Times*, July 1995)

Mott's historical research into the records of the Portuguese Inquisition has brought to light, for example, the story of the Brazilian woman Felipa de Souza who was convicted and tortured in 1591 for having sex with other women; and the queer love letters written around 1664 by Francisco

Correa Netto ('Francisquinha'), the sacristan of the Cathedral of Silves in southern Portugal, to his boyfriend the guitarist Manoel Viegas (Mott and Assunçao, 1989). Mott is concerned with the history of ordinary queers as well as the great queens, but his revelations about previously unknown figures have not provoked an outcry. It is the suggestion that an important historical figure is also a great queen of history that is felt to be threatening and subversive. Why? Because most people appreciate that a person's homosexuality really does matter.

Lists of famous homosexuals

The best-known paradigm of queer cultural history is the list of famous homosexuals. Often this consists of merely a list of names, without any further details, such as a well-known 1970s cartoon by Rick Fiala of a bearded man wearing a T-shirt on which are printed the words 'Walt Whitman Oscar Wilde Sappho Alexander the Great Gertrude Stein Cole Porter Radclyffe Hall Socrates Leonardo da Vinci Colette Valentino George Sand Tchaikovsky … and Me'. Fiala satirizes the slightly preposterous effect of ordinary gay people including themselves in the company of the great queens. Kate Charlesworth similarly parodies the idea of a gay ethnic/cultural identity in her large full-page cartoon titled 'A Short Guide to Britain's GAY HERITAGE' (Gay News 170, 1979), prompted, I believe, by my column in Gay News headed 'The Gay Heritage Guide to Britain'. Charlesworth draws a map of the United Kingdom with arrows pointing to gay sites illustrating, for example:

Bradford – Where Blondes Have More Fun. Birthplace of David Hockney, Artist

Sheffield – Edward Carpenter Lived near here. A must for all gays, socialists, vegetarians, playwrights & thesis-writers

Clouds Hill – T. E. Lawrence's cottage

Reading – Scene of The Incarceration of Oscar

Chelsea – Home of Q. Crisp, noted Stately Homo

Cerne Abbas – Site of 'Unabashed' Iron Age chalk figure, Cerne Giant. Gay men will be fascinated by the proportions of their forebears.

It has to be admitted that the search for our forebrothers and foresisters can be a bit naive. Perhaps Gay Men and Women Who Enriched the World (Cowan, 1988) really ought to be complemented by a companion volume on *Gay Men and Women Who Have Grown Rich from the World* (for example, William Beckford the plantation owner, Krupp the arms manufacturer, etc.), or even *100 Gay Monsters and Queer Serial Killers* (for example, Gilles de Rais, the Marquis de Sade, Countess Erzsébet Báthory, Fritz Haarmann the 'werewolf', etc.). One wonders how well these figures would fit into works such as Martin Greif's *The Gay Book of Names* (1982) or the series of short biographies currently being published by Chelsea House on gays who have made significant 'contributions' to society. When we look at the output of Alyson Publications – *The Alyson Almanac* (1989), *Lavender Lists* (Fletcher and Saks, 1990), *Lesbian Lists* (Richards, 1990), and the superb collections by Leigh W. Rutledge, *The Gay Book of Lists* (1987), *The Gay Fireside Companion* (1989) and *Unnatural Quotations* (1988) – we may feel that such collections are a fairly modern product of popular queer culture.

But initially such homophile apologetics were seen as an important historical argument for the decriminalization and destigmatization of homosexuality. Freud himself objected to the simplistic definition of homosexuals as 'sick', and asked in 1905: 'Should we not then have to classify many great thinkers and scholars of all ages, whose sound minds it is precisely that we admire, as sick men?' (W. Johansson, 'Freudian Concepts', *EH*). Freud cites a list of famous homosexuals in his *Letter to an American Mother* (1935), to show that her son is in good company and therefore reassuring her he is not 'sick'. Benkert in 1869 pointed out that if the Prussian law had prevailed throughout Europe in the past, many leading figures would have been imprisoned, such as Charles IX, Henry II, James I, Pope Julius II, Napoleon I, Louis XVIII, Frederick the Great, Machiavelli, Michelangelo, Bazzi (Il Sodoma), Shakespeare, Mazzarin, Molière, Newton, Winckelmann, Cambacérès, Byron, von Platen, and Eugène Sue (Lauritsen and Thorstad, 1974). Though we smile at the occasional odd entry here, the standard 'homophile' use of the list is neither naive nor irrelevant, as in this classic statement from a 1957 article by Jim Kepner in *ONE Magazine*: 'If perhaps the proportion of degeneracy among homosexuals in our present society seems high, it is because society forces most homosexuals into the role. The names of Ruth and Naomi, Plato, Sappho, Erasmus, Michelangelo, Tennyson, Florence Nightingale, Carpenter, and Gide are testimonials to the fact that homosexuality is not synonymous with degeneracy' (Legg, 1994). Christopher Isherwood remembers seeing in 1930 the film *Gesetze der Liebe* (*Laws of Love*) (1927), a remake of the banned *Anders als die Andern* (*Different from the Others*), a film about the blackmail of homosexuals, made in co-operation with Hirschfeld in 1919 as a plea for repealing the German law against homosexuals. The film contains a dream sequence which shows a 'long procession of kings, poets, scientists, philosophers and other famous victims of homophobia' moving sombrely across the screen, heads bowed, passing beneath a banner inscribed 'PARAGRAPH 175'. The Nazis destroyed all copies of the film, though a partial print was discovered in the Ukraine in 1979 (Miller, 1995). The same reflection was made by Jeremy Bentham as early as 1774:

> What would have become of Aristides, Solon, Themistocles, Harmodius and Aristogiton, Xenophon, Cato, Socrates, Titus – the delight of mankind – Cicero, Pliny, Trajan, Adrian, etc., etc. – these idols of their country and ornaments of human nature? They would have *perished on your gibbets*.

Bentham's views are part of the rational Enlightenment tradition (Greenberg, 1988). In the second year of the French Revolution a group which Hallam (1993) calls 'the Sodomite Liberation Front' published a pamphlet, *Les Petits Bougres au manège* (*The Little Buggers' Reply*), which defended the taste for buggery according to the principles of individual liberty, demanding equal rights for

> orders of being, to whom a kindly nature has given senses that they might use them in the way best corresponding to their tastes and inclinations. ... my prick and my balls belong to me; and ... whether I put them in a cunt or an arse, no one has the right to complain of the use I make of them.

Though this last phrase defends sodomy rather than queers, the pamphleteer refers to a 'class of creatures' and 'orders of being', and illustrates these by an accompanying list of famous homosexuals, from Socrates through to modern French generals. A somewhat earlier pamphlet, *Les Enfants de Sodome* (1790), a petition addressed to the Assemblée Nationale containing proposed Articles of Association for a Society of Sodomites, also includes a list of prominent sodomites.

Most of the modern English-language lists are traceable to two sources: Havelock Ellis's *Sexual Inversion* (German, 1896; English, 1897), particularly the sections assembled by John Addington Symonds, a specialist in Renaissance art history and enthusiast for Greek art and literature; and *Jonathan to Gide: The Homosexual in History* by Noel I. Garde (pseudonym of Edgar Leoni) (1964). *Jonathan to Gide* has been rather unfairly characterized as naive, but it serves as a useful tool, in providing short biographies of some 300 important political or cultural figures cited in various books as having had homosexual relations. For every biography Garde is scrupulous to cite an exact reference containing the 'allegation'.

Although full-length books about famous homosexuals seem to be a product of a homosexual emancipation agenda, shorter lists of the great queens of history go back much further than the nineteenth century. These lists are by no means limited to the modern period, nor are they found only in homophobic contexts (both of which would be required by the social constructionist premise). The pornographic poem *Don Leon* (c. 1836) cites Virgil and Alexis, Epaminondas and Cephidorus: 'How many captains, famed for deeds of arms, / Have found their solace in a minion's arms!' Voltaire in the article on 'L'Amour nommé Socratique' in his *Dictionnaire philosophique* (1764) records a list of famous pederasts. Denis Sanguin de Saint-Pavin (1595–1670), self-styled 'King of Sodom' – usually called a libertine but more rightly styled a proud and self-identified queer – defended homosexuality in his verse, based partly on imitations of Martial, and once sent Condé a poem declaring that 'Caesar was as great a *bougre* as you, but not so great a general.' In 1623 Théophile de Viau (1590–1626) – one of the most interesting premodern queers, unfairly called merely a 'libertine' – addressed an obscene poem 'Au marquis du Boukinquan' (i.e. James I's lover George Villiers, Duke of Buckingham), relating that

> Apollo *with his songs*
> *Debauched young Hyacinthus,*
> *Just as Corydon fucked Amyntas,*
> *So Caesar loved only boys.*
> *One man fucks Monsieur le Grand de Bellegarde [a friend of Viau],*
> *Another fucks the Comte de Tonnerre.*
> *And this learnèd king of England,*
> *Has he not fucked Buckingham?*

Such a list is prima facie evidence of the existence of queer identity during the early seventeenth century: de Viau clearly uses here the conceptual framework of *members of a group* of people with something in common. Any argument that this establishes a group of sodomites rather than a group of queers quite misses the point: it is a group of *persons* rather than *acts*.

Carl Miller (1996) in *Stages of Desire* devotes an entire chapter to 'the roll call of sodomites' in various Tudor plays. The most famous example occurs in Christopher Marlowe's play *Edward II*:

> *The mightiest kings have had their minions;*
> *Great Alexander lov'd Hephaestion,*
> *The conquering Hercules for Hylas wept,*
> *And for Patroclus stern Achilles droop'd.*
> *And not kings only, but the wisest men;*
> *The Roman Tully lov'd Octavious,*
> *Grave Socrates wild Alcibiades.*

In John Bale's *A Comedy Concerning Three Laws of Nature, Moses and Christ, Corrupted by the Sodomites, Pharisees and Papists Most Wicked* (1530s) there is a long list of idolaters/sodomites recited by Sodomy on behalf of himself and Idolatry, including Noah's son Ham, Onan:

> *We made Thalon and Sophocles,*
> *Thamiras, Nero, Agathocles,*
> *Tiberius and Aristoteles,*
> > *Themselves to use unnaturally.*
> *I taught Aristo and Fulvius*
> *Semiramis and Hortensius*
> *Crathes, Hyliscus and Pontius*
> > *Beasts to abuse most monstrously.*

The essence of any list is that it establishes the commonality of those included – otherwise there is no point in assembling a list. A list of apples, peaches, pears, lemons, etc. functions as a list precisely because it establishes or exploits the abstract or generic meaning of 'fruit'. These Renaissance lists, and especially the more positive catalogues of faithful friends, establish queer identities in exactly the same way that medieval literary catalogues of Good Women or Wicked Women are designed to establish the character of certain personality types. Negative lists tend to create stereotypes, while positive lists tend to produce amalgams or composites – the latter are specifically offered as models for behaviour.

We can slowly work our way backward in time. Sixteenth-century Spanish chronicles cite Juan II, Alvaro de Luna and Gonzalo Fernández de Córdoba as famous homosexuals. There is a list of homosexual pairs among the gods in Boccaccio's *Genealogia Deorum* (1375), which influenced later writers. Several twelfth-century debates between Ganymede and Helen or Hebe cite the loves of Jupiter and Ganymede,

Apollo and Hyacinthus, Silvanus and Cyparissus (Boswell, 1980). When Benvenuto Cellini was called a 'dirty sodomite' by one Bandinelli, he humorously replied: 'I wish to God I did know how to indulge in such a noble practice; after all, we read that Jove enjoyed it with Ganymede in paradise.'

Premodern defences of homosexual love were not limited to pagan precedents. When James I made his boyfriend George Villiers the Earl of Buckingham in 1617, he had to defend himself in response to the Privy Council's remonstrations against such blatant favouritism:

> I, James, am neither a god nor an angel, but a man like any other. Therefore I act like a man and confess to loving those dear to me more than other men. You may be sure that I love the Earl of Buckingham more than anyone else, and more than you who are here assembled. I wish to speak in my own behalf and not to have it thought to be a defect, for Jesus Christ did the same, and therefore I cannot be blamed. Christ had his son John, and I have my George.
> (Norton, 1974a)

It is possible that James was consciously using a queer tradition about Christ and St John the 'beloved disciple'. St Aelred of Rievaulx, who had several same-sex unions, called the relationship of Christ and St John a 'marriage'. The blasphemous conviction that Christ and John were lovers was consolidated during the late sixteenth and early seventeenth centuries; the view was claimed to have been held by Francesco Calcagno (investigated by the Venetian Inquisition in 1550), by Christopher Marlowe in an accusation of 1593, by Manuel Figuereido in a Lisbon Inquisition trial of 1618, and by others.

Cultural unification

So what is the purpose of these lists? The social constructionist argument is that lists of the great queens of history are compiled primarily, or even solely, by an oppressed minority in order to refute the stigma attached to homosexuality by mainstream heterosexual culture. In other words, a queer person's sense of shame or inferiority is diminished by identifying a link with people widely admired by society, and the list is therefore constructed entirely in reaction to external society.

The most celebrated example of this kind of motivation is found in Oscar Wilde's famous defence of himself during his trials, when he compared 'the love that dare not speak it name' to the love of David for

Jonathan, and defended its nobility and beauty with reference to works by Plato, Michelangelo and Shakespeare. It was a theatrical *tour de force*, but did not stand up to the testimony of boy prostitutes. Wilde of course lied throughout much of his trials, and this particular line of defence was perhaps hypocritical and well rehearsed, but he really did believe himself to be part of the ancient and noble tradition of *paiderastia*. Using lists to position himself in relation to queer culture, this was really more important than any other motivation: Wilde was first and foremost culturally /aesthetically identified. In particular, he referred to past gay artists, thus declaring himself to be part of a cultural elite, as opposed to heterosexual modern philistines. In the last years of his life, exiled, bankrupt, with no more need to defend his character, he told Frank Harris:

> What you call vice, Frank, is not vice. It is as good to me as it was to Caesar, Alexander, Michelangelo, and Shakespeare. It was first of all made sin by monasticism, and it has been made a crime in recent times by the Goths – the Germans and the English – who have done little or nothing since to refine or exalt the ideals of humanity.

The Wilde defence should also be seen in the context of a queer cultural elitism that was an important factor in some branches of the gay emancipation movement in the 1890s. For example, Adolf Brand, who objected to the 'third sex' theory with its effeminate emphasis, edited *Der Eigene: Ein Blatt für männliche Kultur* (*The Exceptional: A Magazine for Male Culture*) (which ran from 1896 to 1931), and in 1903 he founded the Gemeinschaft der Eigenen (Community of the Exceptional). Brand was a self-proclaimed 'anarchist and pederast' who celebrated the bonding of heroic young athletes in ancient cultures and in the Wandervogelbewegung, the German youth movement. His co-founder Benedict Friedlaender tried to split up Hirschfeld's Scientific-Humanitarian Committee and emphasized the 'physiological friendship' of the ancient Greeks, as in his book *Die Renaissance des Eros Uranios* (1904). Both men were married, as, of course, was Wilde.

The idea that 'homosexuality is exceptional by nature' (Cowan, 1988) is still current, usually related to the supposed insights of our status as outsiders, and a curious amalgam of 'intergrade' features: androgyny, creativity, shamanism. The 'Uranian' poet Ralph Nicholas Chubb in 'Note on Some Water-Colour Drawings' (1929) wrote, 'David and Jonathan, Harmodius and Aristogeiton, Christ and the youthful John, Plato, Socrates, Michelangelo and Shakespeare are company good enough for me.' The bisexual writer Robert McAlmon (1896–1956), lover of the painter Marsden Hartley, once astonished a Paris bartender with a passionate defence of Plato and other 'creative geniuses' who celebrated masculine beauty: 'I'm a bisexual myself,' McAlmon shouted, 'like Michelangelo, and I don't give a damn who knows it' (C. Shively, 'McAlmon', *EH*). This sense of being part of an exceptional group is found among the working classes as well, as in the case of a queer prisoner interviewed by a prison doctor in the early 1920s who listed 'Shakespeare, Coleridge, De Quincey, Rosa Bonheur, Joan of Arc, Beethoven, Wagner and Napoleon' to support his view that 'most of the world's geniuses can be traced directly to the homosexual'; the sex reformer Dr William Robinson said that very many gay men and lesbians in the 1920s made such claims in interviews with him: 'they speak of Shakespeare, Byron and Whitman as belonging to their class, as if their homosexuality ... were a well-established historical fact' (Chauncey, 1994).

But the use of the list to demand greater respect from society is merely a secondary result, not the primary purpose of the list, which is to banish a sense of alienation by rediscovering our own cultural traditions. The list of the great queens of history is compiled by queers in order to find a place for themselves in a historical tradition, to celebrate that they are part of a cultural unity. I think we commit a grave error in dismissing such lists as merely part of an apologetic agenda. One obvious fact about such lists is seldom remarked upon: the figures cited are almost invariably *historical* rather than contemporary. The list celebrates the fact not so much that queers are great, or even that they are creative, or even that they are good, but that queers are part of history: we have a unified historical cultural identity.

The list of the great queens of history is aimed primarily at, and read primarily by, queers themselves, rather than straights; it has the essentialist purpose of establishing *for queers themselves* that they are not unique. Cultural unity comes first; from this comes the strength for the defence against society, which is secondary. How the list functions is illustrated in Richard Meeker's novel *Better Angel* (1933). The central character feels 'as if he had been initiated into some secret fraternity' when he discovers the work of Plato, Cellini, Michelangelo, Shakespeare, Shelley, Ellis, Carpenter and Wedekend, from whom 'he learned that his sin ... was not the unique sport he had believed it to be' (quoted by Austen, 1977); the last scene shows him reading about the myth of Hercules and Hylas: 'Strength here against laughter and derision, strength here for the spectral years ahead, strength, and joy in strength.' In the novel *Goldie*

(1933) by 'Kennilworth Bruce', the hero discovers not only that there are 'more than four million others in the United States who dwelt in that twilight realm of sex' but that he is among the company of

> Diocles, Achilles, Homer, Alexander the Great, Pythagoras, Demosthenes, Julius Caesar, Virgil, Benvenuto Cellini, Michelangelo, Leonardo da Vinci, Shakespeare, Marlowe, Francis Bacon, Leo X, Francis I, Henry IV, Louis XIV, Louis XV, the Marquis de Sade, scions of the House of Orleans, Oscar Wilde, William II, James I, and many others of the world's great geniuses. (Quoted by Austen, 1977)

These great queens did not dye their hair golden and try to organize a homosexual rights group called 'The Twilight League', as does Goldie, but they, and he, are all conceived to be part of this historical and cultural unity.

The queer literary canon is revealed for modern queers by Blair Niles in her novel *Strange Brother* (1931), whose protagonist reads Whitman's *Leaves of Grass*, Carpenter's *Love's Coming of Age*, Plato's *Symposium*, Ellis's *Psychology of Sex*, August Forel's *The Sexual Question*, and others. Her list of the great queens of history includes Caesar, Michelangelo, Leonardo da Vinci, Shakespeare, Sir Francis Bacon, and King James I: 'You find them all the way back, among the artists and intellectuals of their time. ... Kings and Emperors [are] in the list, too.'

A consciousness of the cultural unity of queer history is still an important feature in recent gay novels, notably in Alan Hollinghurst's *The Swimming Pool Library* (1988), in the historical fiction of Chris Hunt, and in the novels and plays of Neil Bartlett. In Bartlett's (1990) *Ready to Catch Him Should He Fall* the continuity of queer history is itself the theme: the identity of the central character, simply called 'Boy', is historically constructed upon a collection of letters all beginning 'My Dear Boy' and signed by Oscar Wilde, John Addington Symonds, Baron Corvo, Robbie Ross, Reggie Turner and E. M. Forster; these are kept in a shoe box together with his collection of portraits of these men, and other cuttings of portraits from newspapers and pornographic or bodybuilding magazines, prized possessions which he regularly arranges in a circle around his bed like a pack of magic cards. Many of the characters function as archetypes, and much of the action is ritualistic, almost folkloristic, in accordance with the heritage of the drag-queen and queer-bar subculture from the 1930s to the 1950s. One chapter called 'The Robing of the Bride' consists of ceremonial charades in which Boy dresses and performs in the various roles of queer culture, such as drag queen, schoolboy, soldier looking for trade, small-town queen, black man and woman. By the end of the novel an exact queer equivalent to The Holy Family has been constructed.

Bartlett acknowledges that his novel 'contains fragments from and reworkings of' Wilde's *The Picture of Dorian Gray*, Corvo's *Hadrian the Seventh*, Forster's *Maurice*, Genet's *Our Lady of the Flowers*, Rodney Garland's *The Heart in Exile* and the screenplay *Victim*. Boy and the Older Man are married in accordance with queer tradition, blessed by Madame (The Mother of Us All), the owner and hostess of The Bar, and when they set up home together the Older Man dreamily describes to Boy how he wants to redecorate their apartment in a fantasia of queer motifs:

> In the centre of the floor I shall have painted a copy of the mosaic panel from Hadrian's villa at Tivoli representing the Ascent of Ganymede, ... and in the centre of each wall [will] hang a grisaille panel depicting scenes from the lives of great men: Antinous drowned and perfect at the age of nineteen . . .; Will Hughes playing the gilded boy mentioned by Piers Gaveston in Marlowe's *Edward the Second*; Rimbaud in the house of glass which he built in Addis Ababa; Federico García Lorca on his first night in New York; Robbie Ross lifting his hat to the passing prisoner in the corridor of the Old Bailey. ... From the centre of the ceiling hangs a recreation of the Pompeian lamp described by John Addington Symonds in his poem 'Midnight at Baiae'. ... On our left, the small stained-glass window, ... depicts the loves of David and Jonathan, Absalom and Saul, John and Christ, and the love of Eli for the Infant Samuel.

Even in a very contemporary American play by an angry AIDS activist, Larry Kramer's *The Normal Heart* (1985), the primary purpose of the list to establish a sense of cultural belonging is still explicit:

> I belong to a culture that includes Proust, Henry James, Tchaikovsky, Cole Porter, Plato, Socrates, Aristotle, Alexander the Great, Michelangelo, Leonardo da Vinci, Christopher Marlowe, Walt Whitman, Herman Melville, Tennessee Williams, Byron, E. M. Forster, Lorca, Auden, Francis Bacon, James Baldwin, Harry Stack Sullivan, John Maynard Keynes, Dag Hammarskjöld. ... These were not invisible men.

Pairs of lovers

The great queens of history usually appear in lists of individuals; but there is an important tradition which records *pairs* of lovers or 'faithful friends'. If we examine this tradition we will appreciate even more clearly how the list functions as a kind of cultural incorporation.

Orestes and Pylades may be taken as the archetype of the queer pair; these two lovers are virtually indistinguishable from one another and no one has been able to determine who was the *erastes* and who was the *eromenos*. There is a similar ambiguity about Achilles and Patroclus. Aristotle in *Politics* praised the lifelong love of the Theban lawgiver Philolaus and the Olympic athlete Dioclese, who 'maintained a single household and arranged to be buried beside each other', whose 'tombs, at Thebes, were a tourist attraction in Aristotle's day' (Boswell, 1995). The Sacred Band of Thebes, the military unit composed of 300 pairs of lovers formed in 368 BC, was cited in lists of famous homosexuals from an early period, for example by Plutarch, who likened their relationships to those of 'the greatest heros of old, Meleager, Achilles, Aristomenes, Cimon, Epaminondas. Epaminondas, in fact, loved two young men, Asopichus and Caphisodorus. The latter died with him at Mantineia and is buried close to him' (trans. Boswell, 1995). Plutarch also mentions Hercules's love for Ioläus, citing Aristotle's statement that 'the tomb of Ioläus was a place where same-sex lovers plighted mutual faith' in the fourth century BC.

The catalogue of faithful friends is a major *topos* of the Renaissance homoerotic 'friendship' tradition (Norton, 1974a). Marsilio Ficino in his Commentary on Plato's *Symposium* lists Achilles and Patroclus, Damon and Pithias, and Orestes and Pylades; Castiglione in *The Book of the Courtier* lists Orestes and Pylades, Theseus and Pirithous, and Scipio and Lelius; and Richard Edwards builds an entire play, *Damon and Pithias* (1564), around the most famous pair of faithful friends.

Virgil's *Aeneid* is the primary source for the story of Euryalus and 'his 's love' Nisus; Cicero's *De Amicitia* is one of the main sources for y of Harmodius and Aristogeiton, to which Montaigne refers cussing his love for Etienne de la Boètie. While it is true that dor plays about Damon and Pithias are not plays about it is nevertheless also true that the characters could be seen in contemporaries, as in Thomas Dekker's *Satiromastix* (1601) puns: 'they shall be thy Damans and thou thy Pithyass' – a vord 'asse'. As Miller (1996) observes, Dekker in his play written for boys to perform 'is quite aware that classical friendship can be used as a metaphor for contemporary sodomy. Indeed, it seems to mock those who cannot see the connection.' The tradition is certainly 'rhetorical', but it is a rhetoric full of meaning, a catalogue used specifically as a queer signifier. It is not generally appreciated that the word 'friend' was very important to the sodomites, as revealed in the records of the Inquisition, and that 'friend' has certainly been pronounced with a special queer intonation since at least the 1910s when members of the gay subculture referred to one another as 'dear friends' as well as 'the girls' (Chauncey, 1985).

In *L'Ile des Hermaphrodites* (*The Island of the Hermaphrodites*), a contemporary satire on the effeminate Henri III (1551–89) and his minions, the author describes the inner sanctum of the palace: 'The walls of one room are hung with tapestries depicting Hadrian's passion for Antinous, another with scenes from the life of Heliogabalus, a third chamber has a bed whose roof depicts the marriage of Nero and Pythagoras' (W. Johansson, 'Henri III', *EH*). These famous male couples are obviously perceived as part of a specifically homosexual tradition in the late sixteenth century. This fictional palace was turned into a reality by Frederick the Great (1712–86), who had a bronze Hellenistic statue of Ganymede in his library at Sanssouci (given to him by the homosexual Prince Eugene of Savoy), a figure of Ganymede at the centre of the great ceiling fresco at his New Palace at Potsdam, and a Temple of Friendship which he had decorated with inscriptions in praise of friendship and portraits of Euryalus and Nisus, Orestes and Pylades, Heracles and Philoctetis, Peirithous and Theseus (Steakley, 1989). The German poet Johann Wilhelm Ludwig Gleim (1719–83) also established a Temple of Friendship at his home in Halberstadt, 'containing more than one hundred portraits of passionate male friends' (Conner *et al.*, 1997), which survives today as the Gleimhaus Museum.

Paired saints

In the Judaeo-Christian tradition several same-sex couples became archetypes in the queer cultural tradition, apparently from an early period, notably David and Jonathan, Jesus and John, or 'the Beloved Disciple', and Ruth and Naomi. Boswell (1995) has charted the early homoerotic traditions of paired saints such as Perpetua and Felicitas, a Christian noblewoman and her female slave, martyred for their beliefs; Polyeuct and Nearchos, Roman soldiers of Greek ancestry who are described in a fourth-century biography as being 'bound to each other by a friendship which was much stronger than blood or relationship, from which passionate union their souls were tightly bound together, each believing that he lived and breathed wholly in the other's body' – St Polyeuct became the patron of sworn oaths between brothers.

An important feature of the ancient Christian office of same-sex union – gay marriage ceremonies – discovered by Boswell (1995) is the recitation of a list of paired male saints and other male couples, particularly Peter and Paul, Peter and Andrew, Jacob and John, the apostles Philip and Bartholomew, Cosmos and Damian, Cyrus and John, and, the earliest, from the late third/early fourth century, the Roman soldiers Serge and Bacchus. From hagiographies since the early sixth century Serge was called 'the sweet companion and lover' of Bacchus, and 'they became the preeminent "couple" invoked in the ceremony of same-sex union'. This catalogue always consists of pairs. Some of these pairs constituted genuine icons; the 'two Theodores' – one a foot soldier martyred in the fourth century, and the other a general invented in the ninth century to form a pair – are often depicted with their arms around one another, and they are paired together with Serge and Bacchus in Kievan icons dating from before the twelfth century. Other paired saints include Marcellus and Apuleius, Cyprian and Justinus, Dionysius and Eleutheris, and George and Demetrius. Just as in the pagan lists, most of these paired Christian saints had military connections, though Boswell refrains from speculating on the survival of a military homoerotic subculture. Typical is an eleventh-century Old Church Slavonic 'Order for Uniting Two Men':

> Lord God omnipotent, who didst fashion humankind after thine image and likeness and gavest unto them life eternal, whom it hath pleased that thy holy and glorious apostles Peter and Paul, and Philip and Bartholomew, be joined together not by the bond of blood but of fidelity and love, who didst deem it meet for the holy martyrs Serge and Bacchus to be united together, bless Thou also these thy servants, [Name] and [Name], joined together not of birth, but of faith and love. Grant unto them to love one another, let them continue without envy and without temptation all the days of their lives, through the power of thy Holy Spirit and the prayers of the Holy Mother of God and all thy saints who have pleased Thee throughout the ages. (Boswell, 1995)

The function of the list is very clear: to bless same-sex pair-bonding. In other words, it is an act of benediction, which I believe even today is invoked in order to establish that same-sex lovers are part of a historically continuous line of queer culture.

Chinese tradition

We have been discussing classical and Christian models, but reference to famous homosexual lovers of the past is also characteristic of Chinese literature. As Hinsch (1990) has amply demonstrated, China has a continuous historical and literary homosexual tradition going back from the nineteenth century to the Bronze Age. The reverence of the Chinese for culture and literature meant that 'Even the conceptions of "homosexuality" as a distinct realm of experience had roots in tradition. In general, homosexuality came to be described through reference to famous individuals of ancient times associated with same-sex love.' The intellectual Xi Kang (223–62) and his lover the poet Ruan Ji (210–63) were so famous that we even have archaeological evidence of their love, in the form of incised stone portraits showing them sitting side by side. Ruan Ji composed an encomium listing pairs of male lovers in the Zhou and Han periods, and his work is full of stock homosexual imagery relying upon history. 'In days of old there were many blossom boys' begins one poem, invoking the tradition of the past, then it goes on to cite the famous couple Lords An Ling and Long Yang who, like Mizi Xia and Dong Xian, 'formed the core of a pantheon of figures seen by later generations as symbols of male love. Literate Chinese throughout dynastic history looked to these ancient icons of homosexuality much as medieval Europeans did to Ganymede.'

Li Yu (1611–79/80) in his stories regularly alludes to the great queens of Chinese history such as Lord E and Emperor Ai. An ancient story from the Zhou period (1122–256 BCE) tells of two students, Pan Zhang and Wang Zhongxian, who 'fell in love at first sight and were as affectionate as husband and wife, sharing the same coverlet and pillow with unbounded intimacy for one another' (translated by Hinsch). When they died they were buried together, and from their grave immediately sprang a tree whose long branches and twigs entwined with one another, a miracle called the 'Shared Pillow Tree', which became one of the icons of Chinese queer literature – a metonym denoting something innate and essential about the relationship. Liu Yiqing (403–44) in one of his works has a complete section on noted male beauties, and his description of the 'sworn brothers', the poet Pan Yue (247–300) and Xiahou Zhan (243–91), as 'linked jade discs' provided another common motif in the homosexual tradition. By the first century there was already a tradition of anthologized biographies of famous homosexuals, for example, *The Biographies of the Emperors' Male Favourites* by the Grand Historian Sima Qian. The sixth-century *History of the North* contains forty biographies of favourites, and other scholarly and official records are similar. These are genuine biographies, not stereotypes. Looking to the models of antiquity is an integral part of being queer.

Queer icons

Many gays and lesbians collect the iconography of queer culture. In particular they collect literal icons: essentialized archetypes of identity. Walt Whitman distributed thousands of photographs of himself to all of the men with whom he corresponded, and they became treasured icons hanging in their rooms. A large circle of 'Calamites' in England in the 1880s and 1890s became proud owners of a Whitman photograph. The iconicization of Whitman increased after his death, and was not limited to intellectuals. Jeb Alexander (pseudonym), a non-literary middle-class fairy in Washington, DC, in the 1920s,

> frequently invoked Whitman in his diary and in his conversations with other gay men. When a former lover confessed to pursuing women as well as men, Alexander reacted negatively. 'I don't like his interest in girls', he noted in his diary. 'The "manly love of comrades" is nobler and sweeter and ought to be sufficient.' After reading the Calamus poems in Whitman's *Leaves of Grass*, he added: 'What a noble, lovable man old Walt was! Often I yearn toward Walt as toward a father, look up at his picture, then close my eyes and feel him beside me, rugged and strong with his gentle hands caressing and comforting me'. (Quoted by Chauncey, 1994)

The exchange of Whitman photographs seems to have been part of a 'living gay tradition'. For example, in 1905 the painter Marsden Hartley met a circle of Whitman admirers in his native Maine, including William Sloan Kennedy, 'who gave Hartley a signed portrait of Whitman which Whitman had given him just before he died' (Lynch, 1976). When Hartley's lover, the German soldier Karl von Freyburg, died in battle in 1914, Hartley painted him as an icon of male beauty with expressionist symbols, and in the 1930s and 1940s he painted all-male holy families and pietas consisting of bare-chested Maine lobstermen holding the dead Christ. The American photographer F. Holland Day was notorious for having had himself photographed as Christ on the cross, surrounded by sheepish-looking Male Physique Roman soldiers.

Jean Genet's personal icon was a newspaper photograph of Eugène Weidmann on the day of his arrest, a handsome young German who murdered six people; tried in 1937 and executed in 1939, Weidman's name is the first word of *Our Lady of the Flowers*. Genet called it 'the image of a bloodied archangel trapped by earthly policemen':

> Lola Mouloudji recalls that when Genet would settle into a new hotel room (or even the Barbezats' house at Décines outside Lyons, next to the family factory) he would immediately hang the photo on the wall. Genet said to her, 'The angel, for me, is Weidmann.'

Wherever Genet lived with his lover Java, off and on from 1947 to 1954, usually in hotels, he would hang his photo of Weidmann on the wall. He gave similar photos to his friend Olga Kechelievitch and to Cocteau (White, 1993).

Camille Paglia's personal icon is a picture of Francis Possenti, Saint Gabriel of the Sorrowing Mother (1838–62, canonized in 1920), which she inherited from her grandmother. Here is how Paglia describes him:

> He is one of the pretty boys who are everywhere in Italian art, notably in the creamy-skinned, homoerotic Saint Sebastian and Saint Michael statues that seemed to me, from my toddler's perspective in the church pew, far more interesting than those of Jesus, Mary, or Joseph. My grandmother's saint locks eyes with the Madonna, typifying the intense relations of mothers and sons in Mediterranean culture. As a monk, he will not marry; like the priests of Cybele, he will remain the son-lover of the goddess. As the years passed, the saint's picture accumulated more and more meaning. It became one of my personal icons, representing not only the sacred omphalos-spot of my grandmother's house but the essence of Italian Catholicism itself, which is both a religion and the nation's cultural identity, descending from pagan antiquity. (Paglia, 1994)

Shortly before his death by hari-kari, Yukio Mishima had himself photographed posing as Saint Sebastian pierced with arrows; the first time he ejaculated occurred after looking at a reproduction of Guido Reni's painting *Saint Sebastian*. The popularity of the great queer icon of Saint Sebastian is partly due to the fact that Sodoma's painting of the saint was printed on holy cards for the Vatican (Conner *et al.*, 1997). The conjunction of male beauty, desire and suffering proved a powerful image, but this is not simply a matter of appropriation, for the source was the queer painter Giovanni Antonio Bazzi (1477–1549) who rejoiced in the name Il Sodoma. The contemporary queer artist Matthew Stradling similarly concentrates on wounds in his paintings:

> The first wounds I started using were in a self-portrait as St Sebastian. Throughout the history of Western art, I've found that a shocking image: a passive male being penetrated by spears and shafts. It has a lot of sexual echoes. I read somewhere that the wound in Jesus's side was symbolic of his universal sexuality, representing a male vagina. I wanted to bring femininity to male figures. Figures in my paintings also show their wounds with pride. (Stradling, 1995)

Physical male beauty is central to queer male culture, and most culture queens have possessed an icon of the beautiful youth. One day in 1860 Henry James

> found his cousin, Gus Barker, posing naked on a pedestal in the large studio [of his friend William Morris Hunt] while the advanced students sketched his 'kinsman's perfect gymnastic figure'. ... He was dazzled both by the beauty of his cousin's body and by William's drawing ... which he obtained and kept for a long time. (Kaplan, 1992)

James himself drew a copy of Michelangelo's *Dying Captive*. Dozens of gay artists and photographers have reworked Flandrin's painting *Nude Boy Near the Sea* (Aldrich, 1993) (thousands of gay men must possess copies of it, and it is even used as the basis of a soft-porn scene in the 1995 Pride Video's *Desertion*). This appropriation/deconstruction/ subversion of an image from 'heterosexual' art has also been applied to Manet's *Olympia* (1863), 'the most quoted classical icon' in Smyth's (1996) study of contemporary lesbian art.

The collecting of queer icons is illustrated by the case of John Addington Symonds, whose professional cultural studies gave him the opportunity to indulge his central aesthetic preoccupation with healthy naked men. What attracted him most in Greek poetry were descriptions of nude youths in the gymnasia; what attracted him most in Renaissance painting were the male nudes of Signorelli, Michelangelo and a host of others. He was fascinated by the male nude, and collected numerous representations of it. He had twenty-one photographs of original drawings by the homosexual painter Simeon Solomon sent to him from London in 1868 ('chiefly classical subjects'), and in 1885 he was trying to get a copy of Solomon's *Sintram*, a work (now lost) meant to symbolize homosexuality. Mme Marville the French photographer was enlisted to photograph Ingres's drawings of the male nude in the Louvre and send them to him. He commissioned Edward Clifford to copy paintings for him, and encouraged Clifford's endeavour to paint 'heroic male beauty'.

Symonds wrote to Henry Scott Tuke praising his *Perseus* for its delicate yet vigorous handling of the nude, and asked him for photographs of his pictures of the nude fisherboys of Falmouth. He asked the critic and poet Edmund Gosse if he did not agree that Tuke's *Leander* had 'the *aura*'. He collected an enormous quantity of photographs of Greek and Roman statues, especially representations of Hadrian's beloved Antinous, about whom he wrote a lengthy biographical study, and photographs of the complete works of Michelangelo, which all curled up due to damp weather and covered the floor of his study like a nest of vipers. He engaged a German artist to photograph models posed in the impossible positions portrayed by Michelangelo in the Sistine Chapel. Symonds had heard that William Hamo Thornycroft's *Mower* was 'a Hermes in the dress of a working man', and he eventually acquired photographs of several statues by Thornycroft including the *Teucer* and *Warrior Bearing a Wounded Youth*, which were 'the delight of my eyes & soul'.

In November 1872 he sent a gift of a bronze statue of a gladiator to Cecil Boyle, former boyfriend of the classics master of Clifton College Henry Graham Dakyns, to both of whom he was attracted; on his own desk was a reproduction of the *Dying Gladiator*, possibly a return gift from Cecil. Horatio Forbes Brown gave him a reproduction of Cellini's *Perseus*, which also went into his study at Am Hof in Davos. He advised Vernon Lee to look at 'photographs from the nude published by Giraudon, which proves how little correction is needed ... to convert a soldier or mechanic into a hero or ephebus'. For more private uses he collected nude photographs by Wilhelm von Gloeden, and he was a personal friend of Guglielmo Plüschow whose *plein air* photographs of nude boys he would send to friends such as Charles Kains-Jackson. He exchanged packets of these photographs with Gosse, who kept stealing glances at one all through the funeral service held for Browning at Westminster Abbey.

In March 1890 he proposed to the Julian School of Art in Paris a prize competition for drawings of the male nude, for which he would contribute three prizes of 200 francs each, and for which he would retain the right to publish the winning entries together with photographs of the live models. He drew after models whom he hired to pose for him as he convalesced, and he photographed them in poses from famous statues or paintings such as the study by Hippolyte Flandrin which formed the subject of his essay on 'The Model'. He made impressionistic photo studies of the Venetian porter Augusto Zanon dressed in various shades of blue against different coloured backgrounds (described in *In the Key of Blue*): 'Of things like this, I have always been doing plenty, and then putting them away in a box. The public think them immoral'.

The lesbian cultural universe

The British lesbian painter Gluck's (Hannah Gluckstein, 1895–1978) mannish *Self-Portrait with a Cigarette* (1925) was used for the cover of Radclyffe Hall's novel *The Well of Loneliness* (1928) – thus the icon of the mannish lesbian was created by a mannish lesbian, not foisted upon lesbians by the sexologists. Gluck's famous *Medallion* portrait of her and her lover Nesta in 1937 also became a dyke icon, and is still being referenced by contemporary lesbian art such as Sadie Lee's *Narcissi* (1991). Veronica Slater's *Soul Identified as Flesh* (1988)

> positions a black and white realist life portrait of her lover, in front of a grid construction of multi-coloured reproductions of the Gluck self-portrait, painted in oils to resemble silkscreen. Subverting Warhol's Marilyn Monroe piece, Slater sets up Gluck as a sex goddess for lesbians and her lover as her descendant, the guardian of the image, extending Gluck's lineage to the present. (Smyth 1996)

The image of Gertrude Stein is also important for contemporary lesbian artists: Deborah Kass 'twists Warhol's *Chairman Mao* into an hilarious *Chairman Ma* (1993) featuring Gertrude Stein, making the rather inscrutable image of Stein comic and friendly, and acknowledging her significant role as a literary icon to generations of lesbians'. (The Uncommon Clout Card, an American gay Visa credit card, uses a card in its advertising on which the signatory is Gertrude Stein.) Millie Wilson's *Fauve Semblant: Peter (A Young English Girl)* is an imaginary 'retrospective' based on the work of Romaine Brooks, with wry allusions to Radclyffe Hall and Rosa Bonheur. 'The metaphor of masquerade is heightened in a large photograph of Wilson in drag as Peter, in her studio, easel at the ready, dressed in a shirt and bow-tie, a cigarette in her hand', recalling both Brooks's and Gluck's self-portraits (Smyth, 1996).

Nicki Hastie (1993) in her evocatively titled essay 'Lesbian Biblio-mythography' has described how reading provides the first connection with lesbian culture, and how 'Libraries are a primordial scene of lesbian activity.' Like many lesbians, Hastie explains, 'I had a way of scanning a page or an entire book, ... able to sense the printed word "lesbian" even before my eyes could properly focus.' Many lesbians have 'cruised the library' for evidence of lesbian culture. Hastie is afraid of being labelled an essentialist and she does not wish to 'support a theory of a universally-shared "lesbian intuition"', but the personal narratives she collates nevertheless almost all tend towards the essentialist position. Audre Lorde's autobiography *Zami: A New Spelling of My Name* (1982) reclaims the continuity of black identity and lesbian identity: 'Audre recognises that her mother is a very powerful woman, somehow quite different from any other women she knows, and "that is why to this day I believe that there have always been Black dykes around – in the sense of powerful and women-oriented women".' For Hastie, 'The journeys into literature taken by Alison Hennegan, Lee Lynch, Maureen Brady, Judy Grahn and Audre Lorde were stimulated by the desire for literary manifestations of selfhood, a quest for identity and a historical basis for that identity.'

Rita Mae Brown's *Rubyfruit Jungle* was inspired by a reading of Radclyffe Hall's *The Well of Loneliness*. A large group of 'pathfinder books' or the 'bookmarks' of lesbian history, ranging from Sappho's poetry to Christine Crow's *Miss X*, interpenetrate one another, seeming to form a mythological 'homeland' of lesbian experience. 'We tell stories which both derive from and help to maintain a collective lesbian "myth of origins". ... Sappho is primary source material for the lesbian. ... This inheritance underlines the importance of naming the source. Yes, I need Sappho' (Hastie, 1993).

In many countries 'lesbian' continues to be an acceptable self-applied label because of its cultural reference to Sappho of Lesbos. Lesbians in India, though they are reclaiming the terms *jami* ('twins'), and *sakhiyana* ('women-to-women bonding'), have also adopted 'lesbian' without much sense of uneasiness, precisely because it does establish a continuum with an ancient historical/cultural lesbian identity that goes beyond the West/East partition (Thadani, 1996). Let us generously acknowledge that the dykes of Des Moines have no greater claim on this distant Greek island than the dykes of New Delhi.

The idea of a lesbian cultural tradition having an unbroken continuity back to the time of Sappho was perhaps made explicit in William King's anti-lesbian satire *The Toast* as early as 1736. He gives an etymology for his semi-fictionalized lesbian character Myra of Dublin: 'Myra is a Corruption of Myrrhina a famous Courtesan of Athens, who first practis'd and taught in that City *Sappho*'s Manner and the *Lesbian* Gambols'; and he claims a lesbian folk tradition in the use of the phrase 'fires of Aetna' (used in Ovid's 'Sappho to Phaon'): 'Since the Days of *Sappho*, this Expression hath been familiarly used by all Tribads'; and he implies that modern lesbian networks use hierarchy and titles.

Donoghue (1993) has established the icons and motifs of the lesbian literary tradition: the pair of female doves, associated with Venus or Diana; Diana the Huntress and the hind or female deer; paired nymphs in pastoral poetry; references to the works of Sappho and to the explicit lesbian stories retold by Lucian, Juvenal and Ovid; the biblical story of Ruth and Naomi and the parable of the wise virgins; the 'tender passion' of romantic friends; 'friendship' used as an exact antonym for 'marriage': 'For the most part lesbians were thought of as connected not over space, in a social network, but over time, as a secret cultural tradition.'

Griffin (1993a) is worried that books of lists such as Richards's (1990) *Lesbian Lists*

> in some respects continue a tradition of display of *curios*, ... inviting the reader to contemplate their content with surprise, pandering to the reader's desire to marvel. Richards's section on 'Amazon Queens and Other Exotics', for instance, by its very title seems to stimulate such wonder.

Griffin fears that they tend to present the lesbian as a rare and endangered species, and are therefore part of the 'pathologizing' of lesbianism. I agree that such lists emphasize difference but that difference is treated in a wholly affirmative manner. Many lesbians in the twentieth century believed they were the only ones of their kind – besides Sappho. No lesbian could read Richards's book and continue to feel isolated. I agree with Lee Lynch's response to *Lesbian Lists* as an important 'resource and a validation. We can never record too many facts about lesbian culture; the act of listing is one of handing down, of passing on, a joyous *we are*!'

Christine Crow's (1990) remarkable novel *Miss X, or The Wolf Woman* is full of the 'Symbols, codes, hieroglyphs, secret metaphors, cyphers' which mark the boundaries of queer culture. (I should make it clear that the following interpretation of the novel is my own, and differs significantly from that offered by Hastie.) The novel is divided into fourteen 'pieces' rather than chapters, corresponding to the fourteen pieces into which Osiris's body was dismembered. Throughout the novel there are numerous analogies to Osiris, Pentheus, Orpheus and Dionysus and other dismembered deities in the mythology central to gay men. Miss X occupies a 'perky turret' surrounded by pine trees, clearly the tip of Dionysus's thyrsus. The narrator's quest is to stitch together all these pieces to recreate Osiris in the person of Miss X. Significant revelations occur beside the river Isis in Oxford. Mrs X is Demeter, Miss X is Persephone, and Mary Wolf is Cerberus.

The lesbian sources are also evident: Mary and Miss X – Head Girl and Headmistress – spend a night together in Oxford at what she mistakenly thinks of as the 'Radclyffe Hall Hotel' near the 'Radclyffe Camera', which 'I at once assumed to be spelt with a "y" after the author of a dull-looking novel in a brown-paper wrap recently discovered in the Parlour one Sunday.' Other novels alluded to include Virginia Woolf's *To the Lighthouse* and *Orlando*, André Gide's *L'Immoraliste* and *Corydon*. Miss X wears a 'wedding' ring set with the sapphire of the secret sapphist, but she has grown up in a repressive era and tries to conceal her homosexuality from others in the school:

> On one occasion violently tearing to shreds in front of her, both literally and metaphorically, an eXcellent essay on Walt Whitman's 'Leaves of Grass'. Seven credits, sorry, detentions, and lines in the 'dinner hour', for suggesting his love poems were addressed to men. (Shakespeare's sonnets too, my Love, what of them? Gide, Proust, Sappho, Vita Sackville-West – must have been 'bi-seXual' like Orlando in her case? So *many* Great Artists, come to that. ... Lawrence of Arabia, André Gide again, Proust, Miss Hilbert [a character in the novel who is discovered in the closet with her female lover], Vita Sackville-West, Shakespeare, Walt Whitman, Sappho, Gertrude Stein, Oscar Wilde and, hélas, Radclyffe Hall (though just because she wrote a Novel about it, you can't be sure).

Crow draws a marvellous satirical portrait of the social constructionist in the person of the lesbian-feminist teacher Annabel, who reads an early draft of the novel and criticizes it:

> Apparently I had failed disastrously to distinguish between 'lesbianism' as an active erotic drive ... and 'lesbianism' in the political sense ...: a mode of eXistence devoted to subverting the whole set of oppressive, phallic assumptions at large in heteroseXist society. ... Far from interpreting the whole thing as the passionate *Defence of HomoseXuality* I intended ... she has taken the whole

thing to be an *attack*! ... in fact the very opposite of the 'Feminist Lesbian Novel' she apparently lectures on in her 'Women's Writing Course' ... where she once told me they also hi-jack, eXplode and dismember certain rabidly 'decadent' nineteenth-century teXts on grounds of heteroseXist hypostatization, phallocentricity, pre-post-modernist recuperation and the like. ... Yes, come to think of it, a white paperback by someone called Monique Wittig – couldn't see the title – was poking upside down from her rucksack.

But after working through all the contradictions of employing a stigmatized label in defining oneself, in the last chapter, or 'piece', the narrator inscribes her name together with that of Miss X on the window-ledge of Miss X's study after her death:

> *Miss X and Mary Wolfe 'Come Out' at last.* The love that dares to speak its name? In joining our names together like that in Public – well, almost – I had broken at last the pledge of secrecy between us, cracked the last ice of the terrible interdict, broken the last taboo on naming the god.

Also carved on the window-ledge is the school motto *Ad astra*, and the novel ends with Mary looking up at the starry constellation of the Goat. Many images of the archetypal scapegoat occur throughout the novel: the narrator describes the goat as 'a form of totem representing the name of the tribe or clan' who becomes the sacrificial scapegoat. By taking the scapegoat role upon herself, by accepting the lesbian labels, whether homophobic or lesbian-feminist, Mary exorcizes their destructive and reductive powers, but nevertheless reaffirms the essential nature of lesbian desire as her birthright.

9

Queer (Sub)cultures

It should be clear from the preceding chapter that a queer cultural identity can exist without a queer subculture. This is most obviously the case among middle-class homosexuals who identify with Plato and Whitman and Wilde, or Sappho and Radclyffe Hall. The placing of oneself within the historical queer cultural tradition is an imaginative act that requires only books rather than cruising grounds. Many have agreed with Oscar Wilde that 'one had ancestors in literature, as well as in one's own race, nearer in type and temperament'. As Gregory Woods says in *This Is No Book: A Gay Reader* (1995): 'Whether you live in the remote countryside or in crowded inner-city alienation, gay readings can turn your solitude into solidarity.' Once a gay man or lesbian plucks up the courage to go to their first queer bar, there they will learn the rich possibilities of being queer, but they were already queer before entering its door, and they already carry with them some notion of the precedents and patterns of queer culture.

There has been much specious theorizing to the effect that a queer identity cannot possibly arise in the absence of a queer subculture, which is usually seen as a 'modern' phenomenon. Greenberg (1988) argues, for example, that classical 'transgenerational' relationships are inherently 'unstable' in the sense that an affair ends when the boy reaches adulthood, *and therefore* no subculture and no concept of self-identity would have arisen in ancient cultures. In fact friendships often continue after the end of the sexual relationship. But Dall'Orto ('Italy', *EH*) has shown that although the basic homosexual relationship in fourteenth-century Italy was adult/adolescent, nevertheless the adult men were accustomed to regularly meeting with one another, and a sodomite subculture arose *between the adults* who had sex with youths. A sharing of sexual tastes rather than sexual coupling *per se* is what cements the relationships in queer subcultures. The pederastic Uranians of the late nineteenth century, who enjoyed markedly transgenerational relationships, possessed a clear 'pederastic' identity and a definite subculture (d'Arch Smith, 1970). There was also a pederastic subculture in premodern Morocco, as well as a pederastic expatriate subculture in modern times. As illustrated in the works of Frederick Rolfe, transgenerational relationships can give rise to a complex multi-layered subculture (perhaps an exploitative one, but that is a separate issue): between the men who share similar tastes, and between the boys when they are 'off duty'. And these two groups further intermingle as the men infiltrate the wider world of boys (and transient labourers, etc.) and as the boys are passed from man to man, entering their wider cultural world and developing a taste for the high life.

There is no simple one-to-one correspondence between identity and subculture. But we can say with some degree of certainty that queer subcultures are created by queer people congregating with their own kind, not by straight society herding misfits into a ghetto. For example, the more recent Italian gay subculture 'is in reality the subculture of the *ricchioni* alone', who think of themselves as very camp men (i.e. fairies) and who do not have sex with one another; an argument that society indirectly creates subcultures by negative labelling of its members is not well borne out in Italy, especially in southern Italy, where there is a high toleration of *ricchioni*, who in turn do not feel guilty for what they are (G. Dall'Orto, 'Mediterranean Homosexuality', *EH*).

Social constructionism is partly informed by the interactionist perspective popular in the 1970s which, despite its name, leans heavily towards the belief that the subgroup has little autonomy and is helplessly moulded by the supra-group. Societal-reaction theory tends to emphasize that nearly all the features and behaviour patterns of a subculture arise in response to hostile stimuli from the supra-culture. Such theories in the queer field draw upon the theory of internalized stigmatization and force sociology back into the confines of personal psychology. The broader historical perspective is seldom broached, and professionals have rarely followed up the grass-roots impression that a homosexual culture resides at the core of the homosexual subculture, and that this core may be quite independent of the heterosexual supra-culture.

Queer historians have inadequately addressed the problems of subculture formation. Evidence drawn from memoirs provides little support for the view that subcultures are 'constructed' in opposition to homophobia. If it were true that a subculture arises solely in response to external pressure, then really the queer subculture could never have emerged: its members were outlaws subject to the death penalty; there was never any secret admiration for queers as there is, for example, for criminals, who are often glamorized and become models for young disaffected men. The straight world has never held double standards regarding queers equivalent to the Victorian gentleman's open exploitation of female prostitutes while placing the 'angel of the house' on a pillar. A historical focus upon specific queer subcultures reveals many features that arose organically from within the subculture and serve no purpose of social control. What it reveals is an ethnic culture. One can adopt this essentialist position without denying the fact that there is obviously some degree of interaction between queer culture and straight culture, and that the parameters of queer culture can often be restricted by regulations imposed by straight culture. But queer subcultures should be considered as examples of queer culture driven underground, retaining some of their original features while developing others to cope with changing moral climates. The proper business of queer history should be to emphasize the generally unrecognized features that are integral to the subculture itself and not a result of oppression. During the 1970s it was the fashion to redefine subcultures as countercultures, in order to emphasize their potential for subversion and revolution. A counterculture of course *does* require a dominant culture to react against, to feel excluded from, to try to transform. Since most gay liberationists were part of the student counterculture – they were not actually part of the gay subculture – they adopted the minoritizing motto, 'No counterculture can define itself independently of the dominant culture' (Bronski, 1984), and regarded the subculture as synonymous with the counterculture. But queer culture, like an ethnic culture, *can* be independent of the dominant culture, self-determined rather than socially controlled.

Queer geography

The Gay Liberation Front introduced the term 'gay ghetto' into its political analysis of the gay subculture, seen largely in terms of sordid or exploitative bars and Greyhound Bus Station urinals. The use of the phrase 'gay ghetto' really prejudges the argument in terms of victimology. Historically and objectively the phenomenon is better described as a queer community or queer quarter rather than a gay ghetto. Gay people are not really rounded up and put into an area cordoned off from society with walls and gates locked at night to keep them in, but it was a useful metaphor to encourage the notion that we did not choose our spaces. 'Ghetto' continues to be the term mistakenly used to denote gay *quartiers* or colonies, which are no more deplorable than the existence of the Jewish enclave in Golders Green or the Pakistani enclave in East Finchley. The poverty of urban areas such as black Harlem is not a feature of 'ghettoization' *per se*, but a reflection of racism. Blacks were not forced into 'poor' areas; they chose these areas long before they were impoverished by the withdrawal of white investment.

In the broad historical perspective (setting aside the period 1950–70), and with the exception of prisons, queers choose their own spaces, where they tend to thrive. The gay subculture that flourished in the naval town of Newport, Rhode Island, in the 1910s was 'neither dark nor secret' (Chauncey, 1985): the gay sailors who called themselves 'the gang' had their headquarters at the Army and Navy YMCA, which was common knowledge to everyone in town for many years; they flaunted themselves openly, loudly talking about their affairs while walking together in the street, even wearing make-up while at work in the naval hospital and refusing to conform despite harassment; everyone knew there were 'floaters' who 'followed the fleet'.

I favour the 'opportunistic' rather than the 'functional' theory of queer subcultures. For example, cruising areas arise in very clear circumstances: first, where there is an opportunity for revealing sexual organs, as in urinals and baths; second, where there is an opportunity of seeing many people in a short period of time in a small area, as on bridges, near theatres after they close and on heavily used paths and roads; and third, where there is an opportunity for loitering without calling attention to oneself (and for making an easy escape if necessary). There is no point in tormenting the data to find out why men are 'driven to sex in public places', and little point in discussing 'tactics' and the 'subversion of boundaries', when the obvious fact about queer geography is that queers congregate wherever they can best make contact with one another. Specialized homosexual bathhouses are first recorded in the last half of the nineteenth century in France and Germany, but public baths have always been notorious as places fostering sexual contact, homosexual as well as heterosexual; 'male stews' are referred to in sixteenth-century London, and visual evidence suggests homosexual relations took place in baths in sixteenth-century Germany and Italy (for example, Dürer's drawing *Men's Bath* and a painting by Domenico Cresti reproduced in Beurdeley, 1994).

Queers are not 'pushed to the margins' of society, as social constructionists would have it. Public cruising grounds and urinals were features of queer subcultures for centuries before the rise of capitalistic competitiveness which, according to Chauncey (1994) and others, supposedly inhibits intimacy between men and encourages 'casual or impersonal sexual transactions, such as take place in twentieth-century public restrooms or baths'. Arnold of Verniolle in the early fourteenth century made some of his pick-ups in the portico connecting the dormitory and latrines of the Franciscan convent of Pamiers and the baths of Ax-les-Thermes (Goodich, 1979). One should also note that not all encounters originate in the 'privy', but partners can be brought there for the sake of privacy: for example, Australia's 'earliest "known" homosexual convict' William Williams in 1828 arranged to meet a sentry, offered him some beer (Williams was a head cook) and then went with him to the privy behind Government House in Sydney, where the suspicious undercook who followed them caught them exposing themselves to one another (the case was dropped for lack of evidence that a specific crime had been committed, though after another incident in 1842 Williams was convicted of sodomy and sentenced to death, which was commuted to transportation for life) (Hay Website).

Possibly the first public urinals in London, the bog-houses built in 1692 in New Square, Lincoln's Inn, near the law courts, were cited as a 'molly market' in 1723; several arrests were made in these bog-houses throughout the eighteenth century, and almost certainly they had been used by the mollies almost as soon as they were built. The area around Lincoln's Inn during the early eighteenth century was frequented by hustlers such as Ned Courtney; several of the butchers who worked in the market at Butcher's Row to the south were known mollies, including the man calling himself Princess Seraphina, and just to the west, on Drury Lane no less, was the Three Tobacco Rolls molly-house. The area was obviously a gay *quartier*, as were Covent Garden market, West Smithfield market and Moorfield Gardens to the north, one path across it being known locally as 'the Sodomites' Walk', where several mollies were entrapped by the police (Norton, 1992). In Amsterdam in the 1760s many sodomites were arrested in the public toilets that were built under the city's numerous bridges; the favourite toilets were even identified with special names, such as The Old Lady or The Long Lady (van der Meer, 1989).

St James's Park was also a noted cruising ground, especially useful for picking up Guardsmen from the nearby barracks. Any area where one has an excuse for loitering is liable to become a cruising ground. Cruising grounds in early twentieth-century New York 'tended to be clustered in theater and retail shopping districts, where many gay men worked and where heavy pedestrian traffic offered cover' (Chauncey, 1994). Queer geography turns around public parks, quays along the waterfront and bridges. In early eighteenth-century Paris queers looked for pick-ups (*pour y raccrocher*) on the Pont-Neuf and then went to taverns where they hired a private room (Rey, 1985). The molly subculture in London was first revealed to the public in 1707, when the members of the Society for the Reformation of Manners set out to entrap the homosexuals who were in the habit of making their pick-ups on London Bridge. For example, Thomas Lane, a foot soldier, was standing on London Bridge, and approached Mr Hemmings (one of the Society's agents), 'and pulling out his Nakedness offer'd to put it into his Hand, and withal unbutton'd the Evidences Breeches, and put his Hand in there'; Hemmings later returned with Mr Baker, another agent, and they apprehended Lane when he approached them again, separately (Norton, 1992). It was not long before at least eight men were arrested, and soon the agents discovered that the Royal Exchange was also a molly market, where further arrests were made, and eventually an extensive subculture of cruising grounds and molly-houses was uncovered. Some forty-three 'He-Strumpets' are supposed to have plied their trade in the Royal Exchange in 1707, and we know that 'Buggerantoes' met one another there as early as 1700.

The dogma that queers are pushed to the outer margins of society has been very much overemphasized: there is nothing 'marginal' about London Bridge or the Royal Exchange or St James's Park, or the main cruising grounds in eighteenth-century Paris – the Tuileries and Luxembourg gardens, the boulevards along the former ramparts or the *quais*. Nor is there anything 'marginal' about the brightly lit self-service cafeteria in the heart of Greenwich Village which was the main meeting place around 1936 for lesbian Lady Lovers 'Clothed in mannish togs, flat-chested, hair slicked tightly back and closely cropped', and pansies wearing heavy mascara, rouge and lipstick (Duberman, 1991). This was not a dark corner in the twilight world, but a centre for flagrant exhibitionism.

By the late eighteenth century the mollies, now more likely to be called 'madge culls' (slang for the female pudenda) had developed a repertoire of secret signs and dress codes by which they could recognize one another in public places. According to an account published in 1781:

These wretches have many ways and means of conveying intelligence, and many signals by which they discover themselves to each other; they have likewise several houses of rendezvous, whither they resort: but their chief place of meeting is the Bird-cage Walk, in St. James's Park, whither they resort about twilight.

They are easily discovered by their signals, which are pretty nearly as follow: If one of them sits on a bench, he pats the backs

of his hands; if you follow them, they put a white handkerchi
thro' the skirts of their coat, and wave it to and fro; but if they a
met by you, their thumbs are stuck in the arm-pits of their
waistcoats, and they play their fingers upon their breasts.

By means of these signals they retire to satisfy a passion too
horrible for description, too detestable for language. (Trumbach,
1977)

Homosexuals in The Hague in 1702 indicated their desires by patting
one hand with the other; the same sign is used today in the Netherlands
to mockingly indicate that someone is a homosexual (van der Meer, 1989).
Homosexuals on the streets of late eighteenth-century Berlin also used
secret signs to recognize one another. They called themselves *warme
Brüder*, still a very common word for 'gay' in modern Germany, which
literally means 'warm brother', but *warme* (like the earlier queer term
schwul/schwül) also means 'passionate' and the phrase is perhaps better
translated as 'hot stud'. Just like the molly-houses in London, Berlin had
its brothel-like inns, known as *Knabentabagie*. In early eighteenth-century
Paris the signals ranged from asking for a pinch of tobacco, to staring in
the face with affection, to pissing on the ground in front of the desired
object (Rey, 1985); contact was often bluntly established, for example by
joking 'What time is it according to your cock?' or by exhibiting one's
rear while pretending to relieve oneself on the *quais*. The direct approach
was not uncommon: *Attends que je te foute* ('Let me fuck you').

'Birth' of the subculture

Trumbach and others refer to 'the birth of the subculture', but I do not
believe there is any particular decade which we can point to and say,
'before this date the queer subculture did not exist'. We learn of the molly
subculture in London in the first decade of the eighteenth century
(Trumbach, 1977, 1989a; Bray, 1982; Norton, 1992), but all of its features
are already fully formed: groups of men meeting regularly at molly 'clubs'
where they use 'maiden' nicknames for one another, dance together,
sometimes imitate women, sometimes dress as women on special 'festival
nights', and have a specialized molly slang. This culture becomes more
extensive and more 'regularized' throughout the century, but its basic
features and queer institutions do not change. Rey (1985) similarly found
that the Parisian queer subculture exhibits no real development: for
example the cruising grounds popular in the 1780s were just as popular

in the 1710s when they were first discovered by police agents, and even in 1706 sodomites met at certain taverns in the St Antoine district, in groups having a 'Grand Master' and a 'Mother in charge of novices'. In other words, the queer subculture seems to have 'emerged' already fully grown. That, I suggest, is impossible. The molly subculture must have existed in London at least two or three generations earlier, during which it had time to go through various stages of development. There is no reason to doubt Ned Ward's statement that his *History of the London Clubs*, first published about 1705, was 'Compil'd from the original Papers of a Gentleman who frequented those Places upwards of Twenty Years' – pushing the date of 'emergence' back at least to 1685. This date would upset Trumbach's theories.

It is almost certain that a queer subculture developed around the theatres of London in the sixteenth century, although the evidence is literary and therefore lacks the kind of precise details revealed by trials (Miller, 1996). Ann Bacon was distressed that her (homosexual) son Anthony moved to the theatre district in Bishopsgate, 'a place haunted with such pernicious and obscene plays and theatres' which 'infect the inhabitants with corrupt and lewd dispositions'. Anthony and his homosexual brother Francis Bacon were both keen on the theatre. Philip Stubbes in his notorious diatribe against the theatre complains that after the performances 'every mate sorts to his mate, every one brings another homeward of their way very friendly, and in their secret conclaves (covertly) they play the *Sodomites*, or worse'. 'There is a general agreement among the satirists that the theatre is a major haunt of late sixteenth-century gay men' (Miller, 1996). Thomas Middleton, Ben Jonson and Michael Drayton, among others, refer to sodomites picking up boy-actors. Edward Guilpin complains of the theatregoer 'who is at every play and every night Sups with his ingles'. Some of the earliest molly-houses in London – where men played the fiddle and danced together and otherwise made merry – resemble the small music-halls, the first one of which was built by Thomas Sadler in 1683.

The British queer subculture did not 'emerge' in 1699 (when a 'gang' and 'confederacy' of sodomites was arrested in Windsor); that is simply the year when it was discovered and revealed in the public prints. It was not born, it was exposed. What is spoken of as 'birth' should really be recognized as 'public knowledge'. Or, to put it another way, the birth of the subculture reflects nothing more than the development of efficient policing and surveillance, and the emergence of the popular press. The massive publicity that followed sodomitical trials in early eighteenth-century England, France and the Netherlands – in poems, broadsides, pamphlets – was made possible by advances in cheap printing technology and an increasing public appetite for 'news'. Our extra-legal knowledge of the English subculture comes from newspapers, which did not exist before 1702, and from proto-newspapers or pamphlets such as *The English Spy* in the 1690s. The fact that the subculture is publicly exposed is closely linked to the rise of a popular press at the turn of the century, and the use of investigative reporters – often called 'spies' – who actively went in search of sensations and scandals in order to feed that press.

I do not believe that a changing 'conceptualization' or ideology of homosexuality has much to do with this 'birth', except in so far as this public exposure is usually connected to the activities of a moral reform movement. It is not correct to infer that around 1700 there was a sudden change either in the roles played by homosexuals or in the social perception of homosexuality. The fact of the matter is that it coincided with the sudden formation of the Societies for the Reformation of Manners (of which there were nine in 1699, and twenty in 1701), and these organizations actively sought out and prosecuted homosexual behaviour; our knowledge of molly behaviour exactly parallels the activities of these Societies. They fostered a moral view for which the general public did not have much sympathy, and we should be careful to note that they represented a very specific and limited social movement, and cannot be taken as evidence for a 'homophobic society' in general. The 'shift' is not a shift in homosexual role, but a shift in prosecution. We know hardly anything about homosexual subcultures before the formation of the Societies for the Reformation of Manners. Most of the sodomites convicted from 1698 to 1709 were entrapped due to the zeal of one man, Reverend William Bray, a leading light in the Society; the raid upon Mother Clap's molly-house in 1725 (which provides the richest data on the molly subculture) was led by Constable Samuel Stevens, another member of the association, who had infiltrated the club by pretending to be the 'husband' of an informant (Norton, 1992). By 1727 the Societies had prosecuted so many people – 94,322 by their own count – that people grew sick of them as officious meddlers, and their popularity declined rapidly. In 1738 they were formally disbanded – and relatively little is known about the queer subculture after that date: not because queers went underground, but because specific groups of moral reformers no longer worked actively to reveal them.

The widespread appearance of queer subcultures across Europe around the year 1700 is almost certainly linked not to the rise of capitalism but to the increase in surveillance. Efficiently organized 'police forces' hardly existed before then. The subculture was *uncovered* as a result of new social regulations rather than created by some tenuous link with economic structures. The discovery of the homosexual subculture of Paris is due entirely to the use of *mouches* (*agents provocateurs*) and later by pederasty patrols (*patrouilles de péderastie*) by the police (Rey, 1989). The already established queer subculture of parks, streets and taverns made it relatively easy for the Paris police in 1725 to compile a list of some twenty thousand sodomites (W. Johansson, 'Police', *EH*). In the Dutch Republic, the legal system was accusatory, acting on charges brought by civilians, until about 1725 when the authorities acquired an independent role in tracing and investigating crimes, and it is only from that date, as agents began gathering information, that the sodomitical subculture comes to light, leading to mass trials (Noordam, 1989). Chauncey (1994) has established that the prosecution of gay men in New York in the 1910s and 1920s

> stemmed from the efforts of the Society for the Prevention of Cruelty to Children, which involved itself in the cases of men suspected of sodomy with boys in order to ensure their indictment and successful prosecution by the district attorney. The fragmentary court records available suggest that at least 40 percent – and up to 90 percent – of the cases prosecuted each year were initiated at the complaint of the SPCC.

Somewhat later, most of the raids upon New York's gay subculture were directed by one man with a mission, John Sumner, leader of the Society for the Suppression of Vice from 1915. Homophobic campaigns are not generated by 'the general public', but by specific named individuals on a moral crusade.

Early queer subcultures

Every feature that is used to characterize modern gay (sub)cultures and identities that allegedly emerged in the late nineteenth century already existed in London at the start of the eighteenth century, with the exception of political organizations. Recognizable queer subcultures in continental Europe can be traced back at least to the early fourteenth century, and there were proto-subcultures, or centres of homosexual activity, in the early twelfth-century Anglo-Norman court of King Rufus, and at the University of Paris in the thirteenth century (Goodich, 1979), and possibly pagan customs surviving as a subculture in medieval Christian Europe

(Boswell, 1980). The trial of Arnold of Verniolle in 1323 for heresy and sodomy reveals not simply the activities of a single operator, but a network of contacts; among the many students who had relations with Arnold were several who had had liaisons with other men as well, and Arnold was aware of the homosexual tastes of Maurand, canon of St Saturnin of Toulouse; at his trial Arnold revealed that 'the bishop would have enough on his hands if he were to apprehend everyone in Pamiers who had been infected with that crime because there were more than three thousand persons' (Goodich, 1979).

The University of Bologna was 'infested' by sodomites in 1375: they were going to be denounced, but were forewarned by a sodomite priest and fled – clear evidence of an efficiently organized network. 'Florence and other early-fifteenth-century Tuscan cities had such a reputation for sodomy that Genoa would not hire Tuscan schoolmasters, and boys walking down the streets of Florence were in greater danger than girls of being sexually assaulted. In Venice, a coterie of homosexual sodomites came to light in 1406' (Ruggiero, 1985; Greenberg, 1988). There is an enormous amount of information, or at least gossip, regarding queer Renaissance celebrities: Pope Leo X, Pope Julius III, the writer Pietro Aloiso called 'the prince of Sodomy', Michelangelo, Leonardo da Vinci who was arrested for sodomy though the charges were dismissed for lack of evidence. Greenberg nevertheless maintains that these do not suggest the existence of anything analogous to the modern homosexual subculture, apparently on the basis that 'Many of the homosexually active men were also actively heterosexual.' Yet this was equally true of the queer subculture in many American cities from the 1940s to the 1960s; gay bars would not have survived during that period without the custom of married men! St Bernardino of Siena in a sermon refers to 'the unhappiness of sodomites' wives': surely this is evidence that substantial numbers of men who preferred men married for convenience during the Renaissance just as they did in the twentieth century.

Dall'Orto has studied the queer subculture in Florence, where sodomites became so conspicuous that a special court, the Uffiziali di Notte (Officers of the Night), was devoted to monitoring their activity. Those accused included Leonardo da Vinci, Sandro Botticelli and Benvenuto Cellini. St Bernardino preached a series of sermons in 1424–7 giving details which clearly revealed a queer subculture: the 'wild pigs' had special meeting places at special times of the night, and congregated at taverns, pastry shops and barber shops (barbers often acted as pimps). Machiavelli implied that boys could be picked up in certain locales such as Borgo Santo Apostolo, Calimala Francesca and Il Tetto de'Pisani. A study of the records for 1478–83 reveals that 'ten per cent of all Florentine boys had to appear before the authorities charged with sodomy'. Among the adult sodomites there were many bachelors and 'recidivists', who enjoyed what can justly be called a 'deviant lifestyle' if not a 'queer lifestyle' (G. Dall'Orto, 'Florence'; 'Venice', *EH*). In Venice, in 1488, the porch of Santa Maria Mater Domini was sealed off by the authorities to stop it from being used by sodomites as a gathering place. In Venice alone there are records of about a thousand homosexual prosecutions during the fourteenth and fifteenth centuries; such investigations often uncovered queer networks of twenty or so people. 'By the fifteenth century Venice had a widespread subculture, centring around apothecary shops; schools of gymnastics, singing, music, dance, and the abacus; pastry shops; and certain dark areas' (W. A. Percy, 'Municipal Law', *EH*; Ruggiero, 1985).

By the late fifteenth century there were queer subcultures in major cities in Germany, France, Spain and most large towns in Italy:

> Male homosexual networks have been documented for the larger French cities of the fifteenth and early sixteenth centuries, including Paris, Rouen, and Cologne; comedies celebrating male homosexuality, a product of these subcultures, were performed as street theater during the annual Carnival season. (Greenberg, 1988)

In countries such as Spain, Portugal and Brazil the queer subculture was first 'discovered' in the late seventeenth century because of the activities of the Inquisition. Luiz Mott has established the existence of a subculture in seventeenth-century Lisbon, consisting not only of street prostitution and a network of go-betweens but also inns patronized by sodomites, private homes where men could meet one another, a vocabulary of queer slang, special modes of dress and the use of female nicknames. There was even a transvestite dance troupe, the Dança dos Fanchonos.

Enough documentary evidence has been uncovered by Gert Hekma, Theo van der Meer, Dirk Jaap Noordam, L. J. Boon and other scholars to establish the historical continuity in the growth and development of the Dutch queer subculture from the late seventeenth century to the twentieth century. From the seventeenth century onwards,

> Brothels and pubs existed in The Hague, Utrecht, Amsterdam, and Leiden. Special go-betweens provided footmen for gentlemen. Public buildings like the Amsterdam City Hall, the Bourse in Amsterdam,

churches, theatres, as well as numerous lavatories which sometimes were specially nicknamed, city walls, specific streets, the underbrush in and outside city walls: all were known to sodomites as places where they either could have sex or find a casual partner. At some of these places they used special codes to make contact with one another, like tapping with one hand on the back of the other, or putting the hands on the hips and hitting with the elbow against that of somebody who did the same thing. (T. van der Meer, 'Netherlands', *EH*)

It should be noted that for Dutchmen in the 1760s the hand on the hip was used quite outside the context of effeminacy, that is as a queer signal *per se*.

As in other European countries, Dutch queer culture was largely a street culture of working-class men, mostly merchants, shopkeepers, peddlers and footmen, which remained relatively constant until giving way in the late twentieth century to the commercialized gay subculture on the one hand, and more intimate, private relationships on the other. As early as 1703 there were cruising grounds in The Hague and circles of men who robbed and blackmailed them; groups of friends met regularly at private houses and inns owned by 'that sort of people' (*mede van dat volk*). In the 1730s, in the provinces of Frisia and Groningen, homosexual men gave each other female names. By the middle of the eighteenth century, in Amsterdam, gay men met not only in public toilets and under the arcades of the town hall but in molly-houses or taverns called *lolhuysen*, 'fun houses'. They developed a sense of gay identity supported by the use of special mimicry, love names and a network of friends and contacts, and some men sealed marriage contracts with blood (Huussen, 1989). Female couples, one of them dressed as a man, tried (sometimes successfully) to get married officially (Noordam, 1989). In The Hague two men sealed a marriage contract agreeing not to have sex with a third party without their partner's knowledge and consent. In early eighteenth-century France the sodomites revealed by police archives constituted the same coherent social group (48 per cent craftsmen and merchants, 26 per cent servants, only 12 per cent nobility and gentry), with the same well-organized subculture; on certain evenings groups of fifteen to thirty men would meet in taverns with shutters closed, where they ate, danced, sang and paired up, and used female nicknames and rituals (Rey, 1985).

Queer diaspora

We should not lightly dismiss the idea that a once-widespread queer culture was driven underground and became fragmented subcultures and clandestine networks, a kind of queer diaspora. For example, homophobia was imported into Russia as part of the modernizing reforms of Peter the Great (who ironically was gay himself), as a result of which eighteenth- and nineteenth-century Muscovite homosexuals went underground. However, features of the queer culture survived 'among the poorer classes and in remote northern regions', especially among the Khlysty and the Skoptsy sects, which 'had recognizable homosexual, bisexual, and sadomasochistic strains in their culture, folklore, and religious rituals' (S. Karlinsky, 'Russia', *EH*); under Stalinist reformers 'the previously widespread homosexual practices in the Caucasus and the Muslim areas of Central Asia were persecuted and punished during the 1920s as "survivals of the old way of life"' – which is precisely what they were.

Albania was relatively untouched by modern Western culture until quite recently, and through the early twentieth century retained vestiges of a queer culture within the peasant culture that probably went back to when the country was heavily influenced by Turkish Islamic civilization. It has been suggested that the Communist dictator Enver Hoxha, though homosexual himself, introduced anti-homosexual legislation after the war not to eliminate Western decadence but because he 'saw homosexuality as a part of traditional culture which he wanted to suppress' (Walderhaug, 1996). The ancient tradition of homosexual marriage survived into modern times and was blessed in Balkan Orthodox churches. As Boswell (1994) says, 'although it was ignored or disguised by anthropologists, gay men in Europe were well aware of the phenomenon and saw no reason to pretend it was anything else.' Lord Byron observed these homosexual unions in Albania in the early nineteenth century, and Paul Näcke, a gay anthropologist, described them with explicit sexual details for the *Jahrbuch für sexuelle Zwischenstufen* in 1908. Christopher Isherwood, travelling down the Danube on a river-steamer in 1933 'kept repeating to himself that they were entering the Balkans – a romantically dangerous region of blood feuds and (so he had been told) male marriages celebrated by priests' (Isherwood, 1977). Isherwood was probably given this information by Magnus Hirschfeld.

At certain periods of history, astonishment is expressed at the large number of sodomites seen by foreign visitors on their travels. It is usually assumed that these are exaggerations. But are they? In more recent periods of history, surrounding instances such as mass arrests when we can accurately count the number of prosecutions, convictions and hangings, the figures are often remarkably high. Forty or fifty mollies used to gather in Mother Clap's molly-house in early eighteenth-century London; if we consider this in terms of the population of London in 1720 and today, such a number would translate into a gathering of 400 gay men today. Obviously that number of men would not occupy the two or three rooms of a molly-house even today, but as a percentage of the population the number should be accorded greater appreciation than it is by historians. What needs recognition is that there has been a large queer population in London for at least three hundred years. And a large population is one of the requirements for the formation of a subculture.

The ample historical evidence of a very high incidence of homosexuality in large urban centres in the premodern period is unwarrantably dismissed by modern historians. The medieval Bernard of Morlaix observed that homosexuals were 'as numerous as grains of barley, as many as the shells of the sea, or the sands of the universe' (Spencer, 1995). Ten thousand men and youths were investigated for homosexuality in Florence in the fifteenth century (and 2,000 were convicted) – a substantial part of the male population. The chronicles of the Inca and Spanish conquests demonstrate that during the fifteenth and sixteenth centuries the northwestern coast of South America was notorious for 'shameless and open sodomy'. Homosexuality was nearly universal in ancient and medieval Islamic countries, where men were openly bisexual and had boys as well as women. A medieval Dominican friar was horrified to observe that 'These Saracens, forgetting human dignity, go so far that men live with each other in the same way that men and women live together in our own land' (Spencer, 1995). (Note that this indicates long-term relationships rather than sporadic acts.) In the nineteenth century Sir Richard Burton observed that commercial travellers in caravans were accompanied by boys dressed as women called their 'travelling wives'. When George Turberville visited Moscow in 1568 he

> was shocked not by the carnage but by the open homosexuality of the Russian peasants. ... Romantic attachments between men and women, if there were any in sixteenth-century Russia, remain unrecorded. What one finds instead, all foreign and domestic observers agree, is that male homosexuality was astoundingly widespread. (S. Karlinsky, 'Russia', *EH*)

A report dated 1723 in the Paris police archives observes, 'Since half of Paris was so inclined, none of the innkeepers was unaware of the practice, and all were on their guard concerning such activities' (cited by Rey, 1985). In Denmark, homosexuals were not regularly prosecuted until the mid-nineteenth century despite the existence of anti-gay legislation; as Ludvig Holberg, a law professor in Copenhagen, observed in 1716: 'the authorities cannot punish vices which are practised by so many, and which are so firmly embedded that to eradicate the evil would be to cause the disintegration of the whole state' (W. Houser, 'Denmark', *EH*).

We do not know how widespread homosexuality was within ancient Chinese society as a whole during the very early periods, though we do know it was very common in court circles, and by the sixth century was frequent among poets and philosophers, gentlemen and officials, and military men; in sixteenth-century China the chronicler Galeote Pereira reported that sodomy was 'a vice very common in the meaner sort, and nothing strange among the best', and the Jesuit missionary Matteo Ricci as early as 1583, shortly after he arrived in China, wrote about 'the horrible sin to which everyone here is much given' and in 1610 witnessed in Beijing 'public streets full of boys got up like prostitutes'; in 1860 a visitor to the port city of Tianjin estimated there were thirty-five male brothels containing some eight hundred boys 'trained for pederastic prostitution' (Hinsch, 1990).

In medieval Japan, Buddhist monks were notorious for homosexual relationships, with other monks as well as with novices. In the sixteenth century, Francis Xavier observed that the practice was 'so general and so deeply rooted that the bonzes [monks] were not reproached for it' (R. P. Conner and S. Donaldson, 'Buddhism', *EH*). In 1655, Margaret Heathcote wrote to her cousin about life in Antigua: 'they all be a company of sodomites that live here' (Hallam, 1993). In 1698 an Englishman told Elizabeth Charlotte, Duchess of Orleans, that 'nothing is more ordinary in England than this unnatural vice' (Greenberg, 1988).

During the great age of discovery, travellers returned from their voyages to report that homosexuality was 'rife' on every continent and among many indigenous people. Repeatedly in the chronicles the shock of the Europeans is due not simply to the fact that homosexuality was tolerated and unashamedly practised, but that it was practised by very great numbers of people. William Lithgow in 1632, while recording his travels through forty-eight kingdoms in Europe, Asia and Africa, claimed that 'beastly sodomy ... is as rife here [in Padua] as in Rome, Naples, Florence, Bologna, Venice, Ferrara, Genoa – Parma not being exempted, not yet the smallest village of Italy' (cited in Norton, 1992). He reported that during his visit to Malta in 1616 he 'saw a Spanish soldier and a Maltese boy burnt in ashes, for the public profession of sodomy' and before night fell 'there were above a hundred *bardassoes* – whorish boys – that fled away to Sicily in a galleot for fear of fire, but never one bugeron [bugger, sodomite] stirred, being few or none there free of it'. Lithgow further claimed there were some three thousand licensed boy brothels in Fez. Many other chroniclers and travellers confirm his findings, with high figures that would indeed shock most modern travellers. Although many Europeans regarded the oriental, eastern and exotic cultures as being 'steeped in vice and luxury', when numerical figures are cited there is no historical justification for dismissing them as exaggerations. In 1845 it was reported to Sir Charles Napier of the East India Company that in the town of Karachi, with a population of only 2,000, there were three brothels of boys and eunuchs. Sir Richard Burton was asked to investigate, resulting in his notorious report about 'the Sotadic Zone'; his attempt to map out the prevalence of homosexuality has been much laughed at, but is more or less accurate geographically, though idiosyncratically analysed.

In some areas of the modern Philippines, where drag shows are very popular cultural entertainment and homosexuals are not held in contempt, 'as many as 80 per cent of the young males from the working and lower middle classes at some point in their youths work as "callboys"' (F. L. Whitman, 'Philippines', *EH*). It has been estimated that as much as 30 per cent of the male population in modern Brazil are predominantly homosexual, and unusually high AIDS statistics seem to bear this out. Brazil is the most gay-positive country in modern Latin America, perhaps partly due to the importation of African slaves with native homosexual traditions, or perhaps even the importation of Portuguese colonists. The early queer subculture of Lisbon seems matched by the very early development of a subculture of *sodomitas* and *fanchonos* (roughly active and passive queers) in the Portuguese bases of Bahia and Rio de Janeiro (L. Mott, 'Brazil', *EH*). Alternatively, there may have been a strong indigenous queer culture. In the sixteenth century the French observed gender variant men among the indigenous Tupi of Brazil, and the Portuguese chronicler Gabriel Soares de Souza 'reported in the sixteenth century that male "brothels" existed among the Tupis where warriors would go to strengthen themselves by engaging in oral or anal intercourse with other men' (Conner *et al.*, 1997). Male prostitution was so pervasive in the Portuguese districts of Rio de Janeiro that the Portuguese Consul in 1846 arranged for the importation of female prostitutes from the

Azores, Poland and France, which drove male prostitutes and transvestites underground (Trevisan, 1986).

Queer migration

Because of the social constructionist dogma that subcultures are formed by outside pressures, the notion that queers, like any ethnic group, carry their culture with them and build it themselves has been largely ignored. Theorists often speak of prostitutes, for example, as if they were simply an economic class, but it is often more accurate to identify hustlers as a specific ethnic class. The hustlers of modern Iran, for example, were specifically young men from the impoverished suburb of Rayy in the south of Teheran, who had their own *lutiyy* or folk-hero types as their pimps (G. Puterbaugh, 'Iran', *EH*). And the hustlers of modern Paris, *les Beurs*, are young Muslim-French men of working-class African origin (W. Johansson, 'Paris', *EH*). The importance of migration to the formation of modern queer subcultures has been studied, but needs to be explored in relation to earlier queer subcultures. The strength of the gay community in San Francisco may be directly related to the purges of gay men and lesbians from the armed forces in the Pacific towards the end of the Second World War, when large numbers, hundreds at a time, were discharged (dishonourably) at that port. 'Unable or unwilling to return home in disgrace to family and friend, they stayed to carve out a new gay life' (D'Emilio, 1992). The right of homosexuals to congregate in public establishments was upheld by California's courts, and by the late 1950s San Francisco perhaps had more gay bars than New York. Word spread along the gay grapevine, and the results can be seen in the census statistics: 'From 1950 to 1960 the number of single-person households doubled and accounted for 38 per cent of the city's residence units.' During the 1970s the 'sexual migration' of gay men and lesbians to San Francisco became even more marked, creating

> a new social phenomenon, residential areas that were visibly gay in composition: Duboce Triangle, Noe Valley, and the Upper Mission for lesbians; the Haight, Folsom, and above all the Castro for gay men. Geographic concentration offered the opportunity for local political power that invisibility precluded. (D'Emilio, 1992)

The Stonewall riots in New York may have captured the gay imagination, but many of the political ideas and strategies of gay liberation were mapped out a dozen years earlier by gay and lesbian activists in San Francisco.

Dr Evelyn Hooker's ground-breaking 1954 study which established a non-pathological paradigm for homosexuals was based upon a study of homosexuals whom she was able to recruit as a result of her personal friendship with a small group of gay men and two lesbians who emigrated to California *as a group*. As she said in an interview with Laud Humphreys much later:

> The core members of this group had met in college, came to California as a group, and lived together ... in an old, ramshackle house on Benton Way. ... A number of prominent, creative homosexuals stayed at Benton Way when visiting Los Angeles; I remember meeting Paul Goodman and many others. My husband and I often went to parties there. We saw a whole cross section of gay society in that house. (Legg, 1994)

The upheavals caused by the Second World War and subsequent demobilization undoubtedly played a role in the relative 'explosion' of queer subculture in America in the 1940s and 1950s. But sexual migration had already been taking place for quite some time. As early as 1910 the Chicago Vice Commission recorded the existence of whole 'colonies' of queer meeting places, ranging from the bohemian area called 'Tower-town' to the hobo area south of the Loop; and queer subcultural 'types' ranging from female impersonators to a queer street gang calling themselves 'The Bluebirds', whose headquarters were in Grant Park. The development of the institutions of the twentieth-century gay subculture that took shape on Chicago's south side

> was owing largely to the tremendous influx of both foreign immigrants and native-born Americans from rural and small town areas who came not only for economic betterment but also to find personal freedom and anonymity by escaping from a more traditional society. Taking root in the 1910s, this diverse subculture flourished openly throughout the 1920s, went underground during the 1930s, and resurfaced in the 1940s. (S. L. Lewis, 'Chicago', *EH*)

Exact numbers cannot be determined, but it is clear from medical case studies, 1930s researchers, interviews and contemporary reports that *very large numbers* of homosexuals migrated to New York between the 1880s and the 1930s, where they quickly found jobs, housing and a social circle through their links with other queers (Chauncey, 1994). The migration of black people to New York contributed not only to the Harlem Renaissance but to a very widespread black gay culture within the community:

> Although some evidence suggests that gay men were more accepted in rural black communities than in comparable white communities, moving to the city made it possible for them to participate in a gay world organized on a scale unimaginable in a Southern town. (Chauncey, 1994)

During the 1930s as many as 8000 black drag queens and black working-class 'flaming faggots' attended the annual Hamilton Lodge Ball. Drag queens and bulldykes were far more publicly visible in black culture, and the influence of 'the life', as queer blacks called it, upon queer white culture is a fact which is generally left unexamined for fear of it being called a racialist slur by respectable African-Americans. Black homophobic scholars and white racist scholars alike ignore the intermingling of black and gay culture in the 1920s and 1930s, specifically the cultural nationalism of the Harlem Renaissance, which owes much to the specifically queer black sensibility of Alain Leroy Locke, Langston Hughes, Countee Cullen, Richard Bruce Nugent, Claude McKay and queer white culturalists like Carl Van Vechten. 'Blues and jazz, especially performed by female vocalists, played a large part in the formation of white gay male sensibility', and many early jazz lyrics explicitly concerned gay men and lesbians (Bronski, 1984). The lively gay nightlife of the bohemian subcultures was significantly shaped by migrating lesbians: 'By the end of the nineteenth century, wealthy and/or intrepid women had consciously migrated not only to Paris, but also to Berlin, Amsterdam, New York, San Francisco, Chicago, and other cities, where they hoped to find other homosexuals' (Vicinus, 1993).

The molly subculture of eighteenth-century London was as demonstrably working-class as the queer subculture of early twentieth-century New York (Norton, 1992). It might well be possible to find patterns of migration which suggest that eighteenth-century mollies moved to London to express themselves more freely just as twentieth-century working men migrated from Hicksville to New York. Although metropolitan subcultures flourished, the provinces should not be considered as being utterly devoid of a subculture: links from the provinces extended into the urban queer subculture. Just as it is quite commonplace today to travel to the major British cities on weekends to participate in queer culture, so it was common even in 1810 for men to travel from thirty miles outside London to go to the White Swan pub-cum-gay-brothel on Sunday nights. In the Victorian period the public postal service – the notorious messenger boys who appeared at Oscar Wilde's trial were just the tip of an iceberg – was significantly staffed by boys who gave their services to men. It is assumed that these 'poor' boys were exploited by middle-class queers, but it is just as likely – by analogy with twentieth-century New York where queer working men took jobs as queers for queers in queer-identified businesses such as pubs, etc. – that queer Victorian boys came to London and went to work for the post office because they knew they could have a better queer life there. The distinction I am making is that any significant manifestations of a queer presence might well suggest queer empowerment rather than sexual exploitation: factors relating to *self-expression* are more important than factors relating to social construction.

At the beginning of the nineteenth century homosexuality was 'scandalously common ... in cities such as Rio de Janeiro – especially among small shopkeepers, where immigrant Portuguese predominated, often keeping their sales clerks as lovers' (Trevisan, 1986). Homosexuality among French troops has been attributed to their service in Algeria. Moral reformers in America blamed the increase of homosexuality during and after the First World War upon American service people's contact with French culture – and the French gay subculture – during the war, a perception which is probably correct (Chauncey, 1994). The inter-relationship of the queer subcultures of different nationalities is something that needs pursuing in order adequately to account for growth and historical development in any specific queer subculture, because many changes probably come more from the intermingling of queer subcultures than from the interaction between queer subcultures and straight cultures. Several interrelationships seem likely: American/French; American influence on British queers (via Whitman, etc.); British influence on American queers (via Wilde, etc.); German influence on the British and on the Americans; Dutch influence on the British during the reign of William and Mary; Italian influence on the rest of Europe.

During the colonial period, immigrant labourers were imported from China to the Philippines, bringing with them their native Chinese queer culture, and, according to the Spanish masters, introducing such tastes to the host population. Many arrests were made in the Chinese enclaves of Manila:

Although the Chinese protested that love between men was an accepted custom in their homeland, the Spanish colonial authorities were intractable. Some offenders were burned at the stake, while others were flogged and condemned to serve as galley slaves. ... To prevent the infection of more Filipinos with this damnable vice, Spanish officials posted notices in the Chinese quarters of the city warning them of the fatal penalties for homosexual acts. (Hinsch, 1990)

In fact an indigenous queer culture has always flourished in the Philippines, and ironically they themselves have become the immigrant labourers stigmatized for their customs: in September 1996 Saudi Arabian authorities sentenced twenty-four Filipino workers to 200 lashes each and subsequent deportation following their arrest for homosexual behaviour. Amnesty International issued an appeal for international protests. Gays formed a significant number of the 117,000 Cubans who emigrated to Florida during the boat-lifts of spring 1980; the National Gay Task Force estimated 2,000 to 10,000, but the *Washington Post*'s figure was nearer 20,000, at least a significant enough percentage for the Cuban government to use that to discredit the boat-lift. Many of the Cuban gay refugees were resettled through the gay Metropolitan Community Church and a gay rights group in Miami (Miller, 1995). Undoubtedly Florida's modern queer culture now has a large Hispanic element. The point to be made about sexual migration is that it contradicts social constructionist theory that the minority culture is invariably shaped by the dominant culture: it is more likely that a native queer culture is shaped by another queer culture imported from outside the boundaries of the dominant culture – or even by a wholly foreign implant.

The Japanese traditionally trace their own queer culture to China. A very famous legend, repeated by Ihara Saikaku in the seventeenth century, among others, states that when the Buddhist monk Kōbō Daishi (also called Kukai) returned from his apprenticeship in China in 806 he introduced Chinese homosexual customs into the monasteries, whence it rapidly spread to the Kyoto aristocracy, and from there to the rest of society. Homosexual behaviour among the native Japanese probably predated Buddhism, but we should not dismiss as 'merely legendary' the possibility that queer cultural values were transmitted in this fashion. Japanese queers in the seventeenth century used the Chinese slang term for homosexual intercourse, *xia zhuan*, whose incomprehensible translation, 'intimacy with a brick', perhaps may be due to confusions between Japanese and Chinese orthography when it was passed to the Japanese by Chinese traders.

Similarly, the 'secret camp language' of polari discussed in Chapter 4 has strong links with the slang of the immigrant Jewish and Huguenot population of London's East End, and even the more ancient language of Mediterranean sailors, Lingua Franca. The importance of great naval ports to the development of queer subcultures can hardly be overestimated. New Orleans seems to have had a queer subculture going back at least to the early nineteenth century.

> The waterfront bars catered, from the beginning, to an unusually high number of Greek seafarers brought to the port by the Mediterranean trade patterns inherited from the city's French and brief Spanish (1763–1800) period. Such Greek bars even today remain heavily mixed, straight and gay. (Lucy J. Fair, 'New Orleans', *EH*)

The conspicuous participation of gays during the Mardi Gras probably dates back to the queer cultural tradition which is integral to the Mardi Gras and its masked balls. Portuguese trading routes may have been important to the development of this tradition in both the New World and the Old World. The port of Algiers has been an important queer cultural centre since the sixteenth century, and Alexandria as early as the first century was a melting pot of queer types: pederasts, effeminate queens and the *galli* of the ancient world. The sailor is the queer icon *par excellence*.

Queer cultural continuity

Queer migration should not be ruled out as a factor in the development of premodern (perhaps even ancient) queer subcultures. Sir Richard Burton put forward the classic suggestion that homosexual practices originated in Greece, were borrowed by the Romans and taken to Rome, whence they extended to the Roman colonies – especially Provence – including Northern Africa and Morocco, with separate strands of importation/migration in the Muslim world and in the Tigris–Euphrates Valley, in particular Iran. In rural Albania the custom of homosexual relations was called *madzüpi*, derived from *madzüp* ('gypsy'). The queer subculture of the Netherlands is hardly recorded until the great wave of persecutions in 1730; the contemporary feeling was that a nadir of sinfulness 'was supposed to have happened on a large scale in 1712–1713 during the negotiations in Utrecht to end the War of the Spanish Succession, when numerous Catholic diplomats visited the city' (T. van der Meer, 'The Netherlands', *EH*). It is not beyond the realm of possibility that contemporary perceptions were correct, and that part of the queer subculture really was an import from southern Europe. No serious research has been devoted to 'the movement of queer peoples', because of the general presumption that homosexuality has its roots in individual personal psychology.

It is not entirely absurd to trace a direct line of continuity between ancient Greece and modern New York. The well-documented institution of Spartan 'pederasty' seems to have been deliberately imported from Crete in the seventh century BC, together with Cretan customs of delayed marriage, nude exercises in gymnasia, etc., as part of a military and legal reorganization; classical Greek writers give the names of the Cretan musicians who introduced such practices from about 630 BC. Slightly less legendary evidence establishes that Solon, chief magistrate of Athens from 594 to 593 BC, visited Crete to study their laws, especially the reforms of Lycurgus in Sparta, and on his return with the Cretan musician Epimenides institutionalized military pederasty. Sicily and southern Italy were colonized by the Greeks in the eighth century BC, when they may have introduced the practice of military pederasty. The Phoenicians later introduced into Sicily the practices of homosexual temple prostitution, eunuchs and effeminacy among young men.

Pederasty proper, along the Cretan model, was introduced into Locri on the tip of Italy by Zaleucus in the mid-seventh century BC. Zaleucus was a student of Onomacritus or Thaletas, who are supposed to have first institutionalized pederasty in Sparta. From Locri it spread quickly to the Greek colony of Sicily. We know virtually nothing about Sicilian sexual practices before that time, but during that period virtually all Sicilian rulers were pederasts. Hiero, pederastic 'tyrant' of Syracuse, was the patron of Pindar, pederastic celebrator of athletes in the Olympian Games; Dionysus, later 'tyrant' of Syracuse, also pederastic, was the patron of Plato and Socrates. Hellenic pederasty common to Sicily became popular throughout the Roman Empire. Many Roman writers, such as Virgil and Petronius, set their homosexual stories in Sicily. The country was dominated by impoverished peasants, and men outnumbered women (due to female infanticide). Sicily became part of the Byzantine Empire and its homosexual culture was strengthened by Arab homosexual traditions. Disparity of males to females persisted throughout the fifteenth century. Sicily was said to be 'plagued' by sodomy in the sixteenth century, and there were attempts at prosecution/persecution. During the late nineteenth century, and even today, Taormina has been regarded as a gay resort. By the mid-nineteenth century Sicily was being exploited by northern industrialists. 'Millions escaped poverty by emigrating to the Americas as well as to northern Italy.' Vast numbers of Sicilian and Neapolitan immigrants to America in the mid-nineteenth century brought their own queer culture with them, and further contributed to the development of American queer culture in a very specific way: 'A significant contribution of the Italian underworld to the American gay subculture was its ownership of gay bars and speakeasies during Prohibition at a time when no respectable businessman would touch such an ill-famed enterprise' (W. A. Percy, 'Sicily', *EH*).

Chauncey (1994) has shown that the institutionalized fairy subculture of New York was specifically a feature of Italian rather than Jewish neighbourhoods, even though as many Jews as Italians emigrated to the city: 'By the late nineteenth century, southern Italian men had a reputation in northern Italy and in the northern European gay world for their supposed willingness to engage in homosexual relations.' Considerable evidence, such as police records, supports this view common to gay folklore. He continues:

> The patterns of homosexual behaviour noted in Sicily appear to have persisted in modified form in the Italian enclaves on the Lower East Side, in Greenwich Village, and in East Harlem. ... it seems likely that an important part of the homosexual culture of fairies and their sex partners visible in turn-of-the-century New York represented the flowering in this country of a transplanted Mediterranean sexual culture.

Partly this is because it was largely a 'bachelor subculture', 'whereas Jewish immigrants more often included whole families rather than single men' (Chauncey, 1994). This working-class bachelor subculture consisted very largely of sailors and seamen, and transients who worked on the waterfront: 'The native-born among them, especially, were part of the immense army of migrant laborers, usually known as hoboes or tramps, who constituted a significant part of the American workforce in the decades before the 1920s.' It is among these two basic groups – travellers on the seas and travellers on the railways – that we find the roots of American queer culture. An investigator for an anti-prostitution society observed in 1917 that the sailors were sex mad. A number of these sailors were with other men walking arm in arm and on one dark street I saw a sailor and a man kissing each other. ... some of the sailors told me that they might be able to get a girl if they went 'up-town' but it was too far up and they were too drunk to go way up there.

Any claim that sailors had 'difficulty finding girls' is of course a nonsense – if anything, they would have had to actively *avoid* the many thousands of female prostitutes working the streets, more of them than at any other time in modern history. Similarly, the notion that fairies were a 'more convenient' substitute for female prostitutes sounds to me like a convenient fiction for the sailors, which should not be taken at face value. The possibility that fairies were easier and cheaper than female prostitutes is not an adequate explanation for what really seems to be a preference for many sailors.

The Seamen's Institute was a major queer resort:

The investigator frequently saw punks and fairies talking with seamen at the Institute, in nearby lunchrooms, and in the park; on one occasion a seaman identified fifteen male prostitutes in the park, sitting 'on separate benches, always leaving room for a [man] to sit down'. (Chauncey, 1994)

Wolf/punk relationships were very often found in circumstances which are now dismissed as 'situational' (prisons, etc.), but in fact they often persisted even when women were available. A seaman working on the lower Manhattan waterfront in 1931 bragged that 'I had one of those punks living with me at the Seamen's Church Institute for quite some time. ... He was a young kid about 15 years old, [and] pretty.' This seaman could have gone to 'sporting houses' (tenement brothels) had he wanted to, but he didn't. Although he did not regard himself as queer, he nevertheless believed that 'a certain kind' of man was more likely than others to be interested in punks: in other words, he had a conception of an intermediate category that avoided the stigma of queer or fairy, which he left undefined but which today he might well have called gay. Fairies were sometimes even 'married' to wolves or jockers, masculine men who positively preferred male sexual partners and who were regarded as being different from normals yet not quite queers.

A 1916 study of vagrants in New York City identified a quarter of them as 'perverts'. Jack London in *The Road* (1907) recalls the standard relationship among hoboes, the teenage 'prushun' protected by, and a slave to, the 'jocker'. Nels Anderson, himself a hobo, in his hobo handbook of 1931 acknowledged that the prevalence of homosexual relations was 'generally assumed to be true among hoboes'. Queer slang and hobo argot overlapped at the turn of the twentieth century just as the molly dialect and thieves cant overlapped at the turn of the eighteenth. Chauncey (1994) argues that

> homosexual relationships appear to have been so widespread among seamen and hoboes that historians need to recognize the desire to live in a social milieu in which such relationships were relatively common and accepted – or to escape the pressure to marry in a more family-oriented milieu – as one of the motives that sent men on the road or to sea.

A somewhat analogous position appertains in Japan, where young itinerant male prostitutes are called 'flyboys' (from *tobiko*, 'travelling child'), originating in the Kansai area of central Japan (Schalow, 1996a). The vagabonds, itinerant labourers and 'masterless men' who roamed England during the late sixteenth and early seventeenth century may have played a role in the formation of the queer subculture. 'It has been suggested that this underworld, which was mostly male, which was ever-changing, absorbing wandering children and orphans, fuelled both the army and navy, provided settlers for Ireland and the New World, and in its sexual practices was largely sodomitical' (Spencer, 1995); this is the charge of contemporary accounts, as in Thomas Harman's *The Fraternity of Vagabonds* (1575).

I mentioned earlier that prison was not chosen as a queer space. However, queer prison subcultures cannot be interpreted as examples of merely 'situational homosexuality'. In America and Australia (where queer prison subcultures have been studied most intensively), we can find evidence of the *importation* of queer culture into prison. As early as 1892 Alexander Berkman noticed the continuity of the queer wolf/punk tradition among hoboes and in prisons (whose population consisted largely of transients): 'It's done in every prison, an' on th' road, everywhere' (cited in Chauncey, 1994). Many of the features of American queer prison subculture can be documented as originating in the hobo queer subculture of the turn of the century, which continues to survive in prison today even after the passing of the hobo culture. The hustler, the hobo and the criminal come from a common pool of working-class men. Prison homosexuality is not simply 'situational' or 'circumstantial' homosexuality, but part of a queer cultural tradition whose origins and cultural development can be documented (W. Johansson, 'Hoboes', *EH*; Chauncey, 1994). It is a subject properly for historical and cultural research rather than sociological or psychological research. The 'deprivation' model, a hypothesis based upon the heterosexual normative assumption, fails to account for the wide range of cultural patterns that do not simply mirror heterosexual patterns; the 'importation' model has factual observation to support it, though it faces the problem of tracing an 'ultimate source' when the patterns are 'brought into' one prison from another (S. Donaldson, 'Prisons', *EH*). Nevertheless, an ultimate source among working-class street punks and queens seems likely. The fact that personal situations rather than social continuities are studied by the professionals reflects the low value placed upon the idea of there being such a thing as a queer culture.

10

Queer Folk and Culture Queens

Ethnic unity

It is commonly asserted that you cannot understand homosexuals without understanding heterosexuals. Clinical psychologists argue that homosexuality cannot be analysed separately from heterosexuality: in other words, only human sexuality is a subject of study. Social constructionists argue that homosexuality does not exist independently from homophobia. But I take the ethnic position: I regard homosexuals as part of an ethnic culture which can be studied in its own relations to itself, in precisely the same way, for example, that gypsy culture can be understood and discussed independently of non-gypsy culture. From an ethnic point of view, the heterosexual/homosexual dichotomy is false: oranges are oranges and apples are apples – to evaluate them against one another is artificial, and certainly less useful than identifying and studying different varieties of oranges and different varieties of apples.

The main difference between queer identity and ethnic identity is that the queer's family of origin cannot pass on experience of managing stigma, for they themselves have not been stigmatized; whereas in an ethnic minority the community will have built up experience in dealing with oppression, and will not itself be a source of oppression for their children. Reading the counselling literature one cannot help but feel that our parents have let us down, even betrayed us: many lesbians and gay men would undoubtedly have lived healthier lives had they been able to escape their families of origin at an earlier age and established a family of choice within the gay community. 'We have a special need for history. Raised as we were in heterosexual families, we grew up and discovered our gayness deprived of gay ancestors, without a sense of our roots' (D'Emilio, 1992). However, to argue that ethnic identity and queer identity are fundamentally different because one is not born into a queer family is to ignore the near certainties that first, queerness is no more a matter of choice than ethnicity, and second, the vast majority of queer people testify to a feeling that they were, indeed, born queer. That feeling may not reflect reality, but we are talking about identity – where the perception *is* the reality.

The other most frequent argument for the proposition that ethnic identity and queer identity are fundamentally different is the assertion that shame is the key factor in queer identity, whereas difference is the decisive element of ethnic identity. But here again, both history and modern testimony make it clear that the perception of mere difference is central to the emerging queer identity; shame is quite localized and historically specific to certain modern cultures during certain eras, but even then it is usually preceded by a vague sense of being 'out of joint with the others'. Ethnic or racial identity and queer identity usually come into focus around the same time – at an age when racial discrimination or homophobia are first encountered in early adolescence – and often they take the same route once that strong sense of difference is perceived, leading to the adoption of a community identity that ranges from a relatively weak socio-cultural identity through to a relatively militant political identity. People who are both queer and black are sometimes aware of a queer identity before they are aware of their black identity. Labi Siffre (1996), writer of the Ivor Novello classic '(Something Inside) So Strong', sang this song at London's Pride 1995, revealing that it was originally written as a song of gay pride, though marketed as a song about racism. At the age of 51 Siffre confides, 'I knew I was gay when I was four, but I didn't know I was actually black until I was seven.'

Although many queers resist identifying themselves within the confines of certain stigmas and stereotypes, many achieve a sense of ethnic identity based upon an awareness of being part of a tribe or race whose culture they 'recognize' the moment they discover it, be it in the first queer novel they read or the first queer bar they enter. They are uneasy, often from a very early age, with a sense of being 'different from the others' in relation to their own heterocentric family and society, but become culturally identified when they embrace 'others like myself'. To observe that it is a struggle to achieve a healthy identity within an atmosphere of anti-gay prejudice is one thing; but to conclude therefore (as sociologists of deviance do) that a gay minority identity emerges only in response to homophobia is entirely mistaken. Queer identity derives from genuine queer folk rather than the demon constructs of homophobia. And although it is fashionable nowadays to refer to homosexualities and gay communities in the plural, Chauncey's (1994) research shows that for the period 1890–1940 'almost all the men in those networks conceived of themselves as linked to the others in their common "queerness" and their membership in a single gay world'.

Homophobic ideology attempts to portray queers as isolated individuals engaging in isolated acts, but a notable feature of queer history are the coteries, cliques, networks, clubs, subcultures and communities formed by queers. 'North American gay (male) communities fit all the criteria suggested by sociologists to define "community" as well as or better than urban ethnic communities do, and lesbian communities exhibit the same features, albeit to a lesser extent' (S. O. Murray, 'Community', *EH*). I believe that one should concentrate on the origin and evolution of queer customs and folklore *in history* rather than engage in a psychological analysis of the individual or socio-political analysis of constructs. In other words, queer folk: folklore; folk speech and folk narratives such as coming-out stories; folk rituals; folk costume; objects of material culture. In eighteenth-century London, for example, male transvestism was not reducible to personal psychology: the wearing of female clothing was part of an ethnic culture – nearly all transvestism and 'lying-in' rituals took place during what the mollies called 'festival nights', which indeed should be perceived literally as folk festivals (datable references suggest that these festivals took place during the last week of December).

> In pre-feminist days describing a lesbian folk costume was a relatively simple matter. ... Plaid flannel shirts or work shirts, bib overalls or jeans, and heavy work boots were standard pieces of apparel. A lesbian might wear a pinky ring ... and cut her hair short. ... With the advent of feminism in the 1970s folk costume became more diversified ...

Thus, lesbians can now choose from woman-identified jewellery (for example, the double-headed axe, or cowrie shells woven into the hair of black lesbians), T-shirts with slogans and special brands of shoes (J. Laude, 'Lesbian Folklore', *EH*). Gay men wore red ties as a badge from 1910 to the 1940s (such figures can be seen in several of Cadmus's paintings). The wearing of pinky rings and a fondness for sapphires was shared by gay men and butch lesbians (Lorena Hickok and Eleanor Roosevelt, whose passionate correspondence suggests that they were lovers, exchanged sapphire rings, a recognized symbol for 'sapphic' love).

Recognizing the role of working-class people and people of colour in the creation of queer culture is an important part of the new queer agenda of creating an alliance of differences. The union of queer identity with ethnic identity is a major theme in contemporary lesbian poetry, by those women born since 1940 whom Faderman (1994) identifies as 'post-lesbian-feminist'. Their postmodernist view unites their lesbianism with their ethnic heritage, seeing both as part of a single integral root of their lives. For example, Irena Klepfisz perceives a similarity between Jewishness and lesbian feminism, and has edited *The Tribe of Dina: A Jewish Woman's Anthology*. Chrystos combines the lesbian voice with that of the Native American Indian. Beth Brant (Degonwadonti), a lesbian Bay of Quinte Mohawk, edited *A Gathering of Spirits* in 1983, 'the first book that brought together works by Native American women, many of whom were lesbian' (Faderman, 1994). Kitty Tsui reconciles her Chinese heritage with her lesbian feminism, and edits *New Phoenix Rising: The Asian/Pacific Lesbian Newsletter*. Suniti Namjoshi and Gillian Hanscombe celebrate lesbian love against the Indian background, and have structured a long work as a dialogue between the two lovers as they visit Namjoshi's home in India, acknowledging a culture that is foreign yet not foreign. Cherri (Lawrence) Moraga combines her lesbian and Latina roots by celebrating her mother's Chicana culture. In general, the early postmodernist game of donning identities like new suits of clothes has been superseded by the more fulfilling post-postmodernist endeavour of reclaiming roots.

It may seem paradoxical, but queer black Americans have often reclaimed their ethnic roots through their queerness, though the passage is a torturous one. James Baldwin's deep conviction that black people had to get beyond colour to discover their true selves probably stemmed from an awareness of his queer self. For him the black self obviously was not sufficient, so he posited a human self to overcome that deficiency. At the same time, he did not wish to be labelled a faggot (though that was indeed his true self), and that led him to a passionate identification with the black struggle against white oppression. The sense of feeling a queer alien in a straight world is the bedrock upon which Baldwin's contribution to the black cultural debate rests. He recognized that American Negroes had an African rather than a European culture, that he was a visitor among people 'whose culture controls me, has even, in a sense, created me'. When asked if he had a sense of African roots, he replied, 'I was an interloper from Africa, but the jungle wasn't my home. I therefore have had to take over white history and make it my own, make it work for me, a part of me on *my* terms' (Weatherby, 1989). This reinvention came full circle on the publication of his gay novel *Giovanni's Room* in 1956, which is partly structured around the biblical story of David and Jonathan (biblical sources often have more relevance to black people than the

Western classical tradition). Baldwin said of a gay bar: 'In this bar a lot of people identify now with *Giovanni*; they feel as oppressed as blacks.'

Richard Wright criticized Baldwin for speaking of a black past stretching back to Africa: 'Roots! Next thing you'll be telling me is that all colored folks have rhythm.' On public platforms, Baldwin adopted the integrationist argument in favour of a human brotherhood rather than a black brotherhood. This is partly because he could never quite accept his queer brotherhood, even though he moved almost entirely in queer circles and was very active in the queer underground of both Greenwich Village and Paris, where he was an exotic eagerly plucked by white men. In public, he tried to control his fairy behaviour so that he would not be recognized for the faggot he knew he was. In private, he joked with Bayard Rustin, organizer of the National Association for the Advancement of Colored People (NAACP), about both of them being 'bastard black queers'. He enjoyed doing imitations of Bette Davis long before it was a popular turn among New York show-business people, and identified with her. He had what were called 'actor's mannerisms', and could become hysterically effeminate when drinking; he was nicknamed 'Martin Luther Queen'. Though by no means closeted, in interviews he avoided the direct answer: 'I love a few people; some are women and some are men. ... if you happen to be homosexual or whatever, you don't have to form a club in order to learn to live with yourself' (Weatherby, 1989). But with increasing self-recognition and a realization of the failure of the civil rights movement, in his later writings he came to reject both white culture and straight culture.

Culturally identified queers

The basic premise of the theory of sexuality is that sexuality is the weak spot of culture, that it constitutes nature and reproduction rather than society and civilization. But the male homosexual's theory of sexuality accords little significance to reproduction; in this respect his sexuality is unnatural rather than natural; for him, sexuality is a *cultural force*. This is somewhat less true for lesbians, who cannot avoid monthly reminders of female nature, although it is not until quite recently that some lesbians have chosen motherhood in their search for a natural rather than a cultural identity. Possibly the earliest, and certainly the most extensive and explicit, defences of homosexual sex, including lesbianism, occur in French Enlightenment literature in which 'libertines' separate sexuality from reproduction and make the case for pleasure rather than procreation as the basis of a civilized, rational, cultured society.

Romantic Hellenism is also a major feature of queer culture, drawing upon the link between homosexuality, masculine beauty and classical civilization. The Corinthian column is a ubiquitous feature of physique photography, though the homoerotic image of the beautiful boy seemingly transcends periods, cultures and nationalities. The Hellenic tradition might have provided cover for some pederasts, but it essentially involves a sincere admiration of young male beauty. As developed by Winckelmann in its revival in the 1760s, and by Walter Pater in its re-revival in the 1860s, it involved an aesthetic that was innately queer (Norton, 1993a). Winckelmann even defined beauty as being essentially homoerotic: 'I have observed that those who are only aware of beauty in the female sex and are hardly or not at all affected by beauty in our sex, have little innate feeling for beauty in art in a general and vital sense.' Robert Aldrich (1993) in *The Seduction of the Mediterranean*, surveying the life and work of some fifty individuals who discovered their queer nature and queer culture in Italy, demonstrates that the image of the homoerotic Mediterranean has remained constant for several hundred years despite the differences in the alleged 'construction' of homosexuality. The 'classical' cultural model for homosexuality continued to inspire gay men even as it became trivialized in the muscle magazines of the 1950s and 1960s, and it really was not until the 1970s that its cultural unity began to break up as gay urban America triumphed.

For several hundred years the artistic temperament has been linked to male homosexuals in the public mind. Ariosto in the fifteenth century reported that 'the vulgar laugh when they hear of someone who possesses a vein of poetry, and then they say, "It is a great peril to turn your back if you sleep next to him"' (cited by Saslow, 1989). The problem facing all social historians is that the people who leave records are almost by definition members of what Harry Hay aptly called the 'chronicling classes'. Most of our information about culturally identified queers comes, not surprisingly, from professional producers of culture, especially writers. Such queers, however, have often focused their energies specifically upon *queer* culture rather than culture *per se*. A queer person's cultural allusions and markers are not simply an effort to establish his or her pretensions to high culture, i.e. gentility and snob appeal. When Bette Bourne (a notorious intellectual) bases the Bloolips drag vaudeville show *The Island of Lost Shoes* (performed at London's Drill Hall in November 1995) partly on works by C. P. Cavafy, it is not because Cavafy represents high culture, but because he represents *queer culture*.

It may not be inappropriate to classify culturally identified queers as 'culture queens', whether they produce or consume culture, but it should also be noted that the queer consumers of queer culture are not simply upper-class twits with more money than sense. A female impersonator who worked in the 'pansy chorus' of a nightclub in 1936 described how he 'reads Oscar Wilde, Dorian Grey [sic] and other authors of this type' (Chauncey, 1994). Cultural identification is important even for those who reject high culture, as musician Mixmaster Morris (a camp Jewish queen, DJ, creator of the albums *Flying High* and *Global Chillage*) explains:

> When I was a boy I was desperate, in that way that little gay boys are, for anything that looked a little like me. I was about 12 and it was about 1980 and the only homos I could name were Oscar Wilde, Tom Robinson and Quentin Crisp. Then I read this piece about Tchaikovsky. Really sad. Said he was in love with this boy. A love that could not be. Broken heart. That kind of stuff. He wrote this piece called *Pathétique* then died a broken man. 'That's me!' I thought and tried to get a copy. I found one in a charity shop. Sadly it was crap. As indeed all classical music is. Seven years later I first heard Brian Eno's *Music for Airports*. It sounded like I thought *Pathétique* should sound. Made me feel how I thought Tchaikovsky felt. And this, apparently, was ambient music. Totally electronic and yet totally human. (*Gay Times*, interview by Richard Smith, April 1995)

Photographs of John Addington Symonds's study at Am Hof, Switzerland, reveal statues of *The Libation Bearer* and Cellini's *Perseus*, and on his desk was the *Dying Gladiator*, all supposedly upper-class queer markers. But in photographs of rooms in Montague Glover's 1950s suburban home in Balsall Heath, Warwickshire, among the ornaments we can also see nude male statues, and a sexy sailor is painted on the wall above the tub in his bathroom; in his photo album is a photograph of his lover Ralph, nude, carefully posing in the same attitude as the figure in the gay artist Glyn Philpot's painting *Melampus and the Centaur*, an illustration of which Monty had cut out and pasted into his scrapbook (Gardiner, 1992). Gardiner's industrious collecting of queer ephemera, which includes the remarkable discovery of Glover's scrapbooks and photo albums, has put on record the existence of a tradition of queer-cultural endeavours among those whose finances limit them to newspaper cuttings rather than antique books. Chauncey's (1994) researches have also established this tradition in America:

Some gay men and lesbians in the early twentieth century left a remarkable record of such gay interpretations by filling scrapbooks with newspaper clippings that they read this way [i.e. with queer associations]: a photo of Greta Garbo and her companion, Mercedes D'Acosta, walking together in pants; an article about two boys filing suit to claim a portion of the estate of the gentleman who had 'kept' them; stories about women suing for divorce because their husbands wanted longtime male companions to share their homes. ... They also preserved pictures that gave them a special gay pleasure: West Point cadets and fraternity boys decked out in drag for a school play, basketball players and other handsome young men performing various tasks in various states of undress. ... Men also learned how to read the papers for news of gay men murdered by the tough young men they had picked up and taken home to their apartments.

Unfortunately Chauncey takes the wrong-headed social constructionist line and views all this as 'appropriation':

Gay men, in other words, used gay subcultural codes to place themselves and to see themselves in the dominant culture, to read the culture against the grain in a way that made them more visible than they were supposed to be, and to turn 'straight' spaces into gay spaces.

Many of the examples in the extract are *not* readings 'against the grain', but accurate readings of queer material genuinely lying between the lines of the news reports.

My own interpretation of all this is that queers placed themselves within the context of queer culture. Gathering the evidence that the straight world suppressed or ignored, they registered and took pleasure in recognizing the queer culture that was obviously being signalled by performers such as Greta Garbo and Cole Porter. The creation of a collage of cuttings showing sailors (a common theme in many scrapbooks, and in 1920s artworks assembled by, among others, Stephen Tennant in England and Gösta Adrian Nilsson in Sweden) demonstrates that queers took pleasure in inferring double meanings in pictures not originally intended for a queer reading. But to interpret such fantasizing as evidence that queers 'construct' their identity is to over-analyse the evidence. Such scrapbooks were designed both to celebrate queer culture and to bear testimony to the existence of gay oppression. William Beckford in the early nineteenth century kept newspaper cuttings of homosexual scandals and prosecutions, some pasted into scrapbooks and some wrapped in gilt-edged paper on which he wrote brief comments. His collection, now in the Bodleian Library, today provides a kind of short cut into the queer history of the period (Norton, 1992). Any suggestion that Beckford was 'appropriating' or 'constructing' or even 'consolidating' a queer history or culture out of nothing is nonsense. He was bearing witness, as in his comment about a newspaper report on the hanging in 1816 of a waiter who had had sex with a stable boy: 'Tomorrow (according to the papers) they are going to hang a poor honest sodomite. I should like to know what kind of deity they fancy they are placating with these shocking human sacrifices.'

Culturally identified dykes

In most homosexual histories effeminate men are associated with culture, but they find their equivalent in mannish women associated with culture in lesbian histories. Nearly all of the women discussed in Collis's (1994) *Portraits to the Wall* were professionally involved with culture (art, acting, painting, the movies), lived as bohemians in the art world on the fringes of society, and wore trousers. Edy Craig set up a *ménage à trois* in 1899 with 'The Boys': Christopher St John (born Christabel Marshall) and Clare Atwood, called 'Tony'; Edy's cousin Olive Chaplain set up home in a house opposite Edy's in Smallhythe with her companion Lucy Gow, who liked to be called 'Lucien'. Edy asked Cicely Hamilton to write a play, *A Pageant of Great Women*, in which Edy played Rosa Bonheur; she appeared as this trouser-wearing painter in several pageants over the years. Rosa Bonheur's lover Nathalie Micas died in 1889, and from about 1897 Rosa lived with the American Anna Klumpke, also a painter; when Rosa died in 1899 she was buried beside Nathalie in Père Lachaise cemetery in Paris; in 1945 Anna was buried beside them: the triune grave bears the inscription *L'amitié, c'est l'affection divine*.

Such women typically moved within a lesbian cultural network. Frances Power Cobbe while travelling in Italy in 1860 met the 'colony' of women who enjoyed longstanding relationships with women, including Charlotte Cushman the American actress, writer Mary Somerville, sculptor Harriet Hosmer and painter Rosa Bonheur; there she met a friend of Cushman's, Mary Lloyd, a woman of independent means who was studying sculpture; the pair remained together until Mary's death in 1898. The composer

Ethel Smyth made a point of establishing contact with Edith Somerville, Helena Gleichen, Vernon Lee and Virginia Woolf, among others.

Just like gay men, lesbians have worked to uncover the history of their tribe. Rosa von Braunschweig, who wrote an article for Hirschfeld's *Jahrbuch für sexuelle Zwischenstufen* in 1903 on Felicita von Vestvali, an actress who played male roles, herself often dressed in drag as a military officer (illustrated in Lauritsen and Thorstad, 1974). One of Romaine Brooks's lovers was the American writer Natalie Clifford Barney (1876–1972), who with her lover Renée Vivien (pseudonym of Pauline Tarn, 1877–1909) are prime examples of the culturally identified lesbian. Vivien wrote four plays about Sappho. Barney, who also wrote a play about Sappho, 'was determined to remove male interpretations from Sappho's life and reclaim the Greek poet as someone whose writings celebrated women's love and friendship' (Miller, 1995). Both women learned Greek in order to read Sappho in the original. In 1904 they went to the island of Lesbos, where they attempted briefly to re-establish the Sapphic school of poetry, though they found its inhabitants irretrievably corrupted by modern society and abandoned the project.

Back in Europe, at her home in Neuilly near Paris, Barney organized the performance of Sapphic plays, 'with guests and performers ranging from Colette to Mata Hari', and she photographed women draped in Grecian robes in her garden. Eventually she succeeded in founding an Academy of Women. She was nicknamed 'Amazon', and used this for the title of her book *Pensées d'une Amazone* (1920). Seventeen of her lovers are listed by Richards (1990). Her first book, published in her early twenties, contains poems addressed to two dozen different women; later in life she compiled a list of liaisons and 'demi-liaisons' with some forty women (excluding casual affairs) (Fletcher and Saks, 1990). In her autobiography she presented a restrained apologist defence for public consumption:

> I considered myself without shame: albinos aren't reproached for having pink eyes and whitish hair; why should they hold it against me for being a lesbian? It's a question of Nature. My queerness isn't a vice, isn't deliberate, and harms no one.

But her life was clearly committed to the notion of lesbian cultural superiority. She became a Fascist and lived in Italy during the war years.

Appropriation seems more common in lesbian culture than in gay male culture, perhaps because of the perceived relative scarcity of genuine lesbian culture. Subversion and appropriation are major themes (derived from social constructionism) in lesbian-feminist theory in the 1990s, notably the view that 'popular culture made for a heterosexual audience can be read against the grain' (Griffin, 1993b). But many of the examples of 'appropriation' that I have seen discussed are more akin to assimilation than subversion. Many contemporary lesbian artists are of course influenced by the work of Andy Warhol, such as Veronica Slater and Deborah Kass, and several have appropriated classic gay male icons (Smyth, 1996). The sculptors Ange et Damnation have reinterpreted Saint Sebastian as Sainte Sebastiane: 'This young man, or should we say homosexual, was presented almost as though he were in orgasmic suffering. To that we added our feminist vision.' Contemporary lesbian photographers and artists have taken over rather than subverted the images of male sadomasochistic homoerotica, and exploited the links between pleasure and pain in much the same way as have gay men. G. B. Jones's *Tom-Girl* series reworks the fetishistic imagery of Tom of Finland, and her *I Am a Fascist Pig #1* (1985) arguably copies rather than subverts Tom's 1964 story-drawing *I Am a Thief*.

Much of the tendency of transgressive appropriation of queer art/literature/cinema has been not to give new meanings to old images, but *to revive and reinscribe their original meanings*. Smyth feels that artists such as Svar Simpson

> draw on a matriarchal heritage and Eastern philosophies in a way that reinvigorates clichéd forms and images that have been hijacked with varying degrees of success by certain cultural feminists. Like [Max L.] White and [China] Marks, she affirms our increasing need for rituals, objects that suggest ritualistic power to make sense of our millennial realities.

I would add my own view that many – perhaps most – lesbian and gay artists continue to find inspiration in their heritage of queer myth and symbol. It is not really a matter of 'subversion' or even 'appropriation', but simply a question of conjuring up changeless meanings and values, as when John Greyson opens his Quebecoise film *Lilies* (1996) with a scene from Gabrielle D'Anunuzzio's *St Sebastian*.

Bradby (1993) conducted a series of interviews with lesbians which illustrated the construction and transmission of the fantasy about the lesbian sexuality of popular female singers such as Madonna, Tracy Chapman, Anita Baker, Sinead O'Connor, Nina Simone, Dusty Springfield and k.d. lang, and how the appropriation of lesbian meanings from mainstream and heterosexual music helps to cement modern lesbian identity. Dykes in the Dublin working-class bar culture clearly preferred mainstream chart music about which they could fantasize, and were not much interested in 'lesbian music' by out lesbians aimed at lesbians (which largely originates from lesbian-feminist recording companies in America, and lesbian folk music of the 1970s). Much of the bar conversation concerns bar music, and lesbian networks outside the bar are fostered by the exchange of cassette tapes. However, the process of 'rumour exchange' on the gay scene does not really support the constructionist theory: the lesbians interviewed by Bradby already had fully formed lesbian identities before they exchanged rumours or elaborated fantasies, and the rumours themselves would not be exchanged if there were no essentialist belief that they might be founded upon reality. It is a linguistic sleight of hand to say that this type of appropriation illustrates construction rather than revelation. One respondent, for example, positively *recognized the inherently queer sound* of k.d. lang when she first heard her, prior to any knowledge or rumours or discussion about her:

> about two years ago, I had gone to bed and Kate came upstairs and, said, you've *got* to *hear* this woman, singing she said, I can bet you *any money* she's a lesbian, she said, it said nothing about her, she just sang one song, but I just *know* she is, and it wasn't until a year later until there was significant press coverage about her and her 'androgynous' sexuality.

The queer tradition

The social constructionist view that queer traditions do not blossom organically but are artificially constructed seems to me to be wholly false. Schalow (1996a) oddly challenges the very notion of a 'Japanese gay literary tradition' even at the same time as he makes it clear that there are numerous gay literary works from the eighth to the twentieth centuries. Depictions of male–male love, *nanshoku* ('the way of men'), clearly constituted a tradition in the ancient and premodern 'temple culture of monks and priests, the samurai culture of the warrior, and the urban townsman's culture of the kabuki theater'. I call this a tradition because there were specific works and even genres devoted to the subject, not merely because of the fact that the subject was included in all works (for example, most Japanese novels have homosexual episodes). Love poems addressed by Buddhist priests to their temple acolytes abound in the imperial anthologies from the tenth to the thirteenth centuries, and there was even a specific gay genre of prose 'acolyte tales', *chigo monogatari*, during the fourteenth and fifteenth centuries (reprinted in the nineteenth century, obviously to cater to gay tastes, in a kind of gay circulation/ distribution network).

The earliest Japanese anthology of homosexual poetry and prose was *Iwatsutsuji*, or *Wild Azaleas*, a collection of thirty-four items of prose and poetry compiled and edited by Kitamura Kigin (1625–1705). The manuscript was compiled for an unnamed private client in 1676. It was eventually acquired by a retired gentleman in Kyoto, and was published in 1713, with illustrations. It was frequently reprinted right up to the mid-nineteenth century. Schalow (1996b) in his essay 'The Invention of a Literary Tradition of Male Love' maintains that it was not published as a defence or apologia, as were some modern gay anthologies such as Edward Carpenter's *Ioläus*, because homosexuality was not stigmatized or unusual in the seventeenth century. But Kigin begins his preface on the defensive note – 'to become intoxicated by the blossom of a handsome youth, not being a woman, would seem to be both wrong and unusual' – although he goes on to demonstrate that it is not unusual because it is part of a long and honourable tradition. The anthology itself is part of the revival of an idealized and romanticized past, but any theory about its public intent or purpose ignores the fact that it was a private venture, compiled at the express request of a wealthy patron and connoisseur of poetry, probably a merchant (but perhaps a samurai) for whom Kigin worked as a tutor in *waka* and *haikai* composition. No broad sociological explanation is required for the simple fact that a connoisseur commissioned a collection to embody and establish his taste.

Schalow in his discussion of the anthology takes the extraordinary view that this work *invented* the Japanese homosexual literary tradition. Certainly it was the first anthology, but like all anthologies it simply collected pre-existing material rather than created it. A tradition cannot be invented by a single individual; a tradition consists of a group of artefacts created by different individuals that have a common link and a series of cross-references. The most that can be said of any pioneering anthology is that it consolidates a tradition that already exists. An anthology is the perfect example of cultural consolidation, and this Japanese anthology is a perfect example of the type.

It is clear that Kigin and his patron thought of male–male love as already constituting a distinct literary tradition, albeit one that had not received sufficiently distinct focus, which they set out to remedy by this anthology. All of the material in it comes from imperial poetic anthologies and other collections, easily identified today. The earliest poem originates from an anthology completed in 905, comparing memories of male–male love with 'wild azaleas bursting into bloom', hence Kigin's title. Kigin was a scholar as well as a poet, and he ascribes this poem to Shinga Sōzu (801–79), a major disciple of Kūkai (Kōbō Daishi, 774–835), who is credited with being the 'originator' of male–male love. 'Wild azaleas' was already an icon of male homoerotic love before Kigin gave his commentary on the poem. Ihara Saikaku includes it in his collection of 'The ABCs of Boy Love' published in 1687, twenty-six years before Kigin's anthology was published. And there were earlier homosexual anthologies: for example, a 1703 collection of gay stories, concerned especially with samurai and kabuki actors, *Nanshoku ki no me-zuke* (*The Pickled Bud of Male Love*) by Urushiya Ensai, which was illustrated, as were many others. One of the very early gay tales, *Ariake no Wakare* ('Partings at Dawn') was famous and frequently alluded to. So when the anthology *Wild Azaleas* was published in 1713, it was part of a well-established homosexual literary tradition, not the invention of that tradition.

Even in the 1670s the anthology can be seen as part of the popular vernacular tradition of *kana-zōshi*, didactic code-books for model behaviour. Of some two hundred *kana-zōshi* books that still exist from the period 1600 to the 1680s, 10 to 15 per cent of them 'treat exclusively or in large part the topic of male love' (Schalow, 1996b). Books of etiquette are specifically designed to function as an aid in the development of social identity, in this case queer identity. But it is foolish to develop an overarching theory about the need for developing a refining samurai model for homosexual behaviour among crude townsmen, when in fact *Wild Azaleas* was simply commissioned for a specific connoisseur who did not publish it, and which probably served as an 'educational' technique of seduction. The notion that this anthology demonstrates a split between heterosexual and homosexual camps that had previously been integrated, or 'a reconceptualization of love poetry on the basis of the sex of the love object' (Schalow, 1996b) is sheer social constructionist dogma.

We should not forget the banal purpose of most anthologies: to gather interesting material together into a single conveniently accessible volume. It does not necessarily pinpoint a sudden historical shift, though it does establish the existence of a culturally identified queer, namely the patron. It is also interesting for showing early efforts at queer interpretations of literature which was not widely identified as queer. For example, Kigin includes a story written between 1330 and 1332 about two men 'amusing themselves' at the Wind and Water Cave because a commentary published in 1621 attributed a queer meaning to it, and observed that 'There are many such cases of male love throughout history.'

So the search for cultural unity and continuity was already well under way in the 1620s. Unlike Schalow, I believe we ought to accept Kigin's own insistence in his preface that he is rediscovering a pre-existing 'tradition' of queer literature rather than inventing or even re-creating it. His sophisticated connoisseur/patron recognized the existence of that tradition, and engaged a scholarly anthologizer to bring it together in a handy form that would make the continuity of the queer cultural tradition more easily recognizable. The compilation of an anthology devoted specifically to homosexual love is certainly a fact worth remarking on, but we must constantly bear in mind that it was a private commission. When the book was issued to the world in 1713, the publisher remarked, 'We hope that men will read the book with youths who are not yet enlightened about this way of love, and that it will be a source of pleasure for many.'

Anti-culture queens

Culture queens are usually thought of as men who identify with high culture. But there are also a good many culturally identified queers who identify with low culture, who see themselves in particular as sexual rebels. One thinks immediately of Rimbaud and Verlaine and other 'decadent' writers, and of Oscar Wilde 'feasting with panthers'. The Victorians were shocked that Wilde deliberately cultivated friendships with the lower classes, and they attacked him as the purveyor of an alien culture, as in an editorial in the *Evening News*: 'He was one of the high priests of a school which attacks all the wholesome, manly, simple ideals of English life, and sets up false gods of decadent culture and intellectual debauchery' (cited by Bronski, 1984).

Even in cultures which have institutionalized some form of homosexuality, the queer nevertheless exists not in the mainstream but at the margins, be they high or low. The space in which he or she fulfils themselves often takes the paradigm of the sacred precinct, a literally taboo region which only he or she can enter relatively unscathed and from which he or she returns, often with a boon for society. This specialness has generally carried over into the concept of high queer culture. But in most modern Western societies this figure at the margins has been criminalized as well as tabooed, and the shaman has become the sexual outlaw.

Jean Genet (1910–86) is the archetype of the queer criminal. At first sight he might seem to be a good illustration of the social constructionist theory that members of a gay subculture organize their lives around a criminal act: that is, acts precede labelling and stigma precedes identity. But like many self-identified sodomites throughout history who did not realize that sodomy was a crime until apprehended, Genet was actively queer before he perceived himself to be a criminal. He was remembered as effeminate in his childhood and youth, and was also a thief from at least the age of 10, when he stole from his foster parents:

> Was I already conscious of the reprobation that was to be my lot because I was a foundling and a homosexual? I dare not say that I was led to steal as an act of rebellion. I already liked boys when I was very young, although I was happy in the company of girls and women. (All quotations are from White, 1993)

Queerness and crime became inextricably interlinked in his imagination and self-concept: 'I think the word "thief" wounded me deeply. Deeply, that is to say enough to make me want, deliberately, to be what other people made me blush about being, to want to be it proudly, in spite of them.' Sartre in his famous study *Saint Genet* (1952) took Genet as the model of the existentialist self-invented outcast, who self-consciously took on the role of the scapegoat by accepting the label of 'thief' as a child, but Edmund White has shown that the image Genet projected was often rationalization after the fact. In reality Genet was never publicly castigated for being a thief during his childhood, though people knew of his thefts. He certainly was not caught and denounced at the age of 10, as Sartre would have us believe. His personality was as much a matter of destiny as choice. Sartre is more correct when he suggests that because he is *named* a thief he becomes a *sacred object* and subverts conventional values. The queer identity is a 'rededication' in the religious sense, rather than a construct. The central theme of Genet's novels is that faggots and criminals and outcasts are empowered by embracing their stigma, by naming themselves with the same word but with a reverse valuation, not that middle-class straights ought to choose a life of crime or homosexuality in order to free themselves from convention.

Genet was star-struck at being the subject of a book by France's greatest intellectual, and he often tried to fit the construct Sartre had imposed upon him. Later in life he admitted that he did not choose homosexuality as Sartre the existentialist had maintained, but that he was born homosexual. As he admitted in 1964:

> Pederasty was imposed on me like the colour of my eyes, the number of my feet. Even when I was still a kid I was aware of being attracted by other boys, I have never known an attraction for women. It's only after I became conscious of this attraction that I 'decided', 'chose' freely my pederasty, in the Sartrean sense of the word. In other words, and more simply, I had to accommodate myself to it even though I knew that it was condemned by society.

Like many queers who look back to the great queens of history, Genet identified himself with the great queer criminals of history. For example, he made a point of visiting the ruined site of Tiffauges where the infamous Gilles de Rais lived; on his return he noticed the fields of broom plant, and recalling that *genêt* is the French word for the broom plant, he identified the yellow broom flowers as 'my natural emblem, but I have roots, through them, into French soil, which is nourished by the dust of children, or adolescents fucked, massacred and burned by Gilles de Rais'. He was an orphan in search of his origins – and he found them in the queer underworld. At the reformatory Mettray he was 'the most sought-after kid'; it was an eroticized paradise where he was 'the high-born lady'. He was ashamed at being shorn and dressed in the infamous uniform; but he embraced his stigma: 'I felt within myself the need to become what I'd been accused of being. I was sixteen years old. I'd been understood: ... I recognized that I was the coward, the traitor, the thief, the faggot that they saw in me.' Acts felt to be degrading become empowering if they are embraced, turning the sinner into a saint (one of Genet's favourite motifs), stigma paradoxically expiating guilt.

But Genet the queer criminal was also determined to find his roots in queer literature. He paid a call on André Gide in Paris in June or July 1933. Genet was 22, and had not yet written anything or attracted fame. He had read *The Immoralist* (1902), though it is not certain if he had read Gide's more openly queer books *Corydon* (1911; revised 1924) and *If It Die* (1920–1). Genet surrounded himself not only with queer thugs, convicts, petty thieves, sailors, hustlers, wrestlers, café waiters, circus performers and the drag queens of Montmartre, but with culturally identified queers: 'Cocteau; the painter and designer Christian Bérard; his lover Boris Kochno, who had directed the Ballets Russes after Diaghilev's death; Jouhandeau; Jean Marais; much younger writers such as Sentein, Laudenbach and Turlais'; Herbert List; the lesbian Violette

Leduc, and others. *Querelle of Brest* was dedicated to Jacques Guérin, a wealthy owner of a perfume factory who became Genet's patron. He (and his brother the painter Jean Guérin, who was also gay) was a culturally identified queer. He collected paintings and autograph manuscripts, including Rimbaud's *A Season in Hell* and many of Genet's works. He even owned 'the bedroom where Proust had died and everything in it' including notebooks, proofs and letters.

It is interesting that Toby Manning in 'Gay Culture', his attack on 1990s mainstream commercial gay culture (in Simpson, 1996), illustrates his alternative 'transgressive' queer culture entirely with examples of high culture posing as low culture: Genet, Burroughs, Cocteau, Denis Cooper (influenced by Genet), Tennessee Williams, Fassbinder, Mapplethorpe, Della Grace, Bruce LaBruce (influenced by Genet), 'new queer cinema' (influenced by Genet: for example, Todd Haynes's *Poison*, 1991; Tom Kalin's *Swoon*, 1992; Cyril Collard's *Savage Nights*, 1992), and queerzines (influenced by Genet). All of his examples used to illustrate mainstream gay culture are drawn from non-literary popular culture, for example gay clubs and gay media characterized by 'dance music, female comediennes, muscular bodies, designer clothes, Calvin Klein underwear, cappuccino, bottled beers and Ikea furniture'. Presumably the key difference is class: the middle class on the one hand, and, on the other, the upper and lower classes in unholy alliance.

In today's commercialized queer subculture, the lower middle classes have purchased a working-class image for themselves. The British weekly magazine *Boyz* consists mostly of features and columns on pop music, and advertisements for clubs and discos, telephone sex lines, escorts and personal ads. The magazine presupposes an expert knowledge of pop music, and promotes that as an essential part of being in the life: 'Call yourself gay and you don't even have a copy of Hazell Dean's "Who's Leaving Who?" in your collection? You're gonna get yourself drummed out of this community if you're not careful, matey' (2 March 1996). This tongue-in-cheek cultural coercion is intended at least half-seriously. *Boyz* sees itself as creating rather than merely reflecting queer pop culture. Being a bad boy is a matter of styling, employing the T-shirts and the scents promoted in its regular 'advertisement features'. But it is not fair to say that the magazine's motive is entirely commercial; the editor genuinely wants to promote queer solidarity, as when he keeps reminding his readers to use the second car on tube trains so that we can recognize our unity as we ride in the 'queer car'. The magazine tries to shape its audience of 'boyz' as slutty bad boys, and from 1995 actively promoted the (black) category of 'ho' ('gangsta slang for whores'), as in its horoscope column called 'Jason Dante's ho'scopes'. You too can become po' white trash. The magazine regularly runs features on how to become the rebellious bad boyz we (allegedly) find so attractive: 'Tattoo, pierce and scar yourself, never shave, never wash', etc. In 1996 *Boyz* published a special guide on how to be working class: 'Use this special Boyz guide to enhance your working class-ness or completely bluff it. Why be boring when you can be a really interesting member of the proletariat?'

Kith and kin

Expressions like 'my own kind' are of course *kinship* expressions. 'In nineteenth-century Japan, students at girls' schools and women's universities formed "S" clubs, calling themselves "sisters" (using the English word) and meeting in secret to discuss their lesbian feelings' (Fletcher and Saks, 1990). Queers in many cultures employ among themselves a set of kinship terms, especially 'sisters', 'aunt' and 'auntie' (*tante* and *Tunte* in the French and German queer subcultures), 'husband' and 'wife', 'brother'. 'Sissy' of course was an affectionate diminutive of 'sister' long before it became an abusive epithet. In the Dutch Republic in the 1720s men indicated their monogamous relationship by addressing one another as *nicht* ('female cousin'), or *nichtje* (the affectionate diminutive form). It has been observed that queer relationships to some extent reflect injunctions against incest and suggest endogamous and exogamous patterns, in so far as 'sisters' seldom marry one another (Chauncey, 1994). But in fact 'brothers' – by far the most frequent queer family/kinship term among men – almost invariably mate with one another, and in the early eighteenth century mollies who both possessed 'maiden names' sometimes lived together as couples (Norton, 1992). King James I signed his many love letters to George Villiers with 'Thy dear dad and husband'. But historians need to resist the 'intuitive' assumption that queer partners always divide themselves along husband/wife gender lines. It is quite common for both gay and lesbian couples to consist of two 'husbands' or two 'wives' (for example, the mollies never used the term 'wife'). Until fairly recently, gay male groupings consisted of a pyramid of many young sisters, several elder aunts, and one 'mother' at the top, who often was literally a female and typically a divorced or widowed woman who was the proprietor of a club or brothel. Nor should we disregard 'queen' as a kind of kinship role, one which is 'the symbolic embodiment of gay culture' (Chauncey, 1994).

It has been observed that in some indigenous cultures of New Guinea institutionalized homosexual relations follow exogamous patterns (which function to avoid incest): for example, a Marind-Anim boy from the age of about 12 or 13 'enters into a homosexual relationship with his mother's brother, who belongs to a different lineage from his own'; while an Etoro boy embarks on a homosexual relationship with his sister's husband or fiancé from about the age of 10 until his mid-twenties, at which point he becomes the partner of another prepubescent boy, 'ordinarily his wife's or fiancée's younger brother', which lasts about fifteen years, and the older youth is called the younger one's 'father' (Greenberg, 1988; Creed, 1994). Among some Australian aborigines, a girl may become engaged to a man at her birth, and while he waits for her to reach marriageable age he takes her older brother as a 'substitute wife', regularly enjoying frottage with him for the ensuing years (Greenberg, 1988). As recently as the 1950s among the Australian Tiwi future brothers-in-law regularly enjoyed (egalitarian) homosexual relations. Greenberg states that among indigenous societies homosexuality 'does not become the basis for imputing a distinct social identity' – and yet he has shown that institutionalized homosexuality is frequently, perhaps even usually, linked to three class identities: the apprentice, the warrior and the 'brother-in-law'. North American Indian *berdache* are occasionally categorized in their villages as everyman's 'sister-in-law' or 'cross-cousin' (Whitehead, 1993).

There does seem to have been male marriage in Fujian, a formal male 'bond' or *qi*, sometimes even called *qu*, the same word used for heterosexual marriage, involving ceremonial rituals of drinking tea and the payment of a bride price to the family of the younger partner. The ceremony included various sacrifices, smearing each other's mouths with the blood of the sacrifice and swearing eternal loyalty to one another, then feasting. A Dutch soldier in the seventeenth century confirmed that the Fujian coast region was full of 'filthy pederasts', and contemporary Chinese writers revealed that men of all classes in Fujian took male lovers, whom they called 'jade bamboo shoots'. The older partner is the 'bond elder brother' (*qixiong*) and the younger is the 'bond younger brother' (*qidi*): thus, there was a kinship tie to organize homosexual relations. (In thirteenth-century China male prostitutes who cruised for custom in restaurants had been called 'elder brothers'.) The men become 'sworn friends' (*qiyou*); in all these words, *qi* means 'written contract'; though it can also denote adoption, the most recent view is that 'bond brother' is a more accurate translation than 'adoptive brother' (Ng, 1989). The 'younger brother' becomes the son-in-law of his husband's parents and moves in with his family. Their marriage can last twenty years, and they can even adopt boys as their sons. Similarly in seventeenth-century Japan one who took on the 'elder brother's role' and one who took on the 'younger brother's role' would pledge a 'troth of brotherly love'.

Heterosexual spouses in ancient Mediterranean societies also called themselves brother and sister. Boswell (1995) points out that the word 'brothers' in Petronius's *Satyricon* is used as a technical term for long-standing homosexual partners; the relationship of the characters to whom it applies, Giton and Encolpius, is called *contubernium* ('cohabitation'), which is 'the form of marriage appropriate when different classes or noncitizens were involved'. Virgil also uses 'brother' (*frater*) to describe Corydon and Amyntas in the *Eclogues*. Most scholars ignore the specifically sexual meaning of *frater* or 'brother' in other languages, as in the description of Enkidu as Gilgamesh's 'brother' (*ahu*), though they are not siblings. Boswell goes so far as to suggest that *frater* actually *denotes* rather than *connotes* a homosexual partner. Martial even calls *frater* and *soror* 'naughty names'.

Abundant evidence has established the existence of legally/socially recognized same-sex unions (among women as well as men) in ancient societies and indigenous cultures, in the East as well as the West, and formal same-sex unions in all of the queer subcultures of Europe from premodern to modern periods. Boswell's extensive analysis of the rites of same-sex union in Slavonic and Greek texts reaches the conclusion that they 'parallel' rather than 'imitate' heterosexual marriage rites. The current argument in favour of gay marriage is based on the notion of equal rights. But the more profound argument is that we are entitled to reclaim gay marriage as part of our queer cultural heritage.

Conclusion: reclamation and reconstruction

When a time capsule was unearthed in 1979 in San Francisco it was found to contain the book *The Great Geysers of California* by the journalist and feminist Laura de Force Gordon, born in 1838. On the flyleaf she had written her message for queer posterity:

> If this little book should see the light of day after 100 years' entombment, I should like the readers to know that the author was a lover of her own sex and devoted the best years of her life in striving for the political equality ... of women. (Richards, 1990)

Every one of us should strive to leave a similar time capsule.

Is queer history the history of a dead or dying culture? Institutionalized and ritualized pederasty vanished long ago. The biography of the last *berdache* has been written. The hobo queer subculture vanished as highway transport replaced railways in the 1920s. Polari was perhaps the last vestige of a queer language – it lingers on as self-conscious nostalgia among those who spoke it in the 1950s – and no other comprehensive body of queer slang and linguistic signs seems to have arisen in its stead. We half-jokingly speculate if someone is 'a friend of Dorothy' or 'a member of the club', but these are as antiquated as the poetic use of 'gay' meaning 'joyful'. George Melly introduced Philip Core's 1984 anthology of *Camp* with the suggestion that it was an 'elegy' on a dying tradition. It may be technically impossible to revive a tradition of which the last link has been severed.

There is a long history of colonial extirpation of homosexuals in the Americas, from the sixteenth century when Vasco Nunez de Balboa ordered forty men dressed as women to be killed by his dogs, to the ostracism of early nineteenth-century missionaries. The Crow *berdache* Osh-Tisch (1854–1929) was denounced by a Baptist minister who came to his reservation in 1903: one Indian informant recalled that the minister

> condemned our traditions, including the badé. He told congregation members to stay away from Osh-Tisch and the other badés. He continued to condemn Osh-Tisch until his death. ... That may be the reason why no others took up the badé role after Osh-Tisch died. (Miller, 1995)

During the late 1940s among the Navajo – where the *berdache* had been held in especially high esteem in the past – only middle-aged and old men continued the tradition; young men ceased taking up the old ways, and the custom more or less died out by the middle of the century.

All indigenous cultural patterns, not just institutionalized homosexual patterns, are rapidly disappearing as the entire world models itself on the colonial paradigms of the West. In Tahiti, by the end of the 1960s there was typically only one single *mahū* (effeminate ritual cocksucker/healer) in each village, and by the 1990s they were dying out and being replaced by the *raerae*, an exclusive masculine homosexual, who live in small groups near to one another in each village (S. O. Murray, 'Pacific Cultures', *EH*).

As China modernized itself, from about 1840 it adopted first a Victorian morality, then the Western medical model to condemn homosexuality, and subsequently declared homosexuality to be a 'Western decadent' perversion of native heterosexual culture:

> Today, most Chinese see homosexuality as rare or even non-existent in China. ... Rather than turning to the examples of antiquity to understand Chinese homosexuality and provide justifications of self-worth and models of behavior, [Chinese homosexuals] now look to New York and San Francisco for examples to emulate. Not only is the native homosexual tradition unknown among critics of homosexuality, but it has also virtually disappeared among homosexuals themselves. (Hinsch, 1990)

China's 2000-year continuum of queer culture has come to an end. Young people can no longer read the ancient Chinese characters, which have been simplified in the cultural reform, and government-controlled printing has totally expunged all references to homosexuality in the Chinese classics. This is effectively a cultural epitaph. Similarly in Japan, during the Meiji era (1868–1912) traditional indigenous *wakashu* ('the way of youths') and *nanshoku* ('the way of men') were refigured as *dōseiai* ('same-sex love', 'homosexuality') and made a taboo subject; male intimacy was either lost or became highly problematical as the Japanese tried to present themselves to Europeans as 'modern'. Yukio Mishima tried to revive the homoerotic samurai tradition, but failed dramatically, in a ritual double suicide with his lover Morita Masakatsu in 1970.

If a really effective scheme of ethnic cleansing is carried out, a cultural tradition can be forgotten in the space of a single generation. In the 1970s and 1980s most gay people were oblivious to the fact that there had once been a thriving gay subculture in San Francisco and New York. Due to a concerted newspaper campaign and the clean-up crusade conducted by Mayor Fiorello La Guardia and Police Commissioner Edward Mulrooney, by 1935 the queens and faggots had quite literally disappeared from the streets of New York (Chauncey, 1994). Arrests for homosexual solicitation more than quadrupled, and the seventy-year-old tradition of drag balls at the Hamilton Lodge came to an end. For the next twenty-five years the New York State Liquor Agency refused to license premises that tolerated 'disorderly' behaviour, by which it meant patrons exhibiting the camp semiotics of swishing hips, limp wrists, high-pitched voices and calling one another 'dearie'; as late as 1963 a bar in Albany was closed because one female customer, of mannish appearance, had held the hand of another female customer. Gay men and lesbians who used to provide a large part of the labour force employed by restaurants, bars and clubs were prohibited from working in them. The increasing risk of serving and employing queers was 'protected' by the involvement of organized crime. Gay and lesbian cultural practices were pushed underground, and the 'closet' – a word absent from queer vocabulary until the 1960s – was constructed. To the extent that culture, even queer culture, is largely a *public* performance (often involving festivals and rituals of public assembly), it was effectively banned.

This gay closet was mistakenly perceived as gay culture, and systematically devalued in the 1970s:

> Many of them [GLFers, mostly young] were still struggling to come to terms with their sexual identity, and they lacked roots in the traditional gay world. Instead, much of their time was spent in the milieu of 'the Movement'. The New Left and countercultural values about community and human relationships that they had imbibed made them recoil from the subculture of Mafia-run bars, seedy bathhouses, butch-femme roles, and anonymous sex. (D'Emilio, 1992)

Some branches of gay liberation ironically finished off certain elements of gay culture that homophobia had not quite succeeded in destroying. The roots of British gay culture 'were cut away during the Great British War on Homosexuality [in the 1950s], and withered still further, with the loss of polare and the older camp tradition, as a sad by-product of the gay liberation movement' (Lumsden, 1982). George Melly feels that the survival of camp

> is threatened not so much by heterosexuals who tend to accept it, although usually at a fairly broad and superficial level, but more by the attitude of the gay community which has emerged and hardened over the last twenty years and created, in itself, a neo-puritanism, a received conformism. (Cited in Core, 1984)

Eddy, who was 16 in 1957, feels that 'The gay scene in those days was much nicer than it is now. There were so many "characters". ... There was much more fun being gay then. We didn't take being gay so seriously as people do now.' P. M. Scott vividly remembers what it was like to be gay in the early 1960s in London:

> Yes, we were well and truly 'in the closet' but we were united by a common bond which, on reflection, has been disappearing under waves of gay liberation and gay politics. ... There were also gay

pubs which were overflowing with gay strangers who were given open invitations to join many of the parties that were held at weekends. Many gays talked in a slang 'in' language and were much more jovial and 'camp' than they seem today. (Cited by Bourne, 1996)

Many feel that discos have destroyed conversation, and drugs have ruined the community. Queer culture and queer 'high culture' are being replaced by commercialized 'pop culture' (Simpson, 1996). Hallam (1993) is nostalgic for the passing of traditional pub drag and the older unsentimental drag queens. Though only 40 years old in 1993, he doesn't think the sanitized gay scene is Sodom any more. People who today have some memory of what queer culture used to be sometimes feel that it is gone for ever. The current revival – rather than survival – of the butch/femme lesbian relationship is considered somewhat artificial and lacking the spontaneous joy it once possessed. Perhaps this is just a matter of 'Fings ain't wot they used to be'.

But AIDS marks a rupture. Gay Sweatshop, Britain's oldest gay theatre company, celebrated its twenty-first birthday in 1996 with Philip Osment's *The Undertaking*, a play whose main image is a journey to scatter the ashes of a man who has died of AIDS. The AIDS epidemic may be too recent for historians to predict its impact upon queer culture and history, but a 50 per cent rate of attrition in the gay male population of San Francisco, a 25 per cent rate in the gay male population of New York, and almost 10 per cent in some European capitals, cannot be less than catastrophic. The AIDS literature that attempts to bear witness to this experience seems to express the view that our memories of the past will help us work through this crisis and are necessary to preserve our culture for the future. Paul Monette in *Borrowed Time* not only politicizes the present crisis, but compares the current position to the situation in ancient Greece, 'as a besieged culture, posed on the verge of extinction, and as a civilization precariously surviving in ruins and fragments' (Suárez Sánchez, 1996). We must salvage the ruins of the past, and stand as sentinels to ensure the survival of at least the ruins of the present into the future.

What can we do to ensure that queers have a future as well as a past? An uprooted people is afflicted by amnesia, and many indigenous queer cultures have been wiped out by missionaries and by acculturation. Can gay and lesbian people 'return to the source' – or has the source been virtually extirpated after centuries of suppression? Does the queer past have too many gaps – the result of suppression and complete breaks with tradition, as in modern China – for us ever to reconnect with our memories? ('Only connect' said Forster!) Or can we only be haunted by its possibilities? Is revival (for example, of the American Indian *berdache* tradition) necessary for survival? Will queer nationalists typically reinvent or idealize the past in light of a desired future?

A large body of queer literature can be literally reconstructed, partly through decoding texts, partly through reinstating the original versions of censored material and partly using material deliberately preserved by queer writers 'against a less hostile day' (for example, Ackerley explicitly provided annotations so that his novels could be reconstructed in their proper queer form). How far are we justified in going along this line? And how can we apply this to history, and perceive the difference between reconstruction and invention? Can a post-colonial analysis help us reclaim our rightful heritage by recovering a queer culture that was driven underground and virtually destroyed by the heterosexual hegemony of modern Western culture?

While it is true that historical continuity cannot genuinely be revived if a link in the chain has been severed, nevertheless it is possible to re-establish *a historical context* for contemporary gay experience. I attribute some of the malaise and weakness of the modern gay community to our uneasy relationship with our past. Queer people cut off from queer history will have a more restricted range of options to explore as they develop their own queer identity. A definition of ourselves solely in opposition to (or as equal to) heterosexuals does not make for cultural stability. Although queer pop (and drug) culture, and gay liberationist politics, have nearly created a distinctively new and self-sufficient queer culture, they seem to be too thinly textured to be deeply satisfying; they can only be empowered and enriched by recognizing links with queer culture through the ages.

References

In the text, the abbreviation *EH* refers to articles in the *Encyclopedia of Homosexuality*, edited by Wayne R. Dynes (Chicago and London: St James Press, 1990).

Abelove, Henry, Barale, Michèle Aina and Halperin, David M. (eds) (1993), *The Lesbian and Gay Studies Reader*. New York and London: Routledge.

Aldrich, Robert (1993), *The Seduction of the Mediterranean*. London: Routledge.

Allen, Paula Gunn (1989), 'Lesbians in American Indian cultures', in Duberman *et al.* (eds) (1989), *Hidden from History*, pp. 106–17.

The Alyson Almanac: A Treasury of Information for the Gay and Lesbian Community (1989). Boston: Alyson.

Austen, Roger (1977), *Playing the Game: The Homosexual Novel in America*. Indianapolis and New York: Bobbs-Merrill.

Bartlett, Neil (1988), *Who Was That Man? A Present for Mr Oscar Wilde*. London: Serpent's Tail.

Bartlett, Neil (1990), *Ready to Catch Him Should He Fall*. London: Serpent's Tail.

Berubé, Allen (1990), *Coming Out under Fire: The History of Gay Men and Women in World War II*. New York: The Free Press.

Beurdeley, Cecile (1994), *L'Amour bleu*, trans. Michael Taylor. Köln: Benedikt Taschen Verlag.

Bingham, Caroline (1971), 'Seventeenth-century attitudes toward deviant sex', *Journal of Interdisciplinary History* 1, pp. 447–68.

Bleys, Rudi C. (1996), *The Geography of Perversion: Male-To-Male Sexual Behaviour outside the West and the Ethnographic Imagination 1750–1918*. London: Cassell.

Boon, L. J. (1989), 'Those damned sodomites: public images of sodomy in the eighteenth century Netherlands', in Gerard and Hekma (eds) (1989), *The Pursuit of Sodomy*, pp. 237–48.

Boswell, John (1980), *Christianity, Social Tolerance, and Homosexuality: Gay People in Western Europe from the Beginning of the Christian Era to the Fourteenth Century*. Chicago and London: University of Chicago Press.

Boswell, John (1989), 'Revolutions, universals, and sexual categories', in Duberman *et al.* (eds) (1989), *Hidden from History*, pp. 17–36.

Boswell, John (1992), 'Categories, experience and sexuality', in Stein (ed.) (1992a), *Forms of Desire*, pp. 133–73.

Boswell, John (1995), *The Marriage of Likeness: Same-Sex Unions in Pre-Modern Europe*. London: HarperCollins (originally published in 1994).

Bourne, Stephen (1996), *Brief Encounters: Lesbians and Gays in British Cinema 1930–1971*. London: Cassell.

Bradby, Barbara (1993), 'Lesbians and popular music: does it matter who is singing?', in Griffin (ed.) (1993b), *Outwrite*, pp. 148–71.

Bray, Alan (1982), *Homosexuality in Renaissance England*. London: Gay Men's Press.

Bronski, Michael (1984), *Culture Clash: The Making of Gay Sensibility*. Boston: South End Press.

Brown, Judith C. (1986), *Immodest Acts: The Life of a Lesbian Nun in Renaissance Italy*. New York: Oxford University Press.

Brown, Judith C. (1989), 'Lesbian sexuality in medieval and early modern Europe', in Duberman *et al.* (eds) (1989), *Hidden from History*, pp. 67–75.

Bullough, Vern L. (1976), *Sexual Variance in Society and History*. Chicago and London: University of Chicago Press.

Burg, B. R. (1985), 'Ho hum, another work of the Devil: buggery and sodomy in early Stuart England', in Licata and Petersen (eds) (1985), *The Gay Past*, pp. 69–78.

Burns, Robert (1976), '"Queer doings": attitudes towards homosexuality in 19th century Canada', *Body Politic*, Our Image No. 6 (December–January), pp. 4–7.

Burton, Peter (1977), 'The gentle art of confounding naffs: some notes on polari', *Gay News*, 120, p. 23.

Carpenter, Edward (1906), *Ioläus: An Anthology of Friendship*, 2nd edn (enlarged). London: George Allen & Unwin.

Carpenter, Edward (1984), *Selected Writings, Volume 1: Sex*, ed. David Fernbach and Noel Greig. London: Gay Men's Press.

Case, Sue-Ellen (1993), 'Toward a butch–femme aesthetic', in Abelove *et al.* (eds) (1993), *The Lesbian and Gay Studies Reader*, pp. 294–306.

Castle, Terry (1995), 'Sister–Sister: Jane Austen's Letters', *London Review of Books*, 3 August; report by Barry Hugill, 'Sex and sexuality: The new key to readings of "gay" Jane

Austen', *Observer*, 6 August; Letters, *London Review of Books*, 24 August.

Chauncey, George Jr. (1985), 'Christian brotherhood or sexual perversion? Homosexual identities and the construction of sexual boundaries in the World War One era', *Journal of Social History*, 19, pp. 189–211.

Chauncey, George (1994), *Gay New York: Gender, Urban Culture, and the Making of the Gay Male World, 1890–1940*. New York: Basic Books.

Collis, Rose (1994), *Portraits to the Wall: Historic Lesbian Lives Unveiled*. London: Cassell.

Conner, Randolph P. Lundschen, Sparks, David Hatfield and Sparks, Mariya (1997), *Encyclopaedia of Queer Myth, Symbol, and Spirit*. London: Cassell.

Core, Philip (1984), *Camp: The Lie That Tells the Truth*. London: Plexus.

Corker, Mairian (1996), *Deaf Transitions: Images and Origins of Deaf Families, Deaf Communities and Deaf Identities*. London: Jessica Kingsley.

Cowan, Thomas (1992), *Gay Men and Women Who Enriched the World*. Boston: Alyson (originally published 1988 by William Mulvey).

Creed, Gerald W. (1994), 'Sexual subordination: Institutionalized homosexuality and social control in Melanesia', in Goldberg (ed.) (1994), *Reclaiming Sodom*, pp. 66–94.

Crompton, Louis (1978a), 'Gay genocide from Leviticus to Hitler', in Crew, Louis (ed.), *The Gay Academic*. Palm Springs, CA: ETC Publications, pp. 67–91.

Crompton, Louis (ed.) (1978b), 'Jeremy Bentham's essay on "Paederasty"', *Journal of Homosexuality*, 3, pp. 383–405; 4, pp. 91–107.

Crompton, Louis (1985), 'The myth of lesbian impunity: capital laws from 1270 to 1791', in Licata and Petersen (eds) (1985), *The Gay Past*, pp. 11–25.

Crow, Christine (1990), *Miss X, or the Wolf Woman*. London: The Women's Press.

Dall'Orto, Giovanni (1989), '"Socratic love" as a disguise for same-sex love in the Italian Renaissance', in Gerard and Hekma (eds) (1989), *The Pursuit of Sodomy*, pp. 33–65.

Dalrymple, William (1993), *City of Djinns: A Year in Delhi*. London: HarperCollins.

Darnton, Robert (1996), *The Forbidden Best-Sellers of Pre-Revolutionary France*. London: HarperCollins.

Davis, Madeline and Kennedy, Elizabeth Lapovsky (1986), 'Oral history and the study of sexuality in the lesbian community: Buffalo, New York, 1940–1960', *Feminist Studies*, 12, 1 (Spring), pp. 7–28.

D'Emilio, John (1992), *Making Trouble: Essays on Gay History, Politics, and the University*. New York and London: Routledge.

Donoghue, Emma (1993), *Passions Between Women: British Lesbian Culture 1668–1801*. London: Scarlet Press.

Dover, K. J. (1978), *Greek Homosexuality*. London: Duckworth.

Duberman, Martin (1991), *About Time: Exploring the Gay Past*, rev. edn. Penguin Meridian (originally published in 1986).

Duberman, Martin, Vicinus, Martha and Chauncey, George Jr. (eds) (1989), *Hidden from History: Reclaiming the Gay and Lesbian Past*. Penguin Meridian.

Dynes, Wayne R. (ed.) (1990), *Encyclopedia of Homosexuality*, 2 vols. Chicago and London: St James Press.

Dynes, Wayne R. (1992), 'Wrestling with the social boa constructor', in Stein (ed.) (1992a), *Forms of Desire*, pp. 209–38.

Dynes, Wayne R. and Donaldson, Stephen (eds) (1992), *History of Homosexuality in Europe and America*. New York and London: Garland Publishing.

Elliman, Michael and Roll, Frederick (1986), *The Pink Plaque Guide to London*. London: GMP.

Epstein, Steven (1987), 'Gay politics, ethnic identity: the limits of social constructionism', *Socialist Review*, 93/94 (May–August), pp. 9–54, reprinted in Stein (ed.) (1992a), *Forms of Desire*, pp. 239–93.

Eriksson, Brigitte (1985), 'A lesbian execution in Germany, 1721: The trial records', in Licata and Petersen (eds) (1985), *The Gay Past*, pp. 27–40.

Faderman, Lillian (1985a), *Scotch Verdict: Miss Pirie and Miss Woods v. Dame Cumming Gordon*. London: Quartet Books (originally published in 1983).

Faderman, Lillian (1985b), *Surpassing the Love of Men: Romantic Friendship and Love between Women from the Renaissance to the Present*. London: The Women's Press (originally published in 1981).

Faderman, Lillian (ed.) (1994), *Chloe Plus Olivia: An Anthology of Lesbian Literature from the Seventeenth Century to the Present*. New York: Viking Penguin.

Fletcher, Lynne Yamaguchi and Saks, Adrien (eds) (1990), *Lavender Lists*. Boston: Alyson.

Foucault, Michel (1978), *The History of Sexuality, Volume I: An Introduction*, trans. Robert Hurley. New York: Pantheon.

Foucault, Michel (1991), *The Foucault Reader*, ed. Paul Rabinow. London: Penguin Books.

Garde, Noel I. (pseudonym of Edgar Leoni) (1964), *Jonathan to Gide: The Homosexual in History*. New York: Vantage.

Gardiner, James (1992), *A Class Apart: The Private Pictures of Montague Glover*. London: Serpent's Tail.

Gerard, Kent and Hekma, Gert (eds) (1989), *The Pursuit of Sodomy: Male Homosexuality in Renaissance and Enlightenment Europe*. New York: Harrington Park Press.

Gilbert, Arthur N. (1985a), 'Conceptions of homosexuality and sodomy in Western history', in Licata and Petersen (eds) (1985), *The Gay Past*, pp. 57–68.

Gilbert, Arthur N. (1985b), Review of Jeffrey Weeks's *Coming Out*, in Licata and Petersen (eds) (1985), *The Gay Past*, pp. 214–16.

Goldberg, Jonathan (ed.) (1994), *Reclaiming Sodom*. New York and London: Routledge.

Goodich, Michael (1979), *The Unmentionable Vice: Homosexuality in the Later Medieval Period*. Santa Barbara, CA, and Oxford: ABC-Clio.

Grahn, Judy (1984), *Another Mother Tongue: Gay Words, Gay Worlds*, updated and expanded edition. Boston: Beacon Press.

Greenberg, David F. (1988), *The Construction of Homosexuality*. Chicago and London: University of Chicago Press.

Griffin, Gabriele (1993a), 'History with a difference: telling lesbian herstories', in Griffin (ed.) (1993b), *Outwrite*, pp. 48–67.

Griffin, Gabriele (ed.) (1993b), *Outwrite: Lesbianism and Popular Culture*. London and Boulder, Colo.: Pluto Press.

Hallam, Paul (1993), *The Book of Sodom*. London and New York: Verso.

Halperin, David M. (1989), 'Sex before sexuality: pederasty, politics, and power in classical Athens', in Duberman *et al.* (1989), *Hidden from History*, pp. 37–53.

Halperin, David M. (1993), 'Is there a history of sexuality?', in Abelove *et al.* (eds) (1993), *The Lesbian and Gay Studies Reader*, pp. 416–31.

Halsband, Robert (1973), *Lord Hervey: Eighteenth-Century Courtier*. Oxford: Clarendon Press.

Hastie, Nicki (1993), 'Lesbian bibliomythography', in Griffin (ed.) (1993b), *Outwrite*, pp. 68–85.

Hay, Bob, 'The Sodomites' Guide to Colonial Sydney', Internet Website <http://lemon.rainbow.net.au/fabfanny/bhay/>.

Healy, Murray (1996), *Gay Skins: Class, Masculinity, and Queer Appropriation*. London: Cassell.

Herdt, Gilbert (ed.) (1994), *Third Sex, Third Gender: Beyond Sexual Dimorphism in Culture and History*. New York: Zone Books.

Higgins, Patrick (ed.) (1993), *A Queer Reader*. London: Fourth Estate.

Higgins, Patrick (1996), *Heterosexual Dictatorship: Male Homosexuality in Post-War Britain*. London: Fourth Estate.

Hinsch, Bret (1990), *Passions of the Cut Sleeve: The Male Homosexual Tradition in China*. Berkeley, Los Angeles and Oxford: University of California Press.

Hirschfeld, Magnus (1922), *Sexualpathologie*, Vol. II: *Sexuelle Zwischenstufen: Das männliche Weib und der weibliche Mann*. Bonn.

Howes, Keith (1993), *Broadcasting It: An Encyclopaedia of Homosexuality on Film, Radio and TV in the UK 1923–1993*. London: Cassell.

Huussen, Arend H. Jr. (1989), 'Sodomy in the Dutch Republic during the eighteenth century', in Duberman *et al.* (eds) (1989), *Hidden from History*, pp. 141–9.

Hyde, H. Montgomery (1970), *The Other Love: A Historical and Contemporary Survey of Homosexuality in Britain*. London: William Heinemann.

Ihara Saikaku (1990), *The Great Mirror of Male Love*, trans. with introd. Paul Gordon Schalow. Stanford, CA: Stanford University Press.

Isherwood, Christopher (1977), *Christopher and His Kind, 1929–1939*. London: Eyre Methuen.

Jeffreys, Sheila (1989a), 'Butch and femme: now and then', in Lesbian History Group (ed.) (1989), *Not a Passing Phase*, pp. 158–87 (earlier version published in 1987).

Jeffreys, Sheila (1989b), 'Does it matter if they did it?', in Lesbian History

Group (ed.) (1989), *Not a Passing Phase*, pp. 19–28 (originally published in 1984).

Johnson, Pam (1989), 'Edith Simcox and heterosexism in biography: a lesbian-feminist exploration', in Lesbian History Group (ed.) (1989), *Not a Passing Phase*, pp. 55–76.

Kaplan, Fred (1992), *Henry James: The Imagination of Genius*. London: Hodder and Stoughton.

Karlinsky, Simon (1991), 'Russia's gay history and literature from the eleventh to the twentieth centuries', in Leyland (ed.) (1991), *Gay Roots*, pp. 81–104.

Katz, Jonathan (1975), *Coming Out: A Documentary Play about Gay Life and Liberation in the United States of America*. New York: Arno Press.

Katz, Jonathan (1976), *Gay American History: Lesbians and Gay Men in the USA*. New York: Thomas Y. Crowell.

Katz, Jonathan (1994), 'The age of sodomitical sin, 1607–1740', in Goldberg (ed.) (1994), *Reclaiming Sodom*, pp. 43–58.

Kennedy, Elizabeth Lapovsky and Davis, Madeline (1992), '"They was no one to mess with": the construction of the butch role in the lesbian community of the 1940s and 1950s', in Nestle (ed.) (1992), *The Persistent Desire*, pp. 62–79.

Kennedy, Hubert C. (1985), 'The "third sex" theory of Karl Heinrich Ulrichs', in Licata and Petersen (eds) (1985), *The Gay Past*, pp. 103–11.

Kenny, Maurice (1991), 'Tinselled bucks: an historical study in Indian homosexuality', in Leyland (ed.) (1991), *Gay Roots*, pp. 113–23.

Kitzinger, Jenny and Kitzinger, Celia (1993), '"Doing it": representations of lesbian sex', in Griffin (ed.) (1993b), *Outwrite*, pp. 9–25.

Klaich, Dolores (1974), *Woman Plus Woman: Attitudes toward Lesbianism*. New York: Simon and Schuster (London: New English Library, 1975).

Koski, Fran and Tilchen, Maida (1975), 'Some Pulp Sappho', in *Lesbian Feminist Writing and Publishing*, special issue of *Margins Magazine*, No. 8.

Lauritsen, John and Thorstad, David (1974), *The Early Homosexual Rights Movement (1864–1935)*. New York: Times Change Press.

Lautmann, Rüdiger (1985), 'The pink triangle: the persecution of homosexual males in concentration camps in Nazi Germany', in Licata and Petersen (eds) (1985), *The Gay Past*, pp. 141–160 (condensed from seminar: *Gesellschaft und Homosexualität*, 1977).

Legg, W. Dorr (ed.) (1994), *Homophile Studies in Theory and Practice*. San Francisco: ONE Institute Press and GLB Publishers.

Lesbian History Group (ed.) (1989), *Not a Passing Phase: Reclaiming Lesbians in History 1840–1985*. London: The Women's Press.

Leyland, Winston (ed.) (1991), *Gay Roots: Twenty Years of Gay Sunshine, An Anthology of Gay History, Sex, Politics and Culture*. San Francisco: Gay Sunshine Press.

Leyland, Winston (ed.) (1993), *Gay Roots: An Anthology of Gay History, Sex, Politics and Culture*, Vol. 2. San Francisco: Gay Sunshine Press.

Licata, Salvatore J. (1985), 'The homosexual rights movement in the United States', in Licata and Petersen (eds) (1985), *The Gay Past*, pp. 161–89 (originally published in 1980; partly based upon a doctorial dissertation of 1978).

Licata, Salvatore J. and Petersen, Robert P. (eds) (1985), *The Gay Past: A Collection of Historical Essays*. New York and Binghamton: Harrington Park Press. (Also published as *Historical Perspectives on Homosexuality*, 1981; originally published as *Journal of Homosexuality*, Vol. 6, Nos 1/2 (Fall/Winter 1980)).

Lister, Anne (1988), *I Know My Own Heart: The Diaries [1817–1824] of Anne Lister (1791–1840)*, ed. Helena Whitbread. London: Virago.

Lister, Anne (1992), *No Priest but Love: Excerpts from the Diaries of Anne Lister, 1824–1826*, ed. Helena Whitbread. Otley, West Yorkshire: Smith Settle.

Lumsden, Andrew (1982), 'Down at the old Piano-Zinc, or how to reclaim your gay culture', *Gay News*, 242, p. 31.

Lynch, Michael (1976), 'A gay world after all: Marsden Hartley (1877–1943)', *Body Politic*, Our Image No. 6 (December–January), pp. 1–2.

MacCowan, Lyndall (1992), 'Re-collecting history, renaming lives: femme stigma and the feminist seventies and eighties', in Nestle (ed.) (1992), *The Persistent Desire*, pp. 299–328.

McIntosh, Mary (1968), 'The homosexual role', *Social Problems*, 16 (Fall), pp. 182–92, reprinted in Stein (ed.) (1992a), *Forms of Desire*, pp. 25–42.

Marwick, Arthur (1989), *The Nature of History*, 3rd edn. London: Macmillan.

Meer, Theo van der (1989), 'The persecutions of sodomites in eighteenth-century Amsterdam: changing perceptions of sodomy', in Gerard and Hekma (eds) (1989), *The Pursuit of Sodomy*, pp. 263–307.

Miller, Carl (1996), *Stages of Desire: Gay Theatre's Hidden History*. London: Cassell.

Miller, Elaine (1989), 'Through all changes and through all chances: the relationship of Ellen Nussey and Charlotte Brontë', in Lesbian History Group (ed.) (1989), *Not a Passing Phase*, pp. 29–54.

Miller, Neil (1995), *Out of the Past: Gay and Lesbian History from 1869 to the Present*. London: Vintage.

Miller, Stephen D. (ed.) (1996), *Partings at Dawn: An Anthology of Japanese Gay Literature*. San Francisco: Gay Sunshine Press.

Minakata Kumagusu and Iwata Jun'ichi (1996), 'Morning fog (correspondence on gay lifestyles)', trans. William F. Sibley, in Miller (ed.) (1996), *Partings at Dawn*, pp. 135–71.

Monter, E. William (1985), 'Sodomy and heresy in early modern Switzerland', in Licata and Petersen (eds) (1985), *The Gay Past*, pp. 41–53 (originally published in French in 1974).

Mott, Luiz and Assunçao, Aroldo (1989), 'Love's labors lost: five letters from a seventeenth-century Portuguese sodomite', in Gerard and Hekma (eds) (1989), *The Pursuit of Sodomy*, pp. 91–101.

Murray, Stephen O. (1989), 'Homosexual acts and selves in early modern Europe', in Gerard and Hekma (eds) (1989), *The Pursuit of Sodomy*, pp. 457–77.

Nanda, Serena (1993), 'Hijras as neither man nor woman', in Abelove *et al.* (eds) (1993), *The Lesbian and Gay Studies Reader*, pp. 542–52.

Nestle, Joan (ed.) (1992), *The Persistent Desire: A Femme–Butch Reader*. Boston: Alyson.

Newton, Esther (1984), 'The mythic mannish lesbian: Radclyffe Hall and the New Woman', *Signs: Journal of Women in Culture and Society*, 9, 4, pp. 557–75.

Ng, Vivien W. (1989), 'Homosexuality and the state in late Imperial China', in Duberman *et al.* (eds) (1989), *Hidden from History*, pp. 76–89.

Noordam, Dirk Jaap (1989), 'Sodomy in the Dutch Republic, 1600–1725', in Gerard and Hekma (eds) (1989), *The Pursuit of Sodomy*, pp. 207–28.

Norton, Rictor (1974a), *The Homosexual Literary Tradition: An Interpretation*. New York: Revisionist Press.

Norton, Rictor (1974b), 'The phoenix of Sodom', *Gay News*, 47, p. 12.

Norton, Rictor (1975), 'Ganymede raped: gay literature – the critic as censor', in Young, Ian, *The Male Homosexual in Literature: A Bibliography*. Metuchen, NJ: Scarecrow Press, pp. 193–205.

Norton, Rictor (1992), *Mother Clap's Molly House: The Gay Subculture in England 1700–1830*. London: Gay Men's Press.

Norton, Rictor (1993a), 'Hard gemlike flame: Walter Pater and his circle', in Leyland (ed.) (1993), *Gay Roots*, pp. 199–206.

Norton, Rictor (1993b), 'The historical roots of homophobia', in Leyland (ed.) (1993), *Gay Roots*, pp. 69–90.

Norton, Rictor (ed.) (1997, forthcoming), *My Dear Boy: Gay Love Letters through the Centuries*. San Francisco: Gay Sunshine Press.

Norton, Rictor, 'The homosexual pastoral tradition', Internet Website <http://www.infopt.demon.co.uk/gayhist.htm>.

Norton, Rictor and Crew, Louie (eds) (1974), *The Homosexual Imagination*, special issue of *College English*, 36, 3 (November).

Oaks, Robert F. (1978), '"Things fearful to name": sodomy and buggery in seventeenth-century New England', *Journal of Social History*, 12, pp. 268–81.

Padgug, Robert (1976), Review of Vern Bullough's *Sexual Variance in Society and History*, *Body Politic*, Our Image No. 6 (December–January), p. 11.

Padgug, Robert (1979), 'Sexual matters: on conceptualizing sexuality in history', *Radical History Review* 20 (Spring/Summer), pp. 3–23, reprinted in Stein (ed.) (1992a), *Forms of Desire*, pp. 43–67.

Paglia, Camille (1994), *Vamps & Tramps*. New York: Vintage Books.

Parker, Peter (1989), *Ackerley: A Life of J. R. Ackerley*. London: Constable.

Plummer, Kenneth (1975), *Sexual Stigma*. London: Routledge & Kegan Paul.

Plummer, Kenneth (ed.) (1981), *The Making of the Modern Homosexual*. Totowa, NJ: Barnes and Noble.

Power, Lisa (1996), *No Bath but Plenty of Bubbles: The London Gay Liberation Front 1970–73*. London: Cassell.

Reade, Brian (ed.) (1970), *Sexual Heretics: Male Homosexuality in English Literature from 1850 to 1900*. New York: Coward-McCann.

Reeder, Greg (1993), 'United for eternity', *KMT: A Modern Journal of Ancient Egypt*, 4, 1, p. 22.

Reeder, Greg, 'Tomb of Niankhkhnum and Khnumhotep', Internet Website <http://www.sirius.com/~reeder/niankh.html>.

Rey, Michel (1985), 'Parisian homosexuals create a lifestyle, 1700–1750: the police archives', *Eighteenth-Century Life*, 9, pp. 179–91.

Rey, Michel (1989), 'Police and sodomy in eighteenth-century Paris: from sin to disorder', in Gerard and Hekma (eds) (1989), *The Pursuit of Sodomy*, pp. 129–46.

Rich, Adrienne (1993), 'Compulsory heterosexuality and lesbian existence', in Abelove *et al.* (eds) (1993), *The Lesbian and Gay Studies Reader*, pp. 227–54 (originally published in 1982).

Richards, Dell (1990), *Lesbian Lists*. Boston: Alyson.

Rocke, Michael J. (1989), 'Sodomites in fifteenth-century Tuscany: the views of Bernardino of Siena', in Gerard and Hekma (eds) (1989), *The Pursuit of Sodomy*, pp. 7–31.

Ruggiero, Guido (1985), *The Boundaries of Eros: Sex Crime and Sexuality in Renaissance Venice*. New York: Oxford University Press.

Russo, Vito (1987), *The Celluloid Closet: Homosexuality in the Movies*. New York: Harper & Row, revised edn 1987 (originally published in 1981).

Rutledge, Leigh W. (1987), *The Gay Book of Lists*. Boston: Alyson.

Rutledge, Leigh W. (1988), *Unnatural Quotations*. Boston: Alyson.

Rutledge, Leigh W. (1989), *The Gay Fireside Companion*. Boston: Alyson.

Saslow, James M. (1986), *Ganymede in the Renaissance: Homosexuality in Art and Society*. New Haven and London: Yale University Press.

Saslow, James M. (1989), 'Homosexuality in the Renaissance: behavior, identity, and artistic expression', in Duberman *et al.* (eds) (1989), *Hidden from History*, pp. 90–105.

Schalow, Paul Gordon (1996a), 'Introduction', in Miller (ed.) (1996), *Partings at Dawn*, pp. 11–19.

Schalow, Paul Gordon (1996b), 'Introduction: the invention of a literary tradition of male love', in Miller (ed.) (1996), *Partings at Dawn*, pp. 97–102.

Scott, Joan W. (1993), 'The evidence of experience', in Abelove *et al.* (eds) (1993), *The Lesbian and Gay Studies Reader*, pp. 397–415.

Siffre, Labi (1996), 'The private life of Labi Siffre', interview by Philip Reay-Smith, *Pink Paper*, 29 November, pp. 15–17.

Simpson, Mark (ed.) (1996), *Anti-Gay: Homosexuality and Its Discontents*. London: Cassell.

Skinner, Gifford (1978), 'Cocktails in the bath', *Gay News*, 135, pp. 21–4; 'The spittoon waltz', *Gay News*, 140, pp. 17–20.

Smith, Timothy d'Arch (1970), *Love in Earnest: Some Notes on the Lives and Writings of English 'Uranian' Poets from 1889 to 1930*. London: Routledge & Kegan Paul.

Smyth, Cherry (1996), *Damn Fine Art*. London: Cassell.

Spencer, Colin (1995), *Homosexuality: A History*. London: Fourth Estate.

Steakley, James D. (1989), 'Sodomy in Enlightenment Prussia: from execution to suicide', in Gerard and Hekma (eds) (1989), *The Pursuit of Sodomy*, pp. 163–75.

Stein, Edward (ed.) (1992a), *Forms of Desire: Sexual Orientation and the Social Constructionist Controversy*. New York and London: Routledge (originally published by Garland, 1990).

Stein, Edward (1992b), 'Conclusion: The essentials of constructionism and the construction of essentialism', in (ed.) (1992a), *Forms of Desire*, pp. 323–53.

Stein, Edward (1992c), 'Introduction', in (ed.) (1992a), *Forms of Desire*, pp. 3–9.

Stradling, Matthew (1995), 'Flesh & pearls' (interview), *Rouge*, 20, pp. 22–5.

Suárez Sánchez, Juan A. (1996), 'Writing AIDS/reading history: AIDS, metaphor, and the historical imagination', *Stylistica*, Monográfico sobre Cultura Homosexual, 4, pp. 49–59.

Summers, Claude J. (ed.) (1995), *The Gay and Lesbian Literary Heritage*. New York: Henry Holt.

Sutherland, Alistair and Anderson, Patrick (eds) (1963), *Eros: An Anthology of Male Friendship*. New York: Citadel (originally published London: Anthony Blond, 1961).

Sweet, Michael and Zwilling, Leonard (1993), 'The first medicalization: the taxonomy and etiology of queerness in classical Indian medicine', *Journal of the History of Sexuality*, 3, 4, pp. 590–697.

Sweet, Michael and Zwilling, Leonard (1996), '"Like a city ablaze": the third sex and the creation of sexuality in Jain religious literature', *Journal of the History of Sexuality*, 6, 3, pp. 359–84.

Symonds, John Addington (1967–9), *The Letters of John Addington Symonds*, 3 vols, ed. Herbert M. Schueller and Robert L. Peters. Detroit: Wayne State University Press.

Symonds, John Addington (1984), *Memoirs*. Manuscript, London Library. About four-fifths was published as *The Memoirs of John*

Addington Symonds, ed. Phyllis Grosskurth. London: Hutchinson, 1984.

Tatchell, Peter (1996), 'Have you slept with Michael Portillo?', *Thud*, 29 November, p. 8.

Thadani, Giti (1996), *Sakhiyani: Lesbian Desire in Ancient and Modern India*. London: Cassell.

Thwaite, Ann (1984), *Edmund Gosse: A Literary Landscape*. London: Martin Secker & Warburg.

Trevisan, João (1986), *Perverts in Paradise*, trans. Martin Foreman. London: GMP.

Trumbach, Randolph (1977), 'London's sodomites: homosexual behavior and western culture in the 18th century', *Journal of Social History*, 11, 1, pp. 1–33.

Trumbach, Randolph (1987), 'Sodomitical subcultures, sodomitical roles, and the gender revolution of the eighteenth century: the recent historiography', in Maccubbin, Robert Parks (ed.) (1987), *Tis Nature's Fault: Unauthorized Sexuality during the Enlightenment*. New York: Cambridge University Press, pp. 109–21.

Trumbach, Randolph (1989a), 'The birth of the queen: sodomy and the emergence of gender equality in modern culture, 1660–1750', in Duberman *et al.* (eds) (1989), *Hidden from History*, pp. 129–40.

Trumbach, Randolph (1989b), 'Sodomitical assaults, gender role, and sexual development in eighteenth-century London', in Gerard and Hekma (eds) (1989), *The Pursuit of Sodomy*, pp. 407–29.

Trumbach, Randolph (1994), 'London's sapphists: from three sexes to four genders in the making of modern culture', in Herdt (ed.) (1994), *Third Sex, Third Gender*, pp. 111–36.

Vicinus, Martha (1993), '"They wonder to which sex I belong": the historical roots of the modern lesbian identity', in Abelove *et al.* (eds) (1993), *The Lesbian and Gay Studies Reader*, pp. 432–52.

Vines, Gail (1992), 'Secret life of the brain', Supplement to *New Scientist*, 28 November.

Walderhaug, Arne (1996), 'Albania: keeping a low profile', *Gay Times*, March, pp. 94–8.

Weatherby, W. J. (1989), *James Baldwin: Artist on Fire*. London: Michael Joseph.

Weeks, Jeffrey (1977), *Coming Out: Homosexual Politics in Britain, from the Nineteenth Century to the Present*. London: Quartet.

Weeks, Jeffrey (1985), 'Inverts, perverts, and Mary-Annes: male prostitution and the regulation of homosexuality in England in the nineteenth and early twentieth centuries', in Licata and Petersen (eds) (1985), *The Gay Past*, pp. 113–34.

Weeks, Jeffrey (1991), *Against Nature: Essays on History, Sexuality and Identity*. London: Rivers Oram Press.

Weinrich, James (1987), 'Reality or social construction?', in *Sexual Landscapes: Why We Are What We Are, Why We Love Who We Love*. New York: Charles Scribner's Sons, reprinted in Stein (ed.) (1992a), *Forms of Desire*, pp. 175–208.

White, Edmund (1993), *Genet*, revised edn. London: Picador (originally published by Chatto & Windus, 1993).

Whitehead, Harriet (1993), 'The boy and the burden strap: a new look at institutionalized homosexuality in Native North America', in Abelove *et al.* (eds) (1993), *The Lesbian and Gay Studies Reader*, pp. 498–527.

Williams, Walter L. (1986), *The Spirit and the Flesh: Sexual Diversity in American Indian Culture*. Boston: Beacon Press.

Index

Browning, Robert 161
Bryson, Bill 118
Bullough, Vern L. 4, 67
Burg, B. R. 139
Burton, Peter 115, 117
Burton, Sir Richard 70, 105, 161, 253, 255, 261
butch/femme 199, 207–11, 291
Butler, William 146
Byron, Lord 252

Cadmus, Paul 269
Caelius Aurelianus 29–30
Cambacérès, Jean–Jacques Régis de 165
camp 20, 22, 26, 74, 112, 114–15, 117, 118–19, 143, 288, 289, 290–1
capitalism 6–7, 10, 28, 61–2, 63, 88, 91–7, 140, 201–2, 242, 247–8
Caravaggio 58–9, 144
Carlini, Sister Benedetta 190
Carpenter, Edward 3, 17, 18, 81, 71, 72, 76, 128, 129, 147, 205, 224, 279
Carpenter, Thelma 181
Castiglione 226
Castle, Terry 184
Castlehaven, Earl of 139
Castlereagh, Lord 80
Cather, Willa 3, 163
Catlin, George 18, 170
Catullus 53
Cavafy, Constantine 182, 272
Cavin, Susan 189
Cellini, Benvenuto 58, 137, 143, 221, 233, 249, 273
censorship 63, 142, 143, 148–9, 152, 153–73, 178–9, 215
Charlesworth, Kate 216
Chauncey, George 6, 34, 46–7, 76, 77, 80, 83, 92, 242, 248, 273–4
China 31, 42, 52, 57–8, 60, 78, 100–2, 105, 106, 107, 110, 155, 157–8, 168, 173, 180, 187, 195, 229–30, 254, 286–7, 288–9
Christina, Queen 207, 211
Chubb, Ralph Nicholas 222
Church, John 122
Cicero 144
Clogher, Bishop of 109
Cobbe, Frances Power 275
Collis, Rose 206, 275
Core, Philip 288
Corneille 154
Corvo, Baron 147, 225
Cory, Donald Webster 22
Cowan, Thomas 98
Craig, Edy 275
Crane, Hart 152, 177
Crete 52, 53

Crisp, Quentin 19–20, 273
Crompton, Louis 138, 191
cross–dressing 17, 51, 73–4, 84–5, 134, 188, 191–5, 269; see also berdache
Crow, Christine 235–7
Cuban refugees 260
Cullen, Countee 72, 166, 258
culture, queer 4–6, 12, 61, 74, 81, 112, 119, 130–3, 149, 153, 156–7, 160, 173, 181, 197, 210, 217, 222–5, 229, 230, 232, 239, 240, 252, 261, 266, 269, 271–4, 281, 284–5, 290–2; see also subcultures
Cumberland, Duke of 177–8
Cybele 38, 107, 113, 231

D'Emilio, John 3, 4, 6, 21, 62, 72, 95–6
Dall'Orto, Giovanni 42, 174, 239, 249
Damian, Peter 94
Damon and Pithias 226
Damon, Gene 152
Daniélou, Alain 131, 157
Dante 142
Daughters of Bilitis 182, 209
David and Jonathan 98, 227
Davidson, Michael 167
Davis, Madeline 209
Day, F. Holland 230–1
Defoe, Daniel 151
DeJean, Joan 183
Dekker, Thomas 226
Demosthenes 52, 87
Denmark 254
Diaghilev, Sergei 155
Dickinson, Emily 163
Dietrich, Marlene 207
Dio Chrysostom 29, 113
Diotimus 31
discourse 25–6, 74, 132–4, 151, 171–2, 178
Donaldson, Stephen 24
Donatello 142
Donne, John 160–1, 175
Donoghue, Emma 51, 110–11, 152, 186, 187–8, 202, 236
Dover, Kenneth 130
Drayton, Michael 246
Duberman, Martin 134, 165
Dürer, Albrecht 242
Dynes, Wayne R. 24, 121

East, Mary 51
Edward II 44
Edwards, Richard 226
effeminacy 19–20, 22, 38, 46, 47, 114, 117, 127, 251, 271, 282
egalitarian model 85–6, 88–90, 95; see also friendship (male)

Egypt 41, 85–6
Eliot, George 75, 163
Eliot, T. S. 164
Ellis, Havelock 70–1, 76, 77, 81, 128,
 208, 218, 224
Engels, Friedrich 95
Enheduanna 189
Epstein, Steven 24
essentialism 4, 5, 9, 11–15, 16, 23, 24,
 31, 91, 99, 102, 113, 151, 152, 186,
 208, 223, 235, 241, 278
ethnic culture 3, 5, 8, 12, 19, 46, 111,
 123, 132, 148, 216, 241, 252, 256,
 267–70, 285–7, 289
Eulenburg-Hertefeld, Prince Philipp Fürst
 zu 26, 75, 99
Euripides 87
exclusive homosexuality 30, 37, 43, 47,
 49, 58–9; see also bisexuality,
 orientation

Faderman, Lillian 153, 165, 188, 203–4,
 270
family unit 93–6
Fausto-Sterling, Anne 33
female husbands 50–1, 138, 192–6, 251
Ferguson, Ann 201
Fiala, Rick 216
Ficino, Marsilio 144, 165, 226
Fielding, Henry 195
Firbank, Ronald 112
Flandrin, Hippolyte 76, 232, 234
Forbes, Bryan 155
Forster, E. M. 129, 142, 225, 292
Foucault 6, 8, 9–10, 25, 30, 37–8, 61–4,
 71, 77, 136, 178
France 37, 38, 42, 44, 90, 95, 106, 109,
 115, 137, 138, 176, 183, 191, 204,
 218, 243–4, 245, 246, 248, 250, 251,
 253, 254, 256
Frederick the Great 4, 176, 227
Freudian theory 28, 30, 51, 53, 78–9,
 203, 217, 262
Freund, Kurt 23
Friedlaender, Benedict 222
friendship (male) 36, 88, 144–7, 170,
 172, 220, 226–7; see also romantic
 friendship (female)
Fuss, Diana 20

Gandhi 156
Garbo, Greta 207, 274
Garde, Noel I. 218
Gardiner, James 273
Garland, Rodney 225
gay, as a term 121–2
Gay Sweatshop 3, 291

gender roles 15, 17, 29, 46, 47, 101, 104,
 171; see also passive roles, role
Genet, Jean 225, 231, 282–4
genetics 14, 32–3
Geneva 138–9, 191
Germany 66–8, 75, 90, 95, 112, 128,
 218, 245, 250
Gesner, Johann Matthias 172
ghetto, gay 241
Gide, André 237, 283
Ginsberg, Allen 3
Gleim, Johann Wilhelm Ludwig 227
Gloeden, Wilhelm von 27, 61, 233
Glover, Michael 13
Glover, Montague 273
Gluck 234
Goodich, Michael 137
Goodman, Paul 257
Gosse, Edmund 26, 161–2, 233
Grahn, Judy 20, 119–20, 173, 189, 211,
 235
Greece and Rome 28–9, 40, 43, 45, 47–9,
 52–3, 86, 89, 100, 105, 158, 190,
 261, 262
Greenberg, David F. 6, 10, 17, 39, 41–2,
 53, 58–9, 87–8, 135, 170, 239, 249,
 286
Greif, Martin 217
Greig, Noel 3
Greyson, John 277
Griffin, Gabriele 236
Griffiths, Drew 3
Guilpin, Edward 246

Haarmann, Fritz 217
Hadrian and Antinous 182, 225, 233
Hall, Murray 196
Hall, Radclyffe 77, 153, 234, 235, 237,
 239
Hallam, Paul 218, 291
Halperin, David M. 6, 27–30
Hamilton, Cicely 168
Hanscombe, Gillian 270
Harmodius and Aristogeiton 47, 88, 226
Harris, Frank 142, 222
Hartley, Marsden 223, 230
Hastie, Nicki 235, 236
Hay, Harry 5, 272
Hays Code 154
Hekma, Gert 250
Hellman, Lillian 150, 155
Hennegan, Alison 235
Henri III 227
heritage 3, 127, 132, 208, 211, 216, 224,
 277, 287, 292; see also tradition
Hervey, Lord 38, 145
heterosexual/homosexual dichotomy 18,
 29, 52, 54, 62, 98, 267, 280

Nijinsky 155
Niles, Blair 224
Nilsson, Gösta Adrian 274
Noordam, Dirk Jaap 250
Novarro, Ramon 177
Nugent, Richard Bruce 258
Nureyev, Rudolf 177

ONE Institute 3, 4, 23, 55, 97, 161
Orestes and Pylades 226
orientation 11, 18, 22, 30, 40, 41, 42–5,
48, 52, 110; see also exclusive
homosexuality
Orton, Joe 177
Osment, Philip 291
Ovid 152, 154, 236

Padgug, Robert 6, 52
Paglia, Camille 9, 10, 73, 182, 231
pair-bonding (female) 50–1, 186–7, 193,
204, 206; see also female husbands,
romantic friendship (female)
Pakistan 54
Palgrave, Francis 145
Park, Frederick William 73, 74
passive roles 17, 29, 39–42, 46, 49,
104–6, 171; see also gender roles, role
Pater, Walter 272
pederasty 24, 30–1, 85, 86–91, 95, 100,
106, 130, 144–5, 172, 222, 239, 262,
288; see also intergenerational model
Pepy II 86
Peter the Great 252
Petronius 262, 287
Petropoulos, Elias 118
Phanocles 31
Philippe de France 56
Philippines 108, 255, 259–60
Philostratus 52, 53
Philpot, Glyn 76, 273
Pindar 262
Pirie, Jane 150
Pitt–Rivers, Michael 167
Plato 48, 65, 68, 72, 111, 144–5, 172,
223, 224, 226, 239, 262
Plautus 53
Plummer, Kenneth 6
Plutarch 45, 52, 76, 87, 145, 161, 226
Plüschow, Guglielmo 233
polari 115–18, 261, 288, 290; see also
language
Poliziano 154
Polyeuct and Nearchos 227–8
Porter, Cole 155, 165, 274
Portugal 128, 250, 255
prostitution 97, 105, 107, 254, 255–6,
264, 265

Proust, Marcel 77, 237, 284
Punshon, E. M. 'Monte' 15

queer 8, 9, 36, 122–3

Raffalovich, Marc–André 128
Rainey, Ma 181
Rais, Gilles de 217, 283
Rambova, Natacha 57
Rawcliffe, Derek 55
Redl, Alfred 177
Reeder, Greg 86
Renaissance 14, 31, 49, 58, 87–8, 90,
142, 154, 172, 175, 190, 218, 220,
226, 232, 249
Renault, Mary 182
Reni, Guido 231
Rey, Michel 245
Rhianus of Crete 30
Rhondda, Viscountess 168
Ricci, Matteo 168, 254
Rich, Adrienne 185–6
Richards, Dell 22, 183, 185, 236, 276
Richardson, Samuel 151
Rimbaud, Arthur 73, 225, 281, 284
Robins, Elizabeth 168
Robinson, Tom 273
role 8, 34, 45–6, 104–9, 114, 188,
208–9, 247; see also gender roles,
identity, passive roles
Rolfe, Frederick, Baron Corvo 240
romantic friendship (female) 24, 153,
166–7, 186, 187, 195–6, 202–6, 209
Roosevelt, Eleanor 163, 269
Ross, Robbie 225
Rossetti, Christina 156
Römer, L. S. A. M. von 128
Rowland, Charles 5
Rowse, A. L. 175
Rubens 154
Rumi 36
Russia 96, 191, 252, 253
Rustin, Bayard 271
Rutledge, Leigh W. 217

Sackville-West, Vita 57, 237
Sacred Band of Thebes 105, 106, 174,
226
Sade, Marquis de 217
Sadler, Thomas 246
Saint-Pavin, Denis Sanguin de 219
same-sex union 87, 88, 159–60, 168,
221, 226–9, 251, 264, 285–7; see also
female husbands, pair-bonding
(female)
Sappho 44, 109, 152, 154, 156, 158,
159, 182, 183, 235–7, 239, 276

Vizzani, Catherine 49–50
Voltaire 176, 219

Wald, Elijah 33
Warhol, Andy 234, 277
Warren, Edward Perry 130
Weber, Bruce 90
Weeks, Jeffrey 6, 8, 25, 61, 93–4, 97, 136, 142
Westphal, Karl Friedrich Otto 69, 71, 72
Whale, James 177
Whitbread, Helena 196
White, Edmund 282
Whitman, Walt 3, 26–7, 71, 72, 87, 88, 129, 147, 224, 230, 237, 239, 259
Wilde, Oscar 26, 55, 72–3, 77, 87, 88, 109, 129, 141–2, 149, 167, 182, 205, 221–2, 225, 237, 239, 259, 273, 281
Wildeblood, Peter 121, 167
Wilder, Frances 72
Wilmot, John 59
Wilson, Millie 234
Winckelmann, Johann Joachim 91, 272

Withers, Thomas Jefferson 165
Wittgenstein, Ludwig 164
Wittig, Monique 238
Wolfe, Elsie de 112
Wollstonecraft, Mary 163
Woods, Gregory 239
Woods, Marianne 150
Woolf, Leonard 142
Woolf, Virginia 177, 182, 237, 276
working class 25, 46, 72, 84, 97, 112, 117, 150, 209–10, 223, 251, 255, 258, 263, 265–6, 269, 281–5
Wright, Richard 271

Xavier, Francis 254
Xenophon 172

Young, Ian 90
Yourcenar, Marguerite 182

Zeno 48, 182
Zschokke, Heinrich 128